D0926500

The
# CELL GAME

# The
# Cell Game

*Sam Waksal's Fast Money
and False Promises—and the Fate
of ImClone's Cancer Drug*

## Alex Prud'homme

HarperBusiness
*An Imprint of HarperCollinsPublishers*

**PJC PENSACOLA CAMPUS LRC**

THE CELL GAME. Copyright © 2004 by Alex Prud'homme. All rights reserved. Printed in the United States of America. No part of this book may be used or reproduced in any manner whatsoever without written permission except in the case of brief quotations embodied in critical articles and reviews. For information address HarperCollins Publishers Inc., 10 East 53rd Street, New York, New York 10022.

HarperCollins books may be purchased for educational, business, or sales promotional use. For information, please write to: Special Markets Department, HarperCollins Publishers Inc., 10 East 53rd Street, New York, New York 10022.

*Designed by C. Linda Dingler*

Library of Congress Cataloging-in-Publication Data

Prud'homme, Alex.
   The cell game : Sam Waksal's fast money and false promises—and the fate of ImClone's cancer drug / Alex Prud'homme.
      p.   cm.
   Includes index.
   ISBN 0-06-055556-4
   1. Waksal, Samuel David.   2. ImClone Systems Incorporated—History.
3. Businessmen—United States—Biography.   4. Antineoplastic agents industry—Corrupt practices—United States.   5. Monoclonal antibodies—Research—United States—History.   6. Cancer—Chemotherapy.   7. Drugs—United States—Testing.
8. Insider trading in securities—United States.   I. Title.

HD9675.A672W35   2004
338.7'61616994061'092—dc22
[B]                                                                                     2003056983

04   05   06   07   08 DIX/RRD 10   9   8   7   6   5   4   3   2   1

*To Sarah*

Scientific theories . . . begin as imaginative constructions. They begin, if you like, as stories, and the purpose of the critical or rectifying episode in scientific reasoning is precisely to find out whether or not these are stories about real life.

—Peter Medawar, *Pluto's Republic*

There is a weird power in a spoken word . . . And a word carried far—very far—deals destruction through time as the bullets go flying through space.

—Joseph Conrad, *Lord Jim*

# *Acknowledgments*

*The Cell Game* was reported and written in nine months, a short time for a book, and I simply couldn't have done it without the help of many extraordinary people. I am grateful to everyone who helped me with this undertaking.

Foremost, I would like to thank all of the cancer patients and their families—most especially Shannon Kellum—for speaking to me openly about a profound and difficult subject. Cancer was thrust upon them, and they had to endure a terrible ordeal, often in great pain. By sharing their stories, they have increased public awareness of the disease and the efforts to combat it. To my mind, they are heroes who deserve to be celebrated. I'd also like to thank the patient advocates, especially Jane Reese-Coulbourne, Fred Santino, Bob Erwin, Nancy Roach, and Frank Burroughs for their help.

I was continually inspired by the hard work and brilliance of the oncologists who have dedicated themselves to combating the terrible set of diseases known as "cancer." I'd like to thank Dr. John Mendelsohn for taking time to vet my reporting on Erbitux and for sharing his life story. I did not have the chance to speak to Dr. Gordon Sato, but his story is impressive. I'd like to thank Dr. Mark Rubin, who tended to Shannon Kellum and played an important role in the development of Erbitux. I'd like to thank Dr. Colin Goddard at OSI Pharmaceuticals for telling me about his work on Tarceva and the difficult business of running a biopharmaceutical company. And I am grateful to the many other cancer specialists who helped me understand just what was at stake in the debate over Erbitux.

This book began life as an article about Sam Waksal—originally suggested by Tina Brown at *Talk,* and then, after the demise of that magazine, adopted and encouraged by Graydon Carter at *Vanity Fair,* where the story ran in the June 2002 issue. I thank both of these fine top editors for their support, as well as the editors, fact-checkers, legal staff, and art departments of those magazines for their hard work.

The crew at the Collins-McCormick Literary Agency—Nina Collins, David McCormick, and Leslie Falk—were steadfast in their support and acute in their observations; they helped me shape a book proposal, choose a title, and bring this book to fruition under sometimes trying circumstances.

At HarperBusiness, I'd like to thank the fine eye, helpful criticism, and grace under pressure of Marion Maneker, Kyran Cassidy, and Edwin Tan.

I could not have written this book without the assistance of other journalists, especially the irrepressible Paul Goldberg and Kirsten Boyd Goldberg, who broke the ImClone story open by publishing excerpts of the FDA's RTF letter in *The Cancer Letter* in January 2001. Adam Feuerstein's informative reports on *theStreet.com* were supplemented by entertaining conversations on the phone. My friend and neighbor Stephen S. Hall not only writes like a dream but was unfailingly supportive; his book on immunotherapy and cancer, *A Commotion in the Blood,* was a valuable resource. Geeta Anand of *The Wall Street Journal* did some of the best reporting on the biotech business in 2001–03, and as we compared notes about ImClone she became a friend.

James Suroweicki was kind enough to include my *Vanity Fair* story, "Investigating ImClone," in a book he edited, *Best Business Crime Writing of the Year.*

Less wittingly, reports by the *60 Minutes* journalists Lesley Stahl and Steve Kroft were insightful, as were stories by Gardiner Harris at *The Wall Street Journal* and *The New York Times,* Andrew Pollack and Constance Hays at *The New York Times,* Justin Gillis at *The Washington Post,* Christopher Byron, John Crudele and others at *The New York Post,* Catherine Arnst at *BusinessWeek,* Stacey Schultz at *U.S. News & World Report,* Andy Serwer at *Fortune,* Matthew Herper at *Forbes,* Jeffrey Toobin at *The New Yorker,* Landon Thomas Jr. and Beth Landman Keil at *New*

*Acknowledgments*

*York,* and Frank DiGiacomo and Ian Blecher at *The New York Observer.* In 1993, Edward A. Wyatt wrote one of the earliest and most important stories about Sam Waksal and ImClone, "Outside the Lab," in *Barron's.*

For the most part, Sam Waksal was gracious, charming, and entertaining; he was generous with his time in the winter of 2001. After mid-January 2002, he refused my many entreaties to discuss the matter. Yet Sam surprised me by giving his blessing so that his old friends Elizabeth Latham and Norma Robert could speak to me; I enjoyed their company and appreciated their observations.

I had a brief conversation with Sam's sister, Patti, and a longer and more fruitful conversation with his former mother-in-law, Shirley Flacks. I wish Jack and Sabina Waksal had returned my calls. I spoke to a number of Sam's friends and acquaintances: Elana Castaneda was particularly insightful.

Those who prefer not to be identified were very helpful: thank you.

Some important figures in the ImClone story refused to speak to me, most notably: Harlan Waksal, Robert Goldhammer, John Landes, and Andrea Rabney at ImClone; Peter Dolan, and indeed everyone else, at Bristol-Myers Squibb. And while Dr. Leonard Saltz and Dr. Larry Norton of Memorial Sloan-Kettering Cancer Center were kind enough to speak to me in late 2001, the hospital declined to make them available once the ImClone scandal made news in 2002.

I interviewed Martha and Alexis Stewart in the winter of 2001, and they were gracious, funny, and helpful. Although I was unable to interview either of them, or Peter Bacanovic, for this book, I appreciate the efforts of our intermediaries.

Special thanks to former ImClone employees who spoke to me on the record: Lee Compton, Irv Feit, Norma Robert, and Ian Alterman. I also extend thanks to the numerous former employees who prefer to remain unidentified; they helped to draw a more complete portrait of a complex and contradictory subject.

Thanks to Phyllis Carter at Merck KGaA, in Frankfurt, Germany.

Thanks to Richard Beleson at The Capital Group, and to my unnamed sources in the investment community.

Thanks to the many people who told me of their experience with Sam Waksal in academia—Lee and Len Herzenberg, among others, at

---

*York,* and Frank DiGiacomo and Ian Blecher at *The New York Observer.* In 1993, Edward A. Wyatt wrote one of the earliest and most important stories about Sam Waksal and ImClone, "Outside the Lab," in *Barron's.*

For the most part, Sam Waksal was gracious, charming, and entertaining; he was generous with his time in the winter of 2001. After mid-January 2002, he refused my many entreaties to discuss the matter. Yet Sam surprised me by giving his blessing so that his old friends Elizabeth Latham and Norma Robert could speak to me; I enjoyed their company and appreciated their observations.

I had a brief conversation with Sam's sister, Patti, and a longer and more fruitful conversation with his former mother-in-law, Shirley Flacks. I wish Jack and Sabina Waksal had returned my calls. I spoke to a number of Sam's friends and acquaintances: Elana Castaneda was particularly insightful.

Those who prefer not to be identified were very helpful: thank you.

Some important figures in the ImClone story refused to speak to me, most notably: Harlan Waksal, Robert Goldhammer, John Landes, and Andrea Rabney at ImClone; Peter Dolan, and indeed everyone else, at Bristol-Myers Squibb. And while Dr. Leonard Saltz and Dr. Larry Norton of Memorial Sloan-Kettering Cancer Center were kind enough to speak to me in late 2001, the hospital declined to make them available once the ImClone scandal made news in 2002.

I interviewed Martha and Alexis Stewart in the winter of 2001, and they were gracious, funny, and helpful. Although I was unable to interview either of them, or Peter Bacanovic, for this book, I appreciate the efforts of our intermediaries.

Special thanks to former ImClone employees who spoke to me on the record: Lee Compton, Irv Feit, Norma Robert, and Ian Alterman. I also extend thanks to the numerous former employees who prefer to remain unidentified; they helped to draw a more complete portrait of a complex and contradictory subject.

Thanks to Phyllis Carter at Merck KGaA, in Frankfurt, Germany.

Thanks to Richard Beleson at The Capital Group, and to my unnamed sources in the investment community.

Thanks to the many people who told me of their experience with Sam Waksal in academia—Lee and Len Herzenberg, among others, at

Stanford, the people who shared a lab with Sam at Tufts, and Dr. Stave Kohtz at Mount Sinai.

As is standard practice, I was not allowed to interview investigators and prosecutors from the U.S. Attorney's Office, DOJ, SEC, and FBI; nor was I able to speak to Judge William H. Pauley III. I found their work illuminating nonetheless. Congressman James Greenwood was witty and thoughtful when we spoke more than a year after the House Subcommittee on Oversight and Investigations held its ImClone hearings; his deputy, the Oversight Counsel Alan Slobodin, was kind enough to explain how such a massive investigation works in practice.

Mitch Gipson at the Audobon Research Park and Karin Duncker at the New York Biotechnology Association were unfailingly helpful. My "landlords" Elise Pettus and David Schwab provided a congenial workspace in TriBeCa. With the long hours required to get this book done, my family had to rely on the kindness of relatives, neighbors, and friends: thank you for your support.

Most of all, I'd like to thank the boundless patience of my wife, Sarah, and our children, Hector and Sophia; they made the hard work worthwhile.

# *Contents*

# Contents

# Prologue

At 9:01 A.M. on December 27, 2001, an unemployed, 27-year-old actress named Aliza Waksal sold 39,472 shares of a small Manhattan biotech firm called ImClone Systems, Inc. It netted her some $2.5 million. At 9:41 A.M., Jack Waksal, Aliza's 80-year-old grandfather, sold approximately 111,336 shares of ImClone, for about $7 million. Both trades had been allegedly prompted by Sam Waksal, who was Aliza's father and Jack's son; he was also the cofounder and CEO of ImClone. A short while later, Sam attempted to transfer an additional 79,797 shares of his own ImClone holdings—worth some $5 million—into his daughter's Merrill Lynch account for another sale. His instructions said the stock transfer was "urgent" and "imperative." But Merrill compliance officers grew wary. This was not normal behavior for a CEO and his family. Because Sam was a company insider, his second trade in Aliza's name was denied. It didn't take long for word of this activity to filter into Wall Street, where the rumor mill reported something fishy at ImClone Systems.

In 2001 ImClone was the undisputed star of biotech. A small Manhattan firm, it owned the license to the hottest cancer drug of the moment—a monoclonal antibody called Erbitux—in the latest class of cancer treatments, so-called targeted therapies. Health care was now a $1.3 trillion industry, and cancer drugs alone constituted a $10 billion-a-year business. A flurry of articles and a *60 Minutes* story had hailed targeted treatments, and Erbitux in particular, as the biotech equivalent of "smart bombs," which promised a new era in the war on cancer.

"Erbitux is going to be *huge,* one of the biggest drugs in the history of oncology—a drug that is going to alter the way cancer therapy is done from now on," Sam declared with an intense, nearly evangelical fervor. And then he'd add: "This drug will be a billion-dollar-a-year product."

He was a charming, reedy, olive-skinned man in his mid-50s, with thinning dark hair, roaming almond-shaped eyes, and a tricky grin. He had cofounded ImClone in the early 1980s with his younger brother, Harlan, to make a fortune conquering "big" diseases such as AIDS and cancer. After years of failure, ImClone had what every biotech company in the world wanted: Erbitux appeared to be a "silver bullet," a seemingly magical cancer drug that would not only help thousands of dying patients, but would also make its sponsors rich and famous.

Sam spent years refining his pitch for Erbitux at investor meetings and leading hospitals across the country, in the halls of Congress, at biotech conferences in Europe and Japan, he'd let people in on a little secret: *ImClone is no ordinary investment,* he seemed to whisper. *Sure, Erbitux will soon be a billion-dollar-a-year drug, but it's more than that. Much more. This is a miracle compound, a cutting-edge biopharmaceutical breakthrough. It will save the lives of thousands of dying cancer patients, and could change the very nature of science. Your investment will bring you not only gold but glory—you could help us to make history!*

It was a very seductive message, coming from a very persuasive man, and many bright and substantial people bought into it. Noted financiers like Robert Goldhammer, former vice chairman of Kidder Peabody, joined the ImClone board. So did world-famous oncologists like Dr. Vincent DeVita, the former head of the National Cancer Institute. Twenty-six leading hospitals around the nation, led by the esteemed Dr. Leonard Saltz, of Memorial Sloan-Kettering, had participated in the drug's clinical trial.

Sam had whetted investors' appetites by predicting that his drug would be on the market by June 2002, well ahead of its nearest competitors—AstraZeneca's Iressa and OSI Pharmaceutical's Tarceva, which were at least a year or two behind (a number of other targeted treatments were behind them, too). In the highly competitive and lucrative pharmaceutical business, such a "first-mover" advantage to market can be critical to a product's success. The market responded by pushing ImClone's stock price up in little excited jumps.

All Erbitux had to do was to pass muster with the U.S. Food and Drug Administration (FDA), the federal body that regulates new drugs. That wouldn't be a problem, Sam promised, because in February the agency had granted his drug special "fast-track" status, the quickest route to approval. Besides, the data spoke for itself: to win the FDA's blessing ImClone had to prove that Erbitux works to quell tumors in 15 percent of the patients in clinical trials; when used with chemotherapy, Erbitux had proved effective in 22.5 percent of patients—far more than what the FDA required.

"Unless I'm sitting here and just boldly lying to you, which I'm not in the habit of doing, I am telling you categorically the FDA told us that these studies will stand alone as full studies for approval," Harlan Waksal assured an analyst in the spring of 2001. "We believe we will cruise through [the FDA approval process]. There will be a groundswell of activity . . . because this drug is setting a new standard. There's never been a drug that's been able to achieve this [result]."

The press began to run prominent stories about the drug, and Im-Clone employees, and even their friends, were bombarded with requests from cancer patients around the country desperate for "compassionate-use" access to the still-experimental drug. ImClone galvanized the entire biotech market, and in September the company signed a record-setting, $2 billion partnership with pharmaceutical giant Bristol-Myers Squibb. From April to July, ImClone's stock price surged from $27 to $53 per share. By early December it had reached $75 a share, and Sam and Harlan Waksal had exercised options with a combined worth of some $111 million.

AND NOW, on December 26, 2001, just as years of painstaking work were about to pay off, something was going wrong. Sam had been vacationing on the resort island of St. Bart's, partying with his art dealer, Larry Gagosian, and Harvey Weinstein, of Miramax, when his brother called with bad news: the FDA was about to reject Erbitux—not because the drug didn't work, but because ImClone's data was sloppy and incomplete.

Keeping mum, saying he'd return to the resort island soon, Sam immediately jetted back to New York on his leased private jet. Arriving back at his 5,000-square-foot loft in SoHo that night, he began to work the phones—first calling his father, Jack, and then, the next morning, his daughter. Unbeknownst to almost everyone, Sam—the highest-paid CEO in biotech—was carrying a personal debt of $80 million, $65 million of which was on margin, secured by his ImClone stock. His monthly margin bill was a cool $800,000. If ImClone collapsed, he would be ruined. He panicked.

Early on the morning of the 27th, Sam instructed Aliza to sell her shares. She sold at $63.20 a share, and the stock began to head down toward $60. Sam attempted to shift some of his own shares to her account. He knew the SEC monitored stock trades by company insiders and their families, but he didn't stop to think about what he was doing; he was just acting. For years he had shuffled money offshore, or through an account he had secretly established in Aliza's name—he'd forged her signature—and he figured it would all work out in the wash. He was doing good for humanity; his drug was about to change cancer medicine. So what if he cut a few corners? But just in case things didn't work out as planned, he took out an insurance policy by buying ImClone "put options" through an anonymous Swiss bank account: if the stock price dropped dramatically, he'd profit by betting against his own company.

At noon, Sam and Harlan—skiing with his family in Telluride—began frantically calling a senior official at the FDA's Center for Biologics to find out if Erbitux would be rejected. The official had no comment.

At 1:43 P.M. that afternoon Martha Stewart had Merrill Lynch execute the sale of all her 3,928 shares of ImClone, for $228,000. (She made a relatively insubstantial profit of $64,000.) Also at 1:43, she called Sam's office. His phone log reads: "Martha Stewart . . . something is going on with ImClone and she wants to know what . . . She is on her way to Mexico . . . she is staying at Los Ventanos."

About an hour later, a Merrill Lynch biotech analyst got on the squawk box to alert the firm's 15,000 brokers: it was rumored that the FDA was about to reject Erbitux. ImClone looked vulnerable. "Sell!"

# PART ONE

# THE $2 BILLION ANTIBODY

ONE

# Cancer Cells Are Smart

Six feet tall, trim, with white hair, a long-featured face, and intelligent hazel eyes, Dr. John Mendelsohn was one of the most accomplished cancer fighters in the world. He wasn't loud or physically imposing, but his fecund mind, forthright demeanor, and implacable resolve drew people to him naturally. The son of a traveling salesman from Cincinnati, Mendelsohn had proven himself a brilliant researcher and teacher, an exceptional administrator and fund-raiser. Yet he was not the kind who took his talents for granted. John Mendelsohn was driven to "use science to improve life."

One prize had eluded him, maddeningly, for over two decades: the commercialization of the monoclonal antibody C225, a potentially revolutionary cancer drug. C225, later called "Erbitux," was Mendelsohn's brainchild. It had alternately inspired and vexed him since 1980, when he and a small group of collaborators at the University of California, San Diego (UCSD), had made their earliest discoveries about "targeted treatment" cancer drugs. The lack of time and money had been their main constraints, as in most creative undertakings, but their novel ideas about how to fight cancer had also met with academic hostility and commercial resistance. Several times Mendelsohn had arranged deals with pharmaceutical companies to develop C225, only to have the agreement fall apart. He was quick to note that this is the nature of science, that developing new drugs is a risky and difficult business, that any worthwhile quest requires trial and error. "You haven't crossed home plate until you've crossed home plate," he'd say stoically.

Mendelsohn was convinced that C225 would one day extend the lives of many cancer victims, that it would be the most significant personal contribution he could make to the war on cancer. When he spoke of his campaign to bring the cancer drug C225 from idea to the laboratory to the marketplace and "get it into patients," Mendelsohn's voice would tighten, his brow would furrow, and his eyes would blaze intensely—revealing for just a moment the steely determination that lay beneath his genial exterior.

At the end of May 2001, Mendelsohn, who was 64, was the guest of honor at a luncheon in New York City for more than 100 members of the nation's social and intellectual elite. The gathering was a fund-raiser for Houston's M. D. Anderson Cancer Center, the nation's largest cancer hospital, which Mendelsohn had run since 1996. The lunch was attended by President George H. W. Bush, a friend from Houston who sat on the board of visitors at the Anderson, and it was hosted by Martin Zweig, a Wall Street tycoon. Encompassing the entire top floor of the opulent Pierre Hotel, on 59th Street and Fifth Avenue, the Zweig apartment was like a castle in the sky: the walls were eclectically decorated with Renoir paintings, Beatles memorabilia, and the sparkling white dress Marilyn Monroe had worn to sing "Happy Birthday" to President Kennedy in 1962. Framed by its expansive windows were breathtaking views over the long greensward of Central Park and around the gray, crenellated cityscape of midtown Manhattan. As he stood in that fabulous aerie at the start of the new century, nibbling canapés, graciously accepting compliments and some $475,000 in donations for M. D. Anderson, no one could begrudge Mendelsohn his feelings of relief, fulfillment, and cautious optimism.

The week before, C225 had been the star of the 37th annual ASCO conference (American Society for Clinical Oncology), the largest gathering of cancer specialists in the world. There, ImClone Systems, Inc., the small Manhattan biotech firm that had licensed Mendelsohn's drug, had made a stunning announcement: in clinical trials, 22.5 percent of colon cancer patients who had used a cocktail of C225 and irinotecan, a standard chemotherapy, had responded positively, meaning their tumors shrank by more than fifty percent. This was the best response rate ever achieved in patients who previously had no hope for survival. The oncology community had reacted with a thundering ovation. There had been a burst of media coverage. ImClone's stock began to climb. And, to cap it all off, ImClone's CEO, Sam Waksal, had begun secret negotiations with the pharmaceutical giant Bristol-Myers Squibb for a landmark deal that finally promised to bring C225 to market.

Circulating in the noosphere of the Zweig apartment, Mendelsohn's gaze slipped out the window, and over the breathtaking views to fix on the bright, indefinite horizon. *After all of the false starts and setbacks,* he wondered, *what could possibly go wrong now?*

THE HISTORY OF modern biotechnology began on April 25, 1953, when James Watson and Francis Crick announced in the British journal *Nature* that they had unlocked the three-dimensional structure of the DNA (deoxyribonucleic acid) molecule. DNA is the "master molecule," the structure of which is encoded with the information needed to create and direct the chemical processes of life. The gracefully spiraled structure, known as the double helix, was the key to understanding the technology of life. Watson and Crick's discovery would earn them the Nobel Prize (Watson was only 34 years old at the time), and would raise many intriguing questions, foremost of which was: Could DNA be manipulated? Could life itself be manipulated?

It was a question, and a challenge, that would motivate an entire generation of scientists to produce some of the most exhilarating medical discoveries in history. It would also set off a philosophical debate: biotechnology was seen as either a Promethean quest to save mankind or a Faustian meddling. In his 1969 book about the discovery of DNA, *The Coming of the Golden Age: A View of the End of Progress,* Gunther Stent described man's ability to manipulate DNA as a sign of the end to social and economic evolution.

As a Harvard junior in 1957, John Mendelsohn became the first undergraduate student in the lab of James Watson. There Mendelsohn was introduced to the exciting new field of molecular biology, which became his intellectual passion in life.

In his first two years at Harvard, Mendelsohn had studied physics and chemistry, but found that he wasn't enjoying himself. As a sophomore he dropped organic chemistry and physics and took a range of humanities courses—philosophy, the government of the Soviet Union—and slowly came to the conclusion that he did not want to devote himself to pure science. How would he apply himself, then? At the time, Watson and his collaborators were learning to apply molecular biology and genetics to the study of cells and the problems of human disease. Once he learned of it, this combination of hard science and humanistic medicine immediately appealed to Mendelsohn. "I liked people," he'd say. "I wanted to be a doctor." He would spend the next two years working at the Watson lab, in addition to carrying his normal course load, playing tennis, and socializing. (He met a Mount Holyoke chemistry student named Anne Charles at a party in Harvard yard; they would marry in 1963.)

The lab work was intensive and nearly all consuming, but Mendelsohn didn't mind. He was thrilled to immerse himself in every aspect of the job—running experiments, delving into research, learning how to analyze data, and even washing test tubes. There were a dozen people in the lab, most of whom were Ph.D. candidates and postdoctoral students, each of whom had a specialty that Mendelsohn could learn from. He enjoyed toiling late into the night, over weekends, and during a hot summer. He researched bacteria and learned about the chemistry of life and how to use new technologies to answer age-old questions. He was paid a modest stipend, which barely covered his housing and food, but he probably would have paid for the opportunity to work for the "brilliant and inspiring" Watson.

Looking back on this apprenticeship, Mendelsohn would recognize these crucial years as the intellectual crucible that shaped his life's work. "I love science," he'd say, "I love teaching. I really love clinical medicine. If you care about what makes people tick, and they have a serious illness, then medicine allows you to get close to them very quickly. All the phony-baloney barriers go down. You help them, not only with your knowledge of disease, but with their human needs."

Mendelsohn's father, a classic "middleman" who traveled from store to store in the Midwest, toting a sample case full of men's apparel—belts, suspenders, cuff links—and his mother, a housewife and active community volunteer, had not been especially inclined toward science or medicine. But they always stressed the importance of education and encouraged John to "follow your nose."

Mendelsohn was always a voracious reader, and as an adult he would be especially drawn to books on religion, philosophy, and history. Indeed, religion is a constant theme for Mendelsohn. He was raised Jewish; his wife was raised half Quaker and half Episcopalian; and they and their three boys attended a Unitarian church. Unlike many scientists, Mendelsohn, who has attended services at synagogues, churches, and Quaker meeting houses, is unembarrassed to say: "I am a religious person." When asked about the tension between science and religion, he answered by paraphrasing Einstein: "Science doesn't have all the answers. When you contemplate the vastness of the universe, you have to believe in a God."

As a 22-year-old Fulbright scholar, Mendelsohn spent a year at the University of Glasgow in Scotland. During the week, he'd study nucleic acids and grow cells in test tubes in the lab. On weekends, he'd backpack through the Scottish highlands—a terrain he fell in love with and still returns to. On holidays, he'd hike the Alps or tour the Continent in a rented car with friends from home. In his diary from this year in Scotland, he wrote that he had decided once and for all to dedicate his life to "using molecular biology to cure human disease."

Mendelsohn returned to the States and graduated from Harvard Medical School in 1963. Over the next three years he did his medical residency at Harvard's Peter Bent Brigham Hospital (now Brigham and Women's Hospital), then went on to study chromosomes at the National Institutes of Health (NIH) in Washington, D.C. At Washington University in St. Louis, he taught and researched hematology and oncology. It would prove a fortuitous combination of experiences and disciplines.

In 1970, the biotech industry did not yet exist and San Diego, California, was not yet one of its most fertile breeding grounds. The war was raging in Vietnam and the nation was about to reach a defining moment. Most young people were far more turned on by tuning out and marching against the Establishment than by spending hour after grinding hour doing scientific research in a lab.

Mendelsohn headed west that year to begin his professional career on the faculty of the two-year-old medical school at the University of California, San Diego (UCSD). As things turned out, his timing and placement would be inspired.

Because cancer is such a widespread and terrible disease—it is the leading killer of Americans, after heart disease—it has long been the focus of intensive medical research. Surgery and radiation remain the most prevalent methods of fighting cancer: "the cold knife and hot rays" have proven relatively effective, "saving" nearly a third of all patients with cancer, which is to say they are still alive five years after their first diagnosis. (This number could be raised to 50 percent, Mendelsohn believed, if people would only take the basic precautions—don't smoke, exercise regularly, eat well, and submit to regular checkups—that have proven to be useful deterrents.)

In the meantime, there has been an ongoing quest for alternative treatments. At the start of the 20th century, the American surgeon William B. Coley treated cancer patients with a rudimentary vaccine made of killed bacteria—an early example of immunotherapy, a form of medicine that helps the body's immune system to fight disease.

In 1910, the German chemist Paul Ehrlich suggested that chemotherapy—that is, treatment with chemicals—might prove to be a "magic bullet" against disease. So-called cytotoxic ("cell killer") chemotherapy (chemo) drugs have proven remarkably effective. Chemo treatments arrest the growth of certain tumors by interfering with cell function. But their success comes at a price. Chemo drugs are in effect poisons, the outgrowth of experiments with mustard gas in World War I, and patients using them become nauseated, shed hair, and lose their appetite and weight.

By the early 1970s, the search was on for a new kind of "magic bullet." It was an exciting time in oncology. Much like the giant strides in physics research in the early 1900s—when Einstein, Bohr, and Heisenberg made their findings about the atom and its powers—the 1970s and 1980s witnessed an enormous upwelling in cancer research in America, with great leaping improvements in surgery and the use of X-rays, radiation, and chemotherapies. These advances were not a random accident. They were the result of a concerted and unprecedented national effort, which would provide both a conceptual launching pad and a practical framework for what Mendelsohn called the "intellectual odyssey" that led him to C225.

In 1971, President Nixon declared a national "War on Cancer," with the objective of curing the disease in time for the nation's bicentennial in 1976. It was a supremely worthy, ambitious and unrealistic goal. The War on Cancer was launched in the midst of the Vietnam War and had been inspired in part by NASA's successful lunar program. Like those grandiose undertakings, the War on Cancer required millions of dollars in federal money and the establishment of a new bureaucracy—in this case, the National Cancer Institute (NCI), which would fund and oversee research into the disease.

"The analogy was the moon shots," Mendelsohn recalled. *(If America can put a man on the moon, then surely it can whip cancer!)* "The feeling was that if the government was willing to bring significant financial resources to bear, there was enough known about the disease that we could make a major breakthrough."

The NCI was smart enough not to be too rigid or specific about how its grants were used. "Scientists often do their best work when they follow their nose," Mendelsohn says. "Often, a result is totally unexpected." He hinted that such unexpected results were the best, or at least his favorite, kind of discovery. Nixon's War on Cancer did not lead to victory. But Mendelsohn believed that it "paid off" in spades, because it lead to the development of important scientific tools and a vast knowledge base from which we continue to benefit.

The first step in battling cancer was to discover how its processes worked and how to interrupt them. It wasn't easy. Part of what makes cancer so difficult to treat is that it is not just one disease: "cancer" is really an umbrella term for about 200 related diseases, each of which is driven by a different set of factors, and which behave in different ways in different patients. Lately, scientists have discovered there are 30,000 genes in the genome: about 500 of them control the critical cell functions that are involved in the proliferation and replication of cells' DNA. When these genes begin to malfunction the cell usually dies off, which is normal; but sometimes the cells divide in an uncontrolled frenzy, which is cancer. But at the time, physicians didn't really understand how cancer cells function.

"When I started at UCSD, in 1970, we didn't have a clue as to what caused cancer," Mendelsohn recalled. "The leading hypothesis was that the disease was the result of a virus," as it often was in lab animals. Cancer was typically diagnosed by a physician looking at a biopsy, or by studying a patient's blood through a microscope. The disease was most often treated with surgery or radiation, although doctors would sometimes consult a list of a few highly toxic chemotherapy drugs. Specific chemo drugs were prescribed for specific cancers—methotrexate for leukemia, say—and then patient and physician would essentially hope for the best. (The first successful use of chemotherapy to cure a cancerous tumor was just a few years earlier, in 1963.)

The belief that viruses were cancer agents led to an intensive period of research. Funded as part of Nixon's War on Cancer, virus research led to several important discoveries and a far more nuanced appreciation for how genetic mechanisms worked. One of these discoveries was the recombinant DNA technique—the process of cutting and recombining DNA fragments as a way to isolate or alter genes—which has proved a huge boon to medicine. In the early 1980s, the use of recombinant DNA helped doctors figure out how the AIDS virus works relatively quickly, which allowed them to devise treatments within a few years.

Research into viruses led to a far more detailed understanding of how cells function, and a surprising discovery. Cancer in humans, it turns out, is not usually caused by a virus. Rather, it is caused when some of the cell's own genes are disrupted and the cell begins to malfunction. Cells normally divide and multiply only as the body signals that it needs them. This process is controlled in part by oncogenes (the genes that stimulate cell growth) and by tumor-supressor genes (which inhibit cell growth). Some cancers occur when a malfunctioning oncogene sends out protein signals that set off a wild division of cells. The resulting cancerous cells spread throughout the body. The tumor-suppressor genes that would normally curtail such proliferation may also be malfunctioning.

In the 1970s and 1980s, researchers slowly built their understanding of this process. In 1977, Dr. J. Michael Bishop and Dr. Harold Varmus identified the first human oncogene, which controlled cell growth. One of the most important molecules produced by an oncogene is called the epidermal growth factor (EGF) receptor. While EGF is found in many normal cells, it is wildly abundant in most cancerous cells. The surface of cells—both healthy and cancerous—have "receptors," which allow the EGF to bind to the cell, and thus trigger a cascade of enzymes inside the cell, which help to stimulate and sustain the tumor. But while the surface of a normal cell may have some 10,000 EGF receptors, cancer cells can have a million or more EGF receptors.

In 1980, it was discovered that a viral oncogene had an internal signaling enzyme called a tyrosine kinase, which stimulates cell growth. Dr.

Stanley Cohen discovered that the portion of the EGF receptor inside the cell was also a tyrosine kinase. His work on EGF and its receptor would win Cohen the Nobel Prize in Physiology and Medicine, and caught the attention of John Mendelsohn and his band of researchers at UCSD. Also in 1980, Dr. Michael Sporn and Dr. George Todero published a paper in *The New England Journal of Medicine* that established the autocrine hypothesis—that cancer cells can bypass restrictions on their growth by making their own growth factors and "autostimulating" receptors on the cell's surface. The growth factor was the mechanism that triggers cell proliferation. This insight suggested wide new possibilities for cancer treatment.

"If we can block the function of the EGF receptor, will that stop cancer cells from growing?" Mendelsohn and Dr. Gordon Sato, his colleague at UCSD, looked at each other with eyebrows raised. It was now the fall of 1980, and the rangy, energetic Mendelsohn and the shorter and quieter Sato would spend weeks brainstorming about what makes cancer cells tick.

Gordon Sato was a *nisei,* a second-generation American of Japanese descent, and during the Second World War he had been interned in a camp in California. After the war he worked as a gardener: while using blood from a slaughterhouse as a fertilizer, he became interested in serum and in learning about how things grow. The president of CalTech was impressed with Sato's inquisitive mind and sponsored his formal education and Ph.D. In 1980, Sato was just finishing a decade's worth of research that demonstrated that serum is required for cells to grow in culture because it provides growth factors.

Sato and Mendelsohn enjoyed each other's company and the intellectual challenge of imagining what was happening inside the body at a microscopic level. Their speculations required deep scientific knowledge, rigorous medical training, creative intuition, and a degree of stubbornness occasionally leavened by flights of pure imagination. Two decades later, Mendelsohn would look back at this rolling conversation with Sato as the moment when "all sorts of half-formed ideas and vague questions were brought into sharp focus." It was the kind of freewheeling and deeply penetrating scientific discussion that he wished he'd had hundreds of times in his life but in fact has had only a few times.

"Cancer cells are smart," Mendelsohn observed, meaning they are adaptive and can proliferate so wildly that they are usually able to circumvent chemotherapy. The word *cancer* is derived from the Greek word for "crab": the disease seems to crawl relentlessly throughout the body; for centuries it was tantamount to a death sentence.

By 1980, it was known that EGF is expressed in a third of all cancers—including tumors of the head and neck, gastrointestinal tract, lung, kidney, breast, and prostate—and several researchers began to research ways to block EGF receptors (EGFr) as a means of attacking the disease. This approach was met with a degree of skepticism. At the time, many in the medical community considered EGF a poor therapy target because it is found in healthy as well as cancerous cells, raising the specter of significant side effects if the growth factor were blocked. Mendelsohn and Sato believed that healthy cells had other growth mechanisms that could compensate for the loss of EGF function.

In the fall of 1980, Sato said: "John, you have a background in immunology and the cell's growth cycle. I have a background in growth factors. Let's sit down and try to figure out a way to block cancer cell growth."

If they could block the receptor, they wondered, would that stop the tumor from spreading? Theoretically it would.

Put simply, if the EGF could not bind to its receptor, and thus could not activate the tyrosine kinase, then a cancer cell would not be able to proliferate. Put more completely, Mendelsohn and Sato hypothesized that a monoclonal antibody—an immune system protein created in the lab rather than in the body—that binds to EGFr and blocks the binding of either EGF or TGF-*a* (transforming growth factor-alpha) could prevent cell proliferation by inhibiting the signaling pathways that depend on EGFr.

In explaining to laypersons how this might work, Mendelsohn said: "If you think of the receptor as a lock, and the growth factor as a key, then the monoclonal antibody works just like sticking gum in the lock. It blocks it up."

For the next two years Mendelsohn, Sato, and a small laboratory team that included Tomo Kawomoto and Sato's son, Denry, worked intensively to develop a monoclonal antibody from mouse cells that would attach to the EGF receptors before the growth factor could. It was slow and grueling work. Finally, the antibody that proved most effective was named "225" because it was the 225th antibody they had tested. (They were conducting experiments in test tubes. The "C" in

C225 stands for "chimera," and would be added later. In Greek mythology a chimera is a monster made of incongruous parts—a lion's head, a goat's body, and a serpent's tail, say. A "chimeric antibody" is made up of part mouse and part human protein.)

AT THIS POINT different cancers were treated as discrete diseases: lung cancer was treated differently than, say, head-and-neck cancer. But in fact as cancer cells metastasize they travel all over the body, so that cancerous cells from a patient's leg could end up in his brain. If C225 worked to block tumor growth, the UCSD researchers concluded, then someday it might be possible to tailor a therapy to combat a *type* of cancer, regardless of where it originated. Today such "targeted therapy" is at the center of modern oncology. But at the time it was a novel approach, and many cancer traditionalists resisted the approach.

When Mendelsohn and Sato applied for funding from the NCI in 1982, they were turned down. "They felt it wouldn't work," Mendelsohn recalled, a bit stiffly. "There's always conservatism in science. Some new ideas are not seen as plausible at first."

Relying on funds from philanthropies, he and Sato pressed on and created a nude mouse colony, one of the first in America, in which to study tumor growth. When they showed that C225 indeed stopped the growth of tumors in mice, Mendelsohn was ecstatic. This was the first real indication that they were onto something, that their wild ideas about "putting gum in the lock" might actually prove correct. But he knew enough not to get carried away. "You can *dream* of the potential, but, well, a lot of times things are discovered that don't end up being important therapies."

In 1983 and 1984, Mendelsohn, Sato, and their colleagues published a series of papers demonstrating that blocking the EGFr with the antibody 225 could inhibit the spread of cancer cells, both in culture and in human tumor xenografts; further, it inhibited the activity of the tyrosine kinase. As things turned out, they had targeted a cellular oncogene. This novel approach—inhibiting tyrosine kinases and oncogene products—has been expanded to include numerous other targets. There is evidence that the combination of an EGFr inhibitor like C225 and chemotherapy or radiation is especially effective against tumors. "I believe this will be the major way that agents that block signaling pathways will be used in the clinic [and] will enhance the efficacy of cancer therapy," Mendelsohn predicts.

Targeted therapy became much discussed among cancer researchers. Mendelsohn and Sato stepped up the pace of their work on C225, and UCSD gave away samples of the antibody to labs around the country, to further research on antibodies and EGF receptors.

In 1984, Mendelsohn and his collaborators were delighted when it was proved that C225 was active against an oncogene, and blocked the signal of cancer-causing genes. "I was able to walk home and say to my wife: 'You know that antibody we made against the EGF receptor? Guess what, that antibody works against an oncogene!' " Mendelsohn would recall with a laugh. He paused, then added: That wasn't our plan. It's just the way it worked out. It was a big moment."

Years later, Mendelsohn would say of the flowering of discovery in the seventies and eighties: "It was a lot of hard work, and a very, very exciting period. We [cancer researchers] discovered how genes work, how they control cell proliferation, how they can malfunction. We know what causes cancer the way we know that germs cause infection. This has all happened in my lifetime. Then we realized that maybe something rational could be designed to treat cancer. In 1980, targeting cancer-causing genes and their protein products was brand-new. Today, it's the mantra for pharmaceutical companies, biotech, and academia. In the future, we're going to develop a long menu of agents, so that when Mrs. Smith's tumor is found to have six abnormally functioning genes, we'll have six therapies against them. That's the dream."

IN 1985, Mendelsohn accepted a prestigious post as chairman of the Department of Medicine at Memorial Sloan-Kettering in New York, which at the time was the nation's premier cancer hospital. Anne took a series of jobs—running an engineering program for Columbia University, overseeing production at a public television station—while their three boys went off to college. (Gordon Sato had left oncology to pursue an answer for world hunger through aquaculture. Today he is developing techniques for raising algae and brine shrimp; his hope is that simple fish farms will provide basic protein for millions of people.)

As a department chair, Mendelsohn was extremely busy, but, as always, he continued to tinker with C225. Although he received NCI funding for his work on the drug, he had come to an important personal decision: he was an academic, a clinician, and an administrator, he realized, not an entrepreneur. He couldn't develop the drug on his own. He needed a business partner, someone savvy enough to turn his experimental drug into a viable commercial product.

U.C. San Diego controlled the license to the patents on C225, but it was the driven Mendelsohn who began to scout around for a partner. Eventually he found a small antibody company called Hybritech. Founded by a colleague from the UCSD lab, it was the very first biotech start-up in San Diego—a city that now boasts at least 200 biotech firms and is one of the leading hubs of the industry. Hybritech licensed Mendelsohn's antibody in 1988 and did a lot of the painstaking groundwork necessary for an experimental compound: conducting phase 1 clinical trials of the drug using the mouse antibody, proving that it was not toxic, scaling up production, and publishing results.

Initially there had been considerable criticism of Mendelsohn's decision to use an antibody, which must be administered intravenously because it is too large a molecule to be absorbed as a pill. Even more worrisome, monoclonal antibodies at that time were made from proteins isolated from mice—murine proteins—which could not be tolerated for long by people.

By 1990 the NCI was interested enough in C225 that it resolved the dispute by paying for the conversion of the C225 mouse antibody into a chimera, with human protein, and to contract a specialty firm to produce it. This was a crucial step that would allow the drug to be tested on human cancer patients.

Mendelsohn's lab at Sloan-Kettering confirmed that C225 was remarkably effective in eliminating tumors in mice, especially when combined with chemotherapy or radiation. Now, after a decade of work on C225, Mendelsohn dared to grow excited about its possibilities.

In 1992, the pharmaceutical company Eli Lilly and Company acquired Hybritech. This was great news: Lilly's deep pockets, long experience with FDA regulators, and marketing savvy meant that C225 would now have a shot at a proper development program and real commercial prospects. Only, Lilly decided that C225 didn't fit into its business plan. This decision may have been based on the fact that Lilly had once burned a lot of time and money on a monoclonal antibody that had failed (a common experience with monoclonal antibodies, at the time). Whatever its motivation, the company decided not to pursue the development of C225, and the drug's license reverted to UCSD, where it again languished.

"It was very sad," Mendelsohn said of Eli Lilly's decision, with a sharp note of frustration piercing his flat Ohio accent. At other times he has recalled this moment differently. "It wasn't a blow," he once insisted, unconvincingly. "There's just a lot of hurdles when you are trying to get a drug from an idea into a patient."

He now faced the very real prospect that C225 might never get out of the lab. Perhaps the science was just too new—despite his encouraging results in the lab, few scientists believed that a monoclonal antibody would prove to be an effective cancer therapy in actual human patients. Perhaps targeted treatments were a pipe dream—many oncologists pooh-poohed his strategy of blocking a growth factor receptor and damned the drug with faint praise when they called it a "promising idea."

Mendelsohn was convinced that if he could only find someone with the time and money and energy to pursue the drug's development, C225 would help suffering cancer patients. "I had no doubt," he said. "I was a believer. I knew the data was compelling, and there was a lot of interest. But it was up to me to find someone who wanted to pursue the drug." This time it had to be the right fit; he didn't want any more setbacks. He wanted to find someone who would fully commit to turning his dream into a reality.

In the spring of 1992, the biotech industry was booming and John Mendelsohn once again set out to find a business partner.

TWO

# The Idea of the New

In 1976, Robert Swanson, a stocky, balding, 27-year-old venture capitalist (VC) from Silicon Valley, heard about a scientific breakthrough and wondered if it had commercial potential. In recent years, the biochemist Herbert Boyer, of the University of California, San Francisco (UCSF), and the geneticist Stanley Cohen, of Stanford, had pioneered a new field called recombinant DNA, now known as genetic engineering. Not fully grasping how important this work was, or how central Boyer was to it, Swanson cold called the scientist and asked if he could drop by to talk. Boyer, a burly and bearded man dressed in faded blue jeans, said he was busy, but granted the young VC 10 minutes of his time. Swanson, dressed in a suit and a red tie, arrived on the green campus of UCSF on a Friday afternoon. When they met, Swanson's enthusiasm captivated Boyer.

"Can recombinant DNA be commercialized?" asked Swanson. "Yes," Boyer replied. They got to talking about the how and why; they went out for a beer; the 10-minute meeting stretched on for three hours. By the time they shook hands that afternoon, Swanson and Boyer had decided to form a new company that they would name Genentech, short for genetic-engineering-technology.

They each chipped in $500, and Swanson's employer, the VC firm

Kleiner-Perkins, added $100,000. At the time a few other start-ups, like Cetus, were trying to bring molecular biology to the marketplace; with funding from the oil and liquor industries, they produced energy products, new vaccines, and bacteria for alcohol production. But Genentech was tightly focused on a unique goal: to use recombinant DNA techniques to create a new kind of drugs—so-called biopharmaceuticals—that could bring potentially huge profits. And with that happy commingling of money and science, a new industry was kick-started: biotech.

Despite resistance from both the academy and business, Swanson and Boyer gathered together a motley crew of about 30 biologists in South San Francisco and pushed ahead with their plan. With a day-and-night effort, using batches of chemicals bought over the counter, the fledgling company managed a heroic feat by August 1977: to produce the first human protein, somatostatin, in a microorganism, the *E. coli* bacteria. This made news, and news brought wider interest. By the time it was published, near the end of 1977, every tech investor in the country had heard of Genentech. (In what would become a time-honored ritual in the business, the company made sure everyone knew about their discovery, by leaking details of the experiments to the public and then holding a press conference to officially state what everybody already knew.)

Genentech scientists went on a tear, wearing T-shirts emblazoned with the legend "Clone or Die!" In 1978, they cloned human insulin, and in 1979 they cloned human growth hormone. The company had the speed and momentum of an onrushing express train.

In 1980, Congress passed the Bayh-Dole Act, which allowed academic and research institutions to license and commercialize the discoveries of their research. These factors combined to unleash a great stampede of scientists and investors into the wide-open fields of biotech. They all seemed to be shouting "To the future!" and heading for the hills in search of scientific bonanzas. Many of them were successful at first.

The word *biotechnology* literally means "life technology," and it refers to the use of living organisms or their products to modify human health and the environment. The word was coined in 1919 by Karl Ereky, a Hungarian engineer who predicted a "Biochemical Age" much like the Stone Age, Iron Age, and Industrial Age. To a large extent, his prediction has been borne out: based on a deepening understanding of the fundamental mechanics of life, we are living in the Biotechnology Age today.

Strictly speaking, biotechnology is some 6,000 years old and dates from prehistoric man's use of yeast cells to raise bread dough or brew beer, and bacteria cells to make cheese and yogurt. But modern "biotech" encompasses some of the most thrilling and controversial science in human history—human genome and stem-cell research, cloned sheep, the Flav'r Sav'r Tomato, biotech drugs for Alzheimer's disease or obesity, even the enzymes used to finish denim blue jeans.

In general, biotech is a growing business "space" that attracts leading scientists and investors who want to be part of something new, mysterious, cool, and exciting. Like dot-coms or independent film, biotech is considered a hip business with a potentially huge upside—Amgen, for instance, the world's leading biotech firm, had total sales of $4 billion in 2001. And while it is an expensive and research-intensive industry, the demand for biotech products has been driving exponential growth. Based on current growth rates, experts predict there will be a "daily doubling of knowledge" in biotech by the year 2016. Revenues from biotech products have increased from $11.2 billion in 1995 to $25 billion in 2001.

Entranced by this success, more and more people, with varying degrees of sophistication, began to throw their money down to get into the game. But while Wall Street aims to maximize its return quickly and reliably, the truth is that biotech is a notoriously fickle and risky proposition. The vast majority of experimental drugs don't make it out of the lab, and those that do take years to eke out a profit.

"You have to contemplate this business in a very strategic manner," said Colin Goddard, the CEO of the biotech firm OSI Pharmaceuticals. "With a 10-year product lifecycle, biotech is an industry where you're constantly managing risk and outcome. One of the main challenges is that while you're growing up and learning new skills, you're also placing a big bet on a key product. Many, many times, biotech companies drop the ball on execution because they fall short on managing [these things simultaneously]. If you live in the now, you're going to lose in the now. You've got to constantly look to the future, and contemplate what the marketplace is going to look like. It can be difficult."

The popular press likes to portray scientific discovery as a steady progression of "breakthroughs" and "revolutions." But biotech discoveries are more often the result of evolution, of long-term, cyclical, and historical shifts. Science can be an exciting voyage into the unknown that ends with a phenomenal insight, such as Watson and Crick's work on DNA; but it is more often an arduous trek of tedious work, failed experiments, and meandering paths to nowhere.

"I think every time a new method is created, you get a spurt of activity where people again exercise their creativity," Charles Weissmann, the noted molecular biologist from the University of Zurich, has said. "After a while, all the easy ideas have become exhausted, and then it's tough going again. You know, it's like with an apple tree. In the beginning you shake it and 90 percent of the apples come down. Then you have to shake it a lot more to get out another 8 percent, and for the last two or three apples you have to climb the tree and crawl along the branches, and that's what happens with every technical breakthrough."

By the late 1970s, biotech scientists were focused on a seemingly amazing protein called interferon, an "antiviral penicillin" that they believed could be a kind of cure-all for everything from herpes to the common cold. Most especially, they thought interferon might work against the viruses believed to cause cancer. In 1979, as biologists, investors, and doctors rushed to find out more about the miracle molecule, *Life* magazine enthused:

> We might use [interferon] to ward off colds all year round and flu in flu season. We might not have to worry about rabies, about shingles or hepatitis or warts or cold sores or eye infections or other familiar ailments. We might be able to regulate our immune systems at will, maintaining our resistance to a variety of diseases in all seasons and at all ages. We could keep our transplanted parts and organs from being rejected. And perhaps we can count on interferon to cure and/or prevent cancer! Was there ever a panacea-hawking, snake-oil salesman at any carnival who ever promised more of his product? Yet, it could all come true some day.

Such was the hype that an all-out race to clone interferon ensued—pitting scientists from Genentech against rival biotech firm Biogen, not to mention Cetus Corp., Hoffman–La Roche, and teams from Caltech,

Stanford, the University of Warwick, England, and the Cancer Institute of Japan. This was biotech as competitive sport, and it drew worldwide attention. *Time* magazine ran a cover story on interferon: "The Big IF."

Despite nearly driving itself into bankruptcy in the process, Biogen, a biotech start-up based in Cambridge, Massachusetts, and Geneva, Switzerland—and whose efforts were being directed by Charles Weissmann in Zurich—ultimately won out. On Christmas Eve 1979, scientists in Zurich finally cloned interferon. It was a legitimate scientific breakthrough. Here at last was a technology with great potential in a wide number of fields—immunology, neurology, endocrinology, embryology, and cell biology. The news that interferon had been cloned broke internationally on January 16, 1980, "the date on which molecular biology became big business," the magazine *Science* reported. A story about the breakthrough ran on the front page of *The New York Times.*

Genentech had placed second in the race and soon identified eight different interferon genes that have yielded great scientific riches. But just as Biogen and Genentech scaled up to produce the molecule, a disturbing pattern became apparent: interferon looked promising in early studies but failed to cure cancer. By the 1981 American Society for Clinical Oncology (ASCO) conference, the future of the drug was in serious question. Interferon was saved by a patient in Texas, A. J. Goertz, who in 1977 had been diagnosed with a rare and lethal cancer, hairy–cell leukemia. He had received various treatments at M. D. Anderson Cancer Center in Houston, but kept relapsing. In July 1982, Goertz's health was failing when his doctors took a chance and gave him a series of experimental injections of interferon. Within two weeks he showed a remarkable improvement. A study of the drug was published in the *New England Journal of Medicine* in January 1984, and the following year the Food and Drug Administration (FDA) approved it for sale.

The race to clone interferon was important for biotech not because it was the first or most significant human gene to be cloned (it wasn't), but because it was the nascent industry's first really big commercial success. By 1996, interferon had been approved for use against seven different diseases and had become the world's first biotech blockbuster (defined as a drug with annual sales of at least $1 billion), with worldwide sales estimated at some $2.7 billion.

This lit a fire under the biotech business. One scientist defined interferon as "a substance you rub on stockbrokers."

For a long time Wall Street didn't quite get these little brainiac start-up companies: the biotechs were not public entities that one could invest in and profit from, and their products seemed incomprehensibly arcane. But in 1979, pharmaceutical analysts began to notice that the big drug companies were buying research from the little biotechs: Eli Lilly licensed an insulin product from Genentech; Schering-Plough invested in Biogen. After a conference entitled "DNA: The Genetic Revolution" was held at the Plaza Hotel in New York in August 1979, biotech was suddenly on investors' radar screens. They began to clamor for more information: Who and what is biotech and how could they put their money into it?

Swanson and Boyer took note. In 1980, Genentech went public and raised an eye-popping $35 million with an initial public offering (IPO) in which its stock price rocketed from $35 a share to $89 a share in less than an hour. It set a record for an IPO and became a classic tale of American wealth building. The gold-rush stories were legendary, especially that of the graduate student who had done a bit of work for the company and became a paper millionaire overnight.

The Genentech sale set off a frenzy of similar, or even more spectacular, offerings. Cetus, for example, which had three Nobel laureates on its scientific advisory board, raised $120 million in its IPO. More and more little biotech firms with big ideas began to pop up, like mushrooms after a rainfall, especially in California and along the Northeast Corridor. Within a few years, there would be more than 100 biotechnology companies underwritten by some $500 million in public capital—a phenomenon so striking that it was dubbed "biomania."

IN THE SPRING OF 1984, a skinny, mercurial young operator named Samuel David Waksal jumped from academia into the raging biomania. He had no job, little money, and no products; but that was okay, because Sam wanted to be an entrepreneur and had plenty of ideas. A few steps behind Sam, less flashy and quick, but steadier, or perhaps more calculating, was his younger brother, Harlan Wolf Waksal.

The Waksal brothers were like two sides of a coin. Sam, the ideas man, would have a brainstorm and Harlan, the nuts-and-bolts guy, would implement it. Charming Sam would make a mess and dutiful Harlan would clean it up. They spoke constantly about everything all the time. "Sam and Harlan are joined at multiple deep levels," said a former ImClone employee, who observed the Waksal brothers' relationship close up. "They absolutely know everything the other is doing. They're symbiotic."

In the early 1980s, biotech was *the* place to be in science. Interferon was making headlines, graduate students were becoming millionaires, and Wall Street investors were lining up for the privilege of funding new companies that had something, or anything, to do with biotech.

Sam Waksal thought: *That's where I want to be.*

In part, he wanted to get in on the excitement. And in part the founding of ImClone represented a means of escape, or reincarnation. Sam had been working as an academic researcher, but it had not been going well. He had caromed from one prestigious post to another, under a darkening cloud. Asked about this pattern years later, he defiantly stuck his chin up and said: "My job in life is to be creative and do important things, positive things, for mankind. The idea of the new, the *aha!* of life, that's what makes it fun. Once I do something, it's over for me, and I want to know what can I do next—what can I do that surpasses that? What next?"

Harlan, too, had reason to look for a change in circumstance. He had aspired to be a pediatrician, but while a medical resident in Boston, he'd been charged with attempting to smuggle two kilograms of cocaine from Florida to Boston. He and Sam would pass the incident off as "a youthful indiscretion," but it sidetracked his career. Now Harlan was working on cadavers, as a pathologist, and was feeling unfulfilled.

Old friends would later maintain that Sam founded ImClone "for Harlan"—to give him something to do, or steer him in a new direction.

In 1984, the Waksal brothers were both working as researchers in New York hospitals, Sam as associate professor of pathology at the Mount Sinai School of Medicine, Harlan as chief resident in pathology at King's County Hospital in Brooklyn. They lived in separate apartments in the same building on 81st Street and Columbus Avenue, on Manhattan's newly trendy Upper West Side.

Sam had no doubt that he would become a star. Physically unimposing, he had always been an intellectual superstar with an offbeat charm. He knew he was smarter than most people and he had no fear of engaging leading scientists in high-minded debates about the latest in scientific thought. "I will win the Nobel Prize," he announced to friends, and they believed him.

SAM WAKSAL was born in France. This was on September 8, 1947, according to the résumé listed in his Ph.D. dissertation from Ohio State University. Or maybe his birthday is in August, not September, as he told colleagues at ImClone who celebrated *their* birthdays in midsummer. Or maybe he wasn't born in 1947 at all, but two years later, on September 8, 1949, as it said on the curriculum vitae he handed out as the CEO of ImClone until he was forced out of the company. Throughout his career, Waksal would fall into regular bouts of delusion, or fabulation, or situational amnesia.

"Oh that's just *Sam,"* his friends say, with a laugh and a wave of the hand, as if to absolve him from any responsibility. To them, everything was explained away by his strange and difficult background.

His parents had survived the Holocaust in Poland and were deeply traumatized by the experience. According to a court filing on Sam's behalf, his mother, Sabina, and father, Jack, met as children in the small town of Yedlinsk, Poland, a village of approximately 700 residents. In 1939, the Germans occupied Poland and the Jews in Yedlinsk were relegated to a ghetto. When she was 19 years old, Sabina Kozlowska, her mother, and her two brothers were sent by the Nazis to a succession of work and concentration camps. Her eldest brother was killed at the first camp. From 1942 to 1944, Sabina was sent with her mother and remaining brother to Pionki, a munitions plant. Then she and her mother were moved to Auschwitz. One day the soldiers came: they began to drag Sabina's mother away, and as she tried to protect Sabina, the soldiers hit her mother in the head with a rifle butt. Before her mother was sent to the gas chamber, she managed to pass her gold wedding ring to Sabina. Sabina used the ring to bribe her way into a job in the camp kitchen, where she survived on potato peels and other scraps. On April 20, 1945, Sabina was one of 700 girls locked in a cattle car to be taken to a gas chamber when Russian troops overran the Germans and liberated the terrified prisoners. Sabina ran into a barn, where she frantically dug a hole and hid "for days." Despite the Russians' attempts to coax her out, she remained in hiding. Later that year, she returned to Yedlinsk, only to discover that she was her family's only survivor.

Jack (Yitzhak) Waksal, meanwhile, was 16 "when the Germans

came." In July 1940, the Jewish ghetto was razed by the Nazis, and Jack, his parents, brother, and two sisters were sent to a work camp in Poland. There Jack witnessed a German soldier place his rifle barrel in the mouth of his three-year-old sister and shoot; his mother and other sister, meanwhile, were sent to Treblinka. In 1942, Jack escaped the Pionki munitions camp. It began on the day the Germans were going to execute his father: Jack volunteered to take his father's place, he recalled in the court filing. "They walked us to the forest, to a big hole, five feet deep, which was already dug. They told us to kneel in single file. I jumped in front of the Gestapo officer and took his revolver as it misfired, then ran into the forest." Jack and his brother and about 10 others fled into the woods. He later learned that the guards had killed his father. Jack and his brother spent the rest of the war in the forests of Eastern Europe, fighting a guerrilla war against the Nazis.

"During the day my father would hide under a corpse in a stone sarcophagus," Sam once recalled. "At night, he would sneak out of the cemetery to steal food and fight the Nazis."

One version of events holds that Jack connected with the French underground and would sneak up to the holding pens where the Nazis herded Jews before sending them on to the death camps; Jack would try to persuade the prisoners to break out, but, mired in a stasis of denial or fear, most of them refused to flee. The experience was harrowing.

Near the end of the war, Jack's brother was shot and killed by the Germans; Jack survived by feigning death in a swamp until the soldiers had passed by. (In 1990, he would return to the spot to say Kaddish, the Jewish prayer for the dead, for his brother.)

Returning to Yedlinsk after the war, Jack and Sabina found one another.

In 1945, Jack and Sabina went to Regensberg, Germany. They may have been placed in a displaced person ("DP") camp there by the Allies, as many Jews were after the war. Jack has said that he was helping the Americans hunt down Nazi war criminals. One day in Regensberg, Sabina pointed out a man on the street who had been an Auschwitz commandant. She called his name; the man turned toward her, then bolted away. Jack gave chase, collared him, and handed him over to the Allied authorities; he was later tried for war crimes.

Scarred by the war, Jack and Sabina Waksal were determined not to bear their first child in Germany. In the summer of 1947, Sam would say, they "escaped" the DP camp and made their way to Paris, where Sabina had family, in time for Sam's birth. They lived in a Paris apartment for three years. Jack worked as a tailor and may have become a skilled trader of black-market goods. But the Waksals pined for America.

In December 1950, the family arrived in Dayton, Ohio, with the help of a sponsoring family that had also come from Yedlinsk. With a group of immigrant friends, Jack bought a truck and went from town to town collecting scrap metal for a local businessman. In 1954, Jack Waksal and his partner, Abraham Stein (whose wife Sabina had helped feed at Auschwitz), bought the scrap yard with the help of a $15,000 bank loan. In the late 1980s, Jack bought out his partner and ran the Dayton Iron and Metal Company until 1997, when he sold it and retired.

Sam would later claim that he was raised in Toledo. After this detail, like his birthdate, had been reported as fact by journalists, and then recycled by other journalists, the story about Sam's hometown became one of many little biographical uncertainties. His impulse to improve on the facts was deeply ingrained; the half-truths or untruths he told came in all shapes and sizes and in all aspects of his life. This need to embellish might have come from an overweening vanity, or perhaps it welled up from a deep insecurity or a mercurial need to be all things to all people. His personality was a contradiction: at once robustly defined and yet fundamentally unformed or malleable.

Self-conscious about his immigrant family, Sam tried hard to blend into his middle-American surroundings. He vividly recalled, at the age of eight, telling neighborhood kids that he had "an older brother in Annapolis," so that he would seem more authentically American.

The Waksal family joined the Beth Jacob Synagogue, an Orthodox congregation in Dayton, and Sam and Harlan and their younger sister, Patti, attended religious school. In 1961, they moved from a cramped apartment into a three-bedroom ranch house.

Jack and Sabina were deeply committed to their children and made sacrifices to give them the best education they could afford. But Sam was a notorious spendthrift and "always in financial trouble," an old girlfriend recalled. "His daddy was always having to bail him out." One consequence of such parental indulgence was that Sam and Harlan were raised to believe that the normal rules did not apply to them. "His parents gave Sam a sense of urgency about life," an old friend observed.

"Their survival had been so miraculous that they had a different sense of how to live. The rules of society didn't really apply."

Their neighbors found Jack and Sabina Waksal to be quiet people who didn't socialize very much. "They're very nice. They don't have a wide social circle. They're extremely family oriented," said Shirley ("Shirl") Flacks, Sam's former mother-in-law, who lived near the senior Waksals. "The father was in the forest in the war, a freedom fighter. He's a pretty feisty guy but he's not very communicative. And she? She's a Jewish mother. She does everything for the children."

The Holocaust was ever-present. As a child, Sam would spend hours leafing through a photo album filled with pictures of the death camps. Those who have met Sabina say that the faded blue identification tattoo from Auschwitz remains visible on her arm. In explaining his mother's "strange sense of humor," Sam described how, when she saw a crowd of people shoving each other in Chicago, she laughed and exclaimed, "It's just like in the camps!" One of Sam's daughters was taken aback by this, but Sabina said: "You have to keep a sense of humor to keep living—even in the worst place on earth." His mother's sensibility rubbed off on Sam: no matter how bad things got, he always had a quick joke or an amusing aside at hand, to break the ice or deflect tension.

Indeed, Sam maintained that the deep reverberations of history shaped his worldview: "My father is an incredible hero. I feel there is nothing I could ever do that could match the things he did. My parents' experience affects me every single day of my life. It drives me. When you grow up in a home where the parents survived a very terrible ordeal in world history, and a lot of other people didn't, then you look at the world from day one in a very different way . . . I look at the world that way, too—in making sure one builds and creates. It's a driving force."

Sam liked to quip that he had been fascinated by science "ever since I was given an Invisible Man kit in the sixth grade." There was just something that drew him to the study of the human body. When asked if Harlan had been interested in science as a kid, his sister, Patti—a thin antiques dealer with big brown eyes, brown curly hair, and a nervous demeanor—snapped: "That's a stupid question!" When asked how it was that both of her brothers pursued careers in medicine, she replied: "Well, that's just what they did. It was like you become a doctor, or you go into business."

When Sam and Harlan were pursuing the business of science at Im-

Clone, they would regale staff members with funny stories about their upbringing. Their colleagues found the tales odd but quite telling.

In one story, the Waksal brothers had been out late one night in Dayton. When they returned home, they turned on the light in the backyard and began to play basketball. Making a racket, they woke up their parents. Sabina turned to Jack, and said: "Go down and *kill* them!" Jack tromped down the stairs and opened the door. The boys looked up and said, "Hi, Dad." Without saying a word, Jack punched one of them in the face. Then he turned around and stomped back upstairs.

Sam and Harlan thought this story was hilarious, and after telling it around the office, they would fall into shudders of laughter.

Another story Sam liked to tell was about the time that he brought a pretty girl home to the family seder. They were seated at a big table, loaded with heavy old-style Jewish food. Sam began arguing with a family member about something. It escalated. Eventually Sam leaped up onto the table and began shouting. The girl was utterly cowed. When Sam drove her home later, she said, "It's really a shame that your family fights like that." Sam looked over at her in surprise, and said: "What fight?"

Sam didn't mind fights. In fact, he seemed to revel in confrontation and transgression. He liked to surmount an obstacle, especially when it afforded him the opportunity to talk his way out of a tight spot. "He loves to pull a rabbit out of a hat," observed an old friend. "He needs that adrenaline rush." Once, Sam said, he had been stopped from entering Egypt from Israel because he didn't have the proper visa. But with a gale of protest and sweet talk he managed to wear down the guards and make his way across the border—an achievement he was especially proud of, an office mate recalled, because he had used his quick mind and quick tongue to "get away" with something forbidden.

SHIRLEY FLACKS first met Sam when he was a very little, very polite, very, very bright twelve-year-old boy. Shirl and her husband were members of a Jewish Holocaust Museum in Dayton where, she remembered, "This little boy would stand up in front of all these older people at these gatherings, most of them survivors, and make these wonderful speeches. He'd talk about how bad the Holocaust was. Even then, he was very, very articulate. Very charismatic. That's Sammy."

He was also very, very interested in Shirl's twelve-year-old daughter,

Cindy. Although they lived only six blocks from each other, Sam and Cindy were in different high-school districts, so it took them awhile to connect. They started dating at age seventeen. "They have different personalities," Shirl noted with a chuckle. "It was a very stormy romance. But Sammy was very persistent."

When they reached college age, Shirl recalled, Sam first went to school somewhere in Florida and Cindy went to Ohio State University (OSU) in Columbus. It wasn't long before Sam had transferred to OSU. Sam and Cindy graduated in 1969, he with a B.A. in history and, his résumé said, philosophy while he was on a pre-medical school track. Dr. Marcus Engelman, who was Sam's roommate at OSU, recalls Sam in college as funny and smart, but also heedless. To gain social favor, he'd promise to help friends or sorority girls with their term papers or class notes; sometimes he'd do what he'd promised, but often he wouldn't. He didn't seem to understand, or care, about the anguish it caused people who had counted on him. "He became known as a flake and a liar," said Engelman. "A 'star-fucker'—always trying to be near the [pretty] people. In the end he wasn't a very popular guy. He burned through people." He also burned through money. Sam would show up for class late and there'd be no parking places left, so he'd just leave his car sitting in the middle of the street; he accumulated so many tickets he set a new OSU record and the police hauled him in. But "his father always bailed him out," said Engelman. "That's Sammy. He never worked. Never had discipline. Never knew the value of money. Never knew about consequences. It's really ironic—his parents tried to give him this great life, and they unwittingly created a monster."

Sam told lies constantly, Engelman said, "he told them so well, and so often, he actually started to believe them himself." For instance, Sam desperately wanted to be a doctor. "He told everyone he had a 4.0 average, when he didn't. He applied to only one med school—Harvard. I warned him he didn't have the grades, and he ought to look around more. But I think he'd convinced himself he'd get in." Sam was not accepted by Harvard Medical School.

Cindy and Sam were out of college for about a year before they married and settled in Cleveland. She was 22 at the time and got a job teaching first grade there, while he began an M.D./Ph.D. program at Case Western University.

If Sam had a fault, friends would say only half-jokingly, it was that he was such an enthusiast that he could not say no; he wanted to see and do everything, to experience life to its fullest. Sam had married Cindy not because he was deeply in love with her, a friend noted, but because he simply could not say no to her demand that they do so.

By 1972, Sam and Cindy had moved back to Columbus, where he worked toward a Ph.D. in immunology at OSU. Cindy had given birth to their first daughter, Elana, that year, and Sam had begun a "special friendship" with his assistant.

HER NAME WAS Elizabeth Latham and she was a strong-willed, striking blonde from Wellington, New Zealand. She had been dragged, weeping, to Columbus by her husband, a Ph.D. candidate in accounting at OSU. She loathed Ohio and she was bored with her husband. At a party one night, her husband drank too much. As he threw up, Elizabeth, clad in nothing but a thin, loose white sheath, with nothing on underneath, leaned over to hold his head. Sam stood there gazing frankly down her top. She stared right back.

Some weeks later she heard a knock on her door. It was Sam and Harlan.

Elizabeth had cut her hair short and was wearing her reading glasses. The first thing Sam said was: "Oh my God, she's got a brain!" They all laughed. Sam said he was looking to hire an office assistant.

Elizabeth was 21 and restless; as far as she was concerned, her husband was self-absorbed and had not been paying enough attention to her. She was intrigued by Sam's humor and his "young philosopher" charm.

He was 24, and one of the brightest and most amusing people she'd ever met. He told her that he needed an assistant to help him write grant proposals and contracts.

"But I don't know anything about immunology," Elizabeth protested.

"It doesn't matter," Sam replied. "I'll teach you."

She signed on. Years later, she'd poke him in the ribs and say: "That's not what you really hired me for, was it?"

"No," Sam agreed, "it wasn't."

They had much in common. She found it significant that his birthday was on September 8 and hers was on September 9. They both liked to spend "lots and lots of money" on good wine and food, nice clothes, and expensive vacations. They shared an irreverent sense of humor and a willingness to push convention. He once convinced an Israeli doctor friend who refused to work with a gentile that Elizabeth was Jewish. When she worried about tripping herself up, he said, "Don't worry, you've been around me long enough to pick it up. Besides, you've got a big nose." Like Jack Waksal, Elizabeth Latham's father had suffered terribly in World War II: he'd been one of three survivors of a horrific battle and was found wandering in a daze with a bloody bayonet in his hand; he had suffered from post-traumatic stress disorder. She had been raised to be independent minded and to question authority.

For four years Elizabeth helped Sam with his paperwork, learned to create tissue cultures in the lab, and would accompany him to scientific conferences all over the country—which was really an excuse, she'd recall, for them to "go off and screw ourselves silly." They fell madly in love. Sam became Elizabeth's tutor and mentor. He made her read all of the serious Russian writers, listen to Mahler, and learn about philosophy. She loved the learning and the attention; she looked up to him; he was her "sexy genius."

Once, when Sam and Cindy and Elana were away, Elizabeth went to their house to collect the mail. Jack and Sabina arrived. Elizabeth had never met Sam's parents before, but the first thing Sabina did was to embrace her warmly, and say, "In France, it's honorable to have a mistress." She knew about the affair and approved, Elizabeth said: "It had nothing to with 'morality.' It was all about Sam's happiness. I made him happy."

In 1974, Cindy gave birth to their second daughter, Aliza (pronounced "Aleeza"), and Sam finished his doctorate, *In Vitro Studies on Thymus Derived Lymphocytes: Differentiation of T-Lymphocytes and Their Function in Tumor Destruction.* They went to Rehovot, Israel, for three months, where Sam worked at the Weizman Institute as a postdoctoral fellow under Professor Michael Feldman—one of the many eminent scientists who would open doors for the promising young man and would later serve as a scientific adviser to ImClone.

Elizabeth stayed in Ohio and collated all of Sam's work for his 83-page dissertation. When asked about a persistent rumor in the biotech community that Sam had never really completed the dissertation, or that there had been some kind of major problem with his work at OSU, Elizabeth fiercely defended him: "That's just more of the same old jealous-boy commentary! There was no issue about his work. I was there. I did all the stuff that needed to be done. There was no problem with Sam's Ph.D." And Sam's adviser, Professor Ronald St. Pierre, a professor of anatomy, would later recall that, "He is one of the brightest students I worked with in 19 years. In fact, the only problem I ever had with him was getting him to slow down and focus on his doctoral dissertation instead of jumping to new projects."

Cindy suspected that her husband and his assistant were up to more than paperwork together, and one day she called Elizabeth's husband to ask him about it. He agreed to look into it. When Sam and Elizabeth returned from a trip to Washington, D.C., her husband confronted his wife politely. "Is there a physical extent to your relationship?" he asked.

She acknowledged that, yes, there was. But her husband was so civilized about it that she found him ridiculous. Everyone was miserable.

Years later, Elizabeth would look back on their early romance as extraordinarily naive and destructive. But she was young and unencumbered by children, and did not understand what effect "the bad karma" of their affair would have on those around them.

It was 1974 when her husband won an assistant professorship at Stanford University and begged Elizabeth to accompany him to California. She agreed, but remained unhappy with him.

Sam, meanwhile, was restless in Ohio. With the help of Dr. Irv Weissman, a Stanford professor who had visited the Ohio State lab and been impressed by the smart young scientist, Sam landed a prestigious job as a postdoctoral fellow in the lab of Dr. Len Herzenberg, the noted Stanford University Medical School geneticist who had invented the FACS machine, which is widely used for sorting blood cells. Sam left Cindy and the girls behind, and headed west, to begin anew.

BY THE TIME Sam arrived in California, he was wracked by guilt and remorse over his family, Elizabeth said. She met him at the Palo Alto Holiday Inn. But their relationship had ceased to be a refuge; it was now a confusing mess and she was "freaking out." When he left that evening, she shouted, "What the fuck is happening to my life?!" and threw a glass at the wall, shattering it. To mollify her, Sam arranged a job for her growing cells in a lab at U.C. San Francisco. He also introduced her to an old friend, Norma Robert, a raven-haired Hispanic beauty who worked in the Herzenberg lab. The two women became roommates and lifelong friends. With Sam, they'd go to the beach and have dinner parties; they both recalled that he drove very fast and not particularly carefully.

When Harlan came to visit, he impressed Norma as, "very young. Very cute. A cherub. His feet were a little more on the ground than Sam's. Sam is an ideas man. Harlan is an implementer."

In the lab, Sam impressed Len Herzenberg and his scientist wife, Lee. "Waksal was a bright guy, a real charmer," Len Herzenberg recalled. "We thought he was absolutely brilliant." In keeping with the time and place, the Herzenbergs ran an unconventional lab, complete with hot-tub parties and a "journal club" that would meet weekly to discuss scientific papers in their bedroom. Norma Robert recalled, "There was always science going on, and always this other aspect in the air. It was a very unusual lab."

Sam immersed himself in the scene. He spent a lot of time with Elizabeth, but there were still other women, and he found himself unable to fully commit to Elizabeth. She grew frustrated and resentful. After six months in Palo Alto, she split for Copenhagen, Denmark, to visit her sister.

The Herzenbergs, too, were having second thoughts about Sam. Not long after he started work in the lab, he told them he had acquired some rare antibodies—proteins that fight foreign matter in the body—from Edward Boyse, of the Sloan-Kettering Institute in New York. "He became a 'big man' in the laboratory by saying he had these antibodies that no one else could get," Herzenberg remembered. He asked Sam to share the antibodies with a researcher who had produced promising results in an experiment using similar material. But the researcher could not reproduce his earlier results using Sam's antibodies. "When the postdoc used them in an experiment, the results weren't right," Herzenberg recounted. "So I called Dr. Boyse, the supposed source of the antibodies, and he had not given them to Sam. I don't know what he had in those test tubes. When I confronted him, Sam insisted they were real. But he was not being straightforward."

Sam explained that the rare antibodies had been sent to his home in Ohio, and that he had the shipping wrapper to prove it. But when Herzenberg demanded to see the wrapper, Sam was unable to produce it. (Boyse has said that records show his lab did ship Sam Waksal a batch of antibodies, but not until 1978, four years after Sam left Stanford.)

The last straw came, Herzenberg says, when, "One day we found

Sam's test tubes—and his only—spilled in the bottom of the lab fridge," which destroyed the evidence.

Elizabeth Latham disputed this version of events. "It's a load of crap," she said. "I was there, and it didn't happen that way. Look, Sam was very smart and sought after. The postdocs were sycophants, fawning all over him. Len was always on the lookout for bright young scientists, and he wanted to suck Sam's brain. And Lee is a revolting woman who tried to control all the young people in the lab. She did everything she could to keep me and Sam apart. She was quite destructive. The scientific world is full of venal people. Anyway, Sam never planned on staying there very long in the first place."

By the end of 1974, Herzenberg had asked Sam to leave the lab. "Years later he called my wife, admitted he hadn't told the truth about the antibodies, and apologized. He said he didn't mean anything by what he'd done, and he hoped we could all be friends. It was very strange. I've never forgotten him. Why would someone so brilliant lie?"

Lee Herzenberg added that she considered Sam a "pathological liar," who liked to use people for his own ends. She remembered Sam saying that he was seeing a psychiatrist and had changed his ways.

In 1975, Sam landed a temporary research job at the National Cancer Institute (NCI), part of the National Institutes of Health (NIH), near Washington, D.C. Missing his two young daughters terribly, he had reunited with Cindy and the girls and set up house there.

William Terry, former head of the immunology branch of the NCI, was the one who hired Sam at the institute and later let him go. Len Herzenberg recalled that he warned Terry about Sam, but, he said, Sam had talked his way around the issue by denying he'd had any problem at Stanford. Terry has said he doesn't recall Herzenberg's warning, and believes he vetted Sam through scientists at Ohio State.

He remembered Sam as "extremely bright, articulate and personable, with a breadth of knowledge on immunology literature."

At the NCI, Sam was involved in many projects with other scientists, but there always seemed to be some kind of strange problem with his work. "When the critical time came to deliver his part of the collaboration, there would be a catastrophe of some sort—a tissue culture would become contaminated or the mice would develop an infection and have to be killed," Terry said to *The Wall Street Journal*. After three years of this, Terry declined to offer Sam a permanent job, effectively forcing him to leave the NCI.

Elizabeth Latham, meanwhile, was in a peripatetic, "Communistic" phase. She had traveled through Europe on the cheap to Corsica, where she caught a ferry to Nice, France. She had been sleeping on beaches and traveled fourth class with Turkish migrant workers on the ferry. As she stepped off the boat in Nice, Sam appeared out of the crowd on the quay. "That shows you how clever he could be," she'd say. He swept her off to a luxurious hotel and used his charm to woo her back. In Paris, he bought her piles of wonderful and very expensive clothes, and they shared some fabulous meals. "We had a wonderful time being financially irresponsible together," she'd laugh.

This time, he swore, he was really going to leave Cindy. To prove that he was a man of his word, Sam found Elizabeth a job in the lab of Dr. Robert Schwartz, a hematologist at the Tufts University School of Medicine in Boston. Elizabeth shared an apartment on Beacon Street with Norma Robert, who also worked for Schwartz, also on Sam's introduction.

In 1977, Sam and Cindy divorced. Elana was five and Aliza was three. Despite the fact that Sam had difficulty paying Cindy alimony, he later paid for their college tuition and, Shirley Flacks said, "was always a very indulgent, loving, adoring father."

Sam moved to Boston, where he joined Elizabeth and Norma in Dr. Schwartz's lab at the Tufts Cancer Research Center, as an assistant professor of pathology. Schwartz had first met Sam at a conference, and would recall that the bright young immunologist had an almost hypnotic effect on him. "Every 100 years, someone like him is born. He's a very persuasive person who can convince you of anything. Within five minutes, you're begging him to work for you."

Dr. Terry, of the NCI, said that even though he was only supposed to confirm that Sam Waksal had worked for him, he had let Schwartz know his misgivings about Sam: "The fact that I was not prepared to keep him on was known by Bob Schwartz." Schwartz did not recall this conversation with Terry, but said that he relied on strong recommendations from two senior scientists who had overseen Sam's work in Israel.

Other former colleagues at Tufts recall Sam as "bizarre." He was rarely in the lab, and odd people would call his extension at all hours— "slimy characters," bill collectors, and his ex-wife, Cindy, irate over the lack of child support. Eventually, Sam's lab mates grew tired of the constant ringing and disconnected his line.

Sam surrounded himself with a coterie of attractive lab technicians—"the profile was tall, long-long legs, big dark hair"—who became known as the Disco Techs. He bought a house in Sudbury, a Boston suburb, and invited a group of friends to help him paint it. He had a big dog that would get carsick. He and Harlan bought motorcycles and raced around at terrifying speeds.

When he was in evidence in the lab, Sam seemed to have difficulty in completing his experiments on time. In one collaborative project, Sam was supposed to produce cell lines for experiments, but never got around to it, a colleague recalled. As an idea man and theoretician, Sam didn't much like the bench science required in a lab. He'd rather oversee others' bench work. "He's one of the most brilliant people I've ever met, and he was doing work, just not on the bench—in his mind," said Norma Robert. "Sam's greatest problem is he never gets things done on time. It's always at the last minute. It tries people's patience. But he's so charming he usually gets his way."

Much of the time Sam's lab space appeared dark and unused. People who were clearly not scientists dropped by late at night carrying brown paper bags. "It was kind of scary," recalled a coworker. A rumor sprung up that Sam was somehow involved with cocaine, although no one ever saw him use it. "The joke was that the only piece of equipment used in his lab was the balance," said a person who worked nearby.

"We worked very hard there," said Norma Robert. "Many times we'd go back to the lab after dinner and work until midnight. I was there not every night, but many nights. I never saw any evidence of cocaine."

Asked about Sam and cocaine at Tufts, Elizabeth Latham replied: "I'd rather not comment on that."

HARLAN WAKSAL graduated from Oberlin in 1975, then joined his brother in Boston and earned his M.D. from Tufts in 1979. Like Sam, Harlan had an irreverent streak. Elizabeth enjoyed a jousting, siblinglike rivalry with him. One of their favorite pastimes was to play practical jokes.

Once, for a quiet afternoon tea at Tufts, everyone was supposed to bring something to eat. One person brought a box of cream puffs. Harlan brought a package and insisted that Elizabeth open it in front of the "boring" people there. When she unwrapped it, she discovered an enormous black dildo. The effect was hilarious, she said.

At other times, she and Harlan would slip into character and see who could outembarrass the other. One day they stopped at a gas station and she jumped out of the car, slammed the door, and began ranting: "I've had enough! No more!"

Harlan got out, and shouted back: "Okay, fine!"

This went on for some minutes, the back-and-forth screaming growing in intensity; finally, he gave in and climbed back in the car, laughing. She had won.

On another occasion, they boarded a train into Boston early one morning. It was crowded. Harlan stood right behind Elizabeth, and in a loud voice said: "I just don't know how you could do this—I work all day, I come home, and you just sit there with the dildo on, vibrating. You don't even have the decency to turn it off!" She turned bright red and didn't dare answer. This time, he'd won.

"We shared lots and lots and lots of laughter," she said.

In 1979, Sam finally committed himself to Elizabeth Latham, and she left him for good. She'd had enough of his melodrama and wavering attention, and she needed a break. Elizabeth called Sam and Norma from Europe: "I'm not coming back," she announced. For months Sam tried to win her back, but to no avail. "I've been told," she'd say, "that I am the only woman who ever left Sam."

Meanwhile, things in the lab had taken their usual turn for the worse. Dr. Schwartz, now a deputy editor of the *New England Journal of Medicine,* said that he first grew suspicious of Sam after a virologist who had worked at the NCI, said: "Watch out for Waksal." It was like a splash of "cold water in my face," Schwartz recalled. He began to watch Sam more carefully and noticed that, "he would tell people the results of experiments he never carried out." In one case, Sam claimed he had bred a particular type of mouse for use in the lab. When Schwartz asked to see the mice, Sam never produced them. Finally, Schwartz sent a technician to the breeding room, but the tech was unable to locate the mice. This led Schwartz to conclude that, "such a mouse never existed."

Sam Waksal, he said, "had an extra gift of creating an illusion."

In 1981, Harlan, by now a medical resident at Tufts–New England Medical Center, was arrested in Miami and charged with possessing cocaine with intent to distribute. Shortly afterward, Sheldon Wolff, the chairman of the department of medicine at Tufts–New England Medical Center, brought yet another complaint about Sam to Schwartz: although not a medical doctor, Sam had allegedly covered for his inconveniently detained brother by seeing Harlan's patients at the center, perhaps dressed in Harlan's lab coat.

"All of these problems put together made me decide Waksal had to go," Schwartz would say. Once nearly hypnotized by Sam's brilliance, he was now fed up. He told Sam: "I want you out."

In 1982, in his last job before leaving academia to start ImClone, Sam Waksal was hired to run an immunopathology lab by Jerome Kleinerman, the chairman of the Pathology Department at the Mount Sinai School of Medicine in New York. It was a prestigious post, but he left after three years: again there are many rumors about why he left, and again he has vehemently denied that he was forced out.

Before hiring Sam, no one at Mount Sinai bothered to call Tufts about him, Dr. Schwartz has said, and so he didn't offer an opinion. Later, when there was trouble, Schwartz recalled, "the man who hired and fired him [at Mount Sinai] called to complain. I said, 'Sir, you never asked for a recommendation.' "

Alexandra Bona, who worked as Sam's assistant professor, recalled that he was friendly, tall, and well dressed; unusually for an academic, his office was fashionably decorated. They had lunch together twice. But one day in 1985, she returned to the lab to discover, "everyone crying and Sam was out of his mind." He and a few technicians had been asked to leave immediately. The circumstances of his departure were kept secret, and she maintained that she never knew exactly what had happened.

Asked about the incident, Sam replied: "There were people at Mount Sinai that I had some big fights with. [They] hate me . . . I, at times, am arrogant and abrasive." In other words, it was a personality clash.

"I don't think anyone *hated* him," said Dr. Stave Kohtz, who worked as Waksal's graduate student at Mount Sinai in the early 1980s. "He just didn't seem appropriate for the position. There were certainly a lot of heated arguments, but that wasn't unusual . . . Sam is very smart, but he didn't fit the stereotype of a rigorous, conservative 'bench' scientist . . . At the time, Sam told me that Dr. Kleinerman [who is now deceased] called him into his office and said, 'I love you like a son, but I can't keep you here.' Sam was very upset. I think it was a bad fit, rather than bad faith."

"It wasn't a bad fit!" Sam snapped. "I left Mount Sinai on sabbatical. I was founding ImClone at the time!" That was the limit to what he'd say on the subject.

Mount Sinai confirmed that Sam worked in the pathology department in the early 1980s, but his file is legally sealed under a confidentiality agreement. But people familiar with the situation told *The Wall Street Journal* that Sam was asked to leave because of evidence that he falsified data. Dr. Bona's husband, Constantin Bona, a Mount Sinai immunologist, has said that in reviewing a paper Sam submitted for publication in a scientific journal, he identified a problem. "I looked at the results. There were discrepancies," Constantin Bona said. "The results in the end were not the same as the lab books." Dr. Sherman Kupfer, then Mount Sinai's senior vice president of research, confirmed that Mount Sinai viewed the discrepancies in Sam's paper as a serious breach: "Is it lying? Not necessarily. But no scientist will accept it as significant proof of a hypothesis. It's viewed as misconduct and is dealt with severely."

Although Stave Kohtz had not seen Sam in years, he had "spent many, many hours thinking about him . . . He affects everybody he comes in contact with. Some people don't approve of him. I admire him, in a sense, although I couldn't *be* him. Most people facing what he's faced in life would have a huge therapy bill, but Sam emerges with one of the biggest biotech deals in history. He's definitely got something to teach the rest of us—I'm just not sure what it is."

Sam defiantly replied: "I don't believe that hitting a roadblock should cause one to go into therapy. Therapy is a great luxury that most people outside of the Upper East Side of New York City don't have. I've never been driven to therapy by issues. When one hits a roadblock, I believe one's job is to be creative, thoughtful and to fix things."

BY NOW the pattern was well established: he would impress someone—a pretty girl, a prominent scientist, someone in a position to open doors—with his humor and intellect; they would undertake an endeavor together; things would begin with great hope and expectations, but then something would inevitably go awry; Sam would push his luck, or fail to do what he'd promised, or he'd betray someone; the experiment or job or relationship would falter, and often it would end in bruised feelings or acrimonious lawsuits. Yet he'd continue to move ahead.

How did Sam Waksal manage to fail upward for so many years? With help. Those who know him point to the long list of influential father figures, well-placed mentors, and powerful friends who continued to open doors for him, bail him out of trouble, and facilitate his career. When things have turned sour, some of these men have staunchly defended their protégé, while others have let the chips fall where they may. "A number of us recognized that Sam was very smart and articulate," said an early champion of his. "We said: 'If there's any way we can help, you let us know.' And when he did, we pushed hard to get him into [prestigious positions]. But then we did site visits later, and his work never seemed to pan out. I felt betrayed."

Others point to a larger systemic problem that Sam's career illustrates: institutions fear being sued for defamation if they give a scientist a poor job review, which allows even compromised researchers to move from job to job with impunity. "Institutionally, we're under the gun to do no more than give [a prospective employer] the most basic information," said the NCI's Dr. William Terry. "It sets up a situation where the bad eggs can move from one place to another with great facility."

Elizabeth Latham believed that it wasn't Sam who was at fault, it was the people around him. "It's the Tall Poppy Syndrome," she explained: Sam had a huge intellect, a fertile creativity, and an independent streak; he could be outrageous and arrogant; he succeeded where others did not, in ways they could not. This made people jealous. It made them want to destroy him, she said. "Sam is his own, special, unique human being . . . He doesn't sit back and wait, he plows straight through things. He breaks norms. And society always bashes down people who break rules. People love to hate him, and always have. Like the tall poppy that stands above the rest, they always want to mow Sammy down."

When asked to explain the unusual pattern of his academic career, Sam shrugged nonchalantly, and said: "I do lots of things in ways that academic centers don't always love to do. Life has ups and downs."

IN 1984, biomania was all the rage. Charming Sam and dutiful Harlan began to kick around some "fun ideas" about changing careers and starting a company. They rounded up $4 million in seed money, and in 1985 Sam left Mount Sinai "on sabbatical" and jumped into the rising biotech tide with both feet. Like the pebble dropped into a pool of still water, his jump would ultimately have a profound ripple effect on a wide range of people and institutions.

Harlan joined Sam. They bought a long-term lease from a bankrupt shoe manufacturer in a huge old building on Varick Street, in SoHo, and began to build their dream. The Waksals named their company (on the spur of the moment, Sam said, en route to an investor's meeting) "Im-Clone Systems, Inc." after the three fields they hoped to enter: immunology, DNA cloning, and medical information systems. But they didn't really know what they were getting into. The general idea, Harlan said, was to "focus on infectious diseases, cancer, and diagnostics, make some products, get rich, and retire early."

# THREE

# *Family Business*

In 1982, Martha Stewart's smile was becoming an increasingly familiar sight. A former model and stockbroker, Martha was 41 years old, with frizzy dark-blonde hair, a thin face, and lively eyes. With the publication that year of the first of her best sellers, a book called *Entertaining,* she was just beginning to transform herself from a Westport, Connecticut-based caterer into a celebrity lifestyle author. *Entertaining* was followed by *Quick Cook* in 1983; *Hors D'Oeuvres* in 1984; *Pies & Tarts* in 1985; and in 1987, the phenomenal *Weddings.* Also in 1987, she inked a deal with Kmart, the giant retailer that would help turn her into a household name. In the 1990s, she signed a deal with the media giant Time Warner and launched her magazine, *Martha Stewart Living,* a television show, and various merchandising deals. Each venture built on the one before, expanded her brand, and helped her to conquer the popular imagination. She worked hard to make it look easy. Martha slept only three or four hours a night, worked her hands almost literally to the bone, and ran roughshod over friends and enemies. But in the process she crafted a message with great resonance: With the right pluck and vigor, and a few pointers from Martha, anyone could transform the messy reality of her life into what Martha called "a good thing"—a calm and ordered existence filled with beautiful homes, delicious meals, and happy people. It was a powerful fantasy, an empowering call to action; and because it tapped into a great American yearning, it would eventually turn Martha Stewart into a billionaire.

Millions of people, it turned out, aspired to the "Martha Stewart lifestyle" just as much as Martha did. Most understood that despite her cool exterior and sophisticated taste, she wasn't exactly what she appeared to be. Born Martha Kostyra, she was the second of six children from an unhappy, middle-class Catholic family of Polish origin from Nutley, New Jersey. Her father was a failed businessman and a mean-tempered alcoholic; her mother a somewhat pinched woman. The purity of Martha's vision and her drive to succeed were a reaction to the world she came from and a clear definition of the world she aspired to inhabit, and did. She was easy to parody, but her Horatio Algeresque success, and her willingness to show others the way, made her message all the more potent. Most people admired the fact that she consistently outfoxed her rivals, outnegotiated her partners, and smiled all the way to the bank. Martha Stewart, it seemed, never put a foot wrong.

She met Sam Waksal at a charity event she catered in the early 1980s. They clicked, and she soon came to think of him as "a very close family friend." They were kindred spirits. Each was smart, ambitious, complex, egotistical, and a bit manipulative. They tended to live in the moment and project into the future. They spoke often on the phone, frequently at six o'clock in the morning, or earlier, by which point they were both at work, hours ahead of the rest of the world.

What Martha liked about Sam, she said, was that he was well educated, extremely intelligent, and devoted to working with the best scholars and scientists and universities. The ImClone board was an illustrious example of that, she pointed out. Also, Sam always gave a good explanation of *what* he was doing and *why* he was doing it. When Sam decided to launch ImClone, Martha was one of his earliest "preinvestors," and then an initial stockholder in the company.

It has been reported that Martha invested in ImClone "as a gesture of support for her friend" Sam. But she recalled a higher purpose. "I am interested in finding *cures*. I'm interested in whatever we can do to help any of the ills of humanity," she said. "Sam and his brother have been extremely interested in finding cures, first for AIDS, and then for certain forms of cancer. I was *so* hoping there would be a cure for AIDS. I was a *staunch* supporter of Sam in that research, but the cure they were close to just wasn't working. When C225 came along, I was a staunch *hoper*" for that drug, as well. And with good reason: Martha knew many people who had been afflicted by these diseases. Her husband at the time, the publisher Andy Stewart, had been diagnosed with cancer in 1977 (he was successfully treated with radiation and chemotherapy); her sister Laura's husband, the actor Kim Herbert, died of cancer; and cancer had killed a number of people in her social circle.

"This is very important work," she said, in the fall of 2001. "And Sam has done a very good job with it. It's thrilling to see."

They were loyal friends and helped each other out in many ways. She designed the kitchen for his SoHo loft, included a photo of him at her backyard birthday party in *Martha Stewart Living,* and featured the wedding of his daughter Elana to Jarrett Posner on the island of Nevis, in her book *Weddings.* She attended Elana's wedding, just as she attended Sam's famous Christmas party every year. She steered other well-known people to invest in ImClone, although she declined to identify them. She had profited from her investment in ImClone and said, "My driver bought a house in Connecticut on [the strength of] his ImClone stock!"

Sam adored Martha and relished her growing celebrity. Like Elizabeth Latham, she was a headstrong, striking blonde woman with a quirky sense of humor and a complicated backstory. He escorted her to parties, cultural happenings, and corporate functions—the sorts of events that both approached as networking opportunities. He made her laugh and allowed her to shine. They shared many friends and several investors in common, like the powerful adwoman Charlotte Beers. As Martha's stature grew, Sam watched and learned how to operate the levers of the money and celebrity machines. The two of them were often photographed together, and she became an essential part of his image, and self-image. He showed her off at every opportunity—to the point where the name "Sam Waksal" was usually followed by the commendation: "He's a friend of Martha Stewart's, you know." Indeed, they seemed so close that many people assumed they were a couple. But both Martha and Sam categorically denied the rumors that they were intimately involved—a view echoed by her daughter Alexis, who *did* date Sam—although many disbelieved them.

On several occasions, Sam offered Martha financial advice. In the mid-1990s, he was one of her counselors during her tortured but ultimately advantageous negotiations with Time Warner. Also, she said, he helped her to invest in several biotech firms and in a number of his side ventures—including Scientia, a biotech holding company, and iBeauty.com, an Internet beauty-products company.

By the fall of 2001, Sam and Martha had been confidants for two decades. She had bought ImClone stock when it was valued at only a dollar or two a share, he pointed out, and since then her investment had appreciated many times over. He was a dear friend and she had always stuck by Sam, she said, through good times and bad.

"I've been through *all* the ups and downs—ImClone has gone up and down, up and down," she said with an easy laugh.

IMCLONE OPENED its doors for business in 1985 with only a handful of employees. The key players were Sam, the chief executive officer (CEO); Harlan, the chief operating Officer (COO); and their friend John Landes, a young attorney, the company's chief counsel.

Landes had forged a bond with the Waksal brothers in Boston, where, according to Norma Robert, he helped Harlan neatly extricate himself from the thorny legal problems around his arrest for smuggling cocaine. Landes's job at ImClone was to advise the Waksals on everything from real estate transactions to technology transfers to employment issues. He was part of the brothers' inner circle, the group of boisterous confidants with whom they shared both professional and personal time. Over the years, Landes would see the company grow from a three-person start-up winging it on a shoestring, into a 400-employee supernova that somehow arranged the largest deal in the history of biotech for a single drug. By 2001, Landes was overseeing a team of six corporate attorneys and was well compensated for it (he made some $2.87 million on stock options alone that year), right up until the day he was forced out of the company for, apparently, failing to police Sam, his patron and boss, with sufficient rigor.

In the earliest days, Sam operated ImClone out of his apartment on West 81st Street, or out of an office in the swooping 9 West 57th Street building (famous for the large, bright orange "9" sculpture that sat on the white sidewalk by its front entrance). In 1985, the fledgling company moved into several thousand square feet of raw space on the sixth floor of an old shoe factory at 180 Varick Street, just south of Houston Street and just north of the entrance to the Holland Tunnel, in SoHo. The far western edge of SoHo was a gritty industrial neighborhood that was better known for its large, moldering industrial spaces than for the funky boutiques and riotous art scene on West Broadway, a few blocks east. The city had not yet figured out how to market itself as a "biotech incubator," and ImClone was only the second biotech firm to set itself up in Manhattan, after Enzo Biologic, which was located around the corner on Hudson Street. The Varick Street space was affordable, and the Waksals had taken canny advantage of low-cost industrial-development revenue bonds to renovate the facility.

A former ImClone employee laughs at the memory of the first days in the building: "We began with just a huge amount of raw, open space. We were the only company on the floor, and this was the only renovated floor in the building. We began by using only a third of the space, leaving the rest empty. You'd open a door in back, and look into a dark, echoing, rat-infested area. They'd use that empty space for all sorts of things. Sometimes they'd shoot movies in there, and people like Dustin Hoffman would be wandering around looking lost."

Sam installed himself in a large corner office. It had white walls, a big window that framed the twin towers of the World Trade Center downtown, and expensive black furniture—a big black leather chair, black desk, black table. His taste was expensive, and the office was impressive—hardly what one would expect from the CEO of a biotech start-up. Which was the point.

Robert Goldhammer joined the ImClone board in October 1984, was named chairman of the board in February 1991, and remained one of Sam's most important confidants and protectors until he, too, finally left the company under a cloud. Once a managing director at the investment bank Kidder, Peabody, Goldhammer is solidly built, with a wide face and silver hair. He struck some as a Patrician gentleman-banker, and others as a brutal corporate shark. He was attracted by the idea of biotech; by the chance to be part of something new, young, and hip; and by Sam's joie de vivre.

"Goldhammer was bored and Sam was exciting," observed a former ImClone employee. "It was like Sam gave him a new lease on life."

They complemented each other: Goldhammer was financially sophisticated in a way that Sam was not, and Sam was flamboyant and socially adept in a way that Goldhammer could never be. "Rubbing shoulders with Sam's famous friends like Mariel Hemingway created adrenaline for Goldhammer," said the ex-employee. "He and Sam taught each other things."

TO GET THE COMPANY up and running, Sam, Harlan, and John Landes recruited a staff of about twenty people from wherever they could be found—hospitals like Mount Sinai, big pharmaceutical companies like Eli Lilly, other biotech firms like Enzo, local universities like Columbia or NYU—through word of mouth, chance encounter, or even from around the neighborhood.

Sam was good with people. He had a knack for conversation and for reading a face. Within a couple of minutes of meeting someone, he would intuit which words or phrases were most important to a person, and then he'd work them into his own sentences with absolute conviction, as if they were his own. He was fascinated by those in power, and developed a network of well-positioned and helpful friends—including Nelson Peltz, of TriArc Industries, which owned Arby's, the media boss Jimmy Finkelstein, and the arbitrageur Carl Icahn, whom he'd met playing tennis in the Hamptons—yet his easy congeniality extended to the common man as well.

Sam liked nice cars, as objects or symbols, but he was a notoriously absentminded driver for whom parallel parking was a personal bête-noir. What he really loved was to be driven around town in a limousine, regardless of the cost. When Sam met Hugh Dunn, a Hell's Kitchen Irishman, he hired Dunn as his driver. Hugh Dunn's son, Charles, essentially grew up with ImClone. For years he was the office gofer—Charlie would run errands for Sam, drive out to Hunt's Point market for a box of fruit, collect photographs of New York City, do anything to help out. He was handy and became the office maintenance man, and eventually he helped to set up ImClone's computer system. (By 2001 Charles Dunn held the title vice president for systems and facilities and made over $3.8 million from vested stock options.)

Waksal impressed building custodians like Jimmy Carter and Robert DeVita with his easy charm, and inspired scientists like Zhenping Zhu, and Alexander Kiselyov with his "free uninhibited exchange of ideas."

"When Sam pays attention to you, it makes you feel special," admitted a former coworker. "He's very seductive. He can be a force."

\*　　　\*　　　\*

NORMA ROBERT followed Sam to ImClone from Mount Sinai in the mid-1980s. She rolled up her sleeves and helped to build the Varick Street space—"this great big place with no walls." A stolid, pleasant, churchgoing woman of Puerto Rican descent, she was in charge of ordering equipment and supplies, and helped the Waksals transform a dirty, disused factory floor into a pristine, brightly lit, antiseptic laboratory. This was the third lab that Norma had helped to build, and she compared the process to knitting: "You start with a ball of yarn, and you knit and you knit, and finally you end up with a piece of clothing. It's very usable and nice to look at. Same thing with a lab."

Varick Street required a huge effort, she recalled. "We bought *a lot* of equipment, and we got the people we wanted to. I don't know about the money details, but it must have taken a lot of resources to do all that."

Norma Robert had first met Sam in 1973, when she was working in a lab at the University of Texas Medical Center in Galveston. He had dropped by for an interview, and although he didn't get the job he made an impression. "You don't forget Sam very easily," she'd say. "He's not forgettable." They reunited two years later in the Herzenberg lab, at Stanford, where, she said, "I didn't see any bad behavior by Sam." Like Elizabeth Latham, Norma said she knew nothing of the disputed antibodies, and believed that Sam was a misunderstood "genius" who was given a bum rap by academic in-fighters.

When the Herzenbergs took a yearlong sabbatical to England, Sam arranged an interview for Norma with Dr. Robert Schwartz, the Tufts hematologist. Norma got the job at Tufts—she never had a title, but her duties were lab assistant/associate and she worked on immunology projects—and was joined there a few months later by Elizabeth Latham (courtesy of Sam). About a year after that, Sam moved to Boston to join the Schwartz lab himself.

Once she joined ImClone, though, the story took a familiar turn. Norma worked in the Varick Street lab from 1986 to 1989—"I spent a lot of time growing cells in these big round plastic bottles, but I had so many jobs there they all run together"—until the day she got into a "big fight" with Sam. It involved a betrayal, the details of which she refused to discuss. Whatever it was, Sam never apologized for it. Norma, feeling hurt and furious, quit ImClone for a job at Bristol-Myers Squibb and refused to speak to Sam for many, many years.

The environment had changed, but Sam Waksal had not.

\*    \*    \*

"A WELL-RUN FACTORY floor is a terribly boring place," goes the familiar saw. But that was an aphorism written for a different era—the rusty and calcified Old Economy. Biotech was a place where cutting-edge science intersected big money and resulted in a gorgeous "new paradigm."

In the 1970s, the epicenter of this new spirit was Silicon Valley—stretching from San Jose to Palo Alto, in Northern California—where a new kind of company had sprung up in the once scenic farmland: Intel, Fairchild, Hewlett-Packard, the giants of the new electronics industry that would change the world. These companies were founded by visionary technologist-entrepreneurs, a type personified by Steven Jobs, the cofounder of Apple Computer. Starting literally in their garages, these young wonks came blinking into the sunlight to proselytize about the wonders of the personal computer. They brought with them not only new gadgets but a new way of doing things. Wall Street could smell money and began underwriting the Valley's pale-skinned geniuses.

The ethos of Silicon Valley shaped Genentech, and the ethos of Genentech shaped the biotech industry. In founding their company, Robert Swanson (who had been a Silicon Valley venture capitalist) and Herbert Boyer (who worked at U.C. San Francisco) knew that in order to recruit and maintain the bright, young, and sometimes eccentric researchers who were the muscle and tissue of their effort, they would have to create a place where the gene cloners would feel comfortable working their brains out. Taking a page from the Valley's playbook, Swanson instituted Friday afternoon "Ho-Hos," beer parties over which he would preside dressed in a bumblebee costume or a grass skirt. The cloners loved it. Further endearing himself, Swanson treated his people humanely, gave out stock options, and allowed his scientists to publish their work. The Ho-Ho ethic became an important part of the Genentech legend and it led to widespread admiration and emulation. *Esquire* went so far as to laud Swanson for creating a "post-industrial management" style, a new type of leadership for a new type of organization.

Swanson also understood the value of the theatrical photo op and the peppy magazine profile. Although he was a moneyman, he, like Sam Waksal, was often photographed in a white coat studiously observing a vial or a complicated-looking fermenter in a lab. But unlike Sam, and most entrepreneurs for that matter, Swanson eschewed the spontaneity of creative chaos for a disciplined approach to building a company with a portfolio of products. *Profitable* products.

Biotech firms typically grow in four stages. The first, or discovery stage, takes place in a research institution, like a hospital or university. With funding from the NIH, a scientist discovers a new process or theory and the institution patents the discovery—as UCSD did with John Mendelsohn's discovery of C225. In the second, or incubator stage, the institution licenses the technology to a biotech company, which raises funding from an "angel," or early stage, investor. In the third stage, the biotech company develops the product to the point where it will attract the bigger money of venture capitalists and can begin to expand its space and staff. In the final stage, the production stage, the biotech company has a commercial product that has been tested in clinical trials and cleared by the FDA and has a defined market. With funding, or a deal with a large pharmaceutical company, the biotech firm acquires a production facility, hires sales and marketing teams, and prepares to enter the marketplace.

"I hate paradigms!" Sam would gripe. "John Stewart Mill said, 'the biggest obstacle to civilization is paradigms.' He was right. I hate them!" Sam was determined to do things his own, antiparadigmatic way. One of his goals at ImClone was to reinvent the biotech business model.

Because of the effort required to develop new drugs—it generally takes a decade and an $800 million investment to prove an experimental drug's effectiveness—the existing business model essentially forced biotech firms to make deals with large pharmaceutical firms. The deals gave the biotechs certain advantages: among them, the big corporations' steady funding, regulatory experience, and huge sales and marketing teams. But such arrangements also cut into the biotechs' profits. Maverick, risk-taking entrepreneurs like the Waksals couldn't "keep their birthright to themselves," as Harlan phrased it, and achieve "one-hundred-percent revenue recognition" from the drugs they developed.

In other words, the Waksal brothers wanted to profit as much as possible: by taking on greater risk, they hoped to achieve far greater reward. The fact that many biotech firms had tried going alone and failed did not deter them. The Waksals never believed the rules applied to them.

\*    \*    \*

IMCLONE'S FIRST THREE PROJECTS were a molecular modeling software, a DNA probe technology, and a monoclonal antibody to fight hepatitis C.

Lee Compton was a scientist who, while earning an MBA from NYU in the mid-1980s, helped ImClone develop the molecular modeling software. In 1987, Compton was hired to be the company's director of product development. He had worked on the modeling software over the summer, and concluded that it was not a great business proposition: he figured the best thing to do would be to sell it off while it was still in development. But Sam had already told his investors it worked. He didn't want to hear any bad news or equivocation—he just wanted the software built. ImClone pulled together a team of a half dozen people to help with the software. At Sam's insistence, they bought a large, expensive installation of Sun Microsystem computer equipment—"it was a huge toy, and it looked good," Compton recalled. "But it was more about the display than the work it could do." Ultimately, ImClone spent about $2.5 million on the development of the software and got little or nothing in return.

The DNA probe group never made much headway, either, nor did the monoclonal group. As often happens, the science did not work out as hoped, or competitors beat ImClone to market, or there wasn't enough money to do the necessary work for a big breakthrough. It was disheartening to many at the firm, but Sam was always onto the next great thing, and the next. He didn't really seem to care about the failures as long as they didn't create too much attention and stop the money flowing in. When he had capital, Sam was free to use funds from any one project to finance others.

THE LOOSE ACCOUNTING kept most people from seeing that his business was foundering while it also continued to support his lavish spending habits.

Throughout the 1980s and into the mid-1990s, the company struggled and its staff never grew beyond 50 or 60 people. Scientists and Ph.D.'s were paid about $60,000 to $70,000, perhaps $100,000 at most, by one in-house estimate. But Sam and Harlan paid themselves considerably more than that. By the mid-1990s, the Waksal brothers were each making nearly $1 million a year.

Sam and Harlan's belief that they could defy gravity and levitate above the biotech fray was eventually punctured by the iron laws of economics. ImClone had to produce income-producing drugs, if not blockbusters.

In a concession to the biotech paradigm, ImClone's business strategy came to rely more on licensing products from other companies, or on forming strategic partnerships, than on developing successful drugs in-house. This pedestrian approach to business was at odds with Sam's incandescent ambition.

By the early 1990s, ImClone had a number of strategic alliances with larger drug companies, like Eli Lilly and Abbott Labs; but none of them were with a "Big Pharma," one of the blue-chip pharmaceutical companies. ImClone had also made arrangements with prestigious academic institutions like Princeton University and Johns Hopkins. The company would pay the universities to license products—a mouse antibody, say—or to have their faculty members, like Princeton's Arnold Levine, or Yale's Vincent DeVita, serve on ImClone's scientific advisory board (SAB). Researchers came to enjoy the perks of their ImClone affiliation: car services, luxe hotels, intimate meals at fine restaurants, sparkling Manhattan parties filled with Sam's glamorous friends.

To pay for these luxuries, Sam was on a constant hunt for money and deals. This search eventually took him abroad, to Europe and Japan. Back on Varick Street, his foreign expeditions became known behind his back as "Sam's offshore drilling."

In the winter of 1990–91, ImClone arranged a strategic partnership with the German pharmaceutical company E. Merck (later known as G. Merck, or Merck KGaA, which had no affiliation with the American drug firm Merck & Co.). It was a $14 million, three-year deal to create a melanoma vaccine, IL6, which stands for interluken sytokine. The day the deal was signed, Sam told colleagues with a giggle, he played it cool; then he went into a bathroom, fell on his knees, and said, "Thank you, Lord!" Payments were predicated on milestones: as ImClone developed the drug in steps, Merck would dole out chunks of money. Every few months, Sam and a team from ImClone would meet with representatives of E. Merck at the company's headquarters, in Darmstadt, Germany, to give them updates. Sam always insisted on traveling first or business class, using limousines, staying in the best hotels, and dining at superb restaurants, a former colleague said. But the work on IL6 had not been going particularly well. One day in the early 1990s, the former ImClone insider recalled, Sam arrived at E. Merck's offices and was told: "We have canceled the meeting. As a matter of fact, we've canceled the project."

Sam appeared unfazed. Turning to his colleagues, he cracked: "Well, we've come this far, we might as well see Germany." So the group toured around the country in high style on ImClone's tab. ["Nobody at the company has any recollection about this deal," said Phyllis Carter, a Merck KGaA spokeswoman.]

The episode was typical of Sam: "It was just another day in the life of ImClone. So many projects failed like that," recalled a person who worked at the company in those years. "There were many periods of nondata, where nothing was going on. If you had joined the company to do science, it was very frustrating."

The company basically survived from one milestone payment to the next, this person said. When money dried up, things became tense, people were laid off, and projects were put on hold; but when times were flush, the ImClone party roared.

"SAM WAKSAL single-handedly made biotech sexy," said Ian Alterman, a former ImClone legal secretary. "He was a pioneer in bringing biotech to New York. It's hard to forget someone like him."

Perhaps if ImClone had been a more boring place, it would not have soared so high and crashed so hard. But that was not Sam Waksal's style. He and Harlan worked overtime to make ImClone a "fun" place to work, in the Genentech mold—only more so. Indeed, some of their employees believed that the Waksals placed a premium on fun to the exclusion of productive and profitable work.

Sam would invite the entire staff out to a "Ho-Ho" party at a local pub, where they'd get drunk "for free," meaning that ImClone picked up the tab. He'd hold office parties at trendy joints like Le Bar Bat, or he'd rent out an entire restaurant for his staff. At Halloween, he'd encourage people to wear costumes to work. At Christmas, he'd dress up as Santa Claus; sometimes he'd ask the women in the office to sit on his lap and tell him what they hoped to find under the tree; then he'd squeeze their rear ends. Some of the women thought it was funny; others considered it vulgar.

Good looks and social enthusiasm seemed to play at least as important a role in one's advancement at ImClone as scientific skill and accomplishment, former employees complained. "You had to play by Sam and Harlan's rules to stay there. I could not, and did not," said a person who left. The ability to drink hard and laugh about it the next morning was a tangible asset. Once, for a holiday party, ImClone hired a boat to take the staff on a circumnavigation of Manhattan Island. There was music and dancing, and a lot of cheer. As the ship pulled into its berth at the end of the evening, a group of mostly young, mostly male ImClone employees lined up along the rail and heaved their guts out.

If you were not a party person you were made to feel bad about it. "I was actually taken aside and told that I needed to socialize more, that it was 'important for my job'—and they were serious about it," recalled a former employee, incredulously. "But I'm not a big partier. And the pressure to have a good time, all the time, made me miserable. I joined ImClone to do science. But finally I realized, you can't even do that here. You don't have to be a good scientist, or even a good employee, to hold a high position at ImClone. You just have to fit Sam and Harlan's mold. I never did. After a while it was just hell to go to work. And I guess it became obvious. Finally, Harlan said: 'Here's a deal. Here's the door.' "

The go-along, get-along culture at Varick Street sometimes turned into a bullying cronyism. One minute a scientist would be hailed as a "golden boy" and placed on a pedestal; the next, he'd be supplanted by a newer, fairer golden boy, or girl, who often had less talent and credentials than the first one. Taking orders from such a person was difficult for experienced scientists. They either made their peace with it or moved on.

While Sam jetted around as the smooth public face of ImClone, Harlan, the workmanlike COO, often ran the company on a day-to-day basis. Balding and medium height, Harlan looked a lot like Sam, although his body and hands were more robust, his face was broader and less creased, and he had a more earnest demeanor. Harlan preferred boxy suits to Sam's slim, tailored European cuts; Harlan and his family lived in the quiet, green suburb of Montclair, New Jersey, far from the edgy cool of Sam's SoHo loft. Harlan had a robust ego, yet he always stood in the shadow of his charismatic older brother.

"Harlan is actually very, very conservative," Sam observed. "I am much more of a risk taker. He won't jump right in when I'm going to. He'll wait a few seconds and watch, to make sure I'm okay, then he'll join me."

Harlan was always described in the press as the "more serious" Waksal brother; the quiet, hardworking scientist, whose "practicality" combined with Sam's "brilliance" to produce "a powerful synergy," John Mendelsohn said. But to those who worked under Harlan, "serious" was an oversimplified characterization.

Harlan was a good enough scientist and had a thorough understanding of how Wall Street worked. But he was not a natural leader or a particularly adept manager of people. He could be a prickly taskmaster who would obsess about details in the lab. He lacked nuance and did not think creatively. Most galling, former employees said, he had a blindspot when it came to his friends at ImClone, a select group who seemed to do as they pleased. Harlan and his friends joined a health club and would regularly disappear from the office for two hours in the afternoon to play racquetball; meanwhile, the scientists who were not invited to join them were expected to keep working in the lab and would be reprimanded for perceived errors. One member of Harlan's clique, a senior manager, appeared to spend most of his work time reading the newspaper. Another Harlan crony got so drunk one night, it was said around the office, that he smashed his car into a tree: he extricated himself from the wreck, stumbled home, and fell into bed; the next morning he had no recollection of the accident until the police showed up at his door asking about the crumpled car with his license plate they'd found.

The sense of entitlement among Harlan's inner circle inevitably led to friction with the rest of the staff. One manager recalled getting into a "nose-to-nose" confrontation with a member of Harlan's claque who had been "pathologically" bullying a shy young researcher who did not speak perfect English. Later, at a company retreat in the Hamptons, the bully and another crony stood outside of the scientist's room making loud, rude remarks about him. They had no fear of punishment, for they were Harlan's boys. "There was more damage done in that office from protecting cronies than you can imagine," the manager recalled, still angry about it years later. "It verged on *Animal House.*"

Indeed, a number of ex-employees remain bitter about their time at ImClone; none of them stepped foot back in the Varick Street offices or stayed in touch with former colleagues. "I am so glad to be out of there," said one. "It was not a healthy place."

Harlan was courteous in public, but could reveal a capricious and unreasoning temper behind closed doors. Once he took a dislike to a person, a former colleague said, there was nothing anyone could do or say to change his mind. In the mid-1990s, there was a female scientific worker at ImClone who was not making the kind of progress that Harlan expected. To make matters worse, she was not especially quick or attractive, and her personality could be grating at times. Yet she was well intentioned and a better scientist than some at ImClone. She desperately sought Harlan's approval and would go out of her way to try to interact with him. He despised her and would express his contempt in petty ways: he'd refuse to say good morning to her, or to give her the time, or to encourage her in any way; he'd humiliate her in meetings. Colleagues felt sorry for the woman but were too cowed to come to her defense. They were afraid that by speaking out they would be driven from the company, as she ultimately was.

Indeed, a number of former staffers believed that female technicians and scientists were not treated on par with their male counterparts. "I constantly had to fight tooth and nail for recognition and credit there," a former employee said. "I always had to work twice as hard to be equal, and never felt comfortable as part of 'the boys' club.'"

Sam would often make crude jokes, or do things to demonstrate his virility. Sometimes it was genuinely funny. "Only Sam would show up to a party with the Russian-hooker version of 'scientists' on his arm," a member of his social set laughed. "He's *incorrigible.*"

Other times it was corrosive. "It's not easy to be a woman at ImClone," recalled an ex-employee. "There was always a sexist issue to deal with. I couldn't stand it."

Not every woman was bothered by the caddishness, though: "Oh, it was a lot of fun," said one. "It's *Sam.* You can't take it seriously."

If you were a woman whom Sam wanted to impress—especially if you were a pretty, blonde celebrity—then he'd go to extreme lengths to charm you. It is said that Sam once developed a crush on the actress Michelle Pfeiffer and for months tried to woo her on a date. She fended him off, in part because she was publicity shy. But, the story goes, she finally relented when Sam offered to rent out an entire restaurant—Provence, a French restaurant in SoHo—so that they could have lunch there in private.

When the actress Mariel Hemingway and her husband, Steven Crisman, started up Sam's Café ("Sam" was Mariel's nickname) in midtown, Waksal loaned them over the course of several years a total of

$722,499. An old friend recalled: "He really liked Mariel, and was willing to share his friendship with her, unlike those people who jealously guard their celebrity friends. That's the nice, extremely generous side of Sam." But when the restaurant's parent company filed for Chapter 11 bankruptcy protection in the early 1990s, Sam had to concede that his judgment had been clouded. The loan, he said, had come out of his own pocket and "was a real error."

IN 1987 Alexis Stewart, Martha's only child, was a senior at Barnard College when she began to date Sam Waksal. Alexis—known to friends as Lexi—was a pretty girl with cascading blonde hair, bee-stung lips, and long legs. She had a reserved demeanor and a slightly melancholy air, but also a quiet determination. She found Sam charming and very smart, and was impressed that "he teaches at Princeton and stuff." They were introduced by a mutual friend one night at a restaurant in Manhattan. Lexi had been walking by, she recalled, and Sam was sitting there and said hi. They struck up a conversation. She ran into him again in the Hamptons over the summer and they took up together—although "it wasn't just a 'summer thing,'" she was quick to point out. At that time she was looking for someone to steady her.

The year 1987 was one of momentous change for the Stewart family: Martha would publish the hugely successful book *Weddings* and sign her landmark deal with Kmart; her husband, Andy Stewart, would leave Martha (for her assistant) after 25 years of marriage; and their daughter, Alexis, would graduate from college. Lexi and her father had never been particularly close, and she had a tight but fraught relationship with her mother. Given these circumstances, it was not altogether surprising that she would be attracted to a smart, funny, solicitous older man like Sam Waksal.

Sam was a great teacher, Alexis said. She learned a lot about science and other things from him. He'd take her to the ballet, or movies, or introduce her to his powerful friends at dinner parties. Their names would appear together in gossip columns and their photo would appear in the *New York Post* or in magazines like *Vanity Fair*. He made her laugh. He reportedly set her up in an apartment just off Madison Avenue. He would do favors, like write a note from "Dr. Samuel Waksal" stating that Alexis "has been under my care . . . for a variety of disorders . . . traced to a chronic inflammatory condition . . . she is unable to perform . . .

jury duty." His air of absentminded distraction worried her when he got behind the wheel—"he's too much of a thinker to drive really well," she'd say—and in general reminded her of the scientist in *The Fly,* who wore the same outfit every day so that he wouldn't have to think about his wardrobe. Sam liked nice possessions, and she would sometimes call him " 'Waste Your Money' Sam." His famous SoHo loft was "okay," she judged, "but not good enough for Sam. It's not that he has bad taste, but he's not a decorator. He needs a woman's touch."

Sam encouraged Alexis to do things she would never have done on her own. One year, he and Harlan took Lexi and Harlan's wife, Carol, for a week of sailing in the Bahamas on a chartered boat, "cockroaches and all." Alexis was scared of the water, she said, and the Waksal brothers didn't make her feel particularly comfortable about being out on the ocean without a professional crew. "They *say* they can sail, but . . . well, luckily we didn't hit any storms," she recalled with a nervous laugh. "We had a good time."

To outsiders her romance with Sam seemed "a bit crazy," as one friend put it, or faintly scandalous. The most obvious thing about it was that Alexis was in her early twenties and Sam was 40 (his daughters were 13 and 15 at the time). There was also the fact that Alexis was the daughter of Sam's good friend, the powerful and controlling Martha Stewart. And, Lolita-like, Lexi would dress in revealing clothes—"skirts up to her crotch," a friend said. "She was too young to know any better."

Sam often seemed more interested in showing Alexis off than in sharing quiet romantic moments alone with her. He liked to go to chic clubs and stand back, observing, while other men clustered around her. "It was so weird the way he treated her like a possession," said a friend. "With all these men just *ogling.* He'd sit there and watch with a big grin on his face."

The generation gap could lead to problems. One night Sam and Lexi and a small group from ImClone went to see a Neil Simon play on Broadway. The CEO and his date struck their companions as unintentionally funny: he was a thin balding man who blinked up at her; she towered over him like an Amazon, dressed in a jacket with padded shoulders and apparently little else. Before the show started, Alexis scowled and huffed in the lobby: it was her 21st birthday, it turned out, and she didn't want to be at *that* show, with *those* people, on *this* night, and she let everybody know it. Sam tried to placate her with soothing words, but they didn't have the desired effect.

Still, Sam and Alexis dated for nearly four years. "I was almost Sam's mother-in-law," Martha declared, "until my daughter just threw him away!"

"I was pretty young," Alexis explained, quietly. "So I don't think it was really meant to last."

Sam and the Stewarts would remain good friends, however, and would spend numerous Christmases and vacations together. And despite his vow to steer clear of the restaurant business, Sam invested "a little bit of money" in Alexis's plan to rehabilitate a stainless-steel diner in Southampton; ultimately, objections from the town convinced Alexis not to proceed.

Looking back on their years together, Alexis said that her favorite thing about Sam was that "you can ask him *anything,* and even if he doesn't know the answer, he'll give you a great answer and make you feel really comfortable. You'll be totally thrilled for a long time. I don't think he's usually wrong."

PETER BACANOVIC, a college friend of Alexis's (he attended Columbia while she was at Barnard), worked in business development at ImClone in the early 1990s. Bacanovic was good looking and talkative, and he, too, would become a frequent visitor to the Stewart household. He was introduced to Sam in the late 1980s by mutual friends, and they struck up an "acquaintanceship." It has been said that Bacanovic introduced Alexis and Sam, but that is incorrect, said an intermediary. Bacanovic met Sam socially in the late 1980s, and was impressed with Sam as "extremely cultivated in a very broad range of topics." In 1990, Bacanovic joined ImClone, and worked there for 25 months, first as a marketing manager and then as the director of business development; in the meantime, he studied molecular biology at the New School. Bacanovic represented ImClone at trade shows, did market research, and worked on "licensing-in" technology (marketing other companies' technology in the United States) and "licensing-out" ImClone products.

Bacanovic was born in 1962 and raised in Manhattan. His mother was an anesthesiologist from Greece and his father was a banker from Belgrade. Peter attended the Lycée Français in New York, and became fond of music, ballet, skiing, and travel. As an adult, he joined in the same fin de siècle social whirl that Sam and Martha were swimming in. He could be spotted at a fund-raiser for the New York Botanical Garden, or in the lobby of the American Ballet Theatre, or orchestrating the seating for an uptown crowd at the downtown restaurant Da Silvano. The writer Brad Gooch, an old friend, observed: "He was incredibly enthusiastic about the society scene, the way other people love movies or Picasso, or other boys follow sports. He mythologized Upper East Side society, which is odd, because generally people who do that are outsiders, and Peter was a [Manhattan] insider. I was writing for *Vanity Fair* [and] he had a line-by-line knowledge of the magazine. Peter, in his early twenties, knew everything about the social network."

A former colleague remembered that ImClone's business and scientific staffs had little interaction; Bacanovic, he said, was, "very beautiful and very smooth. But inexperienced, and not the brightest kid in the world. You'd see him at a fancy restaurant dressed quite well, sitting at a table of older women, and chatting about [frivolous] things."

Bacanovic left ImClone to join Merrill Lynch as a stockbroker, in October, 1993. Initially, his clients were friends from the biotech industry and grad school. But over time he would become one of Merrill's most successful private bankers, managing some $200 million worth of accounts. His clients included a diverse mix of people, from successful business owners to trust-funders to struggling artist friends. The list would eventually include Sam Waksal and his daughters, Elana and Aliza, and Martha Stewart. Martha gave him a modest slice of her stock portfolio to work with. She would be happy with Bacanovic's investment advice, and remained his most prominent client by far. Bacanovic's style was genteel and discreet: a teetotaler, he would never talk about business at dinner parties; rather, he'd opt for private conversations, like an Old World financial adviser.

ImClone was "making a huge number of seminal discoveries in the field of science," Sam claimed, but its first decade in business was not a financial success. The company had developed a number of products in-house, like diagnostics kits and infectious disease vaccines, and licensed them to pharmaceutical firms like American Home Products and Abbott Laboratories. It had research programs devoted to new cancer therapies, like the development of inhibitors of tyrosine kinase receptors (growth factor receptors) of tumor cells, and hematopoiesis (therapeutics that block blood cell disorders). And it was engaged in various clinical and academic collaborations—underwriting research of the P53 tumor suppressor gene by Dr. Arnold Levine, chairman of the Molecular Biology Department at Princeton University; supporting work on a gonorrhea vaccine by Dr. Frederick Sparling at the University of North Carolina at Chapel Hill. Yet few of these ventures provided a significant revenue stream.

"ImClone had some bright people," recalled Lee Compton. "But my greatest frustration there was the lack of focus. There was always a lot of talk about what we were *going* to do, but nothing ever got *done.*" Eventually Compton grew frustrated and decided to leave. "I was glad to go," he said, "and they were glad to have me go."

The lack of focus and profits went hand-in-hand with other serious problems.

IN 1989, Sidney Lumet directed a movie called *Family Business,* about a family of thieves who target a biotech company for a heist. Exterior shots of the company's headquarters show a mirrored-glass building on a generic suburban strip, while the interior scenes of offices and labs were shot at ImClone's office-lab on Varick Street.

The movie's plot is driven by the aspirations and travails of three generations of the McMullen-Gruden family: Jessie (Sean Connery), the Scottish grandfather; Vito (Dustin Hoffman), the Scottish/Sicilian son; and Adam (Matthew Broderick), the Scottish/Sicilian/Jewish grandson—who conspire to steal eight vials of "red-hot agricultural plasmoids" from the unnamed biotech firm. A plan is hatched. They sneak into the building. In ImClone's offices, you see long hallways, cubicles, laboratories filled with scientific instruments and glass vials, a big glass-fronted fridge holding the precious test tubes full of "plasmoids." A guard is bound with duct tape. A logbook is swiped from a desk. The test tubes are snatched from a fridge and carefully placed in a cooler. As the three generations of robbers escape an alarm is tripped. Sirens wail. Legal and familial complications ensue.

Lumet was a friend of Sam's, and Sam—who had invested in movies like *The Last Party,* a political satire starring Robert Downey Jr.— took great pleasure in talking about the filming of the movie in his offices. "They set it all up and shot it in one night," he enthused, "because we had to get back to work the next day." He kept photographs of the movie's stars on his office wall, and mentioned the movie frequently.

What is most striking about *Family Business* in retrospect is that a number of its scenes and bits of dialogue could have been lifted right from the story of Sam Waksal and ImClone. Near the end of the film, for example, Jessie (Sean Connery) interrogates Jimmy Chiu (B. D. Wong), a scheming biotech scientist, about a double-cross gone wrong.

> JESSIE: "Tell me, what was it—an insurance scam?"
>
> JIMMY: ". . . It's not about insurance."
>
> JESSIE: "No?"
>
> JIMMY: "We've been promising this new discovery [the plasmoids] for almost a year. We dug a hole for ourselves. Goddamn thing always looked a week away. Never worked."
>
> JESSIE: "It's a tough game, science, isn't it?"
>
> JIMMY: "We've just gone public with an $80 million offering. The financial community has valued this company based on this new discovery. And your robbery buys us six months' development time."
>
> JESSIE: "So long as the logbook and the plasmoids are never, ever recovered, huh?"

In June 1986, when ImClone was still brand-new, Sam forged the signatures of Harlan and John Landes on a certificate for 12,000 shares of ImClone common stock. It is alleged that he used this deception to swindle a friend and investor, Sherwood M. "Woody" Weiser, out of $90,000. His ruse remained undetected for several years. John Landes said that he only found out about the forgeries in April 1991, when Weiser's attorney came calling. Once the facts had been established, ImClone issued Weiser a genuine and valid stock certificate. In an affidavit, Sam wrote: "The stock was mistakenly purported to be transferred from Biotechnology Holdings Company (BHC) to Mr. Weiser." BHC was one of Sam's myriad side ventures. But BHC "did not and has not held ImClone Systems common stock," he wrote.

Despite the existence of this legal document, both Harlan and Robert Goldhammer would testify before Congress that they and the other ImClone directors learned of this forgery (it may have been Sam's first, but it was not his last) in 2002.

Upon hearing from Weiser's attorney, John Landes, ImClone's general counsel, immediately had a number of conversations with Sam. The forgery was a "crazy thing to do," he said. Sam replied: "I do crazy things sometimes." Neither of them, the government would later charge, disclosed the truth of what Sam had done to Weiser; nor was Sam's indiscretion revealed to the ImClone board of directors or to regulatory authorities because, Landes told Congress, he was convinced that Sam "did not recognize how shares were to be conveyed if you owned them. I believed that . . . this was a good-faith misunderstanding, or lack of knowledge on his part."

At this, Congressman James Greenwood, a Pennsylvania Republican, interrupted the ImClone attorney: "I'm trying to understand how one could have a lack of knowledge about a technical financial matter that would result in one's forging another person's name on a document."

"We were a very small company at the time," Landes replied, shakily. "We were just beginning . . . I did not report it to the board of directors, because, as I say . . . this was a misunderstanding on Sam's part."

Greenwood, a distinguished and laconic type, stared at Landes for a moment, then snorted: "My children know better than that, Mr. Landes."

"SAM IS NOT NAIVE, and he's not a bad person. He never intentionally goes into something trying to burn or hurt someone," observed Elana Castaneda, one of Sam's former girlfriends. "Unfortunately, he has a problem with execution."

"I'm not always charming," Sam admitted, charmingly. "I don't like to be charming all the time. Do you think that's a bad thing?"

One of the things that made him less than charming was Sam's habit of overextending himself. In 1993 Waksal's friend, the venture capitalist Charles Antell, sued him in order to recoup a $100,000 personal loan. "That had nothing to do with the company," Antell explained. "It was personal between me and Sam Waksal. Unfortunately, I felt I had to file suit to get my money back." Antell owned more than 100,000 shares of ImClone stock, and described himself as a close friend of Sam's; he was even sympathetic about Sam's nonpayment: "Sam is too nice a guy sometimes. He's tried to be helpful to people. He made some loans and people took advantage of him."

Sam wrote an $85,000 check to partially repay the debt. The check bounced. The case was eventually settled. In a note to Antell handwritten in his loopy script, Sam said: "Thank you for being a good friend . . . I know I don't deserve it."

There were other serious lapses in the early days of ImClone.

When it came to the company's sputtering projects, "Sam didn't want to hear any bad news," recalled a former ImClone manager. "He needed every product to work out, to keep the money flowing in and the business going." And this person said, "I always had significant questions about ImClone's science."

In at least one case, this person said, "I found evidence of falsified scientific results." The manager discovered discrepancies in the data of a product under development in the early 1990s: after spending hours poring over the lab books and taking notes, he sat down with the lead technician on the product. The tech, who was an aspiring "golden boy" and one of Harlan's racquetball pals, seemed unconcerned. The manager carefully went through his findings, noted "errors of omission and commission," pointed out "willful discrepancies," and asked for an explanation. The tech's only response was to say: "Yes." The message was clear: "Yes, I see there is a problem with the data. No, there is nothing here for us to talk about. End of story." Not satisfied, the manager raised his concern with Harlan, who thanked him politely. There was no further discussion about the matter, no corrective action was ever taken, and the research never resulted in a product.

"I can't *prove* that Sam and Harlan knew about the discrepancies beforehand," the manager said. "It's impossible to know. But as COO and CSO, I don't think what I reported to Harlan could have come as a complete surprise. I suspect that the boys hoped to rescue some value from [the research], but it never happened. The science behind it was too badly compromised."

Falsifying scientific data was an extremely serious matter, one that was not common in biotech. "It was the last straw," said the manager. He quit ImClone without a new job lined up and without vesting valuable stock options. "I had already stayed at the company far longer than I should have because I was really trying to make the job work. But how could you stay at a place like that?"

Sam had a great ability to compartmentalize and was relentlessly optimistic in his outlook. To those who worked with him, he seemed genuinely unaffected by ImClone's bad luck and unconcerned about its bad science.

"I think about doing lots of different things—creative, important things," he said. "Yes, we had some difficult times. But I don't allow roadblocks to stop me. I never have. I find ways to correct and improve, and I move on."

The manager had a different interpretation: "The truth is, I don't think Sam gave a *hoot* what the company did. He didn't give a *hoot* about making 'great scientific advances,' or 'saving people's lives'—all the things he'd talk about. Those things were not all that important to him. He was always just one step ahead of all the people who were trying to make him accountable for his past science, after all . . . You know what Sam's goal was? To build a company, with himself as CEO, and get rich. Period."

MONEY—THE CRAVING OF IT, the acquiring and spending of it, the constant pressure of it—would be the elemental force that impelled Sam Waksal, and would ultimately prove his undoing. So some say. Others say that while attaining wealth was certainly important to Sam, it was only one part of his larger objective. The primary motivator for Sam, these people believe, was status. "He loved the image and the lifestyle," a former colleague observed. "He loved being *that* CEO, the guy with the hot biotech company and the hot drug, the guy who travels everywhere in a limousine or by corporate jet. That kind of status is worth far more than a million dollars to Sam."

The banks and VCs were good for start-up capital, but to fuel significant long-term growth ImClone began to eye the public market—hoping for a spectacular payout, like the ones Genentech and Cadus had achieved a few years earlier.

Sam wanted only the best firm to take ImClone public, naturally. In the late 1980s, Solomon Brothers was the leading underwriter for initial public offerings (IPOs). Sam declared that he wanted Solomon, and only Solomon, to take ImClone public. For weeks, the "Solly" people were seen crawling all over the Varick Street office, until one day they weren't. Suddenly, the name "Solomon Brothers" was forever banished from the halls of ImClone.

ImClone would remain a private business for seven years, but not by choice. In October 1987, the company's first attempt at an IPO was a victim of the stock-market crash. It was only because Sam was able to convince investor friends, like his poker- and tennis-playing buddy Carl Icahn, to keep the company afloat that ImClone was able to launch its second IPO. This took place in November 1991 and raised some $31.7 million. It was a significant sum, yet Sam's spending remained profligate and the company remained deeply in the red.

By the spring of 1992, a number of ImClone's products—most notably its DNA amplification probe and its AIDS drug—had failed to take off. The company was facing bankruptcy. A few people were laid off, others quit, and morale spiraled down. If it was going to stay in business ImClone desperately needed to find a lead product that would generate attention and income.

FOUR

# The "Miracle"

On a crisp blue morning in April 1992, three men sat around a table in a nondescript café on Manhattan's Upper East Side talking in low excited tones. Seated in the middle was Dr. Zvi Fuks, chairman of the radiotherapy department at Memorial Sloan-Kettering Cancer Center. On one side sat his colleague, Dr. John Mendelsohn, who was chairman of the hospital's Department of Medicine. Across the table sat Sam Waksal. Fuks was the matchmaker of this breakfast. He had worked with Mendelsohn for a decade at the hospital, and he had first met Waksal at Stanford, back in 1972. Aside from his duties at the hospital, Fuks sat on ImClone's scientific advisory board (SAB), where part of his role was to scout new scientific opportunities for the company. He had brought his two friends together on this beautiful spring day because each had something the other wanted.

After making the introductions and ordering bagels and orange juice, Fuks sat back and let the two get acquainted. Speaking in the measured tones of his Cincinnati childhood, Mendelsohn explained that he had devoted his career to fighting cancer, and that his pet project over the past dozen years was a potentially revolutionary cancer drug, a targeted treatment called C225. The drug was still in the experimental stage, but it had shown tantalizing hints that it could effectively block

EGF receptors, and thus block tumor growth. Because EGF receptors are found in a third of all solid cancer tumors, the potential market for a drug that works to block them was enormous. "To explain how it works, simply," Mendelsohn said, "using C225 is like putting chewing gum in a lock."

"Yeah, yeah, I get it," said Sam, nodding enthusiastically.

While the science behind C225 was exciting, Mendelsohn said, the development of the drug was time consuming and capital intensive. He was a research scientist and an academic, not an entrepreneur. He was determined to turn C225 into a commercially viable product, but he didn't want to start and run a company by himself. Finally, he arrived at the punch line: "I want to do the research and let someone else take care of the business."

Sam sat straight up, his eyebrows arched, his eyes popped wide, and his grin spread encouragingly. *Those* were the magic words he'd been waiting to hear for a very long time. So what if his company was nearly broke, and he and Harlan had zero experience taking a drug through the FDA regulatory process?

"I want that antibody!" he said.

This breakfast meeting is what Sam would later refer to as the " 'Aha!' moment" in ImClone's history. He sensed the new antibody could be his lifeline. Although C225 was still experimental, Sam believed that its biologics and preclinical data were "solid." And while there were similar targeted treatments under development, Mendelsohn was the farthest along in his research. The more he thought about it, the more Sam grew convinced that a bet on C225, enhanced by Mendelsohn's good name and platinum connections, was "an informed and calculated bet, not a blind one."

The Waksal brothers had no clinical experience, no manufacturing capability, and no sales force. But they decided to shoot the moon, quickly purchased the license for the original C225 mouse antibody for a minimal amount from U.C. San Diego, and converted it into a chimeric, or mostly human antibody, in the lab. Once they had the antibody in usable form, they had to test it in clinical trials—a laborious process—and figure out a way to manufacture the drug and market it.

"Well," he cheerfully announced to friends, "we just bet the company on C225!"

\*     \*     \*

JOHN MENDELSOHN was equally pleased to have found Sam. "I urged him to take it on and I thought it was wonderful when he did," Mendelsohn said. "My personal goal remains to do everything in my power to bring C225 through the approval process and to patients with cancer." Hybritech and Eli Lilly had not been able to move the drug forward. Mendelsohn had pitched his targeted treatment to a number of the Big Pharma companies, but none of them had bitten. Now, after a dozen years' worth of often frustrating work he'd finally found in Sam a partner with "the vision, the desire and the capability to get this new treatment to patients."

Waksal was just the kind of guy Mendelsohn had been looking for: not only had he recognized the drug's potential as a tyrosine kinase inhibitor "faster than anybody else," but he was fully committed to commercializing it. "Previously people had put too much emphasis on C225 as an 'antibody therapy.' Sam saw that we were attacking an oncogene product called the EGF receptor, which is relevant in a large number of human cancers," Mendelsohn said. "I was delighted that there was somebody who seemed to have the energy and the vision to try to bring this forward . . . At the time Sam agreed to do this, people were still skeptical about antibodies. So it took some guts."

Mendelsohn didn't know much about Sam Waksal's background. They had a few things in common: both were bright, Jewish, Ohio natives who lived in New York and were in the cancer business. Beyond that, Zvi Fuks had vouched for Sam. "With his experience and understanding of the science, Sam seemed very credible to me," Mendelsohn said. It seemed enough, and so Mendelsohn didn't dig any deeper. The important thing was that Sam would take the C225 ball from Mendelsohn's hands and run with it.

He did exactly that. "I've watched a lot of companies work, and Sam and Harlan Waksal moved things along as expeditiously as I've ever seen," said Mendelsohn. "I give them credit." On the other hand, in his enthusiasm Sam would occasionally help himself to more credit than was absolutely his due. He claimed that while most people viewed C225 as an antibody, an immunological agent, it was he who had the insight that it blocked cancer cells' enzyme function, like a chemical. "This is not simply an antibody, it's a very specific drug. It mimicked the growth factor, but instead of turning the cell on it shut it off," Sam said. "I just saw it—it was one of those 'Aha' things. I looked at the drug, and felt it should be developed in a certain way. We switched the entire development path of that drug. And John very quickly saw it my way."

Asked about this Mendelsohn let out a gruff laugh and noted, "With all due respect, he's embellishing a little there. Sam said that 10 years after I said it. He's right, but it was not an original idea. The [action of C225] was very clear when Sato and I published it in 1984. He did *not* redirect the development of this drug."

There must have been many moments like this one, and Mendelsohn must have questioned his decision to do business with Sam Waksal. He refused to discuss it beyond saying "I was very disappointed in some of the things I learned about Sam." Years later, he would note: "[ImClone] was a small start-up company instead of a big drug company. But I had no one else to do it."

IN EXPLAINING how ImClone, and not some other, larger, more experienced company managed to acquire the rights to John Mendelsohn's drug, Sam said: "The license for C225 had been lying around for years and no one was doing anything with it. We simply understood the biologics *better* than anyone else. And, you know what? We were right."

There was a problem, though. "We had no money," Sam recalled with a flash of the lopsided grin. "Zero. I mean *none.*"

In May 1993, ImClone undertook a second offering of common stock, which raised $10.4 million. And in 1994, through private offerings, the company raised an additional $5.7 million. But these were weak bulwarks against a steadily rising debt. From its inception in April 1984 through December 1996, ImClone would show cumulative losses of $102 million.

Aside from C225, the company had several other drugs under development in the early 1990s, including two cancer vaccines—105AD7 and BEC-2—and Sam continued to "drill offshore" for deals.

In January 1993, ImClone hopped on the stem-cell research craze. Working with scientists at Princeton University, the company was in a race against other biotech firms to find a ligand—an important stimulating factor—and had formed a strategic alliance with a Japanese company called Chugai Pharmaceuticals. The Japanese money came rolling in like big ocean waves. Chugai's headquarters were located near Mt. Fuji, south of Tokyo, and Sam organized trips to Japan: expensive *Shinkansen* Bullet Trains were taken, fabulous sushi dinners and gallons of sake were consumed, luxurious rooms in ryokan hotels were booked. "It was a pretty good deal for Sam, as usual," one participant remembered. "The Japanese were quite the hosts. They really know how to wine and dine you." But by the end of the year, a large biotech rival, Immunex, had beaten ImClone to the ligand and patented its discovery. Chugai pulled the plug on the deal and the funny money drained away. (The ligand turned out not to be the stem-cell factor that was hoped for.)

Once again, ImClone found itself in a tight spot. This was made immeasurably more difficult by the crash of the biotech market in 1994. Sam pink-slipped a third of his workforce and others left. "It was a really, really awful period," recalled a former employee. "The stock went below a dollar a share. The company was running on a skeleton staff. It got so bad we couldn't get supplies—we kept ordering and ordering, but we didn't pay our bills. The vendors refused to supply us. You'd play a game where you'd exhaust one vendor and then you'd call another and then another. We just kept doing it because we didn't have any money. Sam was frantic."

Sam exhorted his staff to keep plugging away, and had a pyramidal crystal paperweight made that was engraved with the motto of the British Special Air Service (SAS): "Who Dares Wins." ImClone's scientists scrimped to get by and tried to devise clever ways of conducting experiments without having to spend a lot of money. But they grew angry when they learned that Sam was continuing to indulge himself. "Even when ImClone was almost broke, Sam did not stop taking limos everywhere," said a former colleague. "It always bothered me the way he spent the company's—and *investors'*—money."

At one point, Sam was caught with his hand in the till by allegedly using ImClone's money to underwrite the lavish, well-publicized private Christmas party at his loft. Robert Goldhammer sternly reprimanded Sam for this and told the staff that such self-dealing was not acceptable: "Sam will never do this again," he announced.

The jaded ImCloners looked at each other and rolled their eyes.

IT WAS WHILE the outlook appeared most bleak that the company stumbled over what may one day prove its greatest in-house success, an "antiangiogenesis" drug.

For a cancer tumor to grow and metastasize, it needs a steady supply of nutrients and oxygen, which are carried by the blood. The body's process of forming new blood vessels is called angiogenesis. Angiogenesis is caused by the interaction of proteins like the Vascular Endothelial Growth Factor (VEGF) with the KDR receptor, which is found on the surface of growing endothelial cells. When VEGF binds to KDR, a biological signal stimulates the production of new blood vessels. By the mid-1990s oncologists had concluded that the overexpression of VEGF in tumor cells is related to solid tumor growth, and they began to investigate ways to inhibit cancer by starving the tumor of blood, or "antiangiogenesis."

This approach became the focus of intensive scientific study and enthusiastic media scrutiny.

On May 4, 1998, *The New York Times* ran a "special report" on the upper left corner of the front page of its Sunday paper—the lead story in the most widely read edition of the week—indicating that antiangiogenesis drugs were a possible cure for cancer. The story was headlined "Hope in the Lab: A Cautious Awe Greets Drugs That Eradicate Tumors in Mice," and was written by Gina Kolata, an experienced medical reporter. It told about the work of Dr. Judah Folkman, a cancer researcher at Children's Hospital in Boston, who after 30 years of research had discovered two new drugs, angiostatin and endostatin, that cut off the blood supply to tumors in lab mice.

Such was the interest in finding a "cure" for cancer and so enthusiastic was the *Times* story, that it inadvertently set off a frenzy that would not be matched until ImClone's C225 made news a few years later.

Folkman's discoveries were the result of an effort to answer a peculiar 100-year-old question about cancer. Sometimes when doctors removed a tumor with no metastases, all seemed fine until a few months later, when a whole series of new tumors suddenly appeared, spread, and killed the patient. Why did this happen and what could be done about it?

Folkman surmised that cancer tumors made both stimulators and inhibitors of blood-vessel growth: while the main tumor thrived, it sent inhibitors through the bloodstream to snuff out competing metastases; but when the large tumor was removed, it would no longer supply inhibitors, and many smaller metastases would sprout. Folkman and a postdoctoral student, Dr. Michael O'Reilly, confirmed that his hypothesis held true, at least in lab mice. By 1991, Folkman had collected minute amounts of two substances he named angiostatin and endostatin from the mice, and began to test them. He discovered that these were potent inhibitors of blood vessel growth. Using the two drugs together, he was able to go a step further and entirely obliterate the tumors in the mice. "There was no tumor left—we couldn't even find it with a microscope," said a surprised Folkman. Further, the drugs had no apparent side effects.

It was possible, he said, that the two human proteins may "be exquisitely aimed—we do not know why—at cancer." If true, then the antiangiogenic approach promised a significant advance over traditional chemotherapy.

Tumors can become resistant to chemotherapy because cancer cells constantly reconfigure their genetic makeup; this allows mutant cells that are resistant to chemo to spread and grow tumors that are invulnerable to the toxic drugs. Endostatin and angiostatin proved effective in mice because they did not act on the tumors, but rather they blocked the normal blood vessels that feed tumors—by denying tumors nutrients, the drugs antiangiogenically starved them to death. (Normal cells do not shuffle their genes and so do not become resistant to drugs. This explains why chemotherapies continue to destroy normal cells and cause awful side effects—hair loss, nausea, diarrhea, vomiting, bone-marrow suppression—even after the cancer has become resistant to the drugs.)

Folkman's results were hailed in the scientific community, and a biotech company named Entremed was formed to manufacture and market antiangiogenesis drugs. Entremed entered into a deal with Bristol-Myers Squibb, the world's leading oncology drug maker.

But Folkman cautioned that he had yet to test his drugs on human patients. "Going from mice to people is a big jump," he noted. Indeed, there had been a long history of failures in drugs making the interspecies leap: chemotherapies that had worked well in mice proved far less successful in people; immune system therapies worked well in mice but were less effective in people; mice with cancer react well to gene therapy, but human patients have had limited success with this method. This is not to say that drugs cannot make the leap: many do. But after long experience, most oncologists had learned to be wary of what they call "that four-letter word: *cure.*"

"We are all driven by hope," Dr. Jerome Groopman, a Harvard

Medical School oncologist, observed to *The New York Times*. "But a sober scientist waits for the data." Until endostatin and angiostatin were tested in patients there would be no data.

Folkman's work on antiangiogenesis had been written about since 1993, but none of those stories were as enthusiastic as Kolata's front-page *Times* piece five years later. Although she noted that, "the history of cancer treatments is full of high expectations followed by dashed hopes," Kolata also wrote, in the second paragraph: "Some cancer researchers say [Folkman's] drugs are the most exciting treatment that they have ever seen." She went on to quote an official with the National Cancer Institute (NCI), who said: "People were almost overwhelmed . . . the data were remarkable." Most notably, she quoted the Nobel laureate Dr. James Watson, John Mendelsohn's loquacious mentor, saying, "Judah is going to cure cancer in two years." Watson predicted that Folkman would be remembered along with scientists like Charles Darwin as someone who permanently altered civilization.

The public's reaction to this article was immediate, unanticipated, and immense. Although Folkman's drugs had yet to be tested on a single human patient, every cancer center in the nation was deluged with phone calls from patients and their supporters, all desperate for access to the "the cancer drugs we read about in *The New York Times.*" The story led all three major TV network news shows that Sunday night, and it was splashed across the front page of every major newspaper Monday morning. The following week it ran as the cover story of both *Time* and *Newsweek* (their stories were as much about the media coverage as about the drugs' prospects). In less than a day of trading, the price of Entremed's stock soared from $12.06 to $85.

It was the interferon biomania all over again.

The media frenzy soon boomeranged, however, as the *Times* was accused of hyping an unproven drug to frantic patients. The criticism mounted when it was disclosed that Kolata's literary agent was circulating a book proposal based on her story. "In this day of public wailing over media ethics," people might be troubled by such apparent opportunism, the *Los Angeles Times* wrote in a critique. The paper quoted an unnamed "publishing official" who said: "It could be that [Kolata] knew she was breaking the story on Sunday and she prepared the proposal in advance of that." Speaking to the *Washington Post* about this charge, Kolata angrily denied she had prewritten a book proposal and said that she was shocked by the negative reaction to her article. To the charge that she had given dying cancer patients false hope, she said she had been accurate and balanced, and that it would be "arrogant and irresponsible" for reporters to censor stories just because they might raise people's hopes. "It's not for us to say what people are entitled to know," she said, a view backed by most media critics.

The excitement over antiangiogenic drugs would cool due to a lack of encouraging data. But in 2003 it would come roaring back again.

ImClone's efforts to develop an antiangiogenesis antibody—designed to target and block the KDR receptor—began in the mid-1990s and led to a number of patents. The company investigated several ways to prevent the interaction of KDR and its binding proteins, in research that continues today with an investigational product called IMC-1C11. But even this promising work became compromised by Sam's wildly exaggerated claims. In the mid-1990s, he reviewed a study conducted by a collaborator and wrote a press release that proclaimed that ImClone's experimental antiangiogenesis drug would completely block tumor growth. In truth, the data only suggested that such a result was possible. The collaborator protested. But Sam blithely issued his original press release. Investors were impressed by his claims, and, according to a former employee, the company's stock rocketed upward. "It was all lies," said the former ImClone employee. "I felt something important had been betrayed. This was the first time I asked myself: What am I doing here? It wasn't the last time—it became a daily question. Some people at ImClone thought I was crazy to feel that way. They'd say, 'What's the big deal that the science wasn't right?' . . . The science didn't matter there. What mattered was how fast Sam and Harlan could make a buck."

In 1996, Dr. John Mendelsohn was regarded as a longshot when he beat out four other candidates and was named the president of Houston's M. D. Anderson Cancer Center. "The Anderson," as the center's legions of devoted patients, employees, and benefactors knew it, was a Texas legend and the largest cancer program in the nation. Mendelsohn's new post was highly prestigious, paid some $800,000 a year, and exposed him to a new level of connections, power, and influence. Mendelsohn had won the job largely on his reputation as a brilliant cancer researcher rather than on his experience leading large, complex businesses. But as usual, Mendelsohn soon surprised everyone.

The Anderson devotes its vast facilities and $1.7 billion operating budget to just one thing: fighting cancer. Founded in 1941 by the Texas Legislature as both a public hospital to treat cancer patients and a part of the university of Texas system, M. D. Anderson every year ministered to some 65,000 people from around the world—ranging from Saudi oil sheiks, the rocker Eddie Van Halen, Southwest Airlines chairman Herb Kelleher, middle-class people from across the country, and poor local laborers. Spurred by the belief that too much of cutting-edge oncological research languished in the lab while patients ran out of therapy options and died, the Anderson championed a controversial philosophy known as "translational research," which made the latest treatments available to patients through clinical trials. To accomplish this, the Anderson enrolls some 12,000 new patients in 800 clinical trials every year, more than any other hospital.

The hospital's facilities consisted of some four million square feet of labs and operating rooms in three large, pink-granite buildings at the Texas Medical Center. There were vaulted ceilings in the main lobby, colorful aquariums at every turn, a pianist in the food court, a large hotel for outpatients and families to stay in, advocates to help smooth a patient's experience, and a staff for whom the war against cancer was an all-consuming passion.

Mendelsohn had his work cut out for him, though, because behind the bright headlines the Anderson was suffering a form of financial sclerosis. By the early 1990s, managed-care companies had decided that the hospital was too expensive, and began to direct their patients to discounted treatment at hospitals on their lists. The cost of state-mandated care for the indigent, meanwhile, had doubled, and M. D. Anderson was spending millions of dollars on the program. Further, a Texas law prohibiting state residents from being admitted to the hospital without a doctor referral kept many patients away. The crisis grew so severe that between 1993 and 1995 M. D. Anderson faced a $90 million budget cut and was forced to lay off workers.

With a tremendous lobbying and PR effort, hospital administrators convinced the state legislature and the Texas Medical Association to remove the prohibition against self-referral. And when John Mendelsohn succeeded Charles LeMaistre as president in 1996, he worked hard to persuade managed-care companies to start sending their patients back to the Anderson. His pitch was simple but effective: although it was more expensive to begin care at M. D. Anderson, he said, it was actually cheaper for HMOs over the long term. "We have a thousand doctors, and about two-thirds are clinicians who treat nothing but cancer, and one-third are Ph.D.'s who study nothing but cancer. We have a very good chance of doing the right thing the first time," Mendelsohn said.

His message resonated. Over the next few years, the hospital's budget doubled, the number of patients it received rose nearly 40 percent, and fund-raising hit new highs—up to $106.4 million in fiscal 2002. The following year, a *U.S. News & World Report* survey named Anderson the best cancer hospital in the nation for the third time in four years.

Mendelsohn's flair for business had impressed patients and staff and Houston's elite, many of whom, like former President George H. W. Bush, were deeply involved in running the hospital. As his profile was raised, so were his perks. In 1994, Mendelsohn joined the scientific advisory board (SAB) of ImClone, and in 1998 he joined the company's board of directors.

In 1999, he was invited to join a far more prestigious board: that of the famous Houston gas trader Enron—roundly hailed as one of the most successful and dynamic businesses in the world. It was a logical step for him. Enron and its affiliated foundations had an existing relationship with the Anderson, having contributed some $2.5 million to the hospital between 1985 and 2000. (After Mendelsohn took over as president, he is quick to note, Enron's contributions dropped to just 0.1 percent of the Anderson's philanthropic income.) In inviting Mendelsohn aboard, Enron's CEO, Kenneth Lay, asked him to fill the seat being vacated by LeMaistre, the Anderson's previous president. The Enron directors met five times a year and were reportedly paid $79,000 a year, plus stock options and ancillary benefits.

John and Anne Mendelsohn had reached an apotheosis. For the first time in her adult life, Anne—a former chemist at Polaroid, child photographer, and TV producer—did not have a regular job. She joined park, theater, museum and education boards. John Mendelsohn joined the boards of the Houston Grand Opera, the Greater Houston Partnership, an influential business group, and BioHouston, which promotes the local biotech industry. They were one of Houston's most prominent couples. At one point, the Mendelsohns were attending parties 23 nights out of every month, his staff calculated, and they often entertained the city's movers and shakers at their redbrick mansion in the city's museum district.

Life could hardly have been better for Mendelsohn, but for one nagging detail: the sluggish development of C225.

SINCE IT HAD acquired the license to the drug, ImClone had been producing small batches of C225 at a plant in Branchburg, New Jersey, and augmenting the work done at Mendelsohn's lab at Memorial Sloan-Kettering. C225 was tested in combination with several chemotherapies (doxorubicin, cisplatin, and paclitaxel) on lab mice and human tumor xenographs. It was arduous work. But the tests had shown, convincingly, that the antibody was able to destroy human tumors placed in the mice. Now came the big test. As with Folkman's antiangiogenesis drugs, there was always a question about how effective C225 would prove against cancer in human patients.

In December 1994, ImClone began limited testing of C225 in patients at some of the nation's leading cancer hospitals: Memorial Sloan-Kettering, Yale Cancer Center, University of Virginia, M. D. Anderson, and the University of Alabama. The first study, involving a single injection of C225 in 13 patients, was completed in March 1995.

A few weeks later, on May 19, Mendelsohn presented the promising results of these early tests at the 35th annual American Society of Clinical Oncology (ASCO) meeting, which was held in Atlanta, Georgia, that year. Sam would later declare that this was the pivotal moment in the history of C225, because for the first time the industry paid attention. Within 24 hours of Mendelsohn's presentation, Sam claimed, "ImClone's stock began climbing—all the oncologists were buying it! We were able to finance again, turn our drug development around, and start moving forward again."

"That's an exaggeration," Mendelsohn said. "Sam loves to think there are moments of truth. But there was no one moment of truth. We gradually accumulated encouraging evidence in the lab and in clinical trials."

A number of Big Pharma companies began sniffing around for a deal and went so far as to review the C225 clinical data. But an agreement was never reached. This must have been deeply frustrating for ImClone and John Mendelsohn, although the Waksal brothers would spin events another way.

ImClone had always intended to develop C225 on its own, Harlan would claim. He and Sam believed they could develop the drug and shepherd it through the exacting FDA approval process without the help of a seasoned partner. "We decided that this was going to be somewhat of a make-or-break-type of issue with us," Harlan confided to an analyst in the spring of 2001. "We decided we would never give away the U.S. rights, no matter what. We knew this drug would work."

In fact, ImClone *had* attempted to license C225, but the bids from the Big Pharma companies had come in so low that the Waksals felt insulted. In a fit of pique, they decided that they didn't need a partner and would instead go it alone. "We could have licensed [C225] and it would have been in a very different development track," Harlan averred. Instead, "we pushed it along very aggressively. We did it creatively. And other groups are now looking at this as a model for how to get a drug approved quickly in oncology . . . Everybody's not only paying attention to us, we're being *copied*. All the pharma companies with small molecules are following our lead."

IN THE MID-1990s, C225 was not yet a blockbuster, and as ImClone's business faltered its struggle was more about survival than about trouncing the competition.

In aggressively promoting the company's products, Harlan and Sam would make super-optimistic claims. One scientist from that era recalled traveling to pitch strategic alliances: "When the Waksals would tell [a prospective business partner] about the science that I had been working on, I found it tough to listen to. I'd sit there and think: 'Oh, God, that's not what the data says. I *wish* the science did what they said it did.' But it didn't. My work was being exploited to the point where it was made to look far more sensational than it really was." This scientist felt caught between duty to ImClone and duty to self. "You suddenly get interest from [potential partners], but when you don't have anything great to show them later, it backfires . . . When you can't make your science work the way Harlan and Sam said it would, then you get caught in this situation. It wasn't your fault. It was the science. But you get blamed. It was damned if you do, damned if you don't. And then you couldn't get back to reality."

The ImClone researchers were under increasing pressure by management to create new products and get them to market. A steady product stream would lead to a steady revenue stream. But as with most small biotech firms, the ebb and flow of funds hobbled the consistent execution of ideas. With researchers coming and going, and supplies available one minute but not the next, it was left up to an experienced core of scientists to figure out ways to keep the ship afloat. One of their main concerns was the issue of securing and defending patents, or negotiating for the use of others' intellectual property.

It is common in biotech for a company to make broad patent claims on a scientific discovery and to litigate aggressively to protect them. Put simply, he who controls the patent controls the market. In the case of a blockbuster drug for a disease like cancer or AIDS, the defense of a patent can literally make or break a company. The inherent conflict between the protection of intellectual property and the curtailing of intellectual discovery has always been a hotly disputed aspect of the industry. It can be an arcane and expensive lawyers' game. But without patent protection a company has no hope of success.

When one company wants to use another's research, they usually pay a licensing fee or royalty to the patent holder; or they may sue the patent holder, in an attempt to access the science and its revenue; less frequently, a company will try to use another's science without permission and hope for the best.

Sam was not averse to taking competitors to court, as he did with Immunex in the 1990s over an ImClone patent related to HER2, an antibody against breast cancer. The companies struck a deal, in which Immunex agreed to pay a royalty in return for the use of the ImClone patent for its successful anticancer drug Herceptin, a targeted treatment.

BY THE MID-1990s, ImClone was deeply in debt, its stock was trading at half its IPO price of $13 a share, morale was bad, and work was slowing to a standstill. In a do-or-die effort to avoid extinction, Sam pulled a string and arranged a bailout.

In 1992, ImClone had cofounded Cadus Pharmaceuticals Corp. with scientists from Princeton University. The company focused on yeast-based screening systems and chemical compounds that blocked signals within cells. In stock sales of December 1994 and April 1995, ImClone spun off its Cadus subsidiary to Carl Icahn for a mere $6 million. Icahn was a Princeton graduate and had donated a $20 million genomics lab to the university; it is likely that he helped to connect Sam to the Ivy League university and its renowned scientists, like Arnold Levine, who served on ImClone's SAB.

(Another investor in Cadus was a Westport, Connecticut, physician named Dr. Bart Pasternak, whose wife, Mariana, was a good friend of Martha Stewart, the Pasternaks' neighbor and also a Cadus investor.)

With only Icahn's money in the bank, Sam and Harlan decided to roll the dice and focus all of their efforts on one product: C225.

It was a stressful time. Harlan feared that John Mendelsohn's discovery would again become orphaned: "I was sure that something of great value wasn't going to be recognized because we didn't have the money," he would recall. Sam added: "If the drug had failed, that would've been the end of ImClone." Instead, C225 and the company were saved by a remarkable coincidence.

HER STOMACH was twisting and burning, like something was exploding in there, and the pain was wearing her out. As she neatened her desk and filled out expense reports in an attempt to distract herself from the incessant roiling, Shannon Kellum worried: *What is happening to me? What can I do to make it go away? When will it end?*

She was 28 years old, petite, blonde, and athletic. A Florida state tax auditor with a boyfriend and a condo in Fort Myers, Shannon was known around the office for her sprightly good humor. Yet she had been unable to shake free of the strange malaise that had been dragging her down, like a heavy net, for weeks.

It was mid-November 1997. She wasn't pregnant, that much she had determined. The first doctor said that her symptoms might indicate any number of illnesses. Over the next three months he listened to her, poked and prodded her, and ran test after test to get to the bottom of it. She put up with his brusque bedside manner, hoping he'd discover something normal, like she had a stomach flu or food poisoning. In February 1998, a second doctor removed her appendix. After the operation he discovered the appendix was perfectly healthy. Shannon continued to feel lousy. In April, a third doctor discovered a malignant tumor swelling inside her liver, just two inches above where her appendix had been, as well as dark spots—a clear sign of cancer—growing on the outside of her colon. It was something the second doctor should have seen, she said later, but at the time she wasn't concerned with that.

"Wait a minute . . . I have *cancer?!*" Shannon said, staring in disbelief. "But I'm young! I take good care of myself! I thought cancer was a disease you get when you're, like, a grandmother."

She didn't cry. She felt herself go numb. All forward-moving thought ceased. Her happy plans for marriage, children, a successful career, suddenly faded. She drifted in a terrible limbo of fear and incomprehension that set her apart from the rest of the world. She imagined the tumor growing inside her, the cells replicating feverishly: it was terrible, the embodiment of every anxiety she had ever had; pure dread.

Cancer was not something Shannon had given a lot of thought to. Her mother had once had a small malignant tumor removed from her breast, but she had recovered nicely and didn't talk about it much. Of course, everyone knew people who had cancer, but they were all a lot older than Shannon. She was in the prime of her life, with things to do, people to see, places to go. Now these doctors were telling her she had "metastatic colon cancer," whatever that was.

The colon extends from the cecum to the rectum: it is the first five to six feet of the large intestine, part of the body's digestive tract, a long muscular tube that removes nutrients from food and stores waste until it is passed out of the body. Colorectal cancer usually begins with polyps, small growths on the inside of the colon. It is insidious, the second most deadly form of the disease after lung cancer: in 2002 an estimated 148,300 cases of colon cancer were diagnosed and it killed some 56,600 Americans. It is unknown what causes colon cancer, but it is believed to be the result of both genetic predisposition and lifestyle factors, such as tobacco use, lack of exercise, and poor diet. Until the advent of targeted therapies, the standard response to colorectal cancer was to attack it with chemotherapy, radiation, or surgery. But those weapons are of limited effectiveness against a disease that essentially eats a patient up from the inside, cell by cell, and can spread rapidly. The median survival rate for people with colorectal cancer, Shannon's doctor said, is only nine to twelve months.

*Oh no,* she thought, as a cold sweat prickled her brow and her breathing grew shallow. *What do I do now?*

Shannon was referred to a local oncologist, a young doctor named Mark Rubin, who had trained at Memorial Sloan-Kettering in New York. Rubin had been one of the most promising doctors in the cancer center's program, but had opted out of the prestigious life of a research scientist in the big city to return to his native Florida, to work with patients in a clinic.

Rubin was a thin and somewhat nervous man, with a head of curly brown hair and a sympathetic demeanor. Unlike the other doctors, he went out of his way to ask about how Shannon was coping. The answer was that for all her outward cheer and inner strength, she was terrified.

He put her through a battery of tests, which confirmed her worst fears.

Shannon's colon was surgically resected, and over the next year she underwent round after round of chemotherapy to rid her of remaining traces of the disease. It was a long and difficult period, but she tried to remain upbeat. She told friends that she considered herself "lucky" because she wasn't suffering too badly from the nausea often associated with chemo. She continued to work full time—now as an accountant at Southwest Florida International Airport—and to go to the gym. She and her boyfriend got married. Yet as the year wore on, Shannon's cancer returned. Then the tumors began to spread throughout her body.

Dr. Rubin tried the three different chemotherapy regimes that are standard for colorectal cancer: first, CPT-11, or ironotecan, a treatment that is taken intravenously; then, when Shannon's cancer flared again, he moved her on to oxaliplatin; finally, Dr. Rubin prescribed Xeloda, a workhorse version of the old standard chemo, 5FU fluoracil, and the last line of defense.

Shannon's lesions continued to spread. She had tried every kind of chemotherapy available, she told her family and friends, "but nothing even fazed the tumors—they just kept growing."

By the spring of 1999, Shannon's tumors had become, she said, "as big as grapefruits," too big to be removed surgically. Her cancer had progressed from stage 1 right up to stage 4, which meant she was "refractory," or not responding to chemo, and now the disease had reached her liver.

One day at the end of March, Rubin sat down with Shannon and her new husband and gave them the unvarnished truth: "The chemo isn't working," he said. "Basically, we've exhausted all our options." Then he took a deep breath and added: "But I have one more idea. It's a long shot. An experimental new cancer drug called C225 that I helped work on at Sloan-Kettering. It hasn't been approved by the FDA yet, and it has never been used to treat a colon cancer patient. But it's our last hope. Are you willing to try it?"

Shannon had been Dr. Rubin's patient for a year now, and had found him to be compassionate and honest, so she nodded yes. She really didn't have a choice: if the tumors progressed any further they were going to kill her. At this point, she was willing to eat or drink literally anything to buy time. So she volunteered to become "the guinea pig for C225."

Despite his air of academic self-effacement, Rubin was a determined cancer fighter who sometimes strayed from oncological orthodoxy in pursuit of new ways to combat the disease. Most doctors taxonomized cancer growths by where in a patient's body they originated—the breast, say, or the lungs—and based their treatment on the assumption that the cancer was rooted in that part of the body. Rubin, however, looked at cancers on the cellular level, searching for biological weaknesses that would allow him to attack a particular kind of tumor in a particular way, regardless of where it had originated. It was an approach he had learned from his mentor at Sloan-Kettering, Dr. John Mendelsohn.

"Don't put cancer in boxes with labels on them," Mendelsohn had preached. "Open your eyes to what *might* be."

It was a lesson that Rubin, one of the brightest researchers in Mendelsohn's lab, took to heart. Looking at cells taken from Shannon Kellum's tumors, Rubin didn't simply say, "this is colon cancer." He discovered they were of a type that "expressed a high degree of EGF [epidermal growth-factor] receptors." That was significant. Normal cells have small amounts of EGF, but cancerous cells can produce a million or more receptors. With cancer, EGF binds to its receptors on the surface of a cell, then sets off a chain reaction of enzymes inside the cell that keep the tumor nourished: the cell "autostimulates," and grows frantically.

In the Sloan-Kettering lab, Mendelsohn and Rubin had discovered that C225 blocked the EGF receptors in certain cancerous cells, and it had worked especially well against colon cancer. At least it did in test tubes.

The tantalizing question was: would C225 work in a real patient?

By March 1999, Shannon Kellum's body was riddled with tumors.

On a hunch, based on the work he'd done in the lab on C225 a decade earlier, Rubin called Mendelsohn at M. D. Anderson and asked permission for Shannon to try the experimental drug. Mendelsohn replied that he would ask his business partners at ImClone.

At the time, ImClone was running clinical trials that tested C225 on head-and-neck cancer, a form of the disease that generally expressed a high amount of EGF, and was thus a promising target for the drug. But Shannon's colorectal cancer also expressed high EGF and was, at least in theory, vulnerable to C225's "gum-in-the-lock" blocking action. And there was an added consideration: there are many more cases of colorectal cancer than head-and-neck. If the drug helped Shannon, then it might open up a much larger market for C225. ImClone agreed to give Rubin a small amount of the experimental drug.

Shannon was frail and terrified as she lay down on a gurney at Dr. Rubin's hospital in Bonita Springs and watched as his head nurse, Sharon, inserted a needle into a bulging blue vein in the crook of her thin, pale arm. The needle was attached to an IV drip filled with clear liquid: C225 mixed with irinotecan, one of the chemotherapies that had previously failed to help her. She was acutely aware that this was her last, best chance, and that it was a crapshoot.

Our bodies have hundreds of thousands of naturally made antibodies—proteins produced in the blood that destroy or weaken bacteria or poisons—circulating at all times. If you have an infected shin, say, then antibodies carried in the bloodstream swarm to that spot and help to fight the infection. C225 is an antibody made in the lab. As it coursed through Shannon's system, it bumped into many kinds of cells, each of which had many receptors on its surface. A small cell has about 10,000 receptors, but cancer cells have about a million receptors on their surface—one of the traits that allows cancerous cells to co-opt nutrients and go where they are not supposed to in the body.

When the C225 in Shannon's bloodstream bumped into cells with EGF receptors, it bound to them. (Many noncancerous cells also have EGF receptors. C225 bound to them all. For reasons doctors don't fully understand, blocking the receptors in a cancer cell has greater consequences than in a normal cell.) Upon binding, C225 blocked the chemical pathway in the cancerous cell. This had an antiangiogenic effect: that is, C225 blocked the production of molecules that were stimulating the growth of blood vessels feeding the tumors spreading throughout

Shannon's body. Although there is still much to be learned about C225, it gives the patients who respond to it many other advantages: it reduces cell proliferation by producing the P27 molecule; it protects against apoptosis (the lack of cellular death—which is essentially what cancer is); and it "potentiates," or enhances the effects of, chemotherapy and radiotherapy. This is why Mendelsohn calls C225, "a really fascinating drug."

Once a week, for a month, Shannon had doses of the C225/irinotecan cocktail injected into her arm. Although clinicians believe that the only side effect of C225 is a mild skin rash (about 2 percent of patients develop hives, or a severe allergic reaction, that forces them off the drug), Shannon felt nauseated and weak. But she was determined to finish the regime. A few more months, or weeks, of life meant everything.

"Are you sitting down?" It was Sharon, Dr. Rubin's nurse, on the telephone. Sharon always used the same tone of voice whether she was delivering good news or bad, and so Shannon didn't know what to expect. It was the end of May now, a month after she had begun using the chemical cocktail.

"Your tumors have shrunk by 50 percent."

Shannon sat at her desk in stunned silence. After a year of hearing only that her tumors were growing-growing-growing, to hear the word *shrink* was a miracle. She jumped up and suddenly let out a big "Whoop!" and began laughing and shouting, with tears pushing at the edges of her eyelids. It startled her office mates.

Shannon's results astonished everyone. By the end of September, the C225/ironotecan cocktail had shrunk her tumors by an unprecedented 80 percent. By mid-December, the tumors had shriveled to the point where a surgeon could remove them, along with more than half of her liver.

To Shannon there was no question that C225 had saved her life. "It's my miracle drug," she said, again and again. "Although it isn't a cure, it has given me a lot more time than I expected. C225 is the only thing that's worked for me. It's a blessing. I am very, very fortunate."

Dr. Rubin was stunned. Neither he nor any other oncologist had ever seen a stage 4 patient turn her health around like Shannon Kellum had. "It was a tremendous response, although I want to make it clear that it is not a cure," he said, feeling cautiously euphoric. It was his hunch—never acknowledged by ImClone—that C225 could be effective against colon cancer that proved the crucial insight that pushed the drug's development rapidly forward, although perhaps to a degree that was unintended, or unwarranted. (Mark Rubin never had a financial stake in the drug, or in ImClone, as John Mendelsohn did.)

The Waksal brothers were quick to grasp the scientific and marketing implications of Shannon's remarkable recovery. She was photogenic and eloquent. They pushed her to talk to journalists, and for a brief moment she became a media darling. During the May 2000 ASCO conference, her story was featured in two *USA Today* feature stories. On May 22, Shannon appeared on ABC's *Good Morning America*. Smiling in a suit, her face made up and eyes sparkling, Shannon looked the picture of health. Soon would come more interviews, and in June 2001 Shannon would testify before Congress. She was ImClone's (unpaid) angel.

As with the story about Folkman's antiangiogenesis drugs, the story of C225 seemed to take on a life and momentum of its own. Within hours of Shannon's story coming out, ImClone employees, and even friends of friends of the Waksals, found themselves deluged with letters and phone calls and e-mails from cancer patients around the country desperate for access to try ImClone's "miraculous" drug. Between May 2000 and February 2001, Sam said, ImClone received more than 10,000 requests for "compassionate use" of C225. President Clinton reportedly intervened on behalf of a patient, who got the drug. Many others suffering from cancer did not. In time, such favoritism would cause a backlash against the company from angry cancer patients and their advocates.

Shannon's results also had an immediate and profound effect on the development of C225. Shannon Kellum "was a very brave young woman, and [her turnaround] was a very, very fortunate event," Harlan would later say. "Based on its value to this one patient, we decided to take a chance and test C225 on colon cancer." In other words, ImClone had decided to shift the focus of its research from patients with head-and-neck cancer to those with colorectal cancer. This was a highly unusual decision. As Harlan had noted, Shannon Kellum was just one patient: in scientific terms, she represented one data point, which was statistically negligible. "You just don't change course on drug development overnight," said a knowledgeable observer. "It's not done. And for good reason—it's not scientifically sound."

The Waksals ignored any qualms and began to work long hours to seize the moment. Sam compared his attitude to one of the founders of Israel, who had faced great opposition: "It was like David Ben-Gurion in September 1939. The war had begun in Europe, and the British put out a white paper saying there would be no more exodus of Jews to Palestine. Ben-Gurion said, 'We will fight on as if the white paper didn't exist.' And you know what? They [prevailed]."

Moving jackrabbit quick, ImClone stopped enrolling patients in the head-and-neck trial and instead launched a new, 125-patient study of the effects of C225 on colon cancer patients. The study was designed by a team at ImClone, led by Harlan, and carried out at cancer hospitals around the country. The lead scientist on these clinical trials was Dr. Leonard Saltz, known as Len, a highly regarded young oncologist from Memorial Sloan-Kettering.

C225 had been under development for twenty years, and now, almost by chance, and literally overnight, Shannon Kellum had turned it into one of the hottest products in the history of biotech.

# FIVE

# Small and One-Armed

Now ImClone was caught between shadow and light. The company's declining reputation and financial state were counterweighted by the incipient success of C225. The balance could easily tip either way. If Sam could get his drug to market soon, then ImClone would be saved and stood to make a fortune; if not, the company would sink, its people would be cast adrift, and the drug—and the thousands of patients waiting for it—would once again be cast into limbo. As the year 2000 opened, ImClone's fate was largely dependent on getting C225 quickly approved by the U.S. Food and Drug Administration (FDA), the federal agency that assesses whether or not a new treatment is fit for the marketplace.

It takes millions of dollars and months of work to generate the quality and quantity of data required by the FDA. The agency's sometimes baroque regulations, internal politics, and slow-moving bureaucracy can prove trying to even the largest and most experienced pharmaceutical companies. To forestall any problems, biotech firms usually meet with the agency before undertaking clinical trials, to ensure that the FDA's reviewers approve of the protocol design (such agreements are usually made binding through a Special Protocol Assessment). In 2000, the FDA was in turmoil: leaderless, balkanized, underfunded, overworked, and defensive in the face of widespread criticism for being too slow and cautious. And while the FDA's Center for Drug Evaluation and Research (CDER) had used dozens of Special Protocol Assessments for cancer drugs, the agency's Center for Biologic Drug Evaluation and Research (CBER)—the group in charge of ImClone's application—had hardly ever used one for a biologic drug.

The fact that ImClone had never taken an experimental compound through FDA approval before didn't bother Sam. He knocked aside any worries about C225's future and blithely assured friends and investors that ImClone was "working closely" with FDA regulators on its application.

He had reason to be optimistic. In 1998, Merck KGaA of Germany had acquired the right to market C225 in most overseas markets for $60 million plus a sales royalty of less than 10 percent. In May 1999, ImClone's early tests of C225 had made headlines at the ASCO conference. And in September of that year, Shannon Kellum's astonishing recovery had dramatically raised C225's profile in the media and on Wall Street. As the new millennium got underway, ImClone renounced its usual haphazard drug development in favor of a disciplined and strategic approach. The company muzzled Sam, reigned in spending, toned down its public profile, and began to work with a renewed focus and energy. ImClone executives were determined to conduct C225's clinical trials as carefully as possible, organize new financing, build awareness slowly, and convince regulators, investors and the public that they and their drug were for real.

At 22 cancer hospitals around the nation researchers working under the direction of Memorial Sloan-Kettering's Len Saltz conducted two phase 2 clinical trials: one to study the effects of C225 on patients with head-and-neck cancer, the other to study colon cancer patients. The latter trial, known as Study 9923, was designed for colorectal cancer patients and would be the centerpiece of ImClone's data package for the Biologic License Application (BLA). Phase 1 studies are generally conducted in a small group of volunteer cancer patients to test a new drug's safety and proper dosage. Phase 2 studies are larger—they often include several hundred patients—and are designed to test the drug's effectiveness. Once the evidence suggests that a drug works against the disease, phase 3 trials study the drug's effectiveness in a much larger group of patients—from several hundred to several thousand volunteers—and try to compare the new drug to an existing treatment in a randomized way. Phase 4 trials are undertaken once a drug has been approved by the FDA; they typically involve a broad range of participants and evaluate side effects or new uses of existing therapies.

In May 2000, Sam and Harlan attended the 36th annual ASCO conference, in New Orleans. Although Study 9923 was not yet complete, preliminary results seemed to confirm that Shannon Kellum's turnaround was no fluke: 20 percent of the stage 4 colorectal cancer patients in the study had improved when treated with the C225/irinotecan mixture. If these numbers held up over the course of the study, this would be an unprecedented response rate in such a desperate group of patients.

"Physicians involved in the [9923] study kept coming to our booth and telling us, 'Your drug really works,'" Harlan recalled. "We didn't know to what extent, but they were telling us that some patients were responding dramatically."

This was the best news the company had heard in years. It boded well for ImClone's FDA application, and it landed Shannon and C225 on the front page of *USA Today*—twice—during the conference.

Sam and Harlan hoped to use their sparkling data to convince the agency to grant C225 accelerated fast-track approval, a strategy that would allow them to bring their drug to market as quickly and cheaply as possible.

In the standard approval process, the FDA required one or more large phase 3 trials to show that an experimental drug will prolong life compared to a placebo or with an already-approved treatment. This is a difficult standard to meet: such trials can take years, require thousands of patients, and cost hundreds of millions of dollars to conduct. Recognizing that time is of the essence when treating life-threatening illnesses, such as AIDS or cancer, the FDA instituted a fast-track option for certain drugs in 1997. A fast-track designation—also known as "accelerated approval"—allows a company to use smaller clinical trials and less comprehensive data than the standard approval process, and it does not require a control group for comparison. Fast-track trials are usually small—limited to the most desperate patients, those who are "refractory," meaning they have not responded to standard treatments like chemotherapy—and are designed to answer one essential question: does a new drug shrinks patients' tumors or not? This is far easier to answer than the question behind a standard drug trial, which is: does a new drug extend patients' lives?

With Study 9923, ImClone was attempting something unprecedented: to get FDA approval for its drug based on an exceptionally small trial, one that had enrolled only 120 patients. Furthermore, the ImClone study had only one "arm"—that is, it tested how well C225 worked in combination with irinotecan, but it did not gauge how well the drug worked on its own.

This approach was highly unusual, and widely disapproved of, because without testing a drug as a "single agent" (on its own) there was no way to tell how effective it really was: did the patient's tumor shrink because of the irinotecan, or because of the C225? It was impossible to know. As a result, experienced oncologists looked askance at Study 9923.

In a due-diligence report on ImClone's study, a Bristol-Myers Squibb scientist would note that the FDA did not look favorably on such limited trials: "No accelerated approval has ever been granted for an oncology drug for use in a combination therapy."

Indeed, unbeknownst to ImClone, the FDA's primary medical reviewer for C225, Susan Jerian, had written in her notes that she did not believe that ImClone's small and one-armed trial would provide sufficient data to grant the drug fast-track status.

THE FOOD AND DRUG Administration has been described as the most important regulatory agency in the world. Headquartered in Washington, D.C., the FDA regulates the manufacture, transport, storage, import, and sale of $1 trillion dollars' worth of drugs, biologics, medical devices, and food every year—products that account for a quarter of every dollar spent by American consumers. Yet it is a relatively small bureaucracy, with only 9,000 employees and a $1.29 billion operating budget (less than 1/250th of the Department of Defense's budget, by one estimate).

While most of its work is mundane, the FDA occasionally makes headlines: in 1979 it was the agency that monitored radiation leaking from the Three Mile Island nuclear plant; in 1982 the FDA devised a method of inspecting millions of Tylenol bottles after someone killed seven people in Chicago by lacing Tylenol capsules with cyanide; and when terrorists threatened the 1996 summer Olympic Games in Atlanta, Georgia, the FDA oversaw the testing of athletes' food and water for poisons.

The FDA's work is crucial, and its standards are unparalleled in the world, but the agency has long been taken for granted.

In the mid-19th century, counterfeit, contaminated, diluted, and decomposed drugs and poor-quality food were rampant in the United States. The sick were frequently relieved of nothing but their money (and sometimes of their health) by purveyors of worthless "nostrums," which often contained opium, morphine, heroin, cocaine, and live worms. Thousands of useless patent remedies such as "Kick-a-poo Indian Sagwa" and "Warner's Safe Cure for Diabetes" flooded the marketplace. American troops in Mexico suffered when given bad antimalaria medicine. Chemical preservatives and toxic colors in foods went unregulated. Labels did not list ingredients or warn against misuse. Cinchona bark powder, which contained quinine, was far more profitable when cut with nontherapeutic substances. Many of the most established drug firms were engaged in such shady practices. The public suffered.

Although Frederick Accum's "Treatise on Adulterations of Food and Methods of Detecting Them" had been published in London and Philadelphia in 1820, and Britain's first national food law was passed in 1860, America was slow to regulate food and drugs. The existing U.S. food laws dated from colonial times and varied from state to state. Enacted to serve industry and trade rather than the public health, these laws set standards of weight and measure, provided for inspections of meats, fish, and flour, and ensured fair competition among bakers. With the Import Drugs Act of 1848, the federal government began to address the growing problem. And with the expansion of interstate commerce after the Civil War, the need for federal guidelines became obvious.

A lone chemist, Charles M. Wetherill, who established a lab at the Department of Agriculture in 1862 to analyze food, fertilizers, and other agricultural products, was the precursor to the modern FDA. His first published report was a study of grape juice for winemaking, which concluded that adding sugar to increase the alcohol content did not constitute adulteration. Wetherill was joined by other scientists and the group grew; by 1901, it was known as the Bureau of Chemistry, and by 1930 it was known as the Food and Drug Administration.

In 1883, Dr. Harvey W. Wiley, a tall bearded man and a natural showman, was appointed the sixth head of the Division of Chemistry.

In 1902, he focused the nation's attention on food safety by establishing the "Hygienic Table," which the media dubbed the "Poison Squad": a group of young men who volunteered to eat only foods treated with "preservatives" such as formaldehyde, borax, and various sulphurous and benzoic acids. The experiment lasted five years and was designed to determine the effect of such chemicals on digestion and health. It's not clear how the Poison Squad's diet affected the health of its volunteers, but their culinary exploits became an overnight sensation celebrated in minstrel shows:

> *O, they may get over it but they'll never look the same,*
> *That kind of bill of fare would drive most men insane.*
> *Next week he'll give them mothballs, a la Newburgh or else plain;*
> *O, they may get over it but they'll never look the same.*

—from "Song of the Poison Squad,"
Lew Dockstader's Minstrels, 1903

The excruciating diet of Wiley's Poison Squad made headlines and convinced the American public of several important things: that chemical preservatives should be used in food only when necessary; that the burden of proving safety should fall on the producer; and that preservatives should not be used without informing the consumer on the label. These points form the basic principles of today's FDA law and regulations, and were a significant victory over industry resistance and political foot dragging.

With his success, Wiley expanded the division's research, and pushed through a federal law prohibiting the adulteration and misbranding of food and drugs. His cause was further spotlighted by muckraking journalists like Upton Sinclair, whose novel *The Jungle* famously exposed the unsanitary conditions of Chicago's meatpacking industry and brought about greater federal regulation of the food industry.

Finally, in June 1906, President Roosevelt signed the Federal Food and Drugs Act, known as the Wiley Act, which charged the Bureau of Chemistry with overseeing the labeling and sale of food and drugs. The act was largely the result of the Pure Food Movement, a grassroots phenomenon headed by women's groups.

Wiley emphasized the regulation of foods, which he believed posed a greater public health problem than adulterated drugs. Indeed, it usually took a crisis to bring about meaningful change in drug laws.

The Biologics Control Act of 1902 only came about after the death of thirteen children in St. Louis from a tetanus-tainted batch of diphtheria antitoxin, and nine similar deaths in Camden, New Jersey. As the bureau's seizures of misbranded and adulterated drugs increased in the 1920s and 1930s, the 1906 law became outdated. But with opposition to change from industry, a bill updating drug legislation stalled in Congress.

The FDA collected an "American Chamber of Horrors," a display of products that were legal but useless, or worse, legal and deadly: Banbar, a worthless "cure" for diabetes; Lash-Lure, an eyelash dye that blinded many women; Radithor, a tonic made from radium that resulted in an agonizing death; and the Wilhide Exhaler, a worthless cure for tuberculosis.

In 1937, a Tennessee drug company marketed Elixir Sulfanilamide as a "wonder drug" for children. The product was not tested before reaching the marketplace, and it turned out that its solvent was a highly toxic analogue of antifreeze. Elixir Sulfanilamide killed over 100 people, most of them children. The resulting public outcry forced legislative action, and in 1938, President Roosevelt signed the Food, Drug, and Cosmetic Act. It was a watershed moment. The new law brought cosmetics and medical devices under Washington's control and mandated that drugs have adequate safety labeling. It prohibited false therapeutic claims and required manufacturers to prove that new drugs were safe before they could be sold. Within two months of the passage of the act, the FDA began to identify drugs, such as the sulfas, that required a prescription from a physician. The law also resulted in a flood of drugs applications to the agency—some 13,000 by 1962.

That year another crisis was narrowly avoided. It was discovered that Thalidomide, a sedative that was popular in Europe, produced skeletal defects in developing fetuses: some 8,000 infants were born with shortened or malformed limbs. Although the sedative narrowly missed approval for use in the United States, the Thalidomide crisis led to the adoption of the Kefauver-Harris Amendments, which strictly regulated drug efficacy and safety, instituted greater control over drug trials, and granted the FDA greater powers to regulate drug manufacturing and advertising.

Cancer hoaxers were an ongoing problem in the 19th and 20th centuries, and squelching their work was often difficult.

"Of all the ghouls who feed on the bodies of the dead and the dying, the cancer quacks are most vicious and most heartless," wrote Morris Fishbein in his 1965 *History of Cancer Quackery*. The sale of "secret specifics" to the sick and despairing flourished almost unregulated in the 1800s. In 1910, Lyman Frederic Kebler, director of the government's Drug Laboratory, a division of Wiley's Bureau of Chemistry, seized a stockpile of "Johnson's Mild Combination Treatment for Cancer," a worthless product labeled with extravagant and misleading promises. But the trial judge ruled against Kebler, saying, that the Pure Food and Drug Act did not cover claims of effectiveness for drugs. This was corrected in 1912, when Congress passed the Sherley Amendment, which required the Bureau of Chemistry to prove that a drugmaker's claims were both false and fraudulent before judging its treatment illegal.

In the early part of the 20th century, a Dr. Camp began to chronicle the many "sure cures" for cancer in editions of his famous *Nostrums and Quackery*. Yet by the 1950s, the FDA estimated that at least 4,000 cancer charlatans were skimming $50 million a year from terrified and uninformed patients. In 1966, the American Cancer Society published a catalogue of "Unproven Methods of Cancer Treatment" that listed nearly 30 false cures for the disease.

The most successful and notorious oncological mountebank was a glib young man named Harry M. Hoxsey. Originally from rural Illinois, he claimed to have inherited a secret cancer remedy from his father, a self-taught veterinarian who had developed his cure on livestock and then used it on people. (Both of Hoxsey's parents died of cancer, a fact the son long suppressed.) Hoxsey first used his father's secret paste in 1922, when he cured the cancerous lip of a Civil War veteran, a man who would testify for years on behalf of the treatment. Sensing an opportunity, Hoxsey established the Hoxide Institute in Taylorsville, Illinois, and began treating hundreds of patients. When some of them began to die—it was discovered that the remedy's key ingredient was arsenic, a corrosive chemical that ate away patients' flesh and bone—Hoxsey was investigated by the "high priests" of the American Medical Association (AMA). He sued the AMA for libel but the suit was dismissed. In another case, he was charged with the death of a patient, pled guilty to practicing without a medical license, and paid a $100 fine. The Hoxide Institute was closed in 1928, but Hoxsey went on to set up similar ventures in Detroit, Atlantic City, and finally, in 1936, in Dallas, Texas.

Hoxsey's arrival in Dallas coincided with a new public awareness of the ravages of cancer, the early years of the chemotherapy revolution, and, in 1937, the establishment of the National Cancer Institute (NCI). By then, he had narrowly avoided a jail sentence and was licensed to practice in Texas as a naturopath. With aggressive self-promotion, Hoxsey played on people's fear and partial knowledge of the new cancer treatments to drive thousands of cancer victims from around the nation to his Dallas "clinic." By 1956, he was said to be grossing some $1.5 million a year from 8,000 patients.

As he prospered, Hoxsey learned to play the influence game. Frequently in the company of congressmen, he was even proposed as a vice-presidential candidate. That year, the FDA went on a major offensive against him, warning that Hoxsey's treatments were "worthless" and "imminently dangerous," and by late 1957, Hoxsey's operation was shut down. It had taken a decade of litigation and had cost the federal government some quarter of a million dollars.

The FDA was the first agency in the world to establish a scientific basis for the food and drug industries. It defines what is safe and effective and what is not. As a result, the agency has been frequently criticized by the industries it regulates and their political allies. Some have termed it "antibusiness." In fact, by maintaining high standards the FDA gives businesses great credibility in the eyes of consumers.

In the 1970s, the FDA came under fire from antiregulatory conservatives led by Ronald Reagan. (In 1975, Reagan incorrectly claimed that 40,000 tuberculosis patients had died because the FDA had not approved Rifampin, a drug used in Europe. In fact, Rifampin had been quickly approved by the FDA five years earlier. Besides, less than 28,000 had died from tuberculosis from 1968 to 1978, and hardly any of those cases had anything to do with access to drugs like Rifampin.)

By 1989 the FDA was in steep decline. A *New York Times* headline described the agency as "A guardian of health buckling under stress." The AIDS crisis was in full bloom. The number of applications for approval of drugs, devices and other products had tripled, from 4,200 in 1970 to 12,800 in 1989. In the same period, reports of serious reactions to drugs had soared from 12,000 to 70,000 a year. Meanwhile, the national budget deficit had grown onerous, and President George H. W. Bush began to cut jobs and budgets at the FDA. Enforcement of the agency's mandate became difficult, external criticism mounted, and internal demoralization set in.

In May 1989, the Subcommittee on Oversight and Investigations of the House Energy and Commerce Subcommittee (the same committee that would later investigate ImClone) laid bare a corruption scandal involving generic drug companies and crooked FDA reviewers. Test data had been faked, it turned out, and the public's health had been put at grave risk in the quest for profits. The subcommittee's hearings, chaired by Representative John Dingell, Democrat of Michigan, eventually led to the conviction of five FDA employees, along with 55 employees of 15 generic drug companies. Frank Young, the FDA commissioner, was surprised by the scandal; by the end of the year he had been pushed out, leaving the agency leaderless for months. Quoting from Romans, Young framed the dilemma in religious terms: "All have sinned and fallen short of the glory of God."

Dingell put it another way: "This has been a slow, persistent strangulation of an agency, and it has led to the damnedest, most unfair, and inconsistent regulations. This is a terrible mess, the denigration and emasculation of a once-proud agency."

It was also the time when the biotech revolution was starting to gain momentum. As the scientists and venture capitalists reveled in anticipation of the medical and financial windfall from genomics and the budding biomania, FDA regulators began to worry. If the agency couldn't keep pace with existing demands, what would happen when all of these new products came up for approval?

So dire was the agency's predicament that the foxes of the pharmaceutical industry began to aid the hounds of the FDA. Acknowledging that they depended on the agency's reputedly tough regulations to give their products credibility, companies like Johnson & Johnson, Merck & Co., Pfizer Inc., Procter & Gamble, and Upjohn established a lobbying group. Called the FDA Council, it set out to strengthen the agency's "infrastructure . . . so that it can efficiently carry out its mission."

In the meantime, a blue-ribbon government committee was formed to assess the FDA's status. Its members informed the nation that without new resources and support, the floundering agency's troubles would soon damage American enterprise. That message caught people's attention.

One of the committee members was a young man named David A. Kessler. A pediatrician who had studied at the Harvard Medical School, Kessler had also gotten his law degree at the University of Chicago, and by the age of thirty-two had been named director of medicine at New York's Albert Einstein College of Medicine. A moderate Republican, the bespectacled and red-bearded Kessler had worked part time for Senator Orrin Hatch, Republican of Utah, and understood how things got done in Washington.

President Bush named Kessler as FDA commissioner in November 1990. The following March, he was confronted by his first crisis: cyanide in Sudafed capsules had killed a woman in the Pacific Northwest. He organized a national recall and calmed the public. From then on, Kessler made his mark as a tough enforcer.

He won a major battle over accurate food labeling and another against silicone breast implants. But it was his celebrated campaign against the tobacco industry in the early 1990s that put him in the league of Harvey Wiley as a legendary FDA commissioner.

Kessler's tobacco investigations showed that cigarettes deliver nicotine, an addictive drug, in a carefully designed way, and that cigarette makers had specifically targeted children as their primary customers. The debate led to hearings and fines. But while the FDA wanted to tightly regulate tobacco companies, the Supreme Court halted this idea in 2000. Congress should be responsible for such regulation, the court ruled, and the debate has remained open.

By 1994, Bill Clinton was president and the FDA was revitalized. But just as it regained its balance, the agency once again came under attack from conservative Republicans, this time led by Newt Gingrich. He labeled Kessler a "thug and a bully," and charged that the FDA—the "No. 1 job-killer" in America—discouraged innovation and prevented new products from coming to market. One goal of the assault was to sharply curtail the FDA's ability to review new drugs and to turn the job over to private companies hired by the pharmaceutical makers.

Representative James Greenwood, Republican of Pennsylvania, led Congress's FDA reform project, in hearings of May 1996. He claimed that the FDA was too slow and inefficient. "Two-thirds of the drugs approved by the FDA in the past five years were first available overseas

[and] 21 percent of those were available abroad for at least six years," he claimed. He had listened to the patients' message, he said, and "it was powerful: Americans are dying of red tape." But the numbers he used to bolster his attack were reportedly inaccurate.

Kessler fought back. "This is as serious as it gets," he told reporters. "This is about weakening a century's worth of food and drug laws. This is about undermining the safety of the drugs Americans take." Point by point he and allies like Ted Kennedy refuted Greenwood's claims.

With opposition growing on both sides of the House, and even from some in the pharmaceutical industry who feared the FDA bashers were going too far, Gingrich's FDA reform effort petered out by the fall of 1996.

The agency had survived a brutal trial by fire, but it had taken a toll. In 1997, Kessler left the FDA to head the Yale Medical School. Some declared him the best commissioner in the agency's history, while others considered him the worst.

So divided were Democrats and Republicans by the battle over re-form that it took more than a year to find a replacement commissioner. Ultimately an oncologist, Dr. Jane Henney, one of Kessler's deputies, was chosen. But it was during her tenure that the aftershocks of the battle over FDA reform were felt. Pressure from the pharmaceutical industry, abet-ted by acquiescent FDA officials, allowed a number of drugs to enter the market that should not have. From 1997 through 2000, a surge in deaths and injuries from such products were reported, and an unprecedented eleven drugs were yanked from store shelves. One of the most notorious examples was Rezulin, a Warner-Lambert treatment to lower blood sugar levels in diabetics. By 2000, the drug had led to 94 liver failures and 66 deaths before the FDA finally pulled it from the marketplace.

Alarms were ringing. Now, instead of being charged with sloth and overcautiousness, the FDA was accused of irresponsibly rushing drugs through the approval process to market. The agency's reviewers became confused and defensive. An internal survey found that one-third of its medical reviewers felt there was too much pressure to approve new drugs and that proper safety precautions were being overlooked. "Deci-sions should be based more on science and less on corporate wishes," a number of reviewers said.

By the summer of 2000, when ImClone submitted its new drug

application for C225, the FDA was again leaderless (the acting commissioner was Dr. Lester Crawford), underfunded, overworked, and hobbled by internal politicking and self-doubt.

WOODMONT I, an FDA building in Rockville, Maryland, was an awkward and almost otherworldly-looking structure—a tilted pyramid lodged between two six-story cubes with mirrored windows—sited on an exurban strip next to a bustling highway. On August 11, 2000, a team from ImClone arrived at Woodmont I to argue for the accelerated approval of C225.

After introductions were made, the nine-member team took their seats along one side of a conference table. The group comprised Harlan Waksal, the COO and the company's head scientist; three regulatory and clinical experts, including Dr. Michael Needle, the man in charge of Study 9923; and five noted oncologists involved in the C225 study, including Len Saltz.

Facing them were eleven FDA representatives, not all of whom were happy to be there. Earlier that summer, Susan Jerian, the stolid, curly-haired primary FDA medical reviewer for ImClone's drug, had decided that Study 9923 would not be adequate to warrant fast track status for C225. Before the meeting with ImClone, however, Jerian had been overruled by her supervisor, Patricia Keegan.

Keegan is a slim woman with short brown hair and glasses. She was director of the FDA's Center for Biologics Evaluation and Research (CBER), which, since 1987, had been in charge of reviewing biotech drugs. CBER had less experience in approving complex new drugs than its larger counterpart at the FDA, the Center for Drug Evaluation and Research (CDER)—which was descended from Lyman Frederic Kebler's Drug Laboratory, founded in 1906.

In defending her decision to proceed with the C225 review, Keegan pointed out that the FDA had approved irinotecan, the standard chemotherapy for colon cancer, with a 13 percent response rate in patients; irinotecan had later proven itself a valuable and widely used treatment. ImClone's drug, Keegan noted, had shown a 20 percent response rate in refractory colorectal cancer patients—a group that had no therapy options. This, she believed, was evidence enough that ImClone deserved a hearing to make its case.

At the August 11 meeting, Keegan asked the FDA's central question: how had ImClone determined that patients were responding to C225 rather than to the irinotecan it was mixed with?

The ImClone executives answered that they had "pictures"—CT scans—that showed tumors growing while the patients were being treated only with irinotecan, and shrinking once C225 had been added to the cocktail. The FDA group conferred, and Keegan said that with such evidence, Study 9923 was "probably acceptable" for fast-track status.

This was a tremendous victory for ImClone: C225 had cleared its first important regulatory hurdle.

But Susan Jerian and a few other FDA reviewers remained unconvinced.

As part of its package, ImClone had also presented backup studies to show that the drug worked best in combination with chemotherapy in lab mice. While this murine evidence appeared to affirm Study 9923's human results, the inference that the two sets of data were equivalent was later judged "a very risky venture" by Richard Pazdur, a respected oncologist who heads CDER. Animal studies, Pazdur noted, often show different results than human ones. "The correct way of developing this drug," Pazdur later testified, would be to do a "randomized" trial that compared the effects of C225 alone versus the C225/irinotecan cocktail. This comparison was important because of chemotherapy's toxicity, which produces debilitating side effects such as diarrhea, nausea, and vomiting: if C225 worked alone, then patients could avoid chemo altogether.

AFTER MEETING WITH IMCLONE, Keegan and her CBER team continued to debate the value of Study 9923. At the end of December, the FDA told ImClone that C225 had been accepted for fast-track designation. But a week later, in January 2001, Keegan changed her mind and sent the company another letter saying she wanted to see data from an additional, randomized study of how well C225 worked alone. Sam and Harlan were incensed. In the race to market, every minute counted. But there was little they could do about Keegan's about-face.

On January 26, ImClone and the FDA reviewers held a conference call. ImClone protested that its executives had left the August meeting believing that Study 9923 was adequate: "As there was no discussion regarding the need to supply data for [C225 alone] . . . ImClone has not pursued" a single-agent trial, company officials said, although they planned to do so later. Furthermore, to do a large single-agent study would be "unethical" because, they said, C225 does not work as well on its own as it does in combination with irinotecan.

(FDA reviewers would say they had raised the issue of a single-agent trial in the August meeting, but notes of the meeting do not reflect that.)

By the end of the conference call, the two sides had reached a compromise that would allow C225 to move forward. Rather than a large, randomized single-agent study, ImClone would conduct a small single-agent study, enrolling only 20 to 50 patients. Later, CDER's Pazdur would criticize the compromise as fundamentally flawed: "In order for that to work, you had to have a zero-percent [effectiveness] almost in the single-agent study," he said. "So in essence [ImClone] were betting against their own drug to get that combination approved."

On March 27, 2001, three of C225's most prominent supporters—Harlan Waksal, John Mendelsohn, and Len Saltz—arrived at Woodmont I for a second in-person meeting with Keegan and her team from CBER. An argument ensued about the single-agent study: the FDA told the company that it wanted results from the second study to be included in ImClone's new drug BLA. Harlan complained that the agency's request for further data was coming too late in the day. Nevertheless, on April 1, ImClone began to enroll a small group of patients for the single-agent study.

In the meantime, Study 9923 was continuing to generate data on the combination therapy and public interest in C225 was growing by the day. By the spring of 2001 pressure was building on both ImClone and the FDA to bring the drug to market: thanks to the media coverage of Shannon Kellum and other success stories, physicians, investors, politicians, and—most of all—cancer patients eagerly awaited the drug.

RUTH-ANN SANTINO and Amy Cohen had a lot in common. They were both mothers, had colon cancer, had read about Shannon Kellum's success with C225, and had been trying without success to get access to ImClone's drug. They didn't know each other but they were in equally desperate straits when their stories were broadcast on national television.

Ruth-Ann Santino was 49 years old, a third-grade teacher, and the mother of two teenage boys when she noticed blood in her stool in January 1999. Four months before her 25th wedding anniversary, she was diagnosed with colorectal cancer. When she returned home that day, her husband, Fred, who teaches computer skills at Babson College, immediately knew from the look on her face that something was terribly wrong. She broke the news to him in the front hallway of their house, in a Boston suburb. She began to cry. After she collected herself, Ruth-Ann, who was a fit ice-skater and had a sunny disposition, bucked herself up and insisted she would beat the disease.

In April, a surgeon resected her colon, and over the summer she embarked on a chemotherapy regimen. It seemed to help. In September, she returned to teach elementary school, but on her second day at work she fell terribly ill. By November, tests had revealed that Ruth-Ann's cancer had returned. She underwent further surgeries, including a colostomy and hysterectomy, and further chemo treatments. By the summer of 2000, however, the cancer had spread throughout her body.

"We were totally at a loss," Fred recalled. "We were running out of options."

In order to get access to still-experimental drugs—those not yet approved by the FDA—Ruth-Ann could apply to participate in a clinical trial, her oncologist explained. In order to qualify, a patient must meet drug companies' criteria for such things as age, type of disease, and previous treatments.

Ruth-Ann was admitted to a clinical trial at the Dana Farber Cancer Center, which is a teaching affiliate of the Harvard Medical School, for the colon cancer drug oxaliplatin (also called Eloxatin). "Oxali" was a popular treatment in Europe, and its producer, the French drugmaker Sanofi-Synthelabo, was using clinical trials to gather data for FDA approval in the United States. Ruth-Ann's health began to improve within a week of taking oxaliplatin. She was finally able to go shopping again and to sleep through the night. That lasted until the winter, when her cancer again flared up.

In the meantime, Ruth-Ann's oncologist had told her about C225 and said, "This is the drug you *really* need. It might be available in the fall." Fred researched C225 on the Internet, and after reading about Shannon Kellum's recovery, and ImClone's glowing test results announced at ASCO in the *USA Today* articles, came to believe that it had a good chance of saving his wife's life.

When she applied to ImClone, Ruth-Ann was told that she was not eligible for the clinical trial. She spoke to Dr. Michael Needle, the man in charge of Study 9923, who informed her in a not very sympathetic way that she was "too sick to get into the trial."

There was one last resort. It was possible that Ruth-Ann could get access to C225 through a so-called "compassionate use" program—in which a company can, if it wishes, provide an experimental drug to critically ill patients outside of its clinical trials. Compassionate use, or "expanded access" to unapproved drugs, is a highly controversial, ill-defined, and unregulated practice, one that has been whipsawed by competing agendas. Activist cancer patients, like AIDS activists, have increasingly demanded that drug companies provide lifesaving drugs, even if they remain unproven. Their demand has been backed by certain politicians and media outlets—most notably the editorial page of *The Wall Street Journal,* which has used the issue of compassionate use to bludgeon the FDA for being too slow and bureaucratic on the approval of potentially lifesaving drugs.

Some companies view compassionate-use programs as an effective marketing tool—if a drug proves effective, the cancer community will let everyone know. But most drugmakers are leery of giving away their unapproved treatments: they argue that they don't want to raise false hope in sick patients, that the cost (which comes out of their pocket) is prohibitive, and that since they have to report the results of such programs to the FDA they fear that compassionate-use patients—who take the drugs in settings that are not well controlled—will ultimately hurt their drugs' chance of approval.

The Santinos didn't care about the fine points of the debate; they just wanted access to C225 as soon as possible. When they inquired about ImClone's compassionate-use program, they learned it was not well defined, that there were already 2,000 people on the waiting list, and that the company had only produced small batches of the drug.

Ruth-Ann's oncologist, another doctor, and Fred Santino all wrote to ImClone to request access to C225 on a compassionate-use basis. The company never replied. Ruth-Ann became obsessed about phrasing the letters just so, figuring that the right pitch could make the difference between getting the drug or not. "You think about it at night when you go to bed," she'd say. "You wake up thinking about it. You think about it when you're making the kids' lunches. It's constant."

One day a person at Dana-Farber whispered to the Santinos that Bill Clinton had intervened on behalf of a patient, and that the patient was being treated at the hospital with C225 by "special arrangement." This was entirely plausible, as Sam Waksal, who was an enthusiastic Democratic fund-raiser (though he also gave to influential Republicans, like New York Governor George Pataki), had become friendly with the former president and his wife, Hillary Rodham Clinton.

The Santinos heard other rumors: that Mick Jagger had used C225; that Sharon Osbourne, wife of the rockstar Ozzy Osbourne, had used C225; that Sam had been doling out his "miracle" cancer drug to politicians from both parties, to gain influence. The Santinos grew incensed at what they perceived to be ImClone's favoritism.

"Well, if *they* can get [C225], I'm going to start writing my letters," Ruth-Ann announced. She and Fred marched home that afternoon and wrote letters, faxes, and e-mails until midnight—to ImClone, to Sam Waksal, to Senators Kerry and Kennedy, to President George W. Bush and Vice President Dick Cheney. In her January 26 letter to President Bush, Ruth-Ann wrote: "I understand that former President Clinton obtained approval for a patient in the Boston area, and the patient is now receiving treatment. Once again, I'm pleading for your compassion to help me. I am only 51 years old and have two children, 15 and 17. My children need me to get through these difficult years. This request is my last hope I have to beat the disease . . . Please help."

In mid-1998, meanwhile, 32-year-old Amy Cohen was told by her doctors: "You have colon cancer. You should get your affairs in order. You have about six months to live." She and her husband, John, began to shake and stared at the doctors in disbelief. Until then, Cohen believed her life was "perfect": she had a newly born child and was content with her life.

"We just decided at that point that we were not going to take that diagnosis lying down," she'd say. Over the next three and a half years, Cohen underwent a number of surgeries and a series of chemotherapy treatments. But her cancer proved resilient and kept metastasizing. After reading about Shannon Kellum and C225 in the *USA Today* articles, the Cohens became determined to get the drug for Amy. "I'm not banking on a cure," she'd say. "I'm just trying to keep myself alive."

Her doctors told Amy Cohen that C225 could help her, yet they were unable to get the drug for her. So she tracked down ImClone in Manhattan on her own and tried to talk her way into the C225 clinical trial. She was told that she was ineligible. When she asked about compassionate-use access to the drug, she was told that it was not available. Her daughter was now three years old and she felt the door was being slammed in her face.

"Compassionate use is a very difficult topic for ImClone," Sam said, noting that the company had become "overwhelmed" by thousands of requests. "This speaks to how dramatic the medical need is for C225, and how unmet that need is."

Sometimes Sam would say that the FDA had limited ImClone's ability to mount a compassionate-use program. But this was not in fact the case. The agency has no authority over compassionate use of new drugs and leaves the hard decisions—whether to give out an experimental drug, how to do it, and whom to give it to—up to the drug companies. Although FDA regulations on compassionate use are now under review, the agency is afraid that too much regulation might boomerang and cause pharmaceutical firms to suspend such programs.

It is a question with no easy answers. Individual cancer patients—like Ruth-Ann Santino and Amy Cohen—feel angry and humiliated at having to beg for a drug that could save their lives. But pharmaceutical companies with an experimental drug try to generate the most carefully researched data possible, through controlled clinical trials, in order to bring their treatments to as many patients as possible, as quickly as possible.

Over the winter of 2000–01, the Santinos continued to write to ImClone, pleading for access to C225. They never got a response of any kind. In the meantime, Ruth-Ann had qualified to take part in a different clinical trial at Memorial Sloan-Kettering—for a drug designed to improve the body's immune system—but she chose not to participate, in large part because she held out hope for the seemingly magical C225.

"I was pissed that they didn't get back to us," recalled Fred Santino. "I teach business students, and let me tell you this is not how you run a business—especially a company that deals with life and death. You do not ignore letters from cancer patients. I mean, you wouldn't run a *lemonade stand* that way. I [later] told Sam Waksal to his face: 'How can you ignore a dying mother? All you had to do is put a 34-cent stamp on an envelope and tell us yes or no about the drug.' That's all we wanted. Then we would have moved on. Waksal could've hired a college kid or someone to write letters. But he didn't. That is *unacceptable*."

One day Michael Needle, ImClone's vice president of clinical affairs, called the Santinos. In what Ruth-Ann described as a "very cold" voice, he informed her that she was not eligible for compassionate use of C225 and hung up.

She refused to give up. "I want to beat this thing so I can go help others," she'd say to Fred, over and over again.

Vice President Cheney's office took an interest in Ruth-Ann's case. Someone there forwarded her letter to the FDA, contacted the Santinos and gave them a privileged number at the agency (for information about upcoming clinical trials), and ultimately put a producer for CBS' *60 Minutes* in touch with them. In February 2001, a *60 Minutes* TV crew, accompanied by correspondent Lesley Stahl, taped a segment at the Santino's Massachusetts home. Then, with difficulty, Fred and Ruth-Ann traveled to New York to tape another bit in the studio.

With the *60 Minutes* camera rolling, Ruth-Ann called Needle one more time: "Is there any way I could get [C225] if I paid for it myself? No? People that have had three chemos still have other [drugs] to try, but I've been through seven. And it's people like me that could really use it at this point."

ImClone denied her the drug because, Ruth-Ann said, she'd already had too many chemo treatments.

Somehow Amy Cohen had discovered Sam Waksal's direct phone number at ImClone. Early one morning she dialed it. His secretary had not yet arrived to screen calls and Sam picked up the phone. "Please, I need two minutes of your time, sir," said Cohen. "I am a young woman with colorectal cancer that has unfortunately spread. And I need your help. I have a three-year-old daughter. And I need to live. And you need to give me a fighting chance against this disease."

Sam listened patiently and said: "Let me talk to my brother. He's the medical director."

When Amy Cohen spoke to Harlan, he explained that he couldn't simply hand out vials of C225. There was a lot of red tape and paperwork to be negotiated, and even then there was no guarantee she'd get the drug. But Cohen was now highly motivated.

With help from her oncologist, she completed the paperwork and cut through the red tape. Three months later her doctor called to say that ImClone had granted her the drug on a compassionate-use basis. Cohen told *60 Minutes* that the early morning call to Sam saved her life: "I do believe that it opened the door for me to lend a voice, a name, versus just being a patient . . . on a waiting list . . . I'm a real, live person and I have a family, and I really have a very strong will to live."

When Ruth-Ann Santino learned that Amy Cohen had been granted access to C225, she said: "That's not fair. It just makes me angry. And there's obviously an injustice when someone's getting [C225] and someone isn't. And there is no written criteria, or any standards available, to say why they get it. And [ImClone] can't tell you why they gave it to someone and they didn't give it to someone else. To me, that's a true injustice."

In the spring of 2001, Ruth-Ann's health suddenly took a turn for the worse. She was in pain and spent much of her time lying in a bed in her dining room, which Fred had "converted into a hospital ward."

At the end of April her older son, David, a high-school senior, wrote to ImClone: "I'm pleading for your compassion to help my mother. This request is the last hope my mom has to beat the disease. We have exhausted all other possible resources."

The company would later say that its compassionate-use program for C225 had been shut down in January, although Fred Santino said that no one at the company explained that to him at the time.

Ruth-Ann was afraid that she wouldn't live to see David graduate from high school. But on May 1, the school principal came to the Santino's house and in a special ceremony at the foot of Ruth-Ann's bed presented David with a diploma. "She perked right up," Fred recalled. "It was a great moment."

The next day, Wednesday, May 2, the phone rang. David answered. His face lit up and he yelled out in excitement: "Dad! It's ImClone! Maybe they're going to give Mom the drug!" *Yeah, she's finally going to get C225,* he thought, *this is the moment we've been waiting for.*

Sitting by Ruth-Ann's bedside, Fred picked up the phone. He'd been trying to get access to the drug for two years. He'd been writing ImClone letters and faxes and e-mails for months. Now, finally, they were calling. Ruth-Ann's luck was about to turn.

The caller was Harlan Waksal. He didn't ask how Ruth Ann was faring, or apologize for not responding, or offer condolences of any kind.

What Harlan said was: "Look, you're being very unfair to ImClone by going on *60 Minutes.*" Then he asked Fred to pull the story, which hadn't aired yet. "But I had no way to stop that show, and I didn't want to," said Fred.

Bitter and angry, he hung up the phone and looked over at his sons.

"Dad, does that mean Mom isn't going to get better?" George, his youngest, asked. Fred nodded, and the two boys broke down sobbing.

Two days later, on Friday, May 4, 2001, Ruth-Ann died. Two days after that, on Sunday night, *60 Minutes* aired its story about C225.

In a congressional hearing into ImClone's business practices a year later, Congressman Ernie Fletcher, Republican of Kentucky, and a doctor, grilled Harlan about his phone call to the Santinos on the eve of Ruth-Ann's death. Harlan acknowledged making the call and agreed that he had not offered Ruth-Ann access to C225. But he protested that, "the call was not made to take issue with Mr. Santino. In fact, my call was made in a response to the fact that I wanted to correct some points on the record. I wanted him to know that, indeed, we were doing nothing to single out his family, his wife, or patients who could not get access to our drug, but that there was no drug available . . . I didn't offer out hope. I offered what I believed was compassion and understanding."

The *60 Minutes* story had a big impact. While many cancer specialists were glad that the plight of patients and the potential of new drugs like C225 had been spotlighted, some were dismayed by what they felt was an oversimplification of a complex and emotionally wrought debate. The inference of the segment was that those who received the drug [Amy Cohen] would live, while those who didn't [Ruth-Ann Santino] would die. But the fact is that the C225/irinotecan cocktail helps only about 20 percent of colorectal cancer patients, at best. Amy Cohen happened to be one of those lucky few, but she was the exception rather than the rule. As a result, advocates for cancer patients fretted that the show might have unintentionally sent the wrong message and that it could backfire.

"One thing that's really hard about expanded access is that while you want to provide hope for people, you don't want to overblow it and create unrealistic expectations," one patient advocate fretted. "Once in a while there's an amazing Lazarus story [about a patient's recovery], but it's not always the case that if you get the drug you'll be fine. Actually, it's rare. Both of those women might have died, even *with* C225."

Andrea Rabney, ImClone's short, sharp-tongued spokesperson (and sometime girlfriend of Sam's), said that the company had no comment on Fred Santino's version of events, or on the *60 Minutes* segment, which the company had not participated in. Harlan described the show as "very negative" for ImClone. Nevertheless, in the weeks following *60 Minutes,* the company's stock price jumped, a congressional hearing on compassionate use was convened, and thousands of patients grew frenzied to get their hands on the "miracle" cancer drug C225.

ON THE EVENING of Sunday, May 6, 2001, Jane Reese-Coulbourne happened to turn on the television. Flipping through the channels, she stopped at the famous ticking stopwatch of *60 Minutes.* When Lesley Stahl's segment about C225 began, Reese-Coulbourne raised her eyebrows in surprise. "Oh my God, that's that guy, that's that drug—I know all about this!" she exclaimed to her husband. When the segment ended she sighed, and said, "I *knew* something like this would happen. I *knew* ImClone would just whimsically start giving their drug to some but not give it to others."

Jane Reese-Coulbourne calls herself a consultant. Among other things, she is the nation's leading expert on compassionate-use programs—or expanded access programs (EAPs)—for new cancer drugs. She came to this specialty via a circuitous route.

Blunt and amusing, Reese-Coulbourne worked as a chemical engineer until 1990, when, at the age of 36, she was diagnosed with inoperable breast cancer. Her oncologist prescribed a high-dose regimen of chemotherapy, and halfway through the regimen her cancer completely disappeared. This was extremely unusual. After her recovery, Reese-Coulbourne refocused her life and helped to found the National Breast Cancer Coalition, a vocal patient-advocacy group. After that, she took a job at the National Cancer Institute (NCI), where she learned all about oncology drugs and met the key players in the debate over expanded access.

In 1999, while at the NCI, Reese-Coulbourne helped set up the first EAP for Gleevec, an experimental treatment for myelogenous leukemia. "I don't want to be known as 'the EAP person,'" she said. But the fact is that since then, Reese-Coulbourne has designed every significant EAP to date—for the drugs Herceptin, Iressa, and oxilyplatin, some of the most promising cancer treatments of the last few years.

Sam Waksal called her in the spring of 2001. "I got your name from someone at the FDA. He said you'd done the Iressa EAP," he said, in what struck her as a very casual way. "We're thinking about setting up an EAP for C225."

Reese-Coulbourne knew about Sam and his drug. She'd heard that although ImClone did not have an EAP in place, Sam had been doling C225 out to certain people who seemed helpful—like President Clinton's friend—or whose story he found compelling—like Amy Cohen—on what he called "a compassionate-use basis." But Reese-Coulbourne suspected that something might be wrong with the drug. She had even warned her patient-advocate friends: "There's something wrong here. It doesn't take this long to set up an EAP. It's not rocket science. I think something's up with ImClone."

She asked Sam what he expected to get from an EAP. When he answered vaguely, she wasn't surprised. In her experience most companies like the sound of an expanded access program, but don't really understand how involved it can be. Some CEOs will declare: "We want to set up an EAP for the whole world!" without giving thought to trade or intellectual property laws.

Compassionate-use programs are viewed in many different ways: they are a humanitarian way to help suffering cancer patients; they are a marketing tool (word of a successful EAP will spread through oncology circles and create a surging demand for the drug); and they are a means to generate more scientific data about an experimental drug. But since they involve giving drugs away for free, and require administrators and a significant infrastructure to administer, they can also be an expensive proposition. A regimen of a new drug like Gleevec, for instance, costs about $30,000 a year; if the drug is effective, a patient can survive for years. The sponsoring company is legally required to continue to supply the drug, and cover the costs of doing so, for as long as the patient lives.

As she began to explain some of the many carefully orchestrated steps ImClone would have to take to set up an EAP, Sam cut her off, saying, "Yeah, yeah, we know all about that."

Reese-Coulbourne was taken aback.

"Look, I've had all of these patient advocates calling me up, pressuring me to put our drug out," Sam complained. "But I don't have a lot of the drug and it's expensive to produce."

"How quickly do you want an EAP up and running?" Reese-Coulbourne asked, trying to steer him back to the point.

He hesitated for a moment, then said: "Well, I'm not really in a *hurry* to set it up . . ."

"Oh, why is that?"

"We have a lot of other things going on," he said. "And this [EAP] thing is going to be a distraction."

She was flummoxed. Did ImClone want a program or not? If not, then why was Sam calling her? What was this guy really after?

Again he complained about the pressure from the patients: "They keep *pushing* me," for C225, he griped.

Reese-Coulbourne felt compelled to say: "Don't forget, I'm a cancer patient, too." Meaning: *my sympathy is with the patients. They are out of options and are growing desperate. This is not a game. They are fighting for their lives.*

Finally Sam said: *"You* know all of these people who keep calling me. Maybe we can have a meeting with them, tell them you're working on an EAP for us. Leave me out of it."

Reese-Coulbourne mulled his words, then asked, pointedly: "Are you looking to *stall?"*

"Well . . ." Sam answered, his voice lifting with insinuation. Meaning: *Yes.*

Now she understood: it was a ruse. *Oh, no, another crazy person!* she moaned to herself, and instantly decided to "blow him off."

Jane Reese-Coulbourne had no doubt that Sam Waksal was asking her to tell cancer patients that ImClone was putting together an EAP when it really wasn't, or at least not in any meaningful way. Sam wanted a quick fix: he wanted her to snap her fingers and make all of the annoying patients go away; but he did not want to establish a real EAP or to relinquish control of C225. A faux EAP would placate the desperate patients, save Sam a lot of effort—which he could devote to completing Study 9923—and would buy him time to arrange a deal with Bristol-Myers Squibb (an industry secret that she had heard about).

"I don't do that," she answered curtly.

Because of the fierce demand for new cancer drugs, a company like ImClone, or the drug's clinical investigators, are often asked for access to the treatment on a compassionate-use basis. (These are usually the rich and famous, or politically well connected: most people don't know enough to ask for expanded access of new drugs, or whom to ask.) Such special requests are often fulfilled, especially when a drug is in the early stages of development. When a company gives its drug to a patient who is not part of the clinical trial, it is supposed to file an investigational new drug (IND) application with the FDA. In practice, however, this usually doesn't happen. More often, special arrangements are made in an ad-hoc way.

The problem with this system, Americans tend to believe, is that it can lead to graft, influence peddling, and the tainting of clinical data. "The central issue in establishing an EAP is to keep drug access equitable and consistent," said Reese-Coulbourne. "That is crucial. Without that, you have a mess." There are alternatives. In the case of the Gleevec EAP, she advised Novartis, the company behind the drug, to establish an international lottery system to decide which patients would get compassionate-use access to the drug. With so many craving treatment, and Novartis's limited resources, this seemed to be the most fair solution.

In countries like France or Germany, by contrast, drug companies usually give their experimental treatments to oncologists and allow the physicians to decide who gets it and who doesn't. As in the United States, this sometimes leads to favoritism and graft, but in Europe it is considered to be the accepted way of doing business.

Sam took a more European approach. He kept trying to sell Reese-Coulbourne on the idea of a faux EAP, which angered her. "You either want a legitimate EAP or you don't," she said. "There are no half measures."

There was no way she was going to lie to cancer patients or their advocates for Sam Waksal, she had decided.

"Oh well, I guess I'm not interested then," he said, in the casual voice. "I'll do it the way *I* want to."

"Okay, *fine*," she snapped, adding under her breath: "Do it without me—I don't give a shit."

A few weeks later, when Reese-Coulbourne happened to tune into *60 Minutes* and saw that Sam was dispensing C225 to Amy Cohen but not to the equally deserving Ruth-Ann Santino, she was appalled but not entirely surprised. A year later, when ImClone became engulfed in a widening business scandal, she was again appalled. And a year after that, in the summer of 2003, when Sam's attorney, Mark Pomerantz, noted that Sam had always given generously of C225, and "never had to over-

rule his clinical staff and insist that ImClone would have a compassionate-use program"—even as prosecutors revealed that despite thousands
of calls ImClone gave the drug to only 30 patients on a compassionate-
use basis—she was even more appalled.

Her decision not to work with Sam Waksal was one of the easiest
and best choices she had ever made, Reese-Coulbourne believed. "That
was *the* wackiest conversation I'd ever had about an EAP," she recalled
with a sardonic laugh. "I've worked with a lot of companies, and Sam
was not like any other professional person I've ever spoken to, in any situation. It was really *wacky*." Then, in a softer and more reflective voice,
Jane Reese-Coulbourne added: "The part that always gets lost is what
this means to the colorectal cancer patients who haven't been able to get
the drug."

OVER THE COURSE OF 1999 and 2000, ImClone had invited at least seven
major pharmaceutical companies to look at its C225 data as an entice-
ment for a deal. Sam and Harlan were hoping that one of the Big Phar-
mas would take a big enough stake to keep their struggling venture
afloat.

The U.S. pharmaceutical business is one of the biggest and least-
noticed industries in the world. It generates an estimated $400 billion in
annual sales—some $140 billion of which is derived from prescription
drugs. It is highly lucrative and highly competitive. Recently there has
been a wave of mergers and alliances, as the industry consolidates, Wall
Street demands double-digit returns, and companies strive to insulate
themselves from the enormous risks of drug research and development. In July 2002, Pfizer, already the world's largest drug company,
merged with Pharmacia, the tenth-largest, to form a company that controls 14 percent of the market and boasts gross sales of $24 billion.
GlaxoSmithKline, with gross sales of $15.5 billion, was ranked number
two; Merck, with sales of $12.5 billion, was number three; Johnson &
Johnson, with almost $11 billion in sales, was number four.

With annual sales of some $10.5 billion, Bristol-Myers Squibb
(BMS) was the world's fifth-largest pharmaceutical company and the
leading producer of oncology drugs. BMS executives and scientists
knew all about John Mendelsohn and his work on C225. The company
had been talking to him about his ideas for the targeted treatment of
cancer for years. One insider recalled that Bristol had considered licens-

ing C225—for about $100,000—after Eli Lilly had declined to pursue it and before ImClone did, but had concluded that the drug's data was insufficient at the time. In 1985, BMS had given Mendelsohn an open-ended $500,000 grant for scientific research, most of which he applied to his work on C225.

One by one, however, the Big Pharma firms concluded that ImClone's asking price was too high and that its development of C225 was not yet promising enough, and broke off discussions.

"We first approached ImClone in 1999, reviewed their data, and decided to let it wait," recalled Brian Markison, a senior vice president of marketing at BMS. "Their data needed to mature."

By early 2001, things had changed. Bristol was about to lose its exclusive right to market Taxol, the best-selling cancer drug in history. "You need new products," observed an old Bristol hand. "No drugs, no business. That's what we were facing. We were looking around kind of desperately" for a Taxol replacement.

In order to stay in the oncology game, Bristol's new CEO, Peter Dolan, had no choice but to arrange a deal or license a new drug from an outside firm. BMS scoured the marketplace for opportunities, but by then most of the promising compounds were already spoken for. In the spring of 2001, BMS narrowed its focus to what was essentially the last remaining cancer drug with any real potential: ImClone's C225.

# SIX

# A Very High-Risk Opportunity

In 1887, William McLaren Bristol and John Ripley Myers invested $5,000 in a failing health products company in Clinton, New York, and renamed it Bristol, Myers. The partners had two rules: "insist on high quality" and "maintain the firm's good financial standing at all costs."

Bristol-Myers's first successful products were Sal Hepatica, a laxative salt, and Ipana, a disinfectant toothpaste that protected bleeding gums. By 1924, the company was selling its goods in 26 countries and had profits of over $1 million. In 1929, Bristol-Myers was listed on the New York Stock Exchange. In the Depression, the company was forced to shut down its burgeoning pharmaceutical business to concentrate on a dozen successful toiletries. After moving its headquarters into Manhattan, Bristol-Myers became a key supplier of penicillin and other antibiotics for the Allied troops in the Second World War. Flush with cash after the war, the company began a spending spree: they bought up rising companies like Clairol, in 1959, which had turned hair coloring into a successful mainstream consumer product; and they built themselves a billion-dollar research-and-development complex in Wallingford, Connecticut.

The investment in research paid off. By the 1980s, the Bristol-Myers Corporation was the quintessential Big Pharma company, a blue-chip multinational health-care conglomerate. With its headquarters, a nondescript concrete-and-smoked-glass tower at 345 Park Avenue, on the corner of 51st Street—nearby the Waldorf Astoria Hotel, the New York Racquet Club, Mies van der Rohe's Seagram Building, and such stalwarts as Lever Brothers, Colgate-Palmolive, and ITT—Bristol-Myers was at the epicenter of Manhattan's white-shoe business district.

In 1984, Bristol earned $500 million on the sale of more than $4 billion worth of products ranging from Ban antiperspirant to Bufferin to Frost & Tip hair coloring to Drano to No-Doz tablets and O-Cedar mops. The company's profit margin had steadily risen every year since 1972 and it had returned a dividend to shareholders. Though Bristol carried $100 million in long-term debt, it still had $800 million in the bank and employed some 35,000 people in labs, factories, and offices around the world under a strong management team that spent over $200 million (5 percent of sales) on research and development. In 1989, Bristol-Myers merged with Squibb, to create Bristol-Myers Squibb (BMS), the world's second-largest pharmaceutical company.

The company's strength in consumer goods didn't detract from its prowess in selling drugs that combated serious diseases. Bristol first sold cancer drugs in 1956, and by the mid-1980s it dominated the oncology market. This lucrative franchise was largely the work of Bristol CEO and Chairman Richard Gelb (his brother Bruce served as vice-chairman), the son of Clairol founder Arthur Gelb. Dick Gelb struck many as patrician and aloof, but he had survived esophageal cancer, invested heavily in oncology drugs, and was considered "a visionary" by the firm's cancer drug division. Even though surgery and radiation remained the most powerful weapons against cancer, Gelb built Bristol's reputation on so-called cytotoxic ("cell killer") chemotherapies. These drugs stop certain tumors from growing by interfering with cell function in some way—disrupting protein synthesis, say, and halting cell division like shutting down a factory by depriving it of power. These treatments were anything but subtle—they were poisons, after all—and patients using them suffered as a war raged inside their bodies. As the drugs shut down their runaway cells, the patients became nauseated, shed hair, and lost their appetite and weight.

For the oncologist these toxins were the necessary evil to destroy a patient's cancer cells before the person expired. But to many, the chemotherapeutic cure could seem as terrible as the disease. As a result, cytotoxic chemotherapy was long considered "an intellectual stepchild," said Dr. Stephen Carter, Bristol-Myers's chief of cancer drug development. "In the sixties, when I was in training, it was considered something only a few people did," he has said. "Chemotherapy always suffered the criticism that it was not scientific, that most of the drugs were discovered serendipitously, from empirical mass screenings for cytotoxicity. We were very, very defensive. With the success of the late sixties, medical oncology exploded as a specialty. But still, chemotherapy has never come out of the criticism that it was an extremely unscientific, toxic approach to treating cancer."

Chemotherapy had, however, proven very effective against certain tumor types, and so Bristol's franchise grew year after year. Of the top-ten anticancer drugs in 1984, five of them—Platinol, Mutamycin, Vepesid, Blenoxane, and Cytoxan—were Bristol-Myers products. They combined to produce annual sales of $150 million and gave Bristol a 40 percent share of the oncology drug market, which was more than twice the market of its closest competitor.

The cancer drug business had been growing by 25 percent annually since the early 1970s, and analysts predicted that oncology would add $600 million to Bristol sales by 1989. But it was still not a major business segment—especially when compared to blockbuster pharmaceuticals like SmithKlineBeckman's Tagamet, an antiulcer treatment, which boasted sales of nearly a billion dollars per year. But then a single, unlikely cancer drug changed the landscape.

THE PACIFIC YEW TREE, *Taxus brevifolia,* is a slow-growing evergreen with reddish bark and flat, inch-long needles. It grows in the Pacific Northwest and throughout Asia, where it suffers few natural pests because much of the tree contains powerful toxins. In 1958, samples of the Pacific yew were among the 35,000 plant species screened by the National Cancer Institute (NCI) in the hopes of discovering useful new drugs. In 1964, two researchers at North Carolina's Research Triangle Institute, Monroe Wall and Mansukh Wani, began to test these samples for anticancer compounds. Using a process called bioactivity-directed fractionation, they purified a crystalline substance from the bark of the Pacific yew, called compound 17, or "paclitaxel." By 1966, they had shown that the purified substance was an effective deterrent to cancer growth, and Wall named it "Taxol."

Work on Taxol was slow and expensive, but it would prove well worthwhile. By the late 1970s, researchers at New York's Albert Einstein College of Medicine discovered how the drug worked: while most antitumor agents inhibited cell division by preventing the production of microtubules, Taxol did the reverse: it stimulated microtubule growth to the point that the coordination of cell division broke down. In other words, Taxol forced cancer's main weapon—the wild proliferation of cells—to work against itself.

Phase 1 clinical trials of Taxol got underway in 1983, then phase 2, and by 1989, two studies of the compound had shown that it was surprisingly effective in fighting ovarian cancer.

By this point, the pharmaceutical company Bristol-Myers (which had not yet merged with Squibb) was seriously considering licensing the drug. Taxol represented a new kind of chemotherapy, a step beyond the traditional "platinum" therapies that were the foundation of the company's oncology business. But there were problems with Taxol: it was highly toxic and difficult to produce—it took 10,000 to 30,000 pounds of dried Pacific yew bark to produce just one kilogram of the compound. Any company interested in making Taxol would have to go into the logging business, which was not something that pharmaceutical companies embraced.

For a company like Bristol-Myers to get behind Taxol, the drug would need an in-house advocate.

Taxol had first come to Bristol's attention in 1988, when David Ettinger, an oncologist at Johns Hopkins University, called his friend Tom Jordan, a vice president in Bristol's worldwide oncology division, and said: "I want you to meet a young fellow named Eric Rowinsky, who has been working on a drug developed at the NCI that is active in a small group of ovarian cancer patients who failed cisplatinum [a standard chemotherapy, commonly referred to as 'cisplatin']. The NCI had it for years, but it was difficult to work on and they abandoned it. But I think its really good stuff. You ought to take a look at Rowinsky's data."

Jordan was interested. He knew that once a patient failed cisplatin, she was out of options. But here was a drug that seemed to offer succor to patients and a potential new market for Bristol.

He showed the Taxol data to Stephen Carter, the head of Bristol's worldwide oncology drug development program. But Carter, who knew of Taxol from his previous job at the NCI, said he wasn't interested: it was simply too toxic and too difficult to produce. "We have given serious consideration to Taxol," Carter wrote in an October 1988 memo. "In our view, the current formulation is unacceptable for commercial development. . . . If our budget was flexible, I would give it some further consideration, but I surely would not consider it worth replacing any current ongoing project."

Jordan regretfully explained what had happened, but Ettinger insisted that Taxol was an active drug. "You really ought to pursue this," he said. Jordan returned to the Bristol lab, and together with a scientist named Marcel Rozencweig, hatched a plan to make Taxol a Bristol drug.

Tom Jordan was not a typical company man. A bear-sized Floridian who was fond of conversation, cocktails, and cigarettes, he, along with in-house allies like Marcel Rozencweig, worked behind the scenes to virtually hand-build Bristol's oncology business. Jordan was a Vietnam veteran who had served for six months in the Mekong Delta in 1968–69 as a platoon leader for the Ninth Infantry Division (in his first 12 days in-country, he endured five firefights). His wartime experience was harrowing, but he never lost a man in combat; the experience of leading soldiers under fire taught him the value of teamwork and decisiveness. Upon returning home, Jordan earned a college degree on the GI Bill and eventually began selling antibiotics for Pfizer in Nashville, Tennessee. In 1975, he joined Adria Laboratories, where he became national sales manager for Adriamycin, the first significant modern chemotherapy.

In 1982, at age 35, Jordan moved to Meade-Johnson, a Bristol subsidiary in Evansville, Indiana, that had a relatively small, $40 million-a-year oncology drug business. Two years later Jordan and his Bristol counterpart, Bruce Ross, merged Meade-Johnson with Bristol Labs' $100 million-a-year oncology business.

Tom Jordan was the first to admit that he was a businessman, not a cancer specialist. He could talk oncology, but his knowledge was only skin-deep. On the other hand, he was one of the few who really understood the business of cancer and how to market chemo drugs in the spirit of public service.

As a former drug salesman, Jordan knew that in practice oncologists relied on hunches, played around with drug doses, and used treatments approved for one form of the disease against another. He also knew that once the FDA had approved a new drug, the clinical studies usually stopped. His insight was that these two factors presented an opportunity: if Bristol continued to study new compounds after they had been approved, then the company would continue to discover new ways to use its drugs; this, in turn, would give Bristol a scientific rationale for the use of specific therapies rather than doctors' informed guesswork. It would also, of course, allow the company to squeeze higher revenues from its products.

In the early 1980s, oncology was a relatively open field, where there were many more hypotheses than solid theories where academics held sway. If a pharmaceutical company needed to test a new compound, or wanted advice on which drug to develop, or wondered how to structure a clinical trial, or was curious about the competition, the fastest and best answers came from the oncologists who worked on cancer every day. Tom Jordan recognized this. By positioning itself as a fully engaged partner of the academy and not simply as a "rug merchant," Bristol would benefit—and so would the patients and clinicians.

Naturally gregarious, Jordan had built a vast network of friends and collaborators throughout the cancer community. He knew oncologists all over the world, and what they were working on; he remembered their names and the names of their wives and children. He befriended everyone, from Nobel laureates to nurses, patients, lobbyists, regulators, bureaucrats, secretaries, and limo drivers. He slapped their backs, cracked jokes, gossiped, and cut deals. Tom Jordan gave away millions of Bristol-Myers's dollars for cancer research and patient care. He assisted the experts at ASCO and they assisted him. He helped to establish an oncological nurse's advisory board. He worked the halls of Congress.

Shortly after joining the company, Jordan formalized his personal network by establishing Bristol's Physician Advisory Board, a group of a dozen of the nation's most prominent oncologists. Once a year, the board would meet for three days to brainstorm over oncology questions; members advised the company on clinical issues large and small, and raised Bristol's profile in the field. The objective was to give the physicians a chance to influence the development of new and better cancer treatments and to enhance Bristol's status within the academy. The Physician Advisory Board (PAB) was a brilliant success and it remains active today. Its members, some of whom have served for nearly two decades, include a who's who of cancer luminaries, including John

Mendelsohn; Larry Einhorn, of the University of Indiana, who developed the drug cisplatin and the testicular cancer regimen that has cured thousands, including Lance Armstrong; Robert Young, president of Fox Chase Cancer Center, and a leading authority on gynecological cancers; George Canellos, a lymphoma specialist at Dana-Farber Cancer Institute; Richard Schilsky, a dean at the University of Chicago who heads a clinical trials cooperative group; and Charles Coltman, head of the University of Texas, San Antonio, cancer center and chairman of the Southwest Oncology Group.

At the PAB's annual gatherings, Tom Jordan was the master of ceremonies. He'd choose the meeting spots—he favored warm climes, which allowed him to wear his favorite electric-green sports jacket. And he'd orchestrate the evening entertainment—usually karaoke, which he'd grown fond of while traveling in Asia.

In 1989, meanwhile, clinical trials of paclitaxel (Taxol's chemical name) continued, and Bristol-Myers merged with Squibb Corporation. Squibb had been founded in Brooklyn, New York, in 1856 by Edward Robinson Squibb. The company was dedicated to producing pure medicines under the slogan, "The priceless ingredient in every product is the honor and integrity of its maker." After the merger, Bristol-Myers Squibb (BMS) was the second-largest pharmaceutical company in the world.

As the newly merged firms got to know each other, officers from each side showed their wares in workshops—for cardiovascular, antibiotic, and oncology drugs. Tom Jordan and Marcel Rozencweig led Bristol's workshop on oncology, and in the process convinced BMS's senior executives that Taxol was a "must-have" product. A number of senior executives remained opposed to Taxol for various reasons, primarily the lack of a patent protection and the drug's dependence on logging. To produce Taxol, one had to travel to Asia or the Northwest, cut down a Pacific yew, shave off its bark, cook the bark, and slowly extract the active drug substance. This was a labor- and capital-intensive process. "If we could synthesize the drug, we could deal with it," complained the drug's opponents. "But logging? That's just not what we do. No thanks."

In their workshop, Jordan and Rozencweig emphasized how "active" (effective) Taxol was compared to BMS's existing oncology drugs. And by the end of the day, the leaders of the new company—especially

Richard Gelb, BMS's CEO—became convinced that they had to have this toxic, difficult-to-produce new drug.

There was pressure to move quickly. By August 1989, the NCI's clinical trials had demonstrated that Taxol was effective against ovarian cancer, and the National Institutes of Health (NIH), which oversees the NCI, announced that it was seeking a pharmaceutical company to bring Taxol to market. Four companies applied for the NIH's Cooperative Research and Development Agreement, or CRADA, which allows companies to partner on research funded by the government as an incentive to develop new pharmaceuticals. With a proposal deemed far superior to its competitors, Bristol-Myers Squibb won the CRADA. Although BMS could not claim a patent on the drug itself because information about the chemical was already in the public domain, BMS was granted exclusive access to the NCI's data, trademarked the drug's name as Taxol, and went on to patent a number of methods to administer it to patients.

In late 1992, after nearly three decades of research, the FDA approved Taxol for treating ovarian cancer. It was eventually approved as treatment for several types of the disease, including breast and lung cancer, as well as AIDS-related Kaposi's sarcoma.

Tom Jordan stayed in the background, and to this day only a handful of cognoscenti are aware of his central role in the drug's development. He was most proud of two things: that he'd convinced Bristol to trademark the name Taxol, by which everyone knew the drug, and that he established a fair price for the drug—$146.10 for a 30-milligram vial—that remained constant for the duration of Bristol's market exclusivity. (Under terms of the CRADA, once the FDA approved Taxol in 1992, Bristol-Myers was granted five years of market exclusivity.) A patient typically required six or seven vials of Taxol every three weeks; if he responded well to the drug, he would take it for six cycles; if not, he would move on to another treatment. Although the price was criticized as too high, Jordan steadfastly maintained that it was not only fair, but necessary to cover Bristol's expenditures, which included more than 600 clinical trials, extensive research, and the costs of producing the drug.

Once manufacturing began, Taxol became a quintessentially global product: people in China and Nepal were contracted to collect twigs, branches, and leaves of the Pacific Yew. This raw material was shipped to a company in Italy, which made the drug's precursor. The precursor was shipped to Ireland, where Bristol added on the "side-chain," which changed the molecule and turned it into an active cancer drug. From Ireland, the compound was shipped to Puerto Rico, where it was bottled in vials. Finally, Taxol was shipped to the United States and 52 other countries. With Bristol bearing all of these costs, Tom Jordan had little time for those who complained about the drug's expense.

BMS's five years of market exclusivity for Taxol—meaning that generic pharmaceutical companies would not be allowed to produce cheaper clones of the drug—lasted until 1997. Bristol managed to extend its control over Taxol for an additional 30 months by filing patents on ways to administer it and with delaying lawsuits against the generics. From 1991 through 2002, Bristol said it had invested $1 billion in Taxol, conducted hundreds of clinical trials and administered the drug to more than 40,000 patients. With $9 billion in worldwide sales, Taxol was the best-selling cancer treatment in history.

IN 1995, Charles Heimbold, an attorney who had been at the company for 38 years, was named Dick Gelb's successor as chairman and CEO. The company had a reputation as a steady and profitable, if not spectacular, performer. Heimbold was determined to change that, and with a whirlwind of deals he managed to drive the company's revenues to new heights. BMS's stock traded at about $55 a share in 1995, soared over $100 in 1996–97, and held at around $60 a share when Heimbold retired in 2000—by which point his stock options were extremely valuable. *Fortune* magazine praised BMS as "America's Most Admired Pharmaceutical Company" that year, although some observers felt the CEO had pushed the company too hard, too fast, in pursuit of short-term gains. "There was a culture of earnings management at Bristol-Myers that may have gone to unhealthy extremes," noted one analyst.

Certain Bristol insiders had a harsher assessment: "Heimbold is a jerk," said a former Bristol executive.

When he stepped down in 2000, Heimbold, who was a long-time friend and benefactor of the Bush family, was appointed ambassador to Sweden (his wife is Swedish and they own a home in Stockholm). In February 2001, Peter Dolan, a Heimbold protégé and the company's president, was elevated to the top job. Some Bristol veterans were surprised by this, having given the edge to the deeply experienced and well-regarded Donald Hayden, who remained at the company as senior vice president.

At 46 years old, Peter Dolan was the 144-year-old company's youngest chairman and CEO ever. This was not universally seen as a good thing. "Peter Dolan is smart, smooth, polished, a very likeable guy," said a colleague. "But CEO and chairman? He has no experience. He was selling over-the-counter medicines, like Excedrin. What does he know? Heimbold just threw him into the job, and he's not up to it. He might as well be in the entertainment business."

Solidly built, with a helmet of brown hair, rounded metal-framed glasses, and a deep voice, Dolan was polite, reserved and ambitious. Raised in a middle-class Irish Catholic family, he took himself, his job, and the mission of BMS—"to extend and enhance human life"—very seriously. As befit a graduate of Tufts University (where he was president of his fraternity) with an MBA from Dartmouth's Amos Tuck School of Business Administration (where he was president of his class), Dolan competed in triathlons, favored boxy American-made suits, and lived with his wife and two sons in the quietly affluent suburb of Larchmont, New York. Dolan liked to quip that he operates in "the underpromise-and-overdeliver mode."

Like Heimbold, Dolan was not a scientist: he had come up through the marketing department. Indeed, his rapid ascent was symptomatic of a cultural shift within Bristol engineered by his predecessor, which, broadly stated, pitted the young business jocks like Dolan versus the nerdy scientists and conservative old guard. It was a cultural shift that has remained unresolved in the company, and that has hobbled Bristol somewhat ever since.

Dolan's first job out of business school was at General Foods, where he marketed Jell-O and other desserts for five years. But when Philip Morris bought the company, he decided that he didn't want to work for a tobacco company. In 1988, at 32, he landed at Bristol-Myers, and his career took flight. By 1993 he was head of Bristol Myers Products, where he pushed the company to market an old product, Excedrin, in a new way—as the first over-the-counter medicine to be approved for treating migraines. Excedrin sales rose 17 percent in one year, to $240 million.

From then on, Dolan earned a reputation for parachuting into divisions he knew little about, making significant changes, and moving on. By 1996, he was running both the Mead Johnson Nutritional Group, which produced infant formula, and Zimmer, which made artificial hips. Zimmer was in particularly bad shape and Dolan shook the company up—demanding layoffs at its plant in a small Indiana town and selling one of the company's major business units. By 2001, Zimmer was deemed a success and was spun-off to its shareholders.

Widely viewed by Wall Street as a boy wonder, Dolan was criticized for being too aggressive, or too young, or too arrogant, but the way Dolan saw it he had simply never failed. "I don't think I've ever had an experience where, at the end of the day, it didn't work out," he has said. "I may be at my best when I'm underestimated."

One of his first initiatives as CEO was an ambitious strategy he called "MegaDouble," by which he promised to double the company's sales and earnings in five years. But his troubles started almost immediately and he would soon regret his MegaDouble promises.

In his first year as CEO, Dolan dismantled much of Heimbold's empire. He sold Clairol, spun-off Zimmer, and acquired DuPont's pharmaceutical arm for $7.8 billion. His plan was to refocus Bristol on pharmaceuticals, which had traditionally been the company's best growth engine. *"Science,"* Dolan declared, would once again become the company's primary driver. "Our top management needs to be more linked into what's happening in *science.*"

But one of his biggest challenges, a former colleague said, was that to a certain extent BMS remained Heimbold's company. Not only had he anointed Dolan, he had helped to pick many of the company's directors and remained a significant shareholder himself. Heimbold had been involved in the expensive and unrewarding acquisition of DuPont Pharmaceuticals, and Heimbold had allowed BMS's famed oncology division to wither, said a former employee.

Perhaps Taxol's success had blinded Bristol, or perhaps institutional stasis led to bad decisions and missed opportunities. People in the oncology division had been sounding warnings since 1994, but were told, "Don't worry, we'll invent a replacement drug here." Yet, in spite of its in-house labs' best efforts, Bristol had no marketable cancer drugs in its development pipeline at all. When BMS finally lost its exclusive control of Taxol in 2001, it began a desperate search for a new blockbuster cancer drug.

\*     \*     \*

FOUNDED IN 1983, OSI Pharmaceuticals, Inc., was one of the hundreds of small, struggling biotechnology companies that survived by developing new compounds in partnership with Big Pharma companies. Typically, OSI would realize only small royalties from potential sales. One of the drugs that OSI had an agreement to develop, a small-molecule anti-cancer pill called OSI-774—now known as Tarceva—didn't seem to be a blockbuster. OSI had an agreement to develop and market the drug with Pfizer: the deal gave Pfizer the lion's share of future revenue. But in June 2000, OSI had what its engaging CEO, Dr. Colin Goddard, called "a lucky break."

Pfizer, in an effort to win federal approval of its merger with Warner-Lambert Co.—which had a competing drug in the works—gave Tarceva back to OSI at no cost. OSI went from controlling just 6 percent of future sales of Tarceva to owning all of it. OSI's stock price soared, and soon Goddard had raised $431 million in an IPO. Then he began to scout for a partner; or, more accurately, he sat back like the belle of the ball and let the Big Pharma suitors come to him.

Because there were so few promising cancer drugs available, Goddard said, "it's fair to say that absolutely everyone who was anyone in oncologic pharmaceuticals was interested" in doing a deal for Tarceva. "By then it was apparent that EGFr drugs [like Tarceva and Erbitux] had blockbuster potential in the cancer space. And because Tarceva is a once-a-day pill, it was a lot more patient-friendly than an IV drip and chemo cure. There was a lot of interest in our drug."

Bristol-Myers was one of OSI's most ardent pursuers, and went all out in its bid for a deal. "They made a very positive impression, a strong bid," Goddard said. Everyone in the business knew that Taxol was coming off patent, and appreciated Bristol's dilemma, he said. "But frankly people were dubious about the strength of the Bristol pipeline" of future drugs.

In January 2001, Goddard made a deal with two companies, Genentech and Roche Holding AG, to develop and market Tarceva. Between them, these companies are developing a strong list of anticancer agents, including Herceptin, Rituxan, and Avastin. "It's a premier oncology portfolio," said Goddard. In choosing partners, "we weren't simply looking at it from the perspective of 2001, but of 2007."

After losing Tarceva, Bristol executives became doubly concerned about their ability to replace Taxol. "After us, there was only one drug available," Goddard recalled. "Literally the minute we said no to Bristol, they started paying a lot of attention to ImClone."

IN MID-APRIL 2001, the investment bank Lehman Brothers (which represented BMS) called Morgan Stanley & Co. (which represented ImClone) with an intriguing proposition: Would the biotech firm be interested in a deal in which Bristol-Myers Squibb acquired the right to market C225, along with a significant equity stake in ImClone?

On May 3, Sam met quietly with Brian Markison and Peter Ringrose, BMS's chief scientific officer, in New York. They discussed a possible deal, the logic of which was obvious to both sides: ImClone had C225 but needed funding and logistical support, while Bristol had great experience and resources but needed a new cancer drug. Each was a bit more desperate than they let on.

In that meeting, Sam said he envisioned an arrangement that would give BMS a significant stake in ImClone, yet would allow ImClone to remain a publicly traded company. Brian Markison agreed to explore such an arrangement: perhaps Bristol could acquire a majority interest in ImClone in return for BMS common stock, he suggested, along with a separate agreement for the rights to market C225. They shook hands and agreed to continue the conversation.

The following week, 25,000 cancer specialists had gathered in San Francisco for the 37th annual meeting of the American Society of Clinical Oncology (ASCO), the "Super Bowl of cancer research." There, Dr. Leonard Saltz, a highly respected young oncologist from Memorial Sloan-Kettering—who was also the lead investigator on ImClone's clincial trials—announced some "knock-your-socks-off exciting" data: C225 mixed with irinotecan helped 22.5 percent of refractory colorectal cancer patients in Study 9923. These were stunning results, the best response rate ever achieved in colorectal cancer patients who had failed other treatments. Saltz's announcement was met with thunderous applause, an uptick in ImClone's stock price, and headlines about C225's potential. Sam celebrated that night by staging a Doobie Brothers concert. It was an inspired, mind-blowing piece of showmanship that people still talk about.

"Only Sam would have thought of that," said a former colleague. "He's just not like anyone else you'll meet."

ImClone was now *the* biotech story to follow. Many Wall Street analysts deemed Saltz's ASCO presentation "spectacular," and on May 14, 2001, rated the stock an "outperform," as Morgan Stanley did, or a "strong buy," as CIBC World Markets did, or a "buy," as UBS Warburg did.

But not everyone was a believer. A group of short sellers and hedge fund operators had been closely following ImClone and sensed trouble. These were not mom-and-pop traders; they were an experienced, successful, and often cynical group, many of whom held medical degrees or Ph.D's. They understood the fine points of the C225 data, and knew how scrappy biotech companies could massage a press release. These Wall Street insiders would listen to Sam and Harlan Waksal promise that C225 would become "a billion-a-year drug" at investment banking conferences, and would roll their eyes and snicker. "There was something not quite right with ImClone," a member of this group recalled. "It was hard to know exactly what it was, but it was there in the nitpicky details. The Waksals were a little too showy. They'd always put the cart before the horse—telling us how'd they be making billions on this drug before we saw any real data [on C225]. That really rankled a lot of people. It built feelings of mistrust and suspicion. Don't get on stage and make big claims about your drug, just show me the fuckin' data! The data is everything. And I understand it as well as you do—maybe better. We were very skeptical of these guys."

Many of these insiders refused to buy ImClone stock, or "shorted" it. Avalon Research, a boutique research and brokerage firm, issued its first "sell" recommendation for ImClone a month before ASCO. "IMC-C225's clinical results to date ... have been unimpressive," Avalon's research notes for April 6, 2001, read. "As a result, we believe the company's $2.1 billion market valuation, which assumes successful IMC-C225 commercialization ... carries substantial downside risk."

But Wall Street was in the midst of the longest bull market in history, and investors of all stripes were lured by the cachet of biotech and its promise of big returns. They had read about Shannon Kellum in *USA Today* and watched Lesley Stahl's piece on *60 Minutes*. ImClone's stock price rose from $27.94 in mid-March to $55.87 in early June. A few months later, ImClone would be selling for more than $70 a share.

*     *     *

## A Very High-Risk Opportunity

ON JUNE 20, 2001, Congressman Dan Burton, an Indiana Republican, chaired a hearing entitled, "Compassionate Use of Investigational New Drugs: Is the Current Process Effective?" He had convened the hearing at least in part as a response to the *60 Minutes* segment on ImClone's inconsistent EAP for C225.

"To be told that you or someone that you love has a life-threatening illness, shakes you . . . to the very core," Burton said in his heartfelt opening remarks. "The life that you have known is changed forever. Suddenly you are thrown into a maze of medical tests, doctors' appointments, and tough decision-making. You . . . become experts in interpreting complex medical jargon and searching the Internet for treatment options . . . [compassionate use] is a very touchy issue." Later he'd add: "We have had a number of [cancer] cases in my family, one that is current."

As the hearing got underway, a parade of witnesses testified about the lack of protocols for compassionate-use programs, a lack of communication by pharmaceutical companies, the slow approval of lifesaving drugs by the FDA, and the general frustration of trying to cope with fatal diseases like AIDS and cancer.

C225's greatest success story, Shannon Kellum, testified before the committee that day in favor of allowing more cancer patients access to the drug: "I am obviously very fortunate to be here today. It could very easily be my husband up here representing me and me not telling my story. If it was not for C225, I would not be here right now . . . I do not know if there is a fair or an unfair way of administering [C225], and I do not think ImClone liked saying no [to patients who had requested it]. But . . . I think we need to look at the common goal here and that is to find a cure for cancer . . . I do not have that answer. I wish we all had a crystal ball that had the formula in it, but we do not . . . I may be simplifying it, but . . . with a drug that has had this success, we need to get it approved as fast as possible and get it out to everyone. But denying some people the opportunity I do not think is the answer, because had I not gotten it . . . we would not have the knowledge or the capacity to give it to other individuals."

Doug Baxter told about his 16-year-old son, David, who had been diagnosed with colon cancer right after returning from a weeklong trip to watch Major League Baseball's spring training camp in Phoenix.

131

"Cancer does not kill," he said. "It first embarks on a mission of relentless, relentless torture of hundreds of people—family members, friends, and strangers, compassionate strangers that step forward, wanting to help. His entire family suffers as David struggles. Because a child is hurting, his parents are consumed by . . . trying to find help." David was struggling, one of the many patients waiting for permission from ImClone to use C225.

Frank Burroughs, whose 21-year-old daughter, Abigail, had just died from an odd cancer that had started in her tongue, said: "We tried to get Abigail into narrowly defined clinical trials but she did not qualify" for the studies run by ImClone or AstraZeneca. "We worked very hard to acquire the drugs on a compassionate-use basis, but got nowhere." He suggested establishing a public/private foundation that would pay for access to experimental drugs on a compassionate-use basis.

In discussing Ruth-Ann's two-and-a-half-year struggle against colorectal cancer, Fred Santino first lambasted Sam Waksal for ignoring her many entreaties for C225, and then said: "I happen to run four Web sites, and I had trouble finding the information. There are so many Web sites . . . They are not linked. Some of them disagree. Some of them say trials are open . . . I could not find anything about [the experimental drugs], what side effects they were, anything like that." He suggested that clearer channels of communication were required, in every respect.

Sam Waksal told the committee that ImClone had treated some 700 patients with C225 by that point, of which 30 (or 4 percent) were on a compassionate-use basis. ImClone had canceled its compassionate-use program, he said, because of the "onslaught" of over 8,500 requests for the drug in the previous year. Not wanting to give patients false hope, he said, "we decided to concentrate on getting the drug approved because we felt that was the best way to get this drug out to as many people as possible."

Seeming to address Santino, he said: "We . . . set up a hotline right after May 2000 to deal with some of these requests, and we really feel badly. We probably should have put a form letter together. We were unexperienced at the time, and the data that we had generated was really new to us at that point. So would we do things differently in the future or would we have done things differently in the past? The answer is yes . . . There is no answer to give to husbands and fathers and other family members of patients who have died of cancer. And this is not meant as a rebuttal to anyone."

For ImClone, he explained, the biggest hurdle to a fair compassionate-use program was not money or the fear of contaminating clinical trials with outside data: it was the difficulty of manufacturing a protein-based drug. Unlike the small molecules being developed by ImClone's competitors—like AstraZenica and OSI Pharmaceuticals—C225 has very stringent biologic manufacturing standards. In 1994, ImClone built a pilot manufacturing facility that produced just enough of the drug for clinical trials. At present, he said, the company had only enough C225 to supply 10 weeks' worth of therapy for each patient in Study 9923.

At the end of a long and exhausting day, Burton urged ImClone to work at making C225 available to more patients, and pushed the FDA to approve promising new oncology drugs faster.

Shannon Kellum recalled the hearing with decidedly mixed feelings: "It was very, very emotional. I didn't cry, but I felt a little guilty. [The other witnesses] had all lost someone and I was still alive." But six months later, she was feeling frustrated. "I made a big effort. I got up there and testified for four hours, but still nothing's really changed as far as people getting the drug. I feel like I'm spinning my wheels. Who's to blame—the FDA? ImClone? I don't really know. C225 is sitting here in front of us, but if people can't get access to it what good can it do?"


A MONTH AND A HALF after chairing the hearing on compassionate use, Representative Dan Burton's name appeared in a *Washington Post* story about a seemingly unrelated event. On August 7, the *Post* reported, Burton had taken an unusual, government-paid trip to Frankfurt and Bonn, "to investigate the German postal system." While lawmakers sometimes travel abroad, they usually do so in groups and with aides in tow to study specific issues. It is rare for a member of the house to conduct an official fact-finding trip abroad on his own, as Burton did. Ostensibly his purpose was to study German postal reform—which was "one of our top priorities during this Congress," according to Burton aide Kevin Binger. But congressional sources told the *Post* that the congressman's briefings were "only a decoy and that the actual purpose of the trip was for the congressman to visit his wife."

Barbara J. Logan Burton, the *Post* added, was "undergoing experimental cancer treatment at an undisclosed facility" in Frankfurt. I contacted Burton's office to confirm whether Mrs. Burton had been treated with an experimental cancer drug in Frankfurt, and to ask whether she was treated with Erbitux. Congressman Burton did not respond to my calls.

Then I contacted ImClone's European partner, Merck KGaA, which is headquartered in Darmstadt, just south of Frankfurt, to ask the same questions. "I have never heard of this story," said Merck spokeswoman Phyllis Carter. "I don't think it sounds right. It wouldn't [make sense] to uproot a very sick American woman and treat her with Erbitux in Germany. Why wouldn't they do it in Indiana?" Carter added: "Even if she was in a clinical trial here, I wouldn't have that information because patient files are all kept private."

On May 10, 2002, Barbara Burton—a private, soft-spoken woman who had worked for her husband's Indianapolis insurance agency for 30 years—passed away. She asked that memorial contributions be sent to the Colon Cancer Alliance and a breast cancer foundation. (Erbitux is designed for use against colon cancer.)

Although Dan Burton's office would not confirm or deny whether Mrs. Burton was treated with Erbitux, the congressman spoke for many during the June hearing when he said: "I have known people in the medical profession, very highly regarded people, people in our government who were the heads of major agencies that deal with our health care, who were against using treatments outside of conventional medicine. And yet when their loved one, their wife, became terminally ill, they tried everything. They went out of the country, they did everything, because it is different when you are talking about the masses of people and . . . when your wife or your daughter or your son is terminally ill with a disease and there is no hope except that long, long bomb that we are talking about, that you might throw in a football game, with a new drug that might save their life."

IN MAY 2001, as New York City began to heat up for summer, executives from Bristol and ImClone signed a confidentiality agreement so they could begin to negotiate in earnest. BMS's legal and financial advisers embarked on an extensive due diligence review of ImClone's clinical trials, legal affairs, information technology, marketing and sales, tax, finance, manufacturing, intellectual property, and regulatory work.

On June 1, Sam met with Richard Lane, president of BMS's World-wide Pharmaceutical Division, to propose a deal in which Bristol would acquire a 70 percent stake in the biotech firm. Rick Lane was a big man, partial to fine suits, gold cuff links, and expensive black Mercedes automobiles; a relative newcomer to BMS and an aggressive deal maker whose style was characterized as "management by intimidation," he was not well loved at Bristol. But Lane had been promoted by Heimbold over the well-regarded Bristol veteran Don Hayden and was, along with Brian Markison, in charge of making the ImClone deal happen.

ImClone's proposed deal structure launched a spirited debate at Bristol. The discussions included the very highest officers of the company, including Dolan, Lane, Markison, Peter Ringrose, and Chief Financial Officer Frederick Schiff. It is said that a number of Bristol's powerful directors—most notably Louis V. Gerstner, the former chief of IBM, Robert Allen, the former head of AT&T, and James Robinson, the former head of American Express—also took an active role in the discussions. The more they talked about it, the less enamored the Bristol executives were of the deal suggested by Sam. A number of people noted that it was the drug C225, not ImClone, that was the real asset in play. They questioned the wisdom of acquiring a majority stake in a small, struggling biotech firm.

Bolstering their skepticism was Bristol's due diligence report, which had highlighted a number of troubling questions about ImClone. BMS scientists were not impressed by the small, one-armed Study 9923, and were concerned that ImClone had not taken the FDA's request for a single-agent study to heart. As a result, a June due-diligence report warned that the agency might not approve C225: "FDA has requested that data be provided on the antitumor activity of C225 as a single agent. Preclinical data has thus far been provided to FDA . . . but they have persisted in their interest that clinical data be provided. No accelerated approval has ever been granted for an oncology drug for use in a combination therapy."

Two days later, BMS Senior Vice President Laurie Smaldone sent a detailed e-mail to her colleagues Peter Ringrose and Beth Seidenberg that outlined her main concerns about ImClone's work. "On the whole, Smaldone's memo concluded, "it [a deal with ImClone] remains a very high risk opportunity."

This was not a warning that Peter Dolan and his executive team heard. Or perhaps they did hear it, but were so confident about C225's prospects that they chose to disregard it. Or perhaps they weren't confident at all, but were starting to panic: with no replacement for Taxol in sight, it is possible Dolan felt he had no choice but to cut a deal for Erbitux as quickly as possible.

THE BRISTOL-MYERS SQUIBB board had proposed an alternative to Sam's plan. Rather than buy a controlling stake of 51 percent of ImClone, Bristol would agree to acquire a minority stake—20 percent, say—in the company while arranging a separate agreement for the codevelopment, copromotion, and distribution of C225.

In a series of meetings and phone calls in late June and early July, the two companies fine-tuned an agreement under which BMS would, over time, spend almost $2 billion to acquire a 19.9 percent equity stake in ImClone, along with the exclusive rights to sell C225 in North America and Japan. (European rights had already been sold to Merck KGaA, of Germany, for $60 million.)

Two billion dollars was a record amount for a single biotech drug, especially one that had yet to be approved by the FDA.

Yet Sam wanted to sweeten the pot even more. Perhaps sensing Bristol's urgency for a deal, he claimed that ImClone was not interested in a deal unless Bristol took "a significant equity investment" in the company. He added that ImClone's existing stockholders would "benefit most" if Bristol made a tender offer (a time-sensitive offer by a company to purchase another company's shares at a premium) for existing stock rather than having the money go directly to the company for shares that would be issued later. Such an arrangement would be unprecedented for a deal between a Big Pharma company and a small biotech firm; typically these alliances are based on milestone payments. Furthermore, the deal would enrich ImClone insiders and current shareholders in the short term, without guaranteeing the company's long-term prospects.

On July 20, the two sides agreed to a tender offer price of $70 per share, a significant premium over the current ImClone stock price of about $40 per share.

With this framework in place, ImClone's board agreed to lend a total of $35 million to the company's three senior officers—Sam received an $18.2 million loan, Harlan a $15.7 million loan, and Robert

Goldhammer a $1.2 million loan—so that they could exercise stock options and warrants to purchase 4.5 million shares of ImClone stock. This massive stock purchase would allow them to profit to an extraordinary degree from the BMS tender offer.

The deal was still a secret—although one that was beginning to leak out—when, at the end of August, BMS's independent radiology reviewer uncovered further problems with Study 9923. ImClone had overstated the response rate (the number of patients who had improved under the C225/chemo regimen) and the size of the patient pool. BMS's independent radiologist noted:

> In 4 of these confirmed partial responses our radiologists have judged the disease to be only stable at the time of patient's enrollment into the study. If these 4 cases were thrown out, then the highest possible response rate would be 11 + 4/120 = 12.5%. However, we have not conducted a strict review of all of the 120 cases, and it is likely that if we carefully reviewed all of the cases we would throw many out on the same basis. Indeed, it is my understanding that the study sponsor [ImClone] has conducted such an analysis on the basis of its own radiologists' review, and has thereby reduced the denominator of the patient population.

As a congressional report on the ImClone matter later noted, if the denominator, or number of patient cases, in Study 9923 was indeed below 100 (especially if it was as low as 89, as this BMS e-mail indicates it was), then ImClone's data would not have been sufficient to warrant the accelerated approval of C225. Apparently, neither ImClone nor Bristol recognized this as a serious problem.

Another concern was that ImClone had still not released data from its single-agent study of C225, information the FDA had specifically and repeatedly asked for. On September 4, a BMS vice president e-mailed other senior executives: "Based on today's discussions with Susan and Steve our preliminary recommendation is a 'go' decision [for a deal with ImClone]. We are still trying to obtain data from the mono therapy study from ICE [ImClone]. As of 6:30 P.M. today we did not have any more information."

Ultimately, Bristol never received the single-agent data before committing itself to a deal for C225.

\*　　\*　　\*

INSIDE BRISTOL, there was still a rump group that considered a $2 billion bet on an unapproved drug reckless. They questioned Bristol's vetting of C225 and viewed Waksal as an opportunist without any meaningful achievements in science. Some marketing experts complained, too: they pointed out that the deal was not advantageous to Bristol. In the original proposal, BMS would have won a 51 percent controlling interest of ImClone; but the BMS board wasn't interested. Now the company was spending $2 billion for only a 20 percent equity stake, which seemed to these internal critics to be far too much to pay for far too little control.

Furthermore, assuming that they could sell $1 billion worth of Erbitux every year—as Sam had optimistically projected—Bristol would only keep 40 percent of the profits, which, after it had covered its costs, would be negligible. "$2 billion is so much money, and we didn't see how we'd get it back," said a former Bristol executive. "The drug isn't big enough to give 60 percent of the profit to ImClone and make it worth [our] while for 40 percent."

Most jarringly, the terms of the tender offer called for Bristol to immediately buy $1.2 billion in stock from ImClone's shareholders (the remaining $800 million would be doled out in step payments). This meant that none of Bristol's money would remain in ImClone itself: if there was any significant problem with C225—a delay in FDA approval, say—then BMS would be unable to recover its investment, nor would ImClone have the cash to pay for additional research or studies.

Asked about this pointedly by analysts in a September conference call, Fred Schiff, Bristol's CFO, replied: "We have great confidence in C225. We looked at . . . the commercial agreement and equity investment in the aggregate, and we believe that for both our shareholders and the future of that product [C225], we are doing the right thing."

Any qualms the Bristol executives had were said to have been allayed by the eminent scientists Sam had recruited to ImClone's board— John Mendelsohn, Vincent DeVita, and Arnold Levine. They were considered gold-standard oncologists, and if C225 was good enough for them then it would be good enough for Bristol.

The deal, recalled a former Bristol executive, had gained tremendous momentum. "It was moving too quickly. They audited [ImClone's] data, but it was taken on good faith . . . Some people thought Waksal was slippery, but, okay, he's surrounded by these big names and you figured you could put up with slippery. The work [on C225] was done. All we had to do was to sell the drug."

It was said within BMS that at least one prominent Bristol scientist raised a red flag after the audit of ImClone's clinical trial data and plainly stated "there's a problem here" but her objections were squashed. Dolan and his executives, an insider said, "didn't want to hear any bad news. They just wanted to make the deal happen."

WHEN IT WAS ANNOUNCED that a landmark $2 billion deal between Bristol-Myers Squibb and ImClone Systems would close in mid-September, the public reaction was overwhelmingly positive. The scientific community was cheered by the prospect of Bristol accelerating the launch of C225. The financial community viewed the deal as a coup for ImClone and a smart strategic alliance for Peter Dolan. Patients and doctors applauded the arrival of a new, perhaps revolutionary weapon in the war against cancer. The deal would be good for everyone, it seemed. After 20 years of research and an estimated $200 million in development costs, C225 now called "Erbitux," would finally reach the market.

# SEVEN

# The $2 Billion Antibody

At 19,340 feet high, Mount Kilimanjaro, in Tanzania, is the highest peak in Africa. In September 1993, Martha Stewart joined her friend Sandy Hill Pittman—the then-wife of Bob Pittman, founder of MTV—and a group of high-powered women on a six-day climb. Martha disliked the bright red, green, and yellow safety gear that had been issued to the group, preferring to wear instead a khaki-colored *Out of Africa* ensemble. One day Martha hiked ahead of the group and became so camouflaged in the dun-colored brush that she became lost. When she finally rejoined the party, she found herself talking to a tall, blonde, self-possessed native of San Diego named Sharon Patrick. It was Patrick—a self-described "business architect" who specialized in start-ups and turnarounds—who would eventually help Martha find her way out of the tangle of contracts and obligations she had wandered into and establish a uniquely successful media empire.

The two women had different sensibilities but much in common. They were both single and driven, self-made daughters of immigrants who had worked their way through college and had spent time in the financial industry. While at Barnard College in New York, Martha had worked as a domestic and a fashion model, and later worked as a stockbroker on Wall Street. Sharon Patrick had paid for her Stanford education by selling jewelry and swimming with the dolphins at Sea World. After working in corporate finance at General Motors and on the staff of the U.S. Department of Health, Education, and Welfare, she earned an MBA from Harvard in 1978. She made partner at the management-consulting firm McKinsey & Company, and learned the art of negotiating media deals under the tutelage of Cablevision's Charles Dolan at Rainbow Programming Holdings. By the time of the Kilimanjaro trip, Patrick was 51 years old and was finishing a yearlong sabbatical. She was interested to hear about Martha's many scattered businesses and disparate contracts. It sounded to her as if Martha's ventures were unnecessarily "fractured" and convoluted. What Martha needed, Patrick suggested, was to streamline and centralize her operations.

By the end of the year, Martha had contracted Sharon Patrick, who ran her own business-consulting firm, to bring a coolheaded logic to the creative whirlwind that she had built. It was a rare instance of Martha ceding control and acknowledging that she couldn't do it all by herself. They began to spend hours around the kitchen table at her home, Turkey Hill, designing a new kind of multimedia company—one that would be built entirely around Martha Stewart.

At Patrick's urging, Martha sat down and typed up a "vision statement" that clearly defined the company she wanted to build and the role she would play in it. Martha's ideal company would espouse "excellent taste," "family-oriented values," and "quality ideas," she wrote; the CEO would not only lead the enterprise on a day-to-day basis, she would embody the brand; the company would reach as many people as possible through as many different media channels as possible; it would both define the idealized image of a lifestyle and merchandise the particulars of the image to consumers. To a remarkable degree, this document described Martha Stewart Living Omnimedia, the company that would eventually come to be.

Martha had been thinking about this since 1987, when it occurred to her that her string of best-selling lifestyle books could be a springboard to some kind of larger media business—"my own little publishing company," she'd dream aloud. The year 1987 was the same one she signed her promotional deal with Kmart and that her marriage to Andy Stewart had dissolved.

By the summer of 1990, she had taken the first step by creating a prototype for a magazine she called *Martha Stewart Living*. At 130 pages long, the *MSL* prototype wasn't simply a new title, it was an entirely new kind of magazine, one built around a single personality. It featured a photo of Martha on the cover, a "Letter from Martha" inside, and many photographs of Martha—arranging flowers, choosing a Christmas tree, relaxing in a sweater—throughout its pages. Publishers had never seen anything like it and reaction was mixed. Martha showed her prototype to senior executives at Kmart, Time-Life Books, Condé Nast, and Rupert Murdoch's publishing company. Some of the executives, like Condé Nast chairman Si Newhouse, were initially enthusiastic about the idea, but then cooled; others disliked it immediately. In the end, they all rejected the idea.

She must have felt discouraged, but Martha stuck to her concept and went back to Time Inc. for a second pitch. This time she approached the company's magazine group rather than its book division. It happened that her timing was excellent.

The venerable book and magazine publisher Time Inc. was just emerging from a long and costly battle to defend itself from a hostile takeover by Paramount Communications and its rapacious CEO, Martin Davis. To escape Paramount, Time's CEO, J. Richard Munro, had broken off a planned merger with Warner Communications, a Hollywood movie and television company, in favor of buying Warner outright. The result was the largest media company in the world, a conglomerate called Time Warner Inc. The new company also had one of the largest corporate debts in history, over $13 billion. The liability was intentional and strategic: Time Warner had made itself unwieldly in order to make a takeover by Paramount impractical. It was a risky strategy, one largely hatched by Steven J. Ross, Warner's mercurial CEO (Ross would later die of cancer), and now that the external threat had passed the company had to figure a way to lighten its debt load.

Time Warner had created a new paradigm: an enormous, global, multiplatform media conglomerate built on the promise of "synergy," a seemingly magical word that described how Time's book and magazine "content" would be fed to consumers through Warner's film and television "pipes" to millions of consumers. At least that was the theory. Gerald Levin, Time's professorial-looking number two, had preached the gospel of cross-pollination and "content extension," which meant turning magazine articles into books, and books into television and radio shows, and vice-versa. It made perfect sense on paper, and soon other media firms were trying to line up similar deals. It was not yet clear that this model would work in practice, however.

In the summer of 1990 Time Warner was on the hunt for new ideas that would make the promise of synergy real, when Martha presented the mockup for *Martha Stewart Living* to Christopher Meigher, the head of Time Publishing Ventures, the company's magazine development arm. The *MSL* prototype did not immediately appeal to him: it seemed more like a book than a magazine and it was blatantly self-promotional; and Martha was associated with the déclassée retailer Kmart, whose customers were not Time Warner's—or its advertiser's—target market. Yet, overriding these concerns, Meigher recognized that Martha and her magazine had great synergistic potential. She was already a best-selling author with a clearly defined message; she was fast becoming a household name (in no small part due to Kmart's promotions); and she had the right look, ambition, and product to push her eponymous brand into every media outlet in Time Warner's business—books, magazines, radio, television, books-on-tape, and even formats that did not yet exist, like the Internet. Although Meigher complained that Martha's sometimes divalike behavior made her "a terrible pain the ass," she and her magazine were the right package at the right place at the right time. Time Warner agreed to underwrite two test issues of *MSL* and see how they sold, before committing any further.

In November 1990, 500,000 copies of the first test issue of *Martha Stewart Living* hit the newsstands. Typically, a new magazine is judged a success if it sells half the issues printed: *MSL* sold at a rate of 70 percent, which was startling to say the least. Time Warner was further surprised when it received 100,000 subscriptions for *MSL* from a direct-mail campaign. And while the publisher had hoped to sell 20 pages of advertising (at $7,500 for a four-color, full-page ad), the first issue of *MSL* had 25 pages of ads.

The suits at Time Warner didn't really understand Martha Stewart's appeal, but they certainly understood the numbers. And then Kmart, which had refused to underwrite the magazine's start-up, quickly agreed to buy two full pages of ads in every issue of *MSL*.

Martha's innovation was seen as brash at the time, but the success of *MSL* would eventually make possible other titles built around a celebrity editor—most notably *O,* the successful magazine built around television host Oprah Winfrey; *George,* the quasi-successful political magazine edited by John Kennedy Jr.; and *Rosie,* the ill-fated magazine built around comedian Rosie O'Donnell. Yet the sad end of *George* and the very public flame-out of *Rosie*—complete with angry lawsuits filed between O'Donnell and her publisher, Gruner + Jahr—demonstrated the perils of building a media franchise around a single personality: if something went wrong or changed in the life of the editor, the results could be disastrous. After John Kennedy Jr. died in a plane crash, *George* quickly withered; *Rosie* imploded after O'Donnell quit her TV show, announced she was a lesbian, and radically changed her look.

The second test issue of *Martha Stewart Living* came out in February 1991, when the nation was focused on the Gulf War in Kuwait. It, too, was hailed as a great success, and now Martha was on a roll. In May, Time Warner announced that it had signed her to a 10-year contract to publish *MSL.* While the people around her sat back and celebrated, Martha seemed to have expected this unparalleled success. She smiled in happy acknowledgment, then dove back into her increasingly hectic life. When not touring a local women's group around the gardens of her home, Turkey Hill, or acquiring properties in the Hamptons, she was on a book tour for her latest offering, *Martha Stewart's Gardening, Month by Month,* or taping the *David Letterman Show* in New York, or the *Jay Leno Show* in Los Angeles, or appearing at Kmart celebrations across the country. And wherever she went, she plugged her new magazine.

By midsummer, Martha inaugurated the first of her weekly appearances on the *Today* show, and that, too, was a success. "You do everything so well," enthused Faith Daniels, one of the hosts. "If only I could be Martha Stewart in my next life!"

Suddenly, hers was a name on everyone's lips. Martha wasn't simply a cute and smiley lifestyle expert: she was a phenomenon, the embodiment of synergy. Or at least she should have been.

By the spring of 1993, *MSL* had a circulation of 725,000 and Martha began to plan for the next logical step: her own weekly television show, based on her magazine. She had intuitively grasped something that others hadn't: not only would an *MSL* TV show promote the magazine and extend the Martha Stewart brand, but advertisers who wanted their products seen in both print and on TV would help underwrite its costs. There was an elegant simplicity to the scheme. The idea seems obvious, in retrospect, but for some reason Time Warner—the largest media company in the world, the company that had taken "synergy" as its creed—did not appreciate Martha's potential as well as she did. Perhaps one reason for this is that the distinct corporate cultures of Time and Warner had not meshed smoothly; in fact, executives from the two sides of the company were locked in self-destructive turf battles.

When Martha suggested the obvious idea of producing a TV show based on *MSL,* she was infuriated to learn that Time Warner's Warner Brothers—the nation's largest syndicator—was not interested. (Syndicators act like agents for TV shows. A production company produces a "pilot," or sample, episode of a show like *Hard Copy, Baywatch,* or *Oprah,* and the syndicator then tries to convince TV stations across the country to broadcast a given number of episodes in a season. When there is enough interest in a show, the syndicator arranges advertising deals to cover the cost.) No amount of asking, cajoling, or demanding would bring Warner Brothers to the table.

To make her displeasure clear, Martha moved her offices out of the Time & Life Building into a space of her own, on 44th Street. Then she arranged a syndication deal of her own.

In January 1993, the large independent firm Group W announced that it had signed a deal to syndicate a half-hour TV series called *Martha Stewart Living* that would offer "a unique combination of inspiration and how-to information on entertaining, cooking, gardening, restoring, collecting, homekeeping, and decoration."

Before Martha's pilot aired, Group W executives grew concerned that it would come across as elitist, or maudlin, and that it wouldn't sell in major middle-American markets like Detroit and Cleveland. Upon seeing her show for the first time, Richard Sheingold, the executive overseeing the project for Group W, had knots in his stomach. "I'm not sure I can sell this," he told Martha candidly. "Look, the people in the cities where we have to sell this show are in urban environments. They're working-class people. These people don't even have gardens."

"Yes," Martha replied evenly, "but they *want* them."

The show opened to generally poor reviews—"We'd say Martha's working, but the show's not," carped one critic—but that didn't seem to matter to the public.

By May 1993, Group W had sold *Martha Stewart Living* to stations in 80 cities, which represented about 75 percent of the U.S. television market. By September 1993, it was being shown to 82 percent of the U.S. television market. And by the spring of 1996, it was on 1 out of 10 U.S.

television sets and was deemed the most popular women's program on morning TV. By the fall of 1996, the show's format was changed from a half hour once a week to a half hour daily, and her ratings spiked up 10 percent.

By the end of 1998, *Martha Stewart Living* was focused on three main topics—cooking, arts and crafts, and gardening—and was televised for an hour every day. Through sheer force of will, it seemed, Martha had fashioned herself into a certified media star.

Time Warner executives were seething at their missed opportunity and tried to woo her back. But there was little they could do about her deal with Group W or her increasing independence in other areas. The media giant was contractually obliged to underwrite Martha's blooming celebrity with a $400,000 base salary, a $40,000 clothing allowance, a hair-and-makeup allowance, a chauffer-driven Chevrolet Suburban, and, reportedly, a $2 million loan to help her buy a house in East Hampton.

Martha's empire was spreading rapidly, but behind the scenes her business was a mess. She had a book contract with Crown Publishing, a marketing deal with Kmart, a magazine deal with Time Warner, and a television deal with Time Warner and Group W—all without a cohesive plan or a single director guiding it. She knew she had to gain control of her far-flung operations but she didn't know how to do it herself, or even where to begin.

Acknowledging that she couldn't do everything herself, Martha began to reach out to a series of mentors, many of whom were successful women.

One of the first was Charlotte Beers, an outgoing rancher's daughter from Beaumont, Texas, who had risen to become head of the influential advertising agency Ogilvy & Mather, in New York. Beers was a frequent guest at Martha's house in East Hampton, and the two would talk for hours about how Martha needed to communicate more effectively. Martha acknowledged that she could be too blunt and self-centered in business meetings, which turned potential allies against her. Beers counseled Martha to think like an advertiser: instead of focusing only on delivering her message, she should try to tailor her words to elicit the kind of response she wanted from her audience.

But what exactly did she want? She needed help in defining her business goals and in bringing them about. It was just then, in September of

1993, that she hiked Kilimanjaro, got lost, and eventually wound up talking to Sharon Patrick, who had clear, strong, well-informed opinions about what Martha could do to focus her businesses.

"Martha fell in love with Sharon's mind," Charlotte Beers observed.

On New Year's Eve of 1993, Martha sat at a friend's ski lodge in Aspen, Colorado, watching the snow fall while she stewed over her deal with Time Warner. As far as Martha was concerned, she had been responsible for the huge success of her magazine and television show, while the smug executives at Time Warner had done little but condescend to her and drag their feet. Now that she was a legitimate media star, she wanted to be treated with respect and to be compensated for her bright ideas and perseverance.

Hired as a consultant, Sharon Patrick encouraged Martha's ambition to build her own company. The first step was to renegotiate the terms of her deal with Time Warner, and for that they turned to Allen Grubman, a stocky, pugnacious graduate of Brooklyn Law School who had earned his reputation through his deft handling of clients like Michael Jackson, Bruce Springsteen, and Billy Joel. Martha viewed Grubman's wily negotiations with Time Warner on behalf of Madonna—who won a joint-partnership with Warner Records, her own record label, music publishing business and film production company—as a model agreement.

By early 1995, Martha had a new deal with Time Warner. She was now CEO of Martha Stewart Enterprises, which was essentially her own company within the giant media company: it also gave her the chance to expand into the nascent World Wide Web and to sell Martha-branded merchandise to her millions of loyal fans. The new contract was a nearly complete victory, and it did not go unnoticed. On his PBS interview show that summer, Charlie Rose noted: "Everyone around here is talking about how much fun it is to see the largest communication company in the world being dragged around by the nose by a former caterer." Martha's eyes flashed, but she refused to take the bait, saying only, "Yes, but I didn't concentrate on that Charlie," before changing the subject.

By the end of 1995, *Martha Stewart Living* was garnering some $50 million a year in revenues for Time Warner, but tensions between the company and its star were again flaring. After working with a series of publishing executives, Martha was now reporting to Don Logan, a hefty native of Alabama who oversaw all of the media company's magazine operations. Despite reassuring public statements, the two did not get along particularly well. This chafe would become increasingly irksome to Martha as the media business grew superheated, and bigger and bigger deals were hatched every day. The boom had been touched off by the initial public offering of Netscape stock in August 1995—Netscape's $1 billion valuation catapulted into $3 billion within minutes of the offer—and was fueled by deals for companies like Yahoo! and Excite. Any media company with any sort of link to the Web (including Time Warner, which had entered the "Internet space" with its Pathfinder service) saw its value rapidly inflated. Martha Stewart was one of the brightest media stars of the moment, yet her hands were still tied by her contract with Time Warner and she could not participate in the gold rush. Once again, she and Sharon Patrick ensconced themselves at Turkey Hill and worked long hours around the kitchen table, brainstorming ways for Martha to gain total independence.

The biggest problem was money. It would take a lot to buy her way out of Time Warner. *Martha Stewart Living* had a monthly circulation of some two million readers and was generating an estimated $50 million a year in revenues; on top of that, Martha had a syndicated TV show, a string of best-selling books, and a recently introduced mail-order business called Martha by Mail. The exact value of her holdings was not made public, but *The New York Times* suggested that it was worth at least $85 million, while others said it was worth much more. Although Martha was now wealthy, she did not have enough to buy her company back outright.

Ten banks reportedly refused to back Martha unless she gave them significant equity in her company. This arrangement sounded an awful lot like the deal she already had with Time Warner, and Martha was not interested. Around and around in circles they went, until Sharon Patrick finally realized that the answer had been sitting in front of them all along.

In a few months' time, Martha's 10-year contract with Kmart would be up for renewal. Now she could negotiate a new deal from a position of strength. By the mid-1990s, the big retailer's business was failing, and the company had installed a new CEO; Kmart needed Martha and the sale of her branded products to keep itself afloat. Sharon Patrick recognized that not only could Martha ask for generous terms, she might be able to convince Kmart to fund the buyout of her Time Warner contract.

Kmart was founded by Martin Kresge in 1899 as a five-and-dime store in Michigan. It eventually grew into a chain of discount department stores that reached across the nation. By 1976, Kmart was the largest general retailer in the country after Sears, but its management had become insular and calcified at just the time that Wal-Mart, the lean discount retailer from Arkansas, began to eat up market share. Kmart fought back with celebrity endorsements of its products, first with a line from Jaclyn Smith of *Charlie's Angels* fame, then with Martha Stewart, and on with the country music star Kenny Rogers and the race car driver Mario Andretti. But its business model was inefficient, and Kmart continued to lose ground. The year 1993 marked the first time the company had dipped into the red in a decade, and in June 1995, Joe Antonini was supplanted as CEO by Floyd Hall. It was Antonini who, back in 1987, had originally championed Martha with an investment in the rising caterer/book author—Kmart initially paid her $200,000 a year, a relatively minor sum that was greatly enhanced by the national marketing campaign Kmart built around her—that had set her on the road to celebrity. Now, a decade later, Martha again looked to Kmart for a war chest.

Perhaps by design, Martha set the stage for a showdown with Time Warner by making increasing demands: along with her base salary of $400,000 a year plus bonuses, a chauffer, and a clothing allowance, she now demanded 40 percent of the equity in Martha Stewart Enterprises.

Time Warner executives were outraged by what they perceived to be her arrogance. After a difficult negotiation, the two sides agreed to part ways. Sharon Patrick brokered the peace talks and Allen Grubman arranged the details of the buyout.

In February 1997, a muted press release announced the formation of Martha Stewart Living Omnimedia LLC ("MSO"). The new company had four divisions: Publishing & Online; Television; Merchandising; and Corporate. MSO would take over *Martha Stewart Living* and a book series from Time Warner, and would pursue new ventures on its own. Martha Stewart was chairman and CEO. Sharon Patrick was hired full time as president. She described her "backstage" role as the person in charge of developing a coherent structure and strategy for the company, while Martha's "front stage" role was to define the vision, embody the brand, and run the company.

A third important role player at MSO was Susan Magrino, who had worked as a book publicist at Crown Publishing, where Martha had been her star author. She, like Martha and Sharon Patrick, was blonde, energetic, and a self-made success. Magrino left Crown to run her own agency. She represented several interconnected clients, including the celebrity hairdresser Frederic Fekkai (who did work for Martha and her friend Hillary Rodham Clinton, and was a good friend of Sam Waksal's), Elizabeth Tilberis, editor-in-chief of *Harper's Bazaar* (who would later succumb to cancer), and even the French restaurant Lutèce (where many in this social set liked to dine). But Martha Stewart was Magrino's most important—some would say most demanding—client, the so-called doyenne of domesticity, with whom the press seemed to have an endless love/hate fascination.

The creation of Martha Stewart Living Omnimedia was a stupendous and unprecedented media deal. By all accounts, it was Sharon Patrick who had defused the tension with Time Warner and brokered an arrangement that kept both sides reasonably happy. "Sharon is great at bringing warring parties together," said Time's CFO, Joseph Ripp. "Without Sharon, there would have been no deal." Indeed, Patrick was proud to note that Time Warner kept a 6.3 percent stake in MSO and continued to process catalog orders and distribute *Martha Stewart Living* magazine.

"Where did Martha's money come from?" Wall Street wanted to know. There had been no mention of backers in the MSO announcement, and details of the buyout remained a tightly held secret. No one believed that she had $85 million of her own, but Martha would only say that her funds were "internally generated capital." A few months later, *Fortune,* a business magazine owned by Time Warner, reported that Martha had garnered some $16 million in cash as a down payment from her new contract with Kmart. That was significant, but it still wasn't enough to support the buyout.

It would take until the summer of 1999, when MSO was gearing up for its own initial public offering (IPO), that the financial details of MSO's beginning were made public in its prospectus. Martha, it turned out, had not paid anything close to $85 million for her company. Instead, she had paid about $2 million of her own money plus the $16 million advance from Kmart; then she had taken out a $30 million loan, and issued Time Warner 6.3 percent of unregistered shares in MSO stock. (She would eventually use the proceeds of her IPO to buy back those shares and repay the loan.) Once again, Martha Stewart had outfoxed everyone.

It was a little before nine o'clock on the morning of October 19, 1999, when Martha Stewart and Sharon Patrick served 3,000 brioche and croissants with freshly squeezed orange juice to traders on the floor of the New York Stock Exchange (NYSE). At 9:30 they moved upstairs to the famed balcony overlooking the exchange and handed out MSO hats to NYSE chairman Richard Grasso and others. Then, with an MSO banner on the wall behind her, a beaming Martha picked up a mallet and rang Wall Street's opening bell for trading. It was the day of her IPO and she was prepared: she had even designed her own stock certificates.

Since gaining its independence, MSO's business had been a runaway hit, bringing in some $222 million in revenues and $30 million in annual profit. The cachet of Martha's IPO was enhanced by the fact that white-shoe investment bank Morgan Stanley & Co. was her counderwriter on the offering. (Morgan had declined to hire Martha 30 years earlier when she was looking for a job on Wall Street.) On her road show to prospective underwriters—mutual funds, hedge funds, and institutional investors—people were excited to meet Martha. She appeared to be charming and well informed. There was a lurking problem, however. Two years earlier, Martha had filed a $10 million libel and defamation suit against the *National Enquirer,* for a story headlined "Martha Stewart Is Mentally Ill." The story was based on Jerry Oppenheimer's unauthorized biography, *Martha Stewart—Just Desserts,* a best-seller that had alleged Martha had inflicted "self-mutilation" (in a rage over the loss of her husband, she supposedly ripped chunks of hair from her scalp) and had "threatened suicide." The libel case, *Martha Stewart v. National Enquirer et al.,* had dragged on for two years in Los Angeles. And now, on the eve of her IPO, it threatened to spill into public, which would have derailed the offering. On October 18, Martha withdrew her suit. The case files were sealed.

Martha Stewart Living Omnimedia went public the next day. Before trading, the MSO share price had been set at $18 and Martha—who owned 70.4 percent of the stock and held 96 percent of the board's voting power—stood to make $614.7 million. But public interest in the offering had grown intense, and that morning MSO began trading at $37.25 a share. By the end of the day, Martha Stewart was worth $1.27 billion.

For lunch that day, Martha had been invited to the sumptuous triplex apartment of Tina Brown and Harry Evans, on East 57th Street in Sutton Place. They had invited a slew of friends to celebrate, including Diane Sawyer, Charlie Rose, and Diane von Furstenberg. Tina Brown, who was the editor of *Talk* magazine at the time, happily greeted Martha at the front door with a question: "How are you doing?"

Martha smiled broadly and announced, "I'm rich!"

ELIZABETH LATHAM and Sam Waksal had not spoken in 10 years. While he had been building ImClone, she had lived in various places around the world with various men, until she'd settled in a woody, phone-less retreat in Northern California with a man who was nine years her junior, the son of the woman who had managed the Herzenberg lab at Stanford. Elizabeth and her beau had two children and had moved back to her hometown of Nelson, New Zealand. He began philandering, she said, and moved out. She took up with the man across the street, who was an orchardist and hang glider. In September 1997, Elizabeth called Sam to wish him a surprise happy birthday. He was amazed and delighted to hear from her. When she asked how he was, he replied: "I'm really rich—*disgustingly* rich!"

While this might have sounded like a good thing to say to his ex-paramour, it was not strictly true. Sam had a good amount of money at his disposal, but it was nearly all leveraged, and meanwhile his debts had mounted perilously. In the late 1990s, ImClone was struggling and still deeply in the red; Harlan worried that in spite of C225's great promise it would remain undeveloped. ImClone badly needed to find a partner to help bring the drug to market.

For Sam it must have been inspiring but difficult to watch from close range as his friend Martha Stewart went from one great success to the next, in a seemingly effortless way. He has said that he advised Martha during her crucial negotiations with Time Warner. And she—along with Sam's other great friend/benefactor, Carl Icahn—continued to support Sam and his work. He was certainly busy.

In a press release, Sam described himself as a "biotech industry pioneer" who had helped to found over 15 biopharmaceutical companies, including Cadus, Medicis Pharmaceutical Corp, and Merlin Pharmaccutical Corp.

On Sam's advice, Martha invested in several biotech ventures, including Cadus and another side business of his called Scientia Health Group, a small biotech holding company that operated out of ImClone's Varick Street office.

Martha's father had once worked as a pharmaceutical salesman, and perhaps this was one reason for her early and ardent support of Sam Waksal. She had been an original investor in ImClone, and now, with the help of her stockbroker, Peter Bacanovic, she continued to add to her holdings.

In January 1999, Martha paid $80,000 for 2,500 shares of ImClone at $32 a share. This was not a significant investment for her. Even after a stock split in 2000 raised her holding to 5,000 shares, her total investment in ImClone represented only .03 of 1 percent of her post-IPO net worth, by one estimate.

Sam and Martha invested in several other businesses together, including a venture capital firm called the Sudbury Group and iBeauty. com, an online beauty products boutique. At iBeauty, Sam was chairman and chief stockholder, his daughter Elana worked as vice president for corporate development, and his son-in-law Jarrett Posner was a director, as was Martha Stewart.

In the meantime, Sam was spending hours and hours in courtrooms and thousands of dollars on attorneys' fees. Throughout the 1990s, he faced a long list of lawsuits, tax liens, and judgments brought against him from friends, charities, contractors, realtors, hotels, consulting firms, account trustees, businesses, and tax authorities.

Some of these cases have the tincture of personal animus—such as when a man named Melvin Epstein sued Sam for $1 in 1995 (the case was dismissed). The Nancy Davis Foundation for Multiple Sclerosis sued him when he refused to pay the $25,000 he had pledged for "the Race to Erase MS" charity event in Aspen (Ogilvy & Mather, the advertising firm run by Martha's friend Charlotte Beers, paid $7,500 of the debt). He was sued by an auction house for bouncing a $57,886.69 check. He was sued by an investor in Sam's Café, the restaurant he owned with Mariel Hemingway and her husband. He was sued by a Manhattan realtor for paying only two months' rent on a one-year,

$25,000-a-month apartment lease (he claimed the apartment was filled with defects). He was sued by numerous banks, and the Bank of New York won a $184,129 judgment against him. American Express sued and recouped $16,455 from Sam for an unpaid credit card bill. He faced tax liens that ranged from $60,990.37 to $178,772.87.

Many of these extrascientific ventures turned into costly distractions. Sam invested in movies like *The Last Party* (starring Robert Downey Jr.), magazines like *Nylon,* Manhattan real estate including BDB Development, which converted factory buildings into apartments in SoHo and TriBeCa, and several dot-com companies (most of which failed).

In February 2000, Sam was sued by Tina Sharkey, a former executive at Children's Television Workshop, who Sam had recruited as CEO of iBeauty.com. She alleged that he had "misled" her about iBeauty by falsely claiming that the company had $10 million to $15 million in cash, that its revenues were set to triple in 1999, that a sophisticated Web site would be built, and that a top Internet analyst from Morgan Stanley would take the company public. None of these things proved true, her suit claimed. When Sharkey quit iBeauty, Sam refused to pay her salary. She demanded $380,000 in unpaid compensation and legal fees, and $5 million in punitive damages. The suit was settled in 2000; terms of the agreement have not been made public.

In August 2001, just as the deal between ImClone and Bristol-Myers Squibb was about to close, Sam was sued again—to the tune of $57.7 million this time, for "fraud and extreme emotional distress"—by Gabriella Forte, the prickly former head of Giorgio Armani and Calvin Klein, Inc. Sam had recruited Forte as Tina Sharkey's replacement at iBeauty.com. Forte alleged that Sam had lied to her about the company's financial state and didn't pay her salary at a time when her husband was suffering from cancer and heart disease. Within a week of joining iBeauty, Forte charged, she discovered that the company was over $4 million in debt, had shrinking sales, no CFO, was being sued by a major vendor, and was, along with Sam himself, being sued by Tina Sharkey. Although Sam contacted cancer specialists on her husband's behalf, Forte alleged that Sam "willfully and purposefully misrepresented that he would provide funding for iBeauty with the intent of causing Ms. Forte . . . to continue as CEO."

Asked about this, Sam snapped: "Gabriella *quit* iBeauty, she wasn't fired, and then she wanted to be paid all this money. I think the company didn't want to pay her." He waved his hand in front of his face, as if to shoo away a fly, and added, "It's being settled." (Forte had no comment.)

Asked about this remarkable string of legal actions Sam shrugged, and with a slight grin said, "I'm not always charming. I don't like to be charming all the time. Do you think that's a bad thing?"

Yet his charm remained such that many would leap to his defense or recall his spontaneous acts of kindness.

An acquaintance recalled the rainy night she sat on a street corner, crying, when Sam suddenly appeared out of the gloom, sat beside her on the curb, bought her a cup of tea, and walked her home. "He was really wonderful, even though I didn't know him that well. A very generous man. It's so strange to think this was the same person that would get into so much trouble."

In response to an article in *Barron's* that had detailed some of his bad behavior and profligacy, Ian Alterman, a former ImClone legal secretary—known around the office for playing show tunes, hosting ice-cream socials, and living with his mother—wrote: "God knows Sam and Harlan aren't angels; none of us are. But neither are they the unscrupulous, devious, egotists you make them out to be . . . Sam and Harlan have maintained ImClone through the stormiest and most unstable period for new biotech companies."

Sam had great social aspirations, and at the same time that he was promoting C225 to the scientific and financial communities, he was climbing the social ladder of fin de siècle New York. He dated Alexis Stewart, the socialite Patricia Duff, and the actress Fran Drescher *(The Nanny)*. He socialized with Lally Weymouth, heir to the *Washington Post* fortune, and Shirley Lord, wife of *The New York Times* editor Abe Rosenthal. He lunched with Tina Brown at the Four Seasons. He befriended the banker Steven Rattner, the investor Arthur Altschul Jr. (brother of MTV's Serena Altschul), the society photographer Patrick McMullen, and the actor Terrence Stamp, among many others. And in the late 1990s, he began to build a stunning collection of paintings—including works by Picasso, Braque, Chagall, Kandinsky, Twombly, and Gorky—which he displayed in his SoHo loft. He acquired most of these paintings from the high-profile art dealer Larry Gagosian, who has galleries in New York and Los Angeles.

"I heard he'd buy paintings from Gagosian at a huge premium," said an art-world friend of Sam's. "The weird thing is he knew Larry was overcharging him, but he didn't care, because it bought him entrée to that world." Indeed, Sam began to hitchhike rides on Gagosian's private jet and to spend vacations on the Caribbean resort island of St. Bart's with the art dealer. Another member of this social set was Harvey Weinstein, the cohead of Miramax Films, who was both a friend of Sam's and an investor in ImClone and Scientia.

"Sam is a very clever guy, but he's a nebbish—a nerd—whose desperation to be part of the fast crowd is so obvious that people would joke about it," recalled a longtime friend. "The sad thing is, he was always so much smarter than the rest of them. They'd go out in big groups and sit at a restaurant table, drinking and smoking cigars, and rating women as they walked by. It was adolescent. Say what you will about Sam, he is a brilliant scientist. So why would he want to waste his time with these people? He is prepared to do whatever it takes, at whatever cost, to become 'a player.' And from the moment I met him I felt he was going to trip himself up by trying to be something he isn't."

In the summer of 2001, just before the BMS deal closed, another friend of Sam's observed: "Sam Waksal is too good to be true. It won't last. It *can't* last. I don't know how and I don't know when, but he *will* crash—and it ain't gonna be pretty."

AT A LITTLE AFTER eight o'clock on the morning of Tuesday, September 11, 2001, Sam and Harlan gathered their top executives at ImClone's offices in SoHo. At nine they were scheduled to host a conference call with financial analysts and journalists to announce what Sam called "the biggest deal in the history of biotech." (While there have been far larger deals in biotech, such as Amgen's $11.1 billion takeover of Immunex, it was true that the ImClone-Bristol venture was the largest deal between a biotech firm and a pharmaceutical company for a single product.) It was a beautiful, clear blue morning, and all of New York seemed to spangle in the sun. At about 8:50 A.M., just moments before the conference call was to get underway, Sam's private cell phone rang. It was his eldest daughter, Elana Waksal Posner, calling from the sidewalk a few blocks south, in a panic.

Elana was 29, a moon-faced, raven-haired lawyer who was married to Jarrett Posner, grandson of the late corporate raider Victor Posner (whom the SEC barred from securities trading for his role in the Milken-Boesky scandal). Campaigning for a seat on the city's district council that day, Elana, Jarrett, and her mother Cindy had been greeting commuters as they poured out of the subways and the PATH trains from New Jersey. At 8:46 A.M., the hijacked American Airlines Flight 11 roared straight into the north tower of the World Trade Center, directly above them.

"Dad!" shouted Elana. "I'm standing under the World Trade Center and a plane just flew into it! The building's on fire!"

Sam rushed into his large, disheveled office on the southwest corner of the Varick Street building. There, framed in the large plate glass window behind his desk, was the North Tower, a gash scythed at an angle into its striped silver facade between the 83rd and 89th floors. Orange flames and thick black smoke billowed into the azure sky, incongruously. The wind was blowing the smoke plume southeast, so that tons of dust and burned scraps of paper were fluttering down onto lower Manhattan, the East River, and across Brooklyn.

"Elana, get off the street!" Sam shouted into the phone. "Come up here right now!"

He scrambled the ImClone staff into his office, which afforded them a view of the second hijacked plane, United Airlines Flight 175, slashing into the south tower, between the 78th and 84th floors. In a rushed phone call, Sam and Peter Dolan agreed to postpone the announcement of their deal until another time. A crowd gathered in Sam's office. They stood in silence, frowning, arms crossed, watching the chaos at the end of the island and the eventual collapse of both trade towers.

"People were dying just a few blocks away, and it was just too much . . . none of us could concentrate on the deal," Sam recalled. "But the next day we decided that it was important to continue on with our work. What we do is help make the world better. To not do our job allows evil to win. I'm a child of [Holocaust] survivors. What do you say when you walk out of a concentration camp? What do you say when you see people jumping out of the World Trade Center? Camus [ *sic* actually, it was Sartre] said, 'Life begins on the other side of despair.' I believe that. Our job is to move forward."

The next day, on September 12, Charles Heimbold stepped down as Bristol's chairman and CEO. He immediately flew off to Sweden to take up his ambassadorship at a time of great uncertainty and international tension. The transition was smooth, and Peter Dolan picked up where his mentor had left off. Indeed, while there were many people's fingerprints on the ImClone deal, the general perception was that it was "Dolan's baby." But this was incorrect, said a former BMS executive: "Heimbold was fully aware of the deal. He can't push [the responsibility] all off on Dolan. This was just as much Charlie's deal. And I'm sure they all went into it with the best of intentions."

ON SEPTEMBER 19, the deal between ImClone and Bristol-Meyers Squibb was finally signed and announced. Bristol would pay $1 billion to acquire 14.4 million shares, or 20 percent of ImClone's common stock, and another $1 billion to ImClone in three milestone payments tied to the successful development and FDA approval of Erbitux (C225). Sam declared that it was "the first major deal on Wall Street since the terrorist attack."

In a conference call with shareholders that day, he was asked how Study 9923, ImClone's clinical trials of Erbitux, was going. "We completed that trial," Sam answered. "It went very well. We'll be announcing that data at the next available conference that we can announce it at . . . We believe we will be successful in gaining [FDA] approval because of the data that we've generated thus far."

On October 29, 2001, thousands of ImClone's shareholders participated in the BMS tender offer to purchase ImClone stock at $70 a share, a 40 percent premium over its trading price, $50 a share. Although all ImClone shareholders were allowed to tender their shares of ImClone stock to BMS, only the Waksals, Robert Goldhammer, and Dr. Arnold Levine were given loans by ImClone to purchase ImClone stock at the highly discounted price of about $8 a share, and then tender it to BMS at $70 per share. Sam sold 814,674 shares and Harlan sold 776,450 shares, or just more than 20 percent of each of their holdings; together, the Waksals netted some $111 million.

News of the deal jumped ImClone stock 13 percent, to $56.60.

"BRISTOL-MYERS DEAL Gives ImClone Execs a Big Payday," was the title of a report written by Adam Feuerstein, who covered biotech for *theStreet.com,* a Web magazine popular in the investment community. He had been closely tracking the rise of ImClone all year. Most of his stories about the company had a generally positive tone, and he had a good working relationship with the Waksals.

In his September 19 article about the BMS deal, Feuerstein characterized ImClone's loans in June to the Waksal brothers as "sweetheart loans," and the deal as "lucrative and risk-free" for them. He quoted Wall Street executives who questioned the timing and propriety of such a deal and he quoted Sam defending his payout. But the piece was generally upbeat and ended on a positive note, saying that Bristol was confident the FDA would approve Erbitux, which could become a multibillion-dollar product.

"It's a legitimate question to ask whether this deal was as much about the Waksals personal financial gain as it was about the financial interest of other shareholders," said one analyst. And a biotech fund manager said: "Sam and Harlan deserve to make some money for shouldering the risk of [Erbitux] . . . but there is something questionable about these guys cashing out before we even know if this drug is going to get approved." Sam bristled at the idea that he and Harlan were profiting unfairly. "This was a perfectly reasonable thing to do," Sam said. He noted that because ImClone's loans had come in the form of interest-bearing promissory notes, "the company was never out any cash; in fact, it's making money through interest payments." He added that ImClone had received legal advice that concluded the deals were entirely aboveboard. "I and other executives and directors have to tender our shares if we're recommending to our shareholders that they do the same. To not tender our shares would send the wrong message. We have a lot of shareholders who believe that our stock will go much higher than $70 when the FDA approves Erbitux."

The next day, the phone in Feuerstein's office in San Francisco rang. It was Harlan Waksal calling. "How dare you?!" he shouted. "My next call is to my lawyer! We're going to sue you, and we're going to sue *theStreet.com!* You're just jealous because I'm successful!"

Harlan was shouting so loudly that Feuerstein had to hold the phone about two feet from his ear. People in the office began to stare at him and giggle. Harlan eventually calmed down and Feuerstein asked: "Is there anything in the story that is factually inaccurate? Because if there is, I want to correct it."

"No, there's nothing *factually* incorrect," Harlan snapped. "I just don't like your *tone,* the *insinuations* you're making."

After Feuerstein put the phone down, his office mates burst into laughter. *TheStreet.com* stood by the story. Feuerstein never heard from the Waksals again. Indeed, from that point on they labeled him a persona non grata: no one at ImClone would deign to give an interview to him, and the Waksals and their supporters went out of their way to snub him.

He wasn't alone. Analysts and investors who didn't tow the ImClone line found themselves pressured by the Waksals. Sam would do it subtly, with an insinuating wagging of the finger, or a cold shoulder, at investment conferences. Harlan would make phone calls: sometimes they were polite but insistent in tone—"the message was, 'What don't you understand here? We're *right*,'" recalled one financier. At other times, Harlan would yell and berate his listeners. "Harlan got pissed about an [investment] note I wrote," recalled an analyst. "Then Andrea Rabney—not realizing who she was talking to—called our firm 'a bucket shop,' and said we were putting out a lot of bullshit about ImClone. I guess we hit a nerve."

ON OCTOBER 25, Bristol's physician advisory board (PAB) gathered at the Ritz-Carlton in Palm Beach. The group of eminent oncologists had flown in from around the country for a meeting and to toast Tom Jordan. The board's members gathered around large folding tables in a ballroom bisected by a beige soundproof screen. On the second day of the three-day meeting, John Mendelsohn and Susan Arbuch, Bristol's newly appointed chief scientist, presented an overview of the latest Erbitux data. For an hour, Mendelsohn reviewed the role of EGF receptors in cancer and the value of blocking them with his antibody.

"Bristol was very interested in our reaction to Mendelsohn's presentation of the *science*—whether we felt that it [gave] a sufficient rationale for the way the clinical trial was designed," recalled one member of the board. The PAB's answer was a qualified yes. It was qualified, this person said, because it implied a question: *So what?* "If one had delved a little deeper, most of us around that table had long [understood] that basic science underpinnings don't predict clinical outcomes." In other words, one can cull promising data from the lab and clinical trials, but until a new drug is administered to a large group of patients and proves effective, the preclinical data doesn't add up to very much.

Had the PAB been asked to comment on Study 9923, they would

have asked whether all of the patients in the ImClone trial had failed to respond to their previous therapies. "Everybody assumed that if these patients were said to be refractory [not responding] to irinotecan, then they were truly refractory," said the oncologist. "We took it at face value that BMS had done its due diligence." But the PAB wasn't asked to comment on ImClone's clinical trial. Nor were they asked whether they thought ImClone was a good investment for BMS.

By this point, it would later be revealed, Bristol's due diligence had discovered that ImClone's clinical trial was fundamentally flawed: Study 9923 did not include enough eligible patients; the patients' responses to the anticancer cocktail were a good deal lower than ImClone had reported; and, furthermore, the FDA would have to set two precedents to approve Erbitux. First, the agency would have to approve a new drug in a two-drug combination (in this case, Erbitux plus irinotecan), which it had never done; second, it would have to approve the drug without the human data to justify the dose. ImClone's new drug application offered no rationale for the dose it recommended. None of this crucial information was presented by Bristol to its PAB, however.

"The company didn't use the group wisely," said one member, frustrated that his knowledge went untapped for three days. "We don't create the agenda for these meetings. It's their agenda. They showed us the data, and we said 'it looks okay.' What else can you say? . . . Whether this group will continue is uncertain."

On the third and last night of the meeting, the group met in a private dining room at the Ritz-Carlton for a retirement party. The usual cocktails and karaoke setup notwithstanding, there was sadness in the air.

At age 55, Tom Jordan had grown tired of the constant turf wars within Bristol and was retiring to start his own consulting business. He was only the latest to quit, in what was turning into a group exodus from Bristol's once dominant and pioneering oncology group. A brilliant, irascible bunch, these long-time employees felt they did not belong in the "new" Bristol of Peter Dolan and his slick lieutenants—the bright young men who had devised a color-coded system to rank employee effectiveness (Jordan didn't fit into any category, someone noted, and should be given his own color), and had aggressively promoted business strategies that would soon blow up.

Late on the evening of October 27, after heartfelt speeches and a splash or two of cognac, Jordan lumbered to the microphone for a rendition of his signature number, Frank Sinatra's "My Way." Then he attempted a Britney Spears song. Finally, a hotel staff member distributed various hats to the oncologists for a group rendition of the 1980s disco hit "YMCA." It was a sight to behold: Robert Young, the straitlaced chairman of the PAB, wore a hard hat; Frank Greco, a community oncologist from Nashville, and Branimir Sikic of Stanford, wore other macho headgear. They all joined in a song that struck at least one participant as a weirdly appropriate farewell to the youthful, heedless new leadership at BMS:

> *Young man, are you listening to me?*
> *I said, young man, what do you want to be?*
> *I said, young man, you can make real your dreams.*
> *but you got to know this one thing.*
> *No man does it all by himself!*

In New York, meanwhile, Sam Waksal felt a mix of emotions. Relief, most of all. It had been a long struggle, but the Bristol deal was finally done and ImClone was being hailed as the great success he had always promised it would be. Now he had more money in the bank than he had ever dared to dream was possible. It seemed almost unreal, yet absolutely right. "It was a feeling of great vindication," he said. "When you work against the established paradigm for so long, it feels great to finally make it happen. It makes me smile." He shook his head, adding, "But I'm the kind of person who, once he does something like this, he wakes up the next day and says, 'What can I do next that surpasses that?' What's *next?*"

The year 2001 would prove to be the defining one for ImClone and nearly everyone associated with it. That fall they all seemed to be happy and thriving. John Mendelsohn had finally secured the future of his brainchild, Erbitux. Sam and Harlan Waksal were on a roll and gave no indication that any trouble was brewing at the FDA. Martha Stewart had realized her dream with the creation of MSO and was enjoying her best year in business ever. The stockbroker Peter Bacanovic had built a solid client list at Merrill Lynch, and, despite a recession, was enjoying a refined social life. Peter Dolan and his team at Bristol-Myers Squibb were breathing a sigh of relief: it hadn't been easy or cheap, but they had found a replacement for Taxol; now they could get on to other pressing matters.

The complex trajectories of these very different lives had intersected, and for the next few months each of them would exist in a state of heightened grace.

PART TWO

# REFUSAL TO FILE

EIGHT

# *The Letter*

On December 4, 2001, Lily Waiyee Lee, ImClone's chief of regulatory affairs, boarded a train from New Jersey to Washington, D.C. She was en route to an unscheduled visit to the FDA's reviewers at Woodmont I, the FDA's odd, mirrored-cube-and-tilted-pyramid building in Rockville, Maryland. The agency wasn't due to render its verdict on Erbitux until the end of the month, and there was no compelling reason for Lee to visit the FDA at that moment; nor had the agency encouraged such a visit. Nevertheless, Lee, a petite 46-year-old Asian woman, had a convenient excuse: she was going to be in town for a meeting of the Oncologic Drugs Advisory Committee (ODAC), an independent group of academics that advises the FDA on new drugs. While in the capital she wanted to drop off some CT scans—data on 17 patients from the Erbitux single-agent trial. The CT scans could easily have been sent by Federal Express, or even by e-mail, of course, but that wasn't the point.

After boarding the train, Lee typed a quick e-mail to George Mills, the FDA reviewer who headed the Erbitux team, alerting him to her impending arrival.

A balding man of medium height and complexion, Mills appeared to be a government bureaucrat straight out of Central Casting. He and his colleagues worked in cramped offices, and his salary barely edged into six figures, a third of what he could command in private practice. Yet Mills was a skilled diagnostic radiologist, the FDA's expert on assessing cancer tumor response. The reviewers took the responsibility of their position seriously: their decisions about drugs had a tremendous impact on patients, doctors, and the marketplace. And so when people like Lily Lee—well-compensated agents of aggressive drug companies—occasionally dropped by Woodmont I to try to gauge their drugs' prospects, the FDA people resented it.

Mills remembered Lee. In 1999, when she worked for the Lipsome Company, she had presented the FDA with data on Evacet, a new formulation of the cancer drug doxorubicin: the new drug was less likely to cause heart damage than conventional doxorubicin, but was less effective in fighting breast cancer. The agency had turned it down. Erbitux, on the other hand, had an excellent chance of being approved by the FDA.

ImClone wasn't seeking "full approval," which would have required proof of the drug's benefit to patients, but rather "accelerated approval," the fast-track shortcut intended to speed lifesaving drugs to patients. Moreover, whenever an experimental therapy comes to the FDA with political support and visibility in the media, as was resoundingly the case with Erbitux, the FDA tended to shield itself from criticism by deferring to outside advisers like an ODAC panel. Indeed, at investor conferences throughout the fall, Sam Waksal had hinted that Erbitux would bypass the FDA and end up in front of ODAC, most likely in the hearing scheduled for February 2002. Once there, he predicted, Erbitux would quickly gain approval and be on the market by June.

Sam had reason to be confident. In examining a new compound, ODAC has only three hours to hear the data, debate it, and make a recommendation. The committee doesn't always catch mistakes or flawed research. Sam loved to put on a show, and he would pull out all the stops for ODAC. But to get in front of an ODAC panel he would first have to pass muster with the FDA reviewers.

GEORGE MILLS and his colleagues were dismayed by the Erbitux application. Since August 2000, Mills had asked ImClone executives—in face-to-face meetings, phone calls, e-mails, and by fax—about important data that was required but missing. The company's responses had been strangely vague or dismissive.

The FDA's concerns had been clearly stated: ImClone's clinical trial had too few patients and was poorly structured; tumor shrinkage had not been sufficiently documented; the company had violated the study protocol and had not given a justification for its recommended dose of the drug. Plus, the agency had always maintained that the Erbitux-irinotecan cocktail was unacceptable because there was no way to separate the effects of each drug: if a patient's tumors shrank, was it due to Erbitux or the chemotherapy? Perhaps most important, ImClone had failed to document that all 120 patients in the clinical trial met eligibility requirements: in fact, 37 patients proved to be ineligible—a huge number for such a small trial, enough, in fact, to render its results moot.

For months the FDA reviewers had stressed these points. ImClone had acknowledged there were problems with its application, but had done little to rectify them.

Still, Patricia Keegan, Mills's boss and the deputy director at the FDA Center for Biologics Evaluation and Research (CBER), decided to give Erbitux the benefit of the doubt. For patients who had reached stage 4 cancer, she reasoned, a promising drug tested in a flawed trial was better than no drug at all. In August 2001, ImClone and the FDA reached an unusual compromise. The company could continue its two-drug trial, Study 9923, as long as it started a new trial that would test Erbitux alone, Study 0141. Their hypothesis was that the first trial would show that the two-drug combination worked well, while the second would show that Erbitux was less effective as a single agent but perhaps beneficial. This would not be as reliable a comparison as a "randomized trial," where patients are assigned to receive either Therapy A or Therapy B, but it was a workable solution.

The compromise left ImClone little room for error. The number of patients in the two-agent trial was so small that losing a few would have a ruinous effect on the data. In a worst-case scenario, such mistakes could trigger a refusal to file (RTF) letter, an extremely rare event. An RTF letter is the FDA's measure of last resort, an official correspondence that says that a sponsoring company's application is so deficient that it cannot be evaluated. Because there is a good deal of communication between the FDA and the drug companies in the application process, a flawed application is almost always corrected, or withdrawn, before an RTF is sent. No company wants to face the unusual humiliation of an RTF letter.

On October 31, ImClone completed its Biologic License Application (BLA) for Erbitux and submitted its data to the FDA, including the clinical records for Study 9923 and Study 0141. This started a clock ticking: under the fast-track rules, the FDA was required to complete its review of Erbitux within 60 days. Up to this point, the agency had relied on the Waksals' assurances, along with records from their investigational new drug (IND) file, that ImClone's data package would be complete and satisfactory by the time it was all filed.

Once Mills had ImClone's clinical data in hand, however, it was immediately apparent the Erbitux application was flawed. As the FDA review continued into November, significant problems continued to crop up.

An important set of CT scans—those showing that patients' conditions had worsened on a previous therapy with irinotecan—were missing from the ImClone package, for instance. When Mills pointedly asked about this omission, Lily Lee explained that the doctors hadn't ordered the scans, but had relied instead on their "clinical judgment." In other words, there was no record of those patients whose health had worsened despite treatment with irinotecan.

This answer left Mills scratching his head. For a drug to be approved there needed to be careful documentation of every step in its development. The missing CT scans were essential information; someone's "clinical judgment" was beside the point. Now Mills began to wonder about ImClone: was the fast-talking biotech company making innocent mistakes? Were its eminent scientists lax? Or was there perhaps a darker motive at work, and the company was being intentionally vague or misleading?

Trained as a radiologist, Mills repeatedly questioned the company's assessment of tumor shrinkage, and it was here that he discovered something of a "smoking gun" that confirmed his suspicions. Sam Waksal had claimed that in the original trial of 120 colorectal cancer patients in Study 9923—the trial inspired by Shannon Kellum's remarkable turnaround and overseen by Dr. Leonard Saltz—tumors had shrunk by half in 27 patients, a 22.5 percent response rate. Sam Waksal had loudly touted this significant response rate to journalists and investors as a sign of his drug's effectiveness. But upon closer inspection, Mills discovered that the independent radiologists assessing the data had disagreed about the tumor shrinkage in 15 of these patients—a huge percentage in such a small trial, and a salient fact that Waksal had neglected to mention. This meant that patients' response to Erbitux was actually less than half what ImClone had claimed it was.

Mills's sense of alarm grew. When he called ImClone, the company's scientists remained unable or unwilling to explain these missing pieces.

Harlan Waksal, who was in charge of the clinical trials, had an imperious demeanor and showed little willingness to delve into details with the agency. Lily Lee had only been working at ImClone for a few months: when she was hired, some at the FDA had seen her as a breath of fresh air; after all, she had experience representing a drug before the agency and was considered a straight shooter. But now Lee appeared no more credible than her ImClone colleagues.

The FDA's clock was ticking louder and louder. As November tipped into December and the 60-day grace period was running down, it was obvious that the Erbitux application was so deficient that it did not meet the legal requirement of an "adequate and well-controlled" clinical trial. ImClone's maddeningly circular arguments convinced Mills that it would be pointless to proceed until the company provided better data. If it could not do so, then the agency would have no choice but to respond with an RTF letter.

The FDA review team would meet in mid-December to make a group decision about the Erbitux application. Until then, Mills decided, he would reveal nothing about his own very firm opinion.

SAM WAKSAL, in the meantime, had been working overtime to promote ImClone and its drug. In July, *Business Week* had run a lengthy cover story headlined, "The Birth of a Cancer Drug: After more than 20 years and $100 million, IMC-225 is awaiting FDA approval: Will ImClone's big effort pay off?" The article was an informative report on the "radical drug" that "could be a blockbuster"—noting that Erbitux had "demonstrated remarkable success in causing colon cancer to regress in patients who had failed to respond to all other treatments." But in places the line between fact and wishful thinking was blurred. Most notably, the story reported that as a result of using Erbitux Shannon Kellum "remains free of the disease today." This was not true. While Kellum had recovered from certain death and was able to work and exercise, she still had cancer.

The boosterish claim that Erbitux had "cured" her particularly ran-kled Kellum's oncologist, Dr. Mark Rubin. "I never said that," he re-called. "In fact, *Business Week* never bothered to interview me." He added that he thought he knew who the source of such a claim might have been, but declined to name that person. "Journalists will believe any-thing you tell them," he muttered.

The *Business Week* story, along with Sam's insistence to Wall Street that Erbitux "will be huge—a drug that is going to alter the way cancer therapy is done," and would be on the market by June 2002, steadily drove ImClone's stock price up and up. On December 4, nearly a million shares of the company were traded, and by the closing bell its price had reached $71.65.

WHEN GEORGE MILLS received Lily Lee's e-mail that morning, he im-mediately deduced her true intentions. She, or someone at ImClone, was getting nervous about the status of Erbitux, and wanted to find out if the FDA would rebuff them with an RTF letter. Lee was inbound to smoke him out.

Such "impromptu" drop-ins by company representatives were not common at the FDA, but they were not unheard of either. Mills was an experienced regulator and he knew how it would go. After the usual in-troductory pleasantries, Lee would steer the conversation back to some variation of the same question that burned in the mind of every phar-maceutical executive on the FDA's doorstep: *Do you like my drug? Are you going to make me or break me?*

These meetings were invariably tense. Mills sighed and steeled him-self, but out of professional courtesy he agreed to meet Lee in the lobby.

The lobby of Woodmont I was not a comfortable place to talk. Its hard surfaces echoed sound, and the only seats available were a few stone benches in a sunken pit amid anemic plants. Before he descended to the lobby, Mills asked Lee Pai-Scherf, an FDA clinical reviewer, to ac-company him: in a potentially sticky situation like this, he wanted to have another agency person there for backup and corroboration.

When Lee arrived, Mills politely accepted her CT scans and a brief, stiff conversation ensued. As things would turn out, this was a crucial turning point in the ImClone story.

Lee's polite chitchat quickly gave way to a series of leading questions about Erbitux. Mills listened impassively, answered briefly, and made an effort not to betray any sign of his true thoughts through body language. "I characterized it with Dr. Lee very carefully," he would later testify before Congress. "I wanted to maintain a very even balance, while I knew that my recommendation and Dr. Keegan's was that we should refuse to file."

Mills's air of quiet focus must have unnerved Lee. She grew increasingly frustrated. Although she'd deny it when testifying before Congress six months later, Mills and Pai-Scherf recalled that Lee finally blurted out her question, point-blank: "Is there a chance we'll receive an RTF?"

Her voice had taken on an edge. After all the attention Sam Waksal had generated for Erbitux, an RTF letter would have a catastrophic effect on ImClone—not to mention Bristol-Myers Squibb, their investors, and the legions of desperate cancer patients whose hopes had by now been raised to a fever pitch.

Mills paused a beat as he carefully composed his answer. "I reviewed the four options that could occur, but was careful to maintain an even weight to them because we hadn't arrived at a formal decision," he recounted. He told Lily Lee that the FDA had the option to: 1) review the application or 2) issue an RTF letter. ImClone, meanwhile, had the option to 3) revise its Erbitux application or 4) withdraw it altogether.

With that, the alarm bells should have been ringing in Lee's head. Mills's mention of the latter option—that ImClone could withdraw its application—was a clear sign that Erbitux was in trouble. There was no other reason to mention it.

This was certainly the message Mills intended to send, he testified. Lee had taken part in all of the conversations with the FDA and she was well aware of the agency's reservations about the Erbitux data. Furthermore, he pointed out, if she wasn't worried about ImClone's application then why was she standing in the lobby of Woodmont I pumping him for information?

It was a highly charged encounter, Mills told Congress. "It's remarkable to me that at that moment in time, halfway through the review cycle . . . to be able to tell a sponsor that [withdrawal] is a consideration, and you should consider it."

But the significance of Mills's hint apparently escaped Lee. In her testimony, she recalled Mills presenting her with only three options: 1) acceptance of the application by the FDA; 2) amendment of data by ImClone; 3) an RTF letter. "Any drugs that file an application are subject to those three things," she said.

After 10 minutes of standing in the lobby of Woodmont I, the conversation flagged uncomfortably. Mills began glancing at his watch. Pai-Scherf watched the glass elevator sliding up the inside of the atrium. Lily Lee eventually took the hint and left.

The next day, December 5, Mills caucused the FDA review team and they formally agreed to issue ImClone an RTF letter.

ON THE AFTERNOON of December 4, Lily Lee had described her conversation with the FDA reviewers in a phone call to Harlan and in an e-mail that quickly made the rounds at ImClone and Bristol-Myers Squibb. In the e-mail, she neglected to mention option 4, the option to withdraw the Erbitux application. Nevertheless, the more experienced and skeptical Bristol scientists understood Mills's coded message: the drug was in serious trouble. They knew that he would not have bothered to mention an RTF unless it was a very real possibility.

Three days later a BMS expert regulatory affairs executive, Beth Seidenberg, e-mailed colleagues that she was not convinced that ImClone fully appreciated its predicament: "a refusal to file decision doesn't appear altogether unlikely at this point," she wrote.

In retrospect, everyone involved—FDA reviewers and officials at ImClone and BMS—would point to early December as the moment when the tone of the conversations between the agency and the companies changed dramatically.

But at the time, Sam Waksal believed that despite the shortcomings of his clinical trials, and the FDA's many warnings about the paucity of Erbitux data, it seemed probable—even likely—that Erbitux would be approved. As far as he was concerned, the emotional testimony of terminally ill cancer patients like Shannon Kellum, the tremendous amount of media attention and political goodwill garnered by the drug, the comforting presence of the well-regarded Bristol-Myers Squibb, and the huge speculative bets placed on ImClone by large and small investors, all conspired to put the leaderless, underfunded FDA on the spot. How could they say no to a drug that could save the lives of 22.5 percent of patients who had no other options? Especially, he'd point out, when the FDA had approved irinotecan with a mere 13 percent response rate?

Waksal's calculus was likely that the FDA would duck a confrontation over a high-profile drug like Erbitux. The agency would probably ask an ODAC panel to review ImClone's data, as it had done in other cases, and base its ruling on the ODAC's recommendation. There were sure to be tough questions about ImClone's data, or admonitions about the lack of communication with the FDA. But if anyone could mount a persuasive presentation for ODAC it was the scientific impresario Sam Waksal. All in all, then, Sam must have figured that Erbitux's chances for approval were better than even.

At Bristol-Myers, Peter Dolan must have seen the troubling reports about ImClone, but he was desperate for a new oncology drug. Besides, it was not really under his control: ImClone was still handling the Erbitux application to the FDA, not Bristol.

In essence, the two companies just kept running as fast as they could, and hoped that somehow Erbitux would squeeze through the FDA review. The alternative was unimaginable.

AT THE END OF OCTOBER, Tina Brown and Harry Evans hosted a party for the British historian Simon Schama at their Sutton Place home. It was a beautiful, warm night and the crowd was fabulous—Lauren Hutton, George Plimpton, Barry Diller and Diane von Furstenberg, Charlie Rose, Martin Scorsese, Morley Safer, the literary agent Lynn Nesbit, and numerous other recognizable names and faces. Sam Waksal was there, too, lurking under a tree near the bar in the apartment's leafy, walled-in garden. He wore a navy blue suit and seemed ill at ease. His head was cocked to one side and he kept peering around at the crowd, as if trying to spot someone who was angry with him or vice-versa. After a few pleasantries and a quick smile, he skittered off around the edge of the garden with a glass of white wine in hand.

Martha Stewart was dressed in yellow and held forth right in the center of the narrow garden. Everyone was buzzing now, the chatter grew loud, glasses clinked, and the party began to kick into gear. At one point, Martha suddenly toppled over backward, legs in the air, into the azalea bushes. Without dropping her canapé, or her poised expression, she got right back up and continued talking as if nothing had happened. Tina Brown smiled and everyone pretended that he hadn't seen it.

Although the stock market had begun to decline, and MSO's share price had dropped from a high of $37 to trade at around $18 a share,

Martha would say that she loved what she was doing and the way she was doing it. She was actively working to expand her business, with a new office in Manhattan and new products. She was also trying to streamline her personal finances. She'd invested with several brokers in many companies; as part of an overarching plan to simplify, she was thinking of selling off her ImClone holdings.

Although Sam and his younger daughter, Aliza, remained clients of Peter Bacanovic's, the Merrill Lynch broker had distanced himself from Sam. He'd convinced most of his clients to sell their ImClone shares, although for a long time Martha had remained loyal to Sam. ImClone's value had steadily increased, she pointed out, and Erbitux was about to hit the market. Finally, in October, after the Bristol deal had closed, she tried to sell her entire stake in ImClone. The Bristol tender offer was oversubscribed, however, and Martha could only dispose of 1,072 of the shares. That left her portfolio with 3,928 shares in ImClone.

In early November she told me that she had known Sam Waksal for years and years, and both liked and admired him. "The Bristol deal, Erbitux coming to market, all of this [was] a big deal for him," she said. After watching him work so hard, for so long, it was nice to see him become successful.

"Even though people complain that Sam's a wacko, and that he runs around [with women], his attention to real fundamentals of research and science are there," she said. "We've always kept our ImClone stock, believed in it, and profited *handsomely* from it."

IN NOVEMBER, Pete Peterson, the respected chairman of the Blackstone Group, an investment firm, and President Ford's secretary of the treasury, joined the ImClone board. He had met Sam in the Hamptons and had been intrigued; after calling a couple of friends about ImClone, he agreed to join the board.

On November 1, a research report put out by Sterling Financial read: "Based upon our analysis of the efficacy data surrounding Erbitux, we have formed a firm opinion that the drug currently lacks sufficient evidence to meet the FDA's regulatory approval standards."

But in midmonth, Morgan Stanley biotech analyst Doug Lind predicted that the FDA would approve Erbitux by April; he forecasted 2002 revenues for the drug at $167 million.

*     *     *

## The Letter

ON THE EVENING of December 6, Sam Waksal's spacious duplex loft in SoHo was packed with a rollicking, eclectic crowd for his annual Christmas party. Notables like Patricia Duff, Lally Weymouth, Mort Zuckerman, Marvin Traub, Andrew Stein, and Andrew Cuomo commingled with the scientists, lawyers, and bankers associated with their host's biotech firm. This year, one reveler noted, Sam's party featured more Wall Street analysts and fewer long-legged women with perfect cleavage in tiny black dresses than in the past. And there, in the midst of the swirl, was smiling Sam Waksal—whispering naughty gossip to Martha, who sat on the floor, posing with Mick Jagger for celebrity photographer Patrick McMullen, reveling with his guests as if he didn't have a care in the world. The party was a perfect amalgam of all that he had aspired to: big money and serious science spiced with celebrity and New York society, a perfect capstone to the most remarkable year of his career.

That morning—two days after Lily Lee's visit to George Mills at Woodmont I—ImClone stock hit its 52-week high of $75.45 a share, and Harlan had sold 700,000 shares, which netted him $50.35 million, bringing his total cash-out to $104,790,490. The following June, Harlan would testify before Congress that he had not based his exceptionally timely trade on any foreknowledge of the FDA's decision. "My trade was in the works for months," he'd say, claiming that the transaction was done for "tax purposes."

Sam had previously sold stock worth $57.02 million, and by this point had borrowed thousands more from the company. Yet, unbeknownst to nearly everyone—possibly including his brother—his personal debts had reached $80 million. At least $65 million of this staggering debt load was on margin, which was costing him some $800,000 a month to maintain. Yet Sam seemed happy, even giddy, at his party. His ability to compartmentalize allowed him to block out the terrible risks he was taking. In fact, his debt had been secured with his ImClone holdings, which meant that if the company's stock were to tumble he would be instantly wiped out.

"After the Bristol-Myers deal [closed], Sam was God for a while," said Elana Castaneda, a former girlfriend. "We all felt happy for him—he'd finally made it. But when you're at the top there's only one place to go: down."

\*       \*       \*

DECEMBER 2001 was a month of alternating good and bad news.

Sam was under a great deal of financial pressure to get Erbitux to market. Based on his promises of a quick approval by the FDA, investors had by now raised ImClone's market value to some $4.5 billion. And under terms of the Bristol deal, approval would trigger a $300 million payment from BMS to ImClone, which the biotech firm badly needed.

On December 12, the FDA, ImClone and Bristol-Myers Squibb held a tense teleconference. The agency's CBER reviewers asked for more information; they did not reveal that they had already decided to issue an RTF letter.

Five days later, ImClone was one of only seven biotech firms included for the first time in the NASDAQ 100 Index (National Association of Securities Dealers, an index of technology stocks), which was a great honor. Yet some on Wall Street were getting butterflies, and ImClone's stock price began to drop mysteriously.

Adam Feuerstein had written in *theStreet.com:* "Is something amiss at ImClone? . . . Fears of an Erbitux delay seem to be based more on educated guesswork than on real facts. Still, ImClone shares fell 6% Monday and Tuesday and are off another $3.64, or 5.5%, to $62.11 in Wednesday trading . . . unfortunately, all this is just speculation, because no one really seems to know what's going on between ImClone and the FDA . . . anxious investors are just going to have to ride out the storm."

On December 20, before the holiday break, Lily Lee called the FDA to ask once again about the status of Erbitux. An agency representative told her that the FDA would fax ImClone its answer in due course, and that the company should not contact the FDA again. This was plainly a brush-off. There were those at ImClone and BMS who immediately suspected that an RTF was a done deal. But others, like Sam, held out hope for a positive response from the FDA. "We were informed at the time that a decision had been made and that it would be coming sometime in the next week," Harlan recalled.

On December 21, ImClone issued a "blackout" order prohibiting its employees from trading in ImClone stock until after the FDA decision on Erbitux was made public. With nothing better to do, ImClone executives and their families began to scatter for the holidays—Harlan to ski in Telluride, Colorado, Sam to a Caribbean resort aboard a leased private jet.

On December 22, Brian Markison, BMS senior vice president for marketing, called Sam Turner, an attorney at Bennett, Turner & Coleman—Bristol's lobbyists—and asked him to use his back channels to find out how the FDA was planning to rule on Erbitux. On Christmas Eve, Turner called his old friend Richard Pazdur, the eminent oncologist who headed the FDA's CDER. Over the course of a long, amicable conversation, Turner wondered out loud if Pazdur knew the status of ImClone's drug application. According to media accounts and a congressional report, Pazdur let it slip that he was "99 percent sure" that ImClone would be getting a refusal-to-file letter. Turner wished Pazdur a happy holiday, signed off, and immediately called Markison, who was on his way to Christmas Mass.

On Christmas day, Markison called Harlan Waksal, who was skiing with his family in Telluride, Colorado, to warn him that the FDA would be rejecting Erbitux. Harlan called his brother, who, as usual, was spending the holidays at the resort island of St. Bart's with his art dealer, Larry Gagosian. Vacationing with them were friends/ImClone investors like Harvey Weinstein, of Miramax Films, the financier Arthur Altschul, and record producer Clive Davis. At the beach, Sam told a friend he had to return to New York "to take care of some business." He promised he would return to the island in a few days with Andrea Rabney, ImClone's 35-year-old director of communications and Sam's sometime romantic interest.

On December 26, the *Los Angeles Times* proclaimed: "Erbitux . . . is set to make one of the biggest splashes of 2002." The same day, ImClone sent a letter to the FDA in an attempt to stave off an RTF by offering to waive its rights to the 60-day deadline that the FDA had to meet by December 28. The agency declined the offer on the grounds that ImClone could not legally waive the deadline.

On December 26, Sam boarded his leased jet in St. Bart's and flew back to New York City. His friends on the beach were startled by his abrupt departure and wondered what it meant for their investments in ImClone. "Before he left St. Bart's I asked him if I should sell, and he told me the trouble was just people selling short," recalled one of Sam's pals. "He must have had his short list, and I wasn't on it."

Arriving back at his Thompson Street loft that night, Sam began to work the phones—first calling his father, Jack, and then, the following morning, his daughter Aliza. At 9:01 that morning, December 27, Aliza Waksal instructed Merrill Lynch to sell all of her 39,472 shares of Im-

Clone stock. Her broker, Peter Bacanovic, was on vacation in Miami, so his 26-year-old assistant, Douglas Faneuil, handled the trade.

Then, when Sam attempted to transfer 79,797 of his ImClone shares into his daughter's account, for another sale, Merrill compliance officers grew wary. Because Sam was a company insider, his trade was denied. The Wall Street rumor mill began cranking: something strange was happening at ImClone Systems. At 11:07 A.M. the stock dipped below $60 a share.

Sam and Harlan began frantically dialing people they knew at the FDA. Sam couldn't reach anyone until he finally hit upon a senior official at the Center for Biologics, whom he had known at the National Institutes of Health. It was the first time that Sam had personally interacted with the FDA over Erbitux. An internal ImClone note, dated noon on Thursday, December 27, 2001, reads: "Sam and Harlan are calling FDA to try to stop RTF."

AT 10 A.M. that morning, Ann E. Armstrong arrived at her desk and began to take down phone messages for Martha Stewart. It was two days after Christmas, one day after Boxing Day, in the slow week leading up to New Year's. Armstrong, Martha's personal assistant, was not in the habit of noting the time of each phone call. But she remembered speaking to Peter Bacanovic sometime between 10 and 11 A.M. that morning.

Martha's December 27 phone log reads, in part (most names have been omitted):

- Plum pudding was excellent! Thank ____.
- Peter Bacanovic thinks ImClone is going to start trading downward.
- ____ office asked if ____ could be on your helicopter to the boat.
- *Find fact sheet.*
- ____ wants to confirm a new date of ____ for shopping center opening in ____.
- ____ source of 4 tabletop lamps and chaise longue in ____.

At the time, Martha Stewart was thousands of feet up in the air, winging down to Cabo San Lucas, Mexico, where she would celebrate New Year's Eve at Las Ventanas, a resort. Accompanying her aboard her private jet were two old friends, Mariana Pasternak, a Westport Realtor, and Kevin Sharkey, the decorating editor of *Martha Stewart Living.* In the holiday spirit, Martha had surprised them with a resplendent airborne breakfast, which included champagne, caviar, foie-gras, and fresh melba toast. Sated, Martha eased back in her seat and turned her attention to her latest book, *Homekeeping,* a guide to home decoration and maintenance.

At 1:26 P.M., the plane touched down in San Antonio, Texas, to refuel. Martha stepped out to stretch and, while standing on the hot and blustery tarmac, placed a cell-phone call at 1:31 P.M. to Ann Armstrong to check her messages. That routine, 11-minute call would become a defining moment in her life—perhaps *the* defining moment. Armstrong read the message from Martha's broker: "Peter Bacanovic thinks ImClone is going to start trading downward."

Then Armstrong connected Martha, in Texas, with Bacanovic, in Florida, and hung up. At 1:43, Bacanovic's assistant at Merrill Lynch, Douglas Faneuil, executed the sale of all of Martha's remaining 3,928 shares of ImClone for $228,000. She made a relatively insubstantial profit of $64,000. (Had Martha sold her ImClone stock after the release of the FDA's decision, it is estimated that she would have lost $43,000.)

Also at 1:43, she called Sam's office. His phone log reads: "Martha Stewart . . . something is going on with ImClone and she wants to know what . . . She is on her way to Mexico . . . she is staying at Los Ventanos."

About an hour later, a Merrill Lynch analyst got on the squawk box to alert the firm's 15,000 brokers about ImClone. The stock was under intense selling pressure, it was rumored the FDA would issue an RTF for Erbitux, and the stock looked vulnerable.

"Sell!" The traders began dumping ImClone. By the end of the day, more than 7.7 million ImClone shares had been traded and the stock price dropped from $63.49 to $58.30.

ON FRIDAY AFTERNOON, December 28, Sam Waksal was pacing around his office, feeling nervously optimistic. He checked his watch. At any minute evaluators from the Food and Drug Administration were going to fax him a letter informing him whether or not he and his company ImClone could start manufacturing and selling the potentially revolutionary cancer treatment Erbitux—the drug that he believed would "change oncology forever." He was fairly certain the news would be good; there had been a few "bumps in the road," he conceded, but he figured Im-Clone could work those out. As he paced around his large, comfortably disheveled corner office, he glanced out the window at the darkening skyline. It was just days after the winter solstice and dusk was settling early over the Statue of Liberty and New York harbor. A few blocks south, the hole once filled by the World Trade towers began to fill with a harsh white glow from the giant Klieg lights at Ground Zero. At 2:55 P.M., just before the market shut down for the weekend, the fax machine began to spit out a nine-page letter from the FDA. Sam read each page as it came through, his emotions arcing from trepidation to hopefulness to stunned disbelief. In a highly unusual step—he once estimated it happens in less than 4 percent of all new drug applications—the FDA had sent a refusal to file letter, meaning the agency had discovered problems in the Erbitux data and would not consider the application.

The company's Erbitux application was "scientifically incomplete" and "filled with deficiencies," the private letter read. The data from Study 9923 was not "adequate and well controlled."

"I was in shock," Sam recalled a few days later. "I was very, very disappointed."

Sam's vignette is compelling. It makes one feel sorry for all of the dedicated people at ImClone who had toiled to bring Erbitux so far, only to have their hopes dashed by capricious bureaucrats obsessed with "documentation." But in light of evidence gathered in the subsequent investigations, it would become apparent that key executives at ImClone and BMS knew by the morning of December 26, at least, if not much earlier, that the FDA would be issuing an RTF. Also, the FDA faxed Lily Lee, at ImClone's offices in an industrial park in Somerville, New Jersey, first. She then refaxed the RTF to ImClone's Manhattan offices, on Varick Street. It is likely that Sam was not entirely shocked, therefore, when he finally read the letter for himself.

ImClone took its time in announcing the bad news to the public. Eventually, at 7:14 P.M. on Friday evening, the company sent out a terse press release:

> ImClone Systems Incorporated announced today that the U.S. Food and Drug Administration (FDA) has advised the Company that at this time it is not accepting for filing in its current form the Company's rolling Biologics License Application (BLA) for ERBITUX . . . Nei-

ther the acceptance nor non-acceptance of the BLA filing is a determination of the approvability of ERBITUX. The Company intends to meet with the FDA as soon as possible to discuss the requests for additional information made by the Agency in order for the filing to be accepted . . . "We will be working closely with the FDA toward the goal of an expeditious acceptance of our BLA," stated Samuel D. Waksal, Ph.D., President and Chief Executive Officer of ImClone Systems Incorporated. "Our goal is to get ERBITUX FDA-approved as soon as possible."

John Mendelsohn was in his office at M. D. Anderson in Houston that Friday when Sam Waksal called from New York with the bad news. Mendelsohn was taken aback. "Clearly this was a surprise to me," he would say. Adding that he'd had no idea the FDA had such major objections to ImClone's application, he said, "I knew the FDA had been talking with the company about some of the issues raised in the letter. I didn't know they'd be put in this way." Recalling this moment nearly two years later, he'd say: "It was frustrating and difficult. Was there tension? Sure. Disappointment? Sure. Shock? No. I'm an optimist and I've always believed in this drug. The FDA felt there was something missing. My attitude was, Okay, we've got to roll up our sleeves and get busy" fixing the problem.

ALSO IN HOUSTON was Addison Woods, a genial 50-year-old who had once been a successful software salesman but was now a full-time stage 4 colorectal cancer patient. When he learned that Erbitux would not be available in June 2002—if ever—he felt as if he'd just been sucker punched. One minute there's a great new drug that's going to help save your life, or at least buy you time, and the next minute it's like the drug never existed. He felt "betrayed."

Woods didn't know what to do. He didn't have time to wait for the pointy-headed scientists and the Wall Street bean counters and the FDA bureaucrats to get their act together. He didn't have time for any dithering at all. His tumors were progressing. He was beginning to slide and had nothing to grab onto. He could hear the angel wings fluttering around his ears and he didn't like the sound one bit.

Woods had been told—*promised*—that he would be one of the first in line for Erbitux once it had been approved by the FDA. He had talked it over many times with his oncologist, and in the course of those conversations he had convinced himself that Erbitux would save his life. "It's my magic bullet," he'd been telling everyone. It wasn't easy to get started on a new therapy, but he'd tried them all and failed them all, and now he was determined that, just like Shannon Kellum and those other people he'd read about or seen on TV—the friend of President Clinton's and the woman on *60 Minutes*—who'd benefited from the drug, he, too, would become a miracle of modern science and beat cancer.

In anticipation of the long-awaited moment when a stream of the miraculous clear liquid would flow from an IV drip down into his arm and into his bloodstream where it would shrink his tumors and restore order to his insides, he had been preparing himself mentally and physically. He was psyched up. He just knew that this was the one: Erbitux would do the trick. And even though he wasn't able to get into an ImClone clinical trial, he'd been willing to wait. After all, Sam and Harlan Waksal had been assuring him, and thousands of other cancer patients like him, that while ImClone's compassionate-use program had been canceled, "Erbitux will be on the market by June 2002."

"If you just hold on a few more months," they'd said, "the drug will be yours."

So Woods had waited. He had intentionally not tried to get into clinical trials for other drugs, so as to keep his system clear for Erbitux. Then came the RTF letter at the end of December. Now he was reeling with confusion and despair, he was angry, he was desperate to find another treatment. Only there weren't any other treatments.

NINE

# *"We Screwed Up"*

Working the phones over the last weekend of 2001, Sam portrayed the FDA's rejection letter in the best possible light. On Saturday, December 29, Reuters reported: "Sam Waksal, ImClone's chief executive officer, told Reuters that the [FDA] first wants more 'annotation' information, about how the company verified that patients enrolled in its trials had indeed failed previous drug regimens and that subsequent tumor reductions attributed to Erbitux were indeed real. Concerns raised by the FDA mainly involve how the data were presented and do not raise outright concerns about safety or efficacy of the drug, the CEO added."

This wire story was widely seen and discussed. But because an RTF was such a rare event and its contents were kept confidential, most people weren't able to gauge its implications. Many cancer patients and biotech investors were mollified by Sam's upbeat interpretation of the letter. Behind the scenes, however, executives at ImClone and Bristol-Myers had no doubts that the FDA's decision was a worst-case scenario.

For the moment Bristol had no public comment. But over the weekend, a flurry of e-mails zipped between Bristol executives who were surprised and dismayed by the ImClone CEO's attempt to downplay the seriousness of the RTF. On Sunday, December 30, in response to the

Reuters story, one BMS executive wrote: "I agree that some alot [*sic*] of Sam's comments are misleading and at this point we should continue to be silent. As you heard from yesterday's discussion, there's a lot we don't know."

Sam and Harlan had scheduled a conference call with investors and journalists for Monday, December 31, in which they would attempt to explain the RTF and its potential impact on ImClone. This would be a crucial call, and over the weekend the Waksals produced draft documents of their statements. The draft documents were circulated among BMS executives, who now expressed further dismay at their partners' response.

On Sunday, a BMS official e-mailed the following private comments on Sam's proposed remarks: "These draft documents leave me most uncomfortable. They gloss over the seriousness of the RTF letter and make it appear that the integrity of the study results is not in question, when in fact it is . . . We will also need to rewrite major portions of the clinical and pharmacology part of the BLA including a new 9923 study report, new 141 [monotherapy] study report, new ISS and ISE based on these revised reports. I know that this is not what ImClone wants to tell their investors, but I think it represents the reality of this situation."

THE CONFERENCE CALL took place before the market opened on Monday morning. Listening in were dozens of investors and journalists across the country. Speaking in an authoritative way with a raspy voice, Sam said: "I was rather stunned when we got the letter. I have to tell you, this was unexpected. I didn't have plans to end the year this way."

He and Harlan insisted that there was "no question" that Erbitux was a safe and effective cancer treatment, and that the bulk of the FDA's concerns were about improper paperwork. "We feel that this is not a drug that failed to meet its clinical endpoints," Sam said. "However, the company did fail to provide a proper train of documentation which would allow the agency to accept this filing."

Harlan concurred: "Obviously, we did not prepare this documentation well enough."

Sam continued: "If we cannot provide the evidence in such a way that makes the agency accept the package, then the clinical trial is not going to be sufficient for approval. However, that is not what we believe is going to happen. Hopefully, we won't need to prove anything else, because we believe that . . . the data exists in its raw form."

At the end of the call, Sam assured his listeners that ImClone would be able to supply the missing information to the agency by the end of the first quarter of 2002; he said he hoped that Erbitux would be approved by the fall.

It was New Year's Eve and by the end of trading that day the company's share price had tumbled another 19 percent, to $44.10.

THURSDAY, JANUARY 3, was a beautiful sunny day in New York. At 10 that morning, Sam Waksal sat in a shaft of sunlight in a narrow conference room next door to his office. He was dressed in a finely cut charcoal-gray suit with subtle pinstripes, a blue shirt, and dark blue tie. His thinning dark hair was neatly combed over his balding pate. A pair of delicate, round gold-framed glasses was perched on his nose. He greeted me with a smile and a gracious welcome, as always, but then he slumped in his chair with a lost look in his eye. His face looked wan and haggard.

When I asked how it felt to receive the RTF, Sam sighed and said, "I was very, very disappointed . . . I haven't slept a wink since." Sighing wearily, he added: "This is an object lesson in [the difficulty of] drug development."

Again, Sam downplayed the FDA's concerns and insisted that ImClone could supply the agency with the missing documentation. "We were like the kid in math class who writes down the answers to his equations but doesn't show how he got them. The FDA wants to see the work. So now we're working hand-in-hand with our partner Bristol-Myers Squibb to fix it." He said several times that he believed the delay was only temporary, and that Erbitux would be approved by the third quarter of 2002. "Look, this drug works! There's no question!" he insisted persuasively.

Pointedly looking at my reporter's notebook, Sam added: "The most disappointing thing is that in keeping this drug off the market, we really hurt the patients who desperately need it."

When I pressed for detail about the contents of the RTF letter, he snapped, "Who fucked up? That's what you want to know."

After a long disquisition on how the IRAC (Independent Response

Assessment Committee) that ImClone had hired to review the Erbitux data had "not followed its charter," and an explanation of the Byzantine workings of the FDA, he answered his own question: "We did."

Then Sam, gracious even in trying times, shook my hand and disappeared into a hurriedly called meeting down the hall. His assistant, an attractive young woman who bit her lip and frowned with worry, escorted me to the foyer, then hurried away. This would prove to be the last one-on-one meeting I ever had with Sam, although it was not my last significant conversation with him.

EARLY THAT AFTERNOON, Paul Goldberg sat in the office in the basement of his house on a quiet street in northwest Washington, D.C., puzzling over a document not meant for his eyes. It was a confidential letter, a copy of the Food and Drug Administration's RTF letter, a communication so unusual that in 17 years of oncological muckraking Goldberg had never seen one before.

The RTF had landed on his desk the day before. Someone (he claims he's not sure who) had leaked Goldberg the letter by means he refuses to detail, via a source he will not identify, for reasons that he can only speculate on.

Goldberg loved a good conspiracy. Born in Moscow, he was raised in Washington, D.C. and since 1985, Goldberg, who was 42, and his wife, Kirsten Boyd Goldberg, who was 38, have published *The Cancer Letter*, a newsletter for the cancer research community that was founded by his father-in-law. Printed in black, white, and red, and usually running eight pages long, *The Cancer Letter* goes to some 10,000 specialized and influential readers. They do not rely on the Goldbergs for the kind of news that can be found in a general-interest periodical: they look to *The Cancer Letter* for the unvarnished truth about oncologic drug development; to ferret out the telling nitty-gritty of FDA policy; to parse the fine print of NIH grants; to keep them up-to-date on who is doing what, where, and when in the highly competitive world of cancer medicine.

Goldberg's Rolodex of oncology sources was unparalleled, he liked to point out, and his reports have had a widespread impact on the industry. In 1996, he backed breast cancer activists who had accused the White House's choice for special adviser on women's health, Susan Blumenthal, of diverting money from research; Blumenthal, who was then the assistant surgeon general, withdrew her name from consideration. In 1998 he took Stanislaw Burzynski, a Houston oncologist, to task for hyping experimental drugs for terminally ill cancer patients that proved ineffective. Three oncologists who reviewed Burzynski's treatments for *The Cancer Letter* described his data as "not interpretable." And in 2000, Goldberg wrote an investigative report on the National Dialogue on Cancer (NDC), a collaboration of 160 public and private groups working on cancer treatment. He characterized the NDC as a lobbying scheme that was using taxpayers' money to promote a strategy of prevention and control at the expense of research. The NDC's chairman, former president George H. W. Bush, brandished a copy of what he called "that darn *Cancer Letter,"* and vowed that the coalition would seek clearer objectives.

In the opening days of January 2002, Goldberg knew only a little about ImClone. For years the company had struggled on the fringes of the highly competitive biopharmaceutical business without turning a profit; a data hound, Goldberg had largely ignored Sam Waksal's increasingly extravagant claims for his "breakthrough" cancer treatment because ImClone was never willing to share its Erbitux data.

What puzzled Goldberg about the RTF letter was that the story it told about Erbitux was very different from the story that ImClone had been telling cancer patients, doctors, investors, and the public for years. At about three o'clock that afternoon, January 3, Paul Goldberg decided to call Sam Waksal and ask him about the contents of the RTF.

As he did with me that morning, Waksal used a flood of words and numbers to build a logical-sounding case to persuade Goldberg that ImClone's science was "not flawed," and that the company would not have to do another clinical trial. "Look, Paul, this drug works!" he insisted. But when Goldberg began to ask specific, oddly well-informed questions about discrepancies in the concordance data from the Erbitux clinical trials, Waksal knew Goldberg must have a copy of the RTF. The words suddenly began to pile up in Waksal's mouth.

"Uhh, the information?" he stuttered. "Where, uh, uh, where did you get the letter from the, uh, agency?"

"We got it confidentially. From a confidential source," replied Goldberg. "Not from the agency."

"Okay . . . It hasn't been published. And it's confidential information between us and the agency."

"Sure."

The conversation moved on and they discussed the various clinical trials that ImClone was working on. Then Sam veered back to the RTF. His voice rising, he asked, "And what are you doing with the, ah, information from the letter?"

"Quoting pieces of it," replied Goldberg. A static-filled silence, at least eight seconds long, ensued. Goldberg could practically hear the gears spinning inside of Sam's head, as Waksal began to comprehend his dilemma, calculate his options, and bluff his way through with intimidation.

"The exchange between the agency and us is right now a confidential exchange," he said, in a hard and wary voice. "We are working with the agency to try to put together a response that allows us to move forward . . . We didn't release the letter. So whatever you have, you have from an illegitimate source."

"Well, I don't know what is illegitimate. There is such a thing as the First Amendment."

"We're trying to refile our application. As expeditiously as possible. It's important that things not be misinterpreted . . . It's very important that things be interpreted correctly."

"I'm sure they will be."

IT IS POSSIBLE that had the RTF not been leaked to Paul Goldberg, Sam might well have been able to assuage Wall Street, regroup his forces at ImClone, garner the corporate support of Bristol-Myers, win FDA approval, and bring Erbitux to market only slightly behind schedule—whether or not the drug was really as effective as ImClone claimed.

But the letter was leaked and Goldberg did print excerpts of it in *The Cancer Letter*. This precipitated a crisis.

Over the course of 2002, it became something of a parlor game in the interlinked worlds of science, finance, law, politics, and society that Sam Waksal operated in, to sit around guessing who leaked the RTF to Goldberg, how he did it, and what his true motives were. Many assumed that the leaker was someone inside the FDA, who was spurred by a sense of moral outrage and a wish to make an example of the biotech cowboys at ImClone. Others believe that the RTF was leaked by an investor who had "shorted" ImClone stock (bet against it) and wanted to profit from the fallout a leaked RTF would cause. If this were true, such a person would almost certainly have to have been an ImClone insider to profit from the leak, and a coldhearted Machiavellian to boot. While this scenario appears unlikely, many strange things have happened at ImClone, and given some of the personalities involved, it cannot be completely discounted. A third group posits that the leaked RTF originated from ImClone's partner, Bristol-Myers Squibb, which hoped to depress ImClone's stock so that the giant pharmaceutical company could gobble up the little biotech firm at a deep discount. A fourth theory—the most popular—maintains that the letter made its way from someone at the FDA to an influential go-between, like a lawyer or a lobbyist, to the reporter. In other words, like the train passengers in Agatha Christie's *Murder on the Orient Express,* nearly everyone connected to ImClone had a motive to undermine Sam and was a suspect. The true answer will probably never be known.

IF YOU WERE A BIOTECH investment banker who had not planned to attend the annual Hambrecht & Quist conference ("H&Q") in San Francisco, then your plans had now changed.

ImClone had been the darling of the industry only a few days earlier, and Sam its star; the Bristol deal had been the rising tide that had lifted all biotech ships. But now ImClone was sinking fast and threatened to take the industry down with it.

Anyone with even a tangential link to biotech wanted to be at H&Q to find out what had gone wrong, what would happen next, and who would be able to capitalize on ImClone's mistakes. Biotech could be cutthroat.

Hambrecht & Quist (now called J. P. Morgan H&Q) is a venerable Silicon Valley investment bank that is often credited as the biotech business's original underwriter. Every January since 1982, the bank had hosted the H&Q Conference in San Francisco. "H&Q," as the conference is known, is always the first and largest Wall Street biotech and drug-investment conference of the year. It is the stomping ground where everyone in the trade gathers to rub antlers, get caught up, and start doing deals.

January 2002 was the 20th anniversary of H&Q, and it was supposed to be ImClone's moment of shining glory. It was here that the Waksal brothers were going to trumpet the FDA's approval of the Erbitux application, present the results of their latest clinical trial, and announce that the drug would be on the market by June. It was the moment they had been working toward for years.

But Sam and Harlan's December 31 conference call had raised far more questions about the RTF letter than it had answered. Because the RTF was a proprietary communication between the FDA and the company, no one on Wall Street knew what the agency had said or what the letter meant for Erbitux. Such unknowns make the Street nervous. Sam and Harlan were both scheduled to appear at H&Q. So were representatives from Bristol-Myers Squibb. The conference would be the investment community's first chance to ask them how bad the news would be for their very expensive investment.

H&Q was scheduled to begin on Monday, January 7, 2002. As the date approached, excitement began to ratchet up and hotels all over San Francisco were sold out, as more and more people were trying to finagle a way into the invitation-only gathering.

ON MONDAY, January 7, Adam Feuerstein woke at five o'clock in the morning in his San Francisco apartment. As he groggily sipped coffee, he booted up his computer and began to mentally prepare himself for the opening day of H&Q. Sitting in his in-box was the latest issue of *The Cancer Letter*. Feuerstein had never met Paul Goldberg, but he respected *The Cancer Letter*'s enterprising reporting. Double-clicking on the file, he saw a large headline that read: "FDA Says ImClone Data Insufficient To Evaluate Colorectal Cancer Drug C225." The story below included lengthy excerpts from the RTF letter and quotes from Goldberg's conversation with Waksal.

Feuerstein coughed and almost sprayed coffee across his computer screen. "Holy shit!" he said out loud. He bolted forward to speed-read the RTF excerpts. It was the kind of raw, confidential information from the FDA that he had never seen before. He knew immediately that this would hit H&Q later that day like a mortar round.

*The Cancer Letter* revealed that ImClone's problems were far more serious than the Waksals had acknowledged. The Erbitux application was "incomplete" and filled with "substantial deficiencies," the RTF said. ImClone had deviated from the protocol and had not maintained careful patient records. Study 9923, the pivotal clinical trial, was not "adequate and well controlled"—something the FDA had repeatedly warned ImClone about in a series of meetings, letters, and phone calls over the past year and a half. "The application does not contain the data requested to support the proposed dose" for Erbitux—something the agency had warned about since January 1999. The RTF, signed by two reviewers from the FDA Center for Biologics Evaluation and Research, went on and on, in what amounted to a stinging rebuke to ImClone— and, by extension, Bristol-Myers Squibb and all of the investors, patients, and clinicians who had believed Sam and Harlan Waksal's claims for Erbitux.

Feuerstein was now fully awake and he began to work the phones. He could not reach the Waksal brothers, who were scheduled to appear at H&Q in two days' time.

Tapping quickly at his keyboard, Feuerstein sent out his "Tech Stocks" report at just before 9:23 in the morning, pacific standard time. Headlined "ImClone's Erbitux Problems May Be Worse Than Believed," he quoted from the RTF letter and noted that ImClone's stock had already sunk 17 percent since the market opened on the East Coast. "It is impossible at this point to verify the veracity of *The Cancer Letter* disclosure," he wrote. "But if *The Cancer Letter* does have a correct copy of the RTF letter, it suggests that ImClone executives have not given investors and Wall Street analysts a full picture of the Erbitux problems."

He pushed the send key and his story buzzed through the electronic nervous system that is the Internet. Then he printed out a fresh copy of *The Cancer Letter* and ran over to the Westin St. Francis Hotel, off Union Square, where H&Q was just abut to open its doors.

THE CONFERENCE was filled to capacity, with 5,000 people in attendance. Nearly 400 health-care companies were there to pitch to investors. As he passed through the hotel's front doors, Feuerstein noticed that the lobby was jammed with clusters of people, nearly all of whom were hunched around copies of *The Cancer Letter*. Some of them had smudged, flimsy, black-and-white versions of the newsletter that had been faxed by their colleagues in New York. Others had hurriedly printed hard copies at the hotel.

This report was the first indication that ImClone's problems were serious, systemic, years in the making, and apparently well known to Sam and Harlan Waksal. It was the first indication that ImClone had been intentionally misleading about the company's communications with the FDA. And it was the first indication that the superstar drug Erbitux might not be a silver bullet after all.

The din was rising, as everyone buzzed with incredulity and confusion, scribbled down notes, cursed, and shouted into cell phones. Few of them had ever seen an RTF letter before. What he was witnessing, Feuerstein thought, was a collective freak-out.

Wading into the crowd, he bumped into two investors who were trusted sources. The three of them grabbed slices of pizza and huddled in a corner to read through *The Cancer Letter* word by word. Every few minutes one of them would chuckle wretchedly, or look up and say, "Oh my God!"

Many of those at the hotel that morning had believed Sam Waksal's seductive pitch for Erbitux—the cancer drug that he claimed would "change oncology" forever—or at least they believed the drug had real promise. The believers had held "long" positions in ImClone, meaning they weren't looking to make a quick profit.

But now, as a result of the revelations in *The Cancer Letter,* ImClone's share price was in a nosedive and had opened at $34.96 that morning. The mood was so grim that even the financial community's usual gallows humor had leaked away.

Sam and Harlan had repeatedly assured Wall Street that the FDA had green-lighted ImClone's development strategy for Erbitux. When the company filed its Biologics License Application (BLA) the previous summer, the Waksals had told analysts and investors that they were in close contact with senior people at the agency and had worked hard to resolve any questions the FDA had. But now, thanks to *The Cancer Letter,* the Street was learning of an alternate version of events. One of the most puzzling excerpts from the RTF read:

> In order for your application to be considered complete, you were informed during the meeting of Aug. 11, 2000, in our letter of Jan. 19, 2001, and during the telephone conference call of Jan. 26, 2001, that the application must provide evidence that the addition of a toxic agent (irinotecan [CPT-11]) is necessary to achieve the clinical effect.

In other words, if Goldberg had gotten it right, and this was indeed a legitimate copy of the RTF, then it meant that ImClone had consistently ignored the agency's questions since August 2000. The bankers were incensed. Such willful disregard of the regulators' questions was beyond stupid, they felt; it was fraudulent and bordered on the recklessly self-destructive.

As the details of the RTF sank in, the collective freak-out hardened into anger. An analyst told *The New York Times:* "The FDA's communications with the company appear directly at odds with the statements made by the company in 2001."

A fund manager who had been long on ImClone, told Feuerstein: "This gives the entire biotech and drug sectors a black eye. This is going to have investors questioning whether they can ever trust anything that a biotech executive says anymore." Another ImClone investor said: "What's so shocking to me is the letter makes it clear that the FDA has had issues with ImClone and Erbitux for a long time, but the company never told anyone about it."

As people digested the RTF, another suspicious question came up: *What were the real reasons behind ImClone's development strategy for Erbitux?*

According to the RTF letter, FDA reviewers believed the drug would work as a single agent against colorectal cancer. But ImClone had developed Erbitux as a combination therapy with irinotecan. Although the company had conducted a small single-agent clinical trial, the FDA had asked ImClone to conduct larger, controlled trials of Erbitux alone. ImClone had not done so, and now everyone at H&Q wanted to know one thing: why not?

John Mendelsohn and the Waksal brothers had long maintained that the two-drug cocktail was more effective than Erbitux alone. The theory is that Erbitux weakens cancer cells, which allows the more toxic irinotecan to shrink and destroy tumors. The FDA's promotion of Erbitux as a stand-alone therapy, ImClone maintained, was simply misguided.

But now a new theory began to circulate through the H&Q crowd: ImClone had a patent problem, they speculated, and that is what had driven the combination strategy, which led, in part, to the RTF.

Patent issues and intellectual property disputes are complex but common in biotech, as companies lay broad legal claim to whole classes of new drugs. Like lurking icebergs, broad patents are easy to overlook but damagingly expensive for a drug company to run into. According to the patent conspiracy theorists, ImClone knew all along that Erbitux was effective on its own, but competitors like Genentech had already made broad patent claims on the EGFr class of drugs. Genentech—which is helping OSI to develop Tarceva, which will directly compete with Erbitux—is known to aggressively defend its patents. Indeed, the company had already threatened legal action if ImClone didn't agree to license its patents, which can be an expensive proposition. So, the theory went, ImClone had intentionally ignored the FDA's request for further tests of its drug as a single agent, and had patented Erbitux as a combination therapy in order to protect itself legally. The problem was that if the FDA insisted on a large single-agent trial, it would further delay Erbitux's entry to market by a year or more. And with such a delay, ImClone would lose its "first-mover" advantage to market, which could cost it and investors hundreds of millions of dollars.

But Irv Feit, who, as ImClone's former vice president for intellectual property and licensing, helped to secure the Erbitux patent, said that ImClone's claim is solid. Because EGFr antibodies were discovered before Mendelsohn did his groundbreaking work, and UCSD had already obtained patent protection for Mendelsohn's 225 antibody, it was only possible for the company to obtain a patent on the combination therapy. To get the patent for the combination therapy, ImClone had to show that EGFr antibodies demonstrated "synergy" when combined with any standard chemotherapy (not simply with the standard treatment, irinotecan). "We had a good case," said Feit. "We came up with about 10 publications of experiments [various combinations of EGFr antibodies, chemotherapies, and tumor types], and every publication reported synergistic results."

"The patent claim we got covered *any* EGFr antibody in combination with *any* chemotherapeutic agent," he said. "It's a strong patent." The patent was issued in 1997 and lasts for 17 years, meaning that Erbitux will not go generic until 2014.

ImClone's development of the drug, Feit said, was not driven by patent considerations, but by a clinical strategy—Mendelsohn's notion that the combination therapy was far more effective in "sticking gum in the lock" of tumors than either C225 or chemotherapy alone—and by a business strategy—Sam's mad dash to make Erbitux a first-to-market product. While there were thorny legal questions about whether or not the Mendelsohn patent would cover the C225 chimeric antibody or simply the murine antibody (Feit believes it covered both), and while Genentech has made some broad claims on the family of human EGF receptors (HER), Feit believes that these were "arguably nonevents."

IT HAPPENED that ImClone's presentation at H&Q was scheduled for Wednesday morning, January 9. As freshly printed versions of *The Cancer Letter* were handed around the crowded hotel lobby, it summoned an image to Feuerstein's mind: "It was like shoveling hunks of raw meat into a cage full of ravenously hungry and pissed-off lions."

In his early morning report on Wednesday, headlined "Today's Main Course: Grilled ImClone Execs," Feuerstein wrote:

> More often than not, the breakout sessions at investment conferences tend to be rather genteel affairs. Yes, questions can get pointed, but rarely do tempers flare or accusations fly. This isn't *The Jerry Springer Show;* after all, no one throws chairs. But the unfolding ImClone saga has been one shocking surprise after another, so few people are brave enough to predict the outcome of this morning's meeting.
>
> Odds are pretty good that Sam and Harlan Waksal won't get up in front of the assembled throng and admit to being the illegitimate children of Elvis Presley and a three-headed Martian cocktail waitress. But other than that, anything goes.

According to an early version of the conference calendar, Bristol-Myers Squibb had been scheduled to give a thirty-minute talk on Wednesday at 10 A.M., just before ImClone's presentation. But in the final version of the calendar, Bristol's name had disappeared. Indeed, the fund managers were buzzing about Bristol's conspicuous silence on the ImClone matter.

At the Westin St. Francis, the overflow crowd of fund managers and analysts wanted to know: *What was the role of Bristol-Myers in filing the Erbitux application? Would their $2 billion deal implode? And what about ImClone: Who knew what about Erbitux, when did they know it, and what did they do with their knowledge? Was the science bogus? Did the multimillion-dollar stock sales by senior ImClone executives constitute insider trading?*

In their presentations at H&Q, some of ImClone's competitors went out of their way to distance themselves from the Waksals' methods of drug development. While never mentioning the name "ImClone," their audience had no trouble identifying the meaning of the message or its target. Arthur Levinson, CEO of Genentech, for instance, questioned the wisdom of taking "shortcuts" in clinical trials, and noted that his company's experimental cancer drug, Tarceva, was being subjected to multiple clinical trials that were randomized and controlled, with clinical endpoints that included demonstrations of the drug's survival benefit—an implicit jab at ImClone's rapid, stripped-down trials for Erbitux. For good measure, Levinson added that Genentech, "gravitates towards the more rigorous side of things. We might decide to add six or nine months to a clinical trial, but at the end of the day that's a good approach."

ON WEDNESDAY MORNING, the auditorium at the Westin St. Francis was filled to capacity. The air inside was thick and stuffy. Demand for seats had been so great that the hotel had organized two overflow rooms into which the audio was piped. Former Vice President Al Gore was scheduled to give a keynote luncheon speech that day but hardly anyone mentioned it.

At 10:30, Sam Waksal took the stage in a medium-sized conference room. As is typical at such events, he would show slides and deliver prepared remarks for half an hour, then move to a smaller room for a 30-minute "breakout" session of free-form questions and answers.

Feuerstein's challenge was to attend the main presentation and then somehow find a way into the breakout session afterward. Both would be packed. A veteran of many H&Qs, he knew the hotel's layout well. For the main event, he positioned himself in the back of the auditorium, away from the main entrance, near an unmarked door used by waiters.

Sam Waksal walked onstage. His face was pale and drawn and his balding head glistened with sweat in the lights. He had big bags under his eyes. Seeing him in the flesh sent an electrical charge through the hot, agitated crowd. The whispering started immediately: where was Harlan? He had always been a constant shadow at his brother's shoulder, and he had overseen the company's FDA application. But now he'd gone AWOL. Standing onstage in a pool of light, facing a hostile audience without Harlan or Bristol-Myers to back him up, Sam had apparently been left to twist on the cord of his words, alone.

Speaking in a hoarse voice, he began by saying there were several issues he couldn't discuss until ImClone had met with the FDA. Then he tried to warm up the audience with self-deprecating jokes: "It was a wonderful ending of the year for me . . . and I haven't slept a wink since that night [December 28]." The audience murmured, but not appreciatively.

He admitted that ImClone had failed to document the response rate of patients to Erbitux in Study 9923. "It's not an insignificant problem," he said. "The data does not exist."

Then his voice shifted to a more urgent tone and he began to cast blame for ImClone's predicament. First he blamed the Independent Response Assessment Committee (IRAC)—the two oncologists and two radiologists who reviewed the Erbitux data for ImClone—for not adhering to their charter. "They were meant to document refractoriness [*sic*]," Sam said, referring to cancer patients whose health did not improve on irinotecan alone. "When the IRAC didn't document and give the measurements for the refractoriness of the patient population—according to the charter which they were given by the agency—then we didn't have a reviewable package, because it was not well controlled. And therefore this package was turned down by the agency. That is the heart of the [RTF]."

He acknowledged that the FDA had made it clear that lacking such documentation, the agency would not and could not accept the Erbitux application. He admitted: "We did not provide that documentation. It doesn't exist."

Then he blamed Paul Goldberg for publishing excerpts of the RTF in *The Cancer Letter*. "This is probably one of the first situations where somebody puts pieces of a refusal-to-file, or any FDA communication, out there. It certainly is disconcerting, because it's part of a process that we are going through with the FDA, and one that is very important to us."

People in the audience were hanging on Sam's every word, and many of them were furiously scribbling down notes as he spoke. Rather than quell the outrage, though, everything he said seemed to incite the audience further.

Holding his chin up, Sam declared: "There were a lot of questions that people have raised in all of this, and they said that we didn't communicate properly these issues with our shareholders. And that isn't the case at all. We've been communicating, and communicating accurately, all the while."

The crowd shuffled restlessly.

"It's also been suggested that FDA either was disingenuous with us, or we didn't understand these communications as they gave them to us," he continued. "And that is also not the case."

"So what happened?" he asked rhetorically. "What happened was that we put together a faulty BLA package, and we screwed up."

Now the crowd began to rumble.

Sam plowed ahead, insisting that the stock trades that he, Harlan, and other senior ImClone officials had made were "appropriate." He reiterated his belief that Erbitux is a safe and effective anti-cancer agent. He said that ImClone was continuing to work with Bristol and the FDA to fix the mess, although he did allow that "if we can't put together the information that the FDA requires, we will have to do new clinical trials"—which meant the drug's entry to market would be further delayed.

As the lights came up, several attendees noted that Sam had failed to explain why ImClone did not respond to the FDA's many calls for better data since August 2000.

Feuerstein leapt out of his chair, cut right, bolted through the unmarked waiter's door, cut left, ran down a stairwell, and squeezed into the already crowded breakout session. It was held in a small room packed with angry investors. Feuerstein was jammed into a corner; he could barely breathe or take notes. If the mood in the auditorium had been scornful and agitated, here it was a rising anger.

Looking harried, Sam eventually made his way through the crowd. The scene degenerated into bedlam. With none of the usual preamble or pretense of waiting to be called on, financiers began firing questions at him. Sam answered some, ignored others, or gave half-answers. Everyone had seen the RTF and understood how serious it was, but Sam continued to equivocate, which only fueled Wall Street's resentment. Many people were shouting at once, and it was difficult to see who had asked what, or to hear clearly. It was a moment unlike any other Feuerstein had witnessed in his career.

Sam squinted at the mob and tried to establish a sense of order by asking his interlocutors to identify themselves. Someone shouted out a question—it was impossible to hear what it was—and Sam said: "Who'm I talking to?"

A loud, taunting voice called out: "You're talking to all of us!"

And now a derisive snicker rippled through the crowd. Sam had lost them.

The H&Q audience was not impressed with the ImClone CEO's responses. "It was a complete circus," griped a hedge fund manager. "It's clear they don't know what they're doing."

"ImClone still hasn't come clean. They're still glossing over major issues," said another fund manager, who had formerly been bullish on ImClone but had now sold his entire stake in the company.

ImClone had been trading flat that morning, but after the presentation everyone ran to his phone or computer and the stock began to sell off aggressively. By the closing bell, ImClone was down another 13.6 percent, or $5 a share, to finish the day at $31.85. (Only a month before, ImClone had been selling for $75.45 a share.)

The message was clear: whether or not Erbitux was a good drug, Wall Street had lost confidence in the Waksals.

H&Q WAS A FIASCO for ImClone. But there were still some true believers willing to prop up the stock, if only because of the promise of Erbitux. Backed by the good names of the oncologists behind it— Mendelsohn, DeVita, Levine, and Saltz—some investors continued to believe that the drug had inherent value. Even if Sam and Harlan had made a few mistakes, they felt, Erbitux was such a good drug that it would ultimately be approved by the FDA and would succeed in the marketplace.

As the 2002 H&Q wound down to its end on January 10, Nadine Wong, who writes the Biotech Sage Report for *theStreet.com,* posted a column entitled "Don't Write Off ImClone Just Yet," in which she mused:

> [T]he company and its drug still have potential. First of all, common sense tells you that Bristol-Myers Squibb must have seen the medical data and the FDA filing for Erbitux before agreeing to its megadeal with ImClone last September . . . then there's ImClone's presentation at [ASCO] which added credibility to [the] science . . . so all is not lost

with Erbitux; it's simply traveling along a winding path with some roadblocks along the way.

The high-profile story of ImClone has definitely added some spice to the biotech sector. And if this is any indication of how this sector will behave in 2002, the tempo is going to be fast and exhilarating.

# PART THREE

# CLINICAL TRIAL

TEN

# *Inquiries*

Alan Slobodin had never heard of ImClone before the last few weeks of 2001. At that time, he had volunteered to help a cancer patient find out how to access Erbitux, which the patient had heard about through the drug's widespread media coverage. Slobodin quickly discovered that the patient was not eligible to participate in an Erbitux clinical trial, and that the company's expanded-access program had been shut down. When he called ImClone, the message he got from the company was the same one that other cancer patients like Addison Woods had gotten: "Just hold on another few months; the drug will be available by June." In late December, Slobodin was surprised to read in *The Washington Post* that ImClone had received an RTF letter, just weeks after he had spoken to company representatives. Slobodin knew this meant a further delay for Erbitux, and that the patient would be devastated by the news. Yet on the conference call of December 31, Sam and Harlan had insisted that the RTF was really no more than a bump in the road, a matter of "documentation," and that the drug would be available by the fall. Then *The Cancer Letter* excerpted the RTF in early January, revealing that ImClone's troubles were far more serious than Sam had admitted. "There was a whole bunch of awfully strange things going on here,"

Slobodin recalled. "And with our concerns about corporate integrity, we had all of the elements of a 'perfect storm.' "

Slobodin mentioned ImClone to his bosses, Congressman W. J. "Billy" Tauzin and Congressman James Greenwood. They assigned him to investigate the company.

Slobodin was, in many ways, the antithesis of the high-powered players in the ImClone saga. A dedicated public servant, he was a 43-year-old Jewish Republican. Raised in suburban New Jersey, he was broad shouldered and balding, with dark, brooding, wide-set eyes; he spoke in a deep voice with a deliberate cadence. His manner was simultaneously calm and intense; he could appear distracted, but he could also suddenly become impassioned and decisive.

Billy Tauzin, a florid Louisiana Republican of the old school, headed the influential Committee on Energy and Commerce, which, at age 206, was the oldest legislative standing committee in the U.S. House of Representatives. The committee maintains principal oversight of a wide range of issues, including food and drug safety, public health, air and environmental quality, telecommunications, consumer protection, energy, and commerce.

To manage its workload, the committee relies on six subcommittees, including the Subcommittee on Oversight and Investigation, headed by Congressman James C. Greenwood, Republican of Pennsylvania. In 1988, the subcommittee led the inquiries into insider trading by Michael Milken and Ivan Boesky. Also in 1988, the subcommittee, under the leadership of John Dingell, accused the noted scientists Robert Gallo and David Baltimore of falsifying scientific data. The celebrated case dragged on for nearly a decade, and ultimately the scientists were absolved. The congressional investigators looking into ImClone were mindful of the lessons of the Baltimore case.

By 2002, Alan Slobodin was one of the subcommittee's chief investigators; his portfolio included oversight of the National Institutes of Health and the FDA. On Friday, January 18, he sent out three versions of a letter that announced that the House subcommittee was "investigating questions about the conduct of ImClone Systems, Inc., in the development of its colorectal cancer drug, Erbitux." One copy of the letter went to Sam Waksal at ImClone, one to Peter Dolan at Bristol-Myers Squibb, and one to Dr. Bernard Schwetz, the acting commissioner of the Food and Drug Administration.

Each five-page letter laid out the recent history of ImClone and Erbitux, noted that "many observers were stunned to learn" the details of the FDA's RTF letter, and pointed with dismay to the fact that ImClone insiders had sold a total of 2.1 million of their shares to Bristol-Myers for $150 million at a time when the FDA was warning that the drug was in trouble. The letter quoted from *The Cancer Letter, theStreet.com, The New York Times,* and *The Wall Street Journal:*

> Given these recent [press] reports, we have several serious concerns. Available information seems to conflict with ImClone's descriptions of the contents of FDA's RTF letter and its clinical research. The RTF letter is not a public document; investors only learned about the details from the excerpts of the RTF letter reported in the Cancer Letter. Without the Cancer Letter article, investors would have had to rely on ImClone's questionable descriptions.
>
> We are also interested in learning about the true nature of the pivotal clinical trial for Erbitux, and whether ImClone knew or should have known about the insufficiencies detailed in FDA's RTF letter. It is important that the hopes of cancer patients are not falsely raised and that the integrity of biomedical research is maintained. The available information demands that this Committee, which is entrusted with the oversight of public health and consumer protection laws, get additional information about ImClone and the Erbitux matter.

Each of the recipients was asked to provide specific information. Congress asked Dr. Bernard Schwetz for all records pertaining to ImClone and the RTF, and wrote: "For the sake of protecting patients and investors from deception, we are interested in learning whether FDA laws need to be clarified to permit the FDA . . . in appropriate circumstances, to share non-public information with other federal agencies." In the letter to Sam Waksal, the committee asked for all records relating to Study 9923, the FDA, and the RTF. And in the letter to Peter Dolan, the committee asked for information about BMS's due diligence and internal audits of ImClone: "Did BMS draw on the expertise of its Oncology Advisory Board to assess the Erbitux data before the ImClone deal was completed? If not, why not? What information did BMS rely on in assessing the Erbitux data?"

The letters were signed by Congressmen Tauzin, John D. Dingell,

Democrat of Michigan, James C. Greenwood, Republican of Pennsylvania, and Peter Deutsch, Democrat of Florida.

Three weeks after Tauzin and Greenwood's ImClone letters went out, the Subcommittee on Oversight and Investigation would again make headlines for its hearings into the notorious accounting practices of Arthur Anderson and the collapse of the Houston energy trader Enron. It was in the dark light of Enron that the ImClone scandal began to unfold.

NOW MANY THINGS began to happen at once. ImClone's stock was in free fall, having lost nearly 50 percent of its value. The company was facing at least a dozen class-action lawsuits claiming that ImClone had actually known—or should have known—that it would receive an RTF letter and had defrauded shareholders by not informing them.

The usually garrulous Sam Waksal had been muted by his lawyers and public relations handlers. It must have been unbearable. Sam loved the attention of the press. He had scrupulously courted reporters for years—playing to their vanity, pretending to be put-upon by their curiosity, yet teasing them onward with tantalizing gossip or wild stories and inviting them to parties at his house. But now journalists felt they had been used by Sam, and turned against him.

On January 14, the business reporter Christopher Byron, writing in the *New York Post,* had run a gleefully mean-spirited column about ImClone's predicament, deeming it the "newest scandal to sweep Wall Street" and opining that "Sam has been loitering at the fringes of the New York society crowd for two decades, leaving an oil slick behind him that has been colorful, to say the least."

At about eight o'clock the next evening, I had bundled up in my winter coat and was about to turn off the office lights when the phone began to ring. I was tired and running late. But when I finally picked up the receiver, I heard the staticky, muffled sound of someone calling from a cell phone while walking. Amid the sound of hard-soled shoes clacking across a cement floor, car doors slamming shut, and people shouting in an echoing space, a familiar, gravelly voice said: "Uuuuuuh, about the story . . ."

It took me a minute to identify the voice. "Sam?"

"Yeah, hi . . ." It was the supposedly incommunicado Sam Waksal calling from a parking garage.

For the next 45 minutes Sam engaged in an alternately charming, arrogant, funny, sad, angry, pleading, swearing, rambling monologue. It was an extraordinary moment. Astutely jumping on and off the record, he hotly contested many of the facts in Byron's *Post* story and complained that he was becoming the target of unfair "slam pieces." "I hope *you* don't do that to me," he cajoled.

He justified himself at length. He assured me that all was well at ImClone, that he wasn't worried, and that everything was going to work out just fine.

In a tone that swung from combative to self-pitying, he gave his version of events: "2002 was going to be our big year—and it's still going to be a big year. It just didn't begin the way I thought it would," he insisted. "The truth is Erbitux works. Yes, there are regulatory hurdles, but there have been for tons of drugs. This will go away. And ImClone will be a very successful company."

He noted that the FDA did not question the drug's efficacy; it simply refused to accept ImClone's application, which he acknowledged is highly unusual. Sam refused to discuss the FDA's decision, saying only, "The FDA is as fair as can be. Our conversations are confidential." He added that Merck KGaA's clinical trials had shown the same results as ImClone's own trials. In the summer of 2002, he said, Merck KGaA planned to file an application for Erbitux's approval in Europe.

As for the criticism about a deal ImClone executives made the previous July, in which Sam borrowed $18.2 million, Harlan borrowed $15.7 million, and Robert Goldhammer, chairman of the board, borrowed $1.2 million from ImClone in order to acquire 4.2 million more shares of the company's stock, he insisted that it was "perfectly legal." (Shares in ImClone were trading at $45 at the time, but the Waksals, along with other insiders, bought their shares from the company at a steep discount of about $8. After the Bristol-Myers deal, the ImClone executives then sold part of their ImClone holdings to Bristol-Myers at a price of $70 a share; the net totaled some $111 million for the Waksal brothers alone.) The timing of these transactions had raised eyebrows on Wall Street because they seemed to indicate foreknowledge of the FDA's decision not to accept the Erbitux application. Harlan told *The Wall Street Journal* that "No one at ImClone had any [foreknowledge of] the FDA's" decision.

"We were buying stock!" Sam angrily shouted into his cell phone.

"Harlan actually ended up with one million *more* shares than he had at the beginning of last year."

He strenuously defended ImClone's loans to company insiders, and insisted that "it was actually good for the company," because rather than using stock sales to exercise their options, which might have hurt the stock, they used loans, which were repaid with 8 percent interest. "The implication is that I'm taking money from the company," he scoffed. "I sold stock. It's money I have now. This isn't the company's money."

He said he planned to donate to charity and invest in biotech and health-care start-ups. "Has anybody ever said to Bill Gates: 'Jesus, you've made a lot of money on a company you built—that's really terrible'?!'"

ON JANUARY 23, Harlan conducted a conference call with institutional clients of Morgan Stanley. Doug Lind, a Morgan analyst (at the time, he rated ImClone stock "outperform"), asked about the RTF.

Harlan answered: "The RTF letter did raise other issues, and we take them all very seriously . . . I want to stress that we've been very forthright and clear in the characterization of our interactions over time with the FDA during the entire process."

When Lind asked about the congressional investigation, Harlan said: "We were very surprised to hear about the investigation, but on reflection it may be a good opportunity for us to go ahead and clear the air on many of the issues that have been raised." He added that he was confident that Congress would find no evidence of wrongdoing. "We believe we can re-file [the Erbitux application] with this existing study, with appropriate guidance from the FDA" and Bristol-Myers Squibb.

When Lind asked if ImClone had been questioned by the Securities and Exchange Commission (SEC), Harlan replied, "We don't comment on discussions with government agencies, but we are happy to provide the SEC with any information that it may deem useful."

The next day, the SEC announced that it had launched an "informal investigation" of ImClone. As part of its inquiry, the commission sent a letter to Paul Goldberg at *The Cancer Letter,* which read in part: "We are trying to determine whether there have been any violations of the federal security laws. The investigation does not mean that we have concluded that anyone has broken the law."

On Friday, January 25, the U.S. Justice Department announced that it had become the third federal agency to investigate whether ImClone had misled investors about Erbitux. Newly released SEC documents revealed that both Sam and Harlan had been hit with margin calls the week before, on January 18: Bank of America sold about 2.6 million ImClone shares pledged by Sam as collateral for loans by the bank; and UBS Paine Webber sold another 213,000 of his shares, also pledged as collateral for a loan. "The sales of [Sam Waksal's] shares were made involuntarily pursuant to margin calls," the SEC filing read.

On the same day, Bank of America sold 72,754 of Harlan's Im-Clone shares—shares that he had pledged to guarantee loans made to Sam. That afternoon, ImClone stock tumbled another 21.8 percent, to $15.31, a drop of nearly 80 percent from a month before.

In what amounted to a final exclamation point to the week, Pete Peterson, the eminent chairman of The Blackstone Group and former secretary of commerce, resigned from the ImClone board after serving for only two months; he cited "time constraints."


ON THE MORNING of January 9, 2002, Charles Miller picked up the newspaper in his Houston, Texas, penthouse and cursed out loud. There, in big bold type, was a headline about the deepening problems at ImClone. His first thought was: *Not this! Not on top of Enron!*

Dr. John Mendelsohn, the famed oncologist and president of M. D. Anderson Cancer Center, the man whom colleagues characterize as "unimpeachably honest," "squeaky clean," and "a Boy Scout," was the only person to be a director at both ImClone and Enron—two companies that by early 2002 were considered among the most avaricious of the many greedy self-dealers in an era of extraordinary corporate cupidity.

Charles Miller was the chairman of the University of Texas system's board of regents, the state body that governs M. D. Anderson. He put down his newspaper and immediately dialed R. D. "Dan" Burck, chancellor of the University of Texas, who had read the same headline. As the men talked, their concern grew.

Mendelsohn refused to discuss the scandals at ImClone or Enron in any detail with me. But in December 2002, he spoke at length with Geeta Anand of *The Wall Street Journal,* as did others in Houston. According to her account, Miller and Burck began to work the phones. They called Mendelsohn, who protested that he had done nothing wrong and pointed out that he could not have known about the problems at the two embattled companies because their executives had acted clandestinely.

Then Miller and Burck began to call powerful friends who ran Houston's leading pharmaceutical companies, banks, and law firms—including former President George H. W. Bush, who was chairman of the Anderson's board of visitors—to gauge the potential damage to the Anderson and formulate ways to limit it.

Patrick C. Oxford, a member of the board of regents and managing partner of the law firm Bracewell & Patterson, called the Mendelsohn situation a "fireball of epic proportions." Like the others, his foremost concern was to limit the harm done to his beloved Anderson.

Compounding Mendelsohn's unease was the way Houston's tightly knit social/business/philanthropic network had suddenly grown tense. It wasn't that people had judged him guilty of anything, exactly. But there was a new wariness. One patron of M. D. Anderson said that if Mendelsohn had acted inappropriately, then, "it would have affected donorship." Anderson staff, meanwhile, grew nervous that their president would become so embroiled in trying to defend himself against the investigations and shareholder lawsuits against ImClone and Enron that the cancer center would suffer. Or, they fretted, he might crack under the pressure. Where would that leave them?

Mendelsohn assured his colleagues that he was doing fine and that his work would not suffer. He appeared unflappable.

Behind closed doors, however, John and Anne Mendelsohn were deeply troubled. They cleared their usually hectic social calendar and instead spent several evenings in their living room, quietly discussing the predicament. In an unusual moment of candor, the usually reticent Mendelsohn told Anand: "We worried this would hurt my lifelong goal, this would tarnish friendships."

Mendelsohn had joined the Enron board the Houston way. Enron had a longstanding affiliation with the cancer center: between 1985 and 2000, the company, its subsidiaries, and its foundations pledged $2.5 million to M. D. Anderson. Mendelsohn knew Kenneth Lay, the congenial and enigmatic Enron CEO, and "admired him."

When Lay called Mendelsohn with a rare and enticing offer—a board seat at the seemingly invincible gas trading company, the seventh-largest corporation in America, that would soon be vacated by Mendelsohn's predecessor at the Anderson—Mendelsohn was flattered. He had joined ImClone's board in 1998, but Enron was a much bigger deal. "I thought I could contribute something and I'd learn something about managing an expanding business," he told Anand.

He agreed to join the Enron board in May 1999. Each director was paid $79,000 to meet regularly five times a year, plus stock options and other benefits. Mendelsohn was asked to participate in two of the board's four committees—finance, audit, compensation, or nominating. He didn't know much about finance, so he chose the nominating committee, which advises on personnel, and the auditing committee, on the theory that since audit committees generally examine deals that have already been done, he wouldn't be required to evaluate complicated transactions.

An old friend says that Mendelsohn loved being on the Enron board: "He enjoyed working with the high-rollers there."

In June 1999, Mendelsohn attended his first Enron board meeting. There, the board unanimously agreed to allow Andrew Fastow, the company's CFO, to run a private partnership called LJM Cayman LP. This was one of two "LJM partnerships" that produced large amounts of reportable income for Enron, in part by buying Enron assets and allegedly making the company appear more profitable than it really was. Corporate governance experts say the arrangement also presented an obvious conflict of interest for Fastow, because he had a duty to act in Enron's best interest, yet the LJM partnerships could have made money at Enron's expense.

The June 1999 board meeting is one of several that later attracted the scrutiny of federal investigators. Mendelsohn told Anand that he understood the complex LJM deals, but didn't notice any irregularities with them at the time. Enron management, he said, had assured the board of directors that Fastow's arrangement was lawful.

As of the autumn of 2003, Fastow had been indicted by a Houston grand jury on 109 counts alleging wire fraud, money laundering, falsification of Enron's accounting records, and other crimes. Fastow pleaded not guilty. His wife, Lea, who also worked at Enron, has been charged separately with fraud, money laundering, and tax violations. Enron filed for bankruptcy protection in December 2001.

In a meeting at former President Bush's ninth-floor office in Houston, in January 2002, Bush and Peter Coneway—a former Goldman Sachs Group partner, who was the incoming chairman of M. D. Anderson's advisory board—questioned Mendelsohn for an hour about his involvement in ImClone's botched clinical trial. They were concerned about how the worsening ImClone situation would affect him and the cancer center.

"We were trying to determine if there was a smoking gun," Coneway told Anand. "We asked him many questions."

Mendelsohn replied that he was not personally involved in the Erbitux trial and "hadn't known anything that put him in an awkward position." Mendelsohn said he was involved in discussions about the design of the trial, but that he wasn't involved in the details of collecting evidence and determining patient eligibility; nor was he responsible for the mistakes made in the Erbitux application submitted to the FDA, he said.

"I spent the great majority of my time running M. D. Anderson," he assured them.

Anand points out that virtually everyone in Houston society knew someone who had been treated at M. D. Anderson, which elicited sympathy for Mendelsohn. After all, he and his team had helped to save lives. Further, many of the men pondering his fate had themselves been directors or advisers to company boards; as they watched him struggle, they felt, as one said, "There but for the grace of God go I." Malcolm Gillis, president of Rice University, phrased the same emotion in Texan: "All of us at one time or another have been up to our elbows in alligators."

Joseph Simone, who was Mendelsohn's boss at Sloan-Kettering, noted that by this time Mendelsohn had become a Houston insider: "He became one of them."

"Johnny, are you okay?" It was late January and Patrick Oxford, the Bracewell & Patterson attorney, had dropped by Mendelsohn's corner office on the 11th floor of the M. D. Anderson clinical building. He was there on behalf of the board of regents. "I've talked to the troops, and you're fine." M. D. Anderson officials had agreed to support Mendelsohn's continued leadership of the cancer center, on the condition that he would update them on the ImClone and Enron investigations, and be honest with them about how the pressure was affecting his work. They also established an emergency succession plan, in which three vice presidents would assume Mendelsohn's presidential duties should he be forced to step down.

Mendelsohn resumed his 12-hour workdays and his nights of socializing and fund-raising. He and Anne attended a dinner to welcome Chinese President Jiang Zemin, another for the queen of Thailand. He played tennis with the British ambassador at the prestigious River Oaks Country Club. Life was getting back to normal.

By all accounts, John Mendelsohn was innocent of wrongdoing at Enron. Many notable figures are asked to join the boards of aggressive companies, in part for their outsider's eye and expertise, in part for their cachet. Such directors don't always have the wherewithal to carefully supervise management's every move. And sometimes the directors get burned.

Mendelsohn said he felt no remorse about the way he handled himself at ImClone and Enron. He said he didn't see how he could have acted any differently than he did given what he knew at the time. But in the next breath he allowed that the failures of those companies have caused him "great disappointment."


BY THE END OF January 2002, it was clear that the biggest single-product deal in the history of biotech was quickly turning into the industry's biggest fiasco. ImClone faced three federal investigations and at least two dozen shareholder lawsuits. Sam was being pilloried in the press and hired Abernathy MacGregor, a well-regarded crisis-management firm, to advise him. ImClone's stock price had plunged to about $16 a share and would keep plunging. The company's problems were dragging down the entire industry, as fund managers bailed out of biotechnology as fast as they could.

"The biotech sector depends on positive investor expectations," said Jon Alsenas, of ING Furman Selz Asset Management. "ImClone [is] acting like a wet blanket . . . with new revelations coming out seemingly every few days. Then we've seen a series of clinical trial disappointments from other companies. With this kind of pessimistic outlook, biotech valuations are going to contract."

It wasn't just the big institutional investors who were hurt by ImClone, of course; plenty of individual investors got their fingers jammed as ImClone's swinging door shut.

In Washington, D.C., members of Congress started to hear from constituents who had been burned by ImClone. The story took on a new political dimension and a debate suddenly flared up about the disclosure of communications between biotech firms and the FDA.

Stock analysts and scientists pointed to the impact *The Cancer Letter*'s excerpting of the RTF letter had on the market: if it had not been for the leak, the public would not have known how faulty the Waksals' science really was. Although ImClone was a rare case, it was not unique. Aggressive biotech firms, working under grueling pressure, sometimes misrepresent their communications with the FDA.

The FDA should make its correspondence with drug companies public, the critics maintained, so that people could make informed decisions about their investments; biotech firms, in particular, should be subject to greater disclosure because most of them have meager revenues. "All you have to go on is some scientific data and the companies' claims about how the FDA responded," a biotech analyst named Steven Harr said to *The Wall Street Journal*. "That's like trying to evaluate Enron without looking at its financial statements."

But others disagreed, saying such disclosures would scare away investors and upset the delicate balance between drugmakers and regulators. "You would be asking the FDA to render decisions before there was a full review of the data," a regulatory affairs officer at a pharmaceutical association said, "and that's not appropriate."

BRISTOL-MYERS HAD TAKEN a chance on ImClone, and now it looked like a sucker. Bristol's CEO, Peter Dolan, appeared weak and wrongheaded, and he was criticized both inside and outside the company.

After acquiring its stake in ImClone and licensing Erbitux for $1 billion, BMS had paid the biotech company a first step payment of $200 million. Had the FDA accepted the drug application, ImClone stood to receive a $300 million step payment from its partner, and marketing approval would have brought a further $500 million. Now, however, the spigot of money had been turned off.

Rick Lane, president of Bristol-Myers Squibb's worldwide medicines group and one of the architects of the ImClone deal, told *Business-Week* that the company remained confident about the future of Erbitux: "There is no doubt it works."

Yet at the end of January, Bristol was forced to write down some $735 million of its $1.2 billion investment in ImClone. The write-off was the result of "new accounting rules," the company maintained, and not due to ImClone's travails. But Fred Schiff, Bristol CFO, warned that BMS might require further write-offs on its remaining $465 million Im-Clone investment. As ImClone's stock had tanked, so had Bristol-Myers Squibb's, down to $45.33, a five-year low.

Peter Dolan was incensed. A growing consensus held that the earnest and aggressive Dolan had been manipulated by the more supple and wily Waksal brothers. Central to the criticism was the issue of due diligence. Critics, like Martyn Postle, of Cambridge Pharma Consulting, charged that, "Whatever due diligence BMS did, it was clearly not enough." Theresa Agovino wrote in the Associated Press: "No one will ever call . . . Peter Dolan meek, or stingy. The question is whether he'll eventually be seen as visionary or will remain what he appears now, a high-stakes gambler on a losing streak . . . Analysts and investors are dying to know how a sophisticated company, noted for its expertise in cancer drugs, could have failed to detect ImClone's problems."

UBS Warburg analyst Jeffrey Chaffkin said: "[BMS] is a company that has taken really big bets and pretty much missed them all . . . I can't say that I'm happy with [Dolan's] performance to date."

In December 2001, before the bad news hit, I asked Brian Marki-son, Bristol's president of oncology and virology and one of BMS's point men on the ImClone deal, about the company's due diligence of its biotech partner. He replied: "We felt there could be synergy and we did an extraordinarily rigorous [due diligence]—we looked at every scrap of paper, verified all the lab data, X-rays, CT scans, manufacturing specifications, toxicity, every single thing." Since that conversation, however, Bristol officials refused to return my calls. (The next time I heard Markison speak was under oath, as he was being grilled at a con-gressional hearing.)

"NEEDLESS TO SAY, we couldn't be more disappointed in the turn of events since the [Erbitux] filing," said Peter Dolan, his normally deep and confident voice strained with frustration. This was on a conference call with analysts and investors on January 24. He said that although Bristol's due diligence of ImClone had included "multiple groups in our company, including R&D, science, commercial, legal etcetera," as well as outside experts, "we aren't happy with where we are."

In what sounded like an emotional and unscripted aside, he said:

"Now I am sure that all of you on this call have additional questions on ImClone. I would, too, if I were in your position. However, I'd ask you to refrain from asking for more information . . . so as to not further complicate the present situation."

But Wall Street wanted answers. When Bridget Cowan of Dresdner Associates pointed out that Bristol was now a part owner of ImClone and asked about Bristol's legal liability for ImClone's "improper actions," Dolan answered stiffly: "We think our legal position is very sound. And we're not going to comment on their situation based on statements made before or after December 28."

When David Hines of Avalon Research asked whether Dolan would sign off on a joint press release about a meeting between the FDA and ImClone, Dolan verbally bristled: "I'm not going to make that commitment . . . We'll continue to work to ensure that the statements ImClone is making are consistent with what we most believe."

The Bristol CEO sounded vexed and determined to set things right. He hinted to those listening carefully that significant moves were afoot. "Let me assure you, this is a matter of top priority to BMS, me, and my senior management team," he said, in an even voice. Then he added, cryptically: "We will consider *all* options in pursuing any actions that will preserve the interests of Bristol-Myers shareholders."

# ELEVEN

# The Disconnect
# That Wouldn't Go Away

On Monday, January 14, 2002, Peter Dolan snapped. He summoned Sam uptown, to Bristol-Myers Squibb's Park Avenue headquarters, and dressed him down. In Dolan's large, quiet office, appointed with rich wood paneling, deep carpeting, and fine paintings high above 51st Street, the Bristol CEO had said he would no longer entrust the development of Erbitux to ImClone. It was a short, uncomfortable meeting. He said he wanted Sam and Harlan to temporarily step down from the company they had founded and let Bristol take over communications with the FDA. He said that Bristol would sharply reduce the amount of money it would pay them. If things didn't improve immediately, Dolan said evenly, then it was all over: Bristol was prepared to exit the barely four-month-old, $2 billion deal and cast Erbitux to the wind.

In early February, Dolan made these demands public in a startling announcement: Unless Sam and Harlan Waksal were removed from day-to-day responsibilities at ImClone—at least until the FDA approved Erbitux—then Bristol-Myers Squibb was prepared to walk away from its landmark agreement.

"We are taking this action because we believe Erbitux has great potential to treat cancer patients, and we want to move the process forward as quickly as possible," Dolan told the press. He was worried about Erbitux. He was worried about Bristol's declining business and tarnished reputation. He was worried about keeping his prestigious, lucrative job. The fracas had the aspect of an elephant trying to stomp a mouse, but Dolan did not like to be humiliated.

That evening, the Bristol CEO met with Robert Goldhammer, chairman of the ImClone board. He suggested that while Sam and Harlan temporarily stepped aside, Goldhammer run ImClone. At first blush, the offer made sense. Robert Goldhammer was 70, a former partner at Kidder Peabody, and now a partner at Concord International Group, a money management firm. Perhaps Dolan felt that Goldhammer would be a more sophisticated and rational partner, a kindred corporate spirit, in a way that the fast-and-loose entrepreneurs Sam and Harlan Waksal could never be. Sam, in particular, seemed to push all of Dolan's stylistic buttons in the wrong way.

But Dolan's suggestion betrayed a misreading of the situation and of the personalities involved. Goldhammer had been with ImClone since the beginning. To many inside the biotech firm, he was a silver-haired mystery, rarely, if ever, seen around the Varick Street offices. To those who knew him, Goldhammer seemed to delight in the Waksals' company, and former insiders speculate that he helped tutor Sam in finance. Although he had occasionally yelled at Sam—for spending a rumored $120,000 of company money on his private Christmas party, for example—Goldhammer had been their staunch defender and protector, and thus a powerful enabler of their erratic and irresponsible behavior, since 1984. He declined Dolan's offer.

In response to Bristol's ultimatum, ImClone released a languid press release that said: "We will review their proposal and respond appropriately in due course."

Behind the scenes, "unnamed people close to ImClone" were talking to members of the press that night. These people pointed out that while Dolan had basically accused Sam of misleading Bristol and of lying to Wall Street, BMS's own regulatory filings had described a thorough due diligence of ImClone and Erbitux. The unnamed sources noted that in June a dozen senior Bristol officials had reviewed the complete FDA regulatory file, including all correspondence with the agency.

And, these people noted, Bristol had been given regular updates as the Erbitux application was filed. These countercharges were duly reported in the next day's papers.

With the news of Dolan's take-charge offensive, the stock of both companies rose slightly. (On February 8, ImClone's shares had hit a two-year low of $13.77.) But worries lingered. To some observers, Dolan had been a bully who had overplayed his hand with a strong emotional reaction. This had left Bristol with little leverage or room to maneuver on the ImClone deal. Dolan's tactical error gave Sam, Harlan, and Goldhammer an edge to exploit. "I'm expecting ImClone to tell Bristol to go home," predicted Eric Hecht, a Merrill Lynch analyst. "Then it'll be up to Bristol to come up with the next move."

On February 11, a special committee of ImClone's board met all day to discuss the situation; Sam and Harlan were recused from the meeting. The next day, Goldhammer called Dolan's bluff.

A meeting between ImClone and the FDA had been scheduled for February 26, to discuss rehabilitating the Erbitux application. If the talks went well and Dolan had exited the ImClone deal, then one of Bristol's competitors could form a quick and cheap partnership with the Waksals and bring Erbitux to market with only a short delay.

ImClone had made Dolan blink. With so much money and prestige at stake, Bristol could not really walk away from the deal.

ON FRIDAY, February 13, Carl Icahn, the brazen corporate raider—he preferred the more genteel appellation "investor activist"—who built an estimated $5 billion fortune by snapping up distressed stocks like TWA cheaply, suddenly filed his intentions to buy $500 million worth of ImClone common stock. This acquisition would give Icahn control of 40 percent of the biotech concern, about the same percentage that Bristol had.

Icahn and Sam had a deep and complex history. They were tennis partners in the Hamptons and poker-playing buddies in the city, which didn't mean they trusted each other. In May 2001, Icahn engaged in what *The New York Observer* characterized as, "a little on-camera towel-snapping," when he told CNBC's *Business Center,* "You know, I play a little tennis pretty badly . . . But I could beat Sam Waksal. That's about the only guy."

Along with Martha Stewart, Icahn had been an early investor in Im-

Clone, and like Robert Goldhammer, Icahn had long been one of Sam's protectors. In 1990, he rescued ImClone from bankruptcy by buying stock and assets for $2 million. In 1994–95, he again rescued Sam with his $6 million purchase of the ImClone subsidiary Cadus Pharmaceuticals. In October 1999, Icahn filed a "13-D" form with the SEC, reporting that he led a group that owned a 5.1 percent stake in ImClone; he reportedly sold most of those shares. And in 2001, when Icahn was making a play for Visx, Inc., an eye-surgery company, he included Sam in his slate of nominees for Visx's board. (The deal never transpired.)

Then there was the Princeton connection. Icahn had majored in philosophy at Princeton University before starting his career as a stockbroker in 1961. In 1999, as part of the 250th anniversary of the university's charter, he made a $20 million gift to construct the Carl C. Icahn Laboratory, which Princeton described as "a state-of-the-art laboratory . . . home to Princeton's new interdisciplinary Institute for Integrative Genomics . . . [where] investigators from the widest range of scientific disciplines will work together to translate the wealth of advanced information on the human genome into important discoveries about biological processes."

Sam claimed to have taught at Princeton, and ImClone's Somerville, New Jersey, lab and manufacturing facility is not far from the university campus.

Icahn's curiously well-timed announcement—that he planned to purchase half a billion dollars' worth of depressed ImClone stock in February 2002—seemed a clear victory for Sam. With a shareholder of Icahn's stature on board, it would be difficult for Bristol-Myers to bully ImClone. By the end of trading Friday, ImClone stock was up 4 percent, to $18.22.

But as several analysts pointed out, Icahn is first and foremost an opportunistic investor who is most concerned with maximizing his return. Such an investor cannot necessarily be relied on, even by his friends. What, for instance, would stop him from suddenly turning around and teaming with Bristol-Myers to oust Sam and Harlan? Nothing.

What were Icahn's true intentions? Was his announcement a vote of confidence in beleaguered ImClone, or a precursor to a takeover attempt, or both at once? It wasn't entirely clear.

Some observers believed that Icahn was intentionally sending mixed signals, as part of an elaborate arbitrage in ImClone common stock. "Icahn is a complex guy. He looks for value and can be loyal, but he could also be looking for an arbitrage situation through the creation of value through a control situation," said Peter Crowley, head of health-care corporate finance at CIBC. "You don't know whether it was done for optics or economics."

Showing its worry, ImClone's board quickly announced a shareholder-rights plan that included a "poison pill" antitakeover defense plan. A poison pill dilutes a company's outstanding shares when any investor acquires more than a 15 percent stake, making it easier for the company to defend itself. Naturally, the same defense could be used to forestall any hostile moves by Bristol-Myers.

Some on Wall Street were left scratching their heads over all the sub-rosa maneuvering. "Do drug companies do hostile takeovers? Not very often," observed Lawrence Blumberg, principal of biotech fund Blumberg Capital. "Would Icahn take over ImClone in a leveraged buyout? Not likely."

To further muddy the waters, Russell Glass, the longtime president and chief investment officer of Icahn Associates, abruptly quit the firm on February 27. No reason was given, although many inferred that Glass's departure had something to do with the ImClone bid. Still, Glass remained as CEO of Cadus Pharmaceuticals, the former ImClone spin-off, on the board of which Icahn sits.

Whether his intentions were genuine or not, the mercurial Icahn never followed through on his plan to purchase 40 percent of ImClone. Reportedly, he was worried that Bristol would abandon the troublesome biotech firm and that competing drugs, like AstraZeneca's Iressa, were fast gaining ground on Erbitux. An Icahn insider told Reuters: "While Icahn likes [ImClone] and thinks it has a good drug, he has concerns that the drug may take a couple of years to hit the market, leaving room open for competition." Icahn did not become a multibillionaire by making stupid bets.

THE ICAHN HEADLINES made for good sport, but in truth they were a sideshow. The real $2 billion question hanging over ImClone and Bristol-Myers Squibb was: What would the FDA require for the approval of Erbitux?

Things were coming to a head now. The companies' meeting with the agency was only a week away, and they were still squabbling over which one of them would take the lead and how to present the most recent Erbitux data. In preparation for the meeting, Sam was working hard to clean up his image. On February 14, he reimbursed ImClone the $486,051 he had made on sales of company stock that may have violated insider-trading regulations. He did this to avoid the mere appearance of impropriety, newspapers said.

Yet, try as he might to appear the responsible CEO, this was not his true nature, which once again began to assert itself.

A FEW WEEKS LATER it was revealed that while repaying his possibly illicit trading profit to ImClone on February 14, Sam had also filed a Form 5 with the SEC, which detailed 50 trades—acquisitions, sales, and gifts—he had made in ImClone stock since 1992 but had failed to report within the proscribed 45 days. In fact, he had never reported them.

According to SEC regulations, corporate officers, directors, and investors holding 10 percent or more of a company's stock are obliged to file a Form 4 when there is a change in their holdings. The form is due within 10 days of the close of the month in which the transaction took place. A Form 5 can be used by people who forget to file a Form 4, but even Form 5 has a deadline of six weeks. Fifty trades over 10 years is a lot of trades to forget about. Securities lawyers said the SEC, which rarely presses charges against executives for missing filing deadlines, might just warn Sam or they might fine him heavily. Given his recent history, the betting was on the latter.

"He's in very dangerous territory," said Peter Romero, an attorney at Hogan & Hartson LLP who specialized in insider trading. "I'd like to know if I was the SEC why some of these filings are ten years late."

This latest piece of news upped the chatter about ImClone: every week, it seemed, there were new damaging revelations about Sam and his wayward company. What'll it be next?

THIS TIME, Paul Goldberg had gotten his hands on the most important Erbitux document aside from the RTF letter: ImClone's clinical trial protocol. The protocol was the scientific plan, or guideline, used by ImClone to develop its cancer treatment. Like the RTF it was confidential. Like the RTF someone had leaked it to him. Only this time he had solicited the leak and knew perfectly well who the leaker was. Not that he'd ever tell. For weeks, Goldberg had been asking a wide variety of sources for the Erbitux protocol, and although such a thing is a rare and coveted internal document, reserved only for those who were actually working with the drug in the lab or in a clinic, someone had eventually come through for him.

It would not do to simply run excerpts of the protocol; it was very technical and wouldn't make sense to most people. He needed someone to analyze it for him, someone who understood it and could translate it into lay language. For the latest issue of *The Cancer Letter,* Goldberg asked three respected oncologists to review the Erbitux trial design and write up their assessment. All three reviewers agreed, Goldberg paraphrases, that, "you couldn't write a worse protocol if you tried."

The Erbitux clinical trial, Study 9923, tested the hypothesis that colon cancer patients who were "refractory—that is, they had already failed the standard chemotherapy, irinotecan—would respond to a combination of Erbitux plus irinotecan. ImClone had enrolled 120 irinotecan refractory patients, which is an extremely small trial, and claimed a remarkable 22.5 percent response rate. But the entry criteria for patients in Study 9923, the protocol showed, were poorly defined. That is, the protocol defines "refractory" so broadly that, Goldberg says, "you couldn't tell who responded to what. It was a mess."

The open question was: had patients in the study responded to the chemo, or to the chemo-Erbitux cocktail?

"The protocol generates far more questions than it could ever answer. It is a blueprint for the production of vague findings," wrote Dr. Otis Brawley, a professor of oncology at Emory University Winship Cancer Institute and a member of the FDA's ODAC. "Overall, this is a protocol that asks the wrong questions, and then is not tightly written and efficient . . . Indeed, the fact that this drug received a lot of hype and positive press means a physician hoping to do the best for his or her patient might use the vagueness of the inclusion and exclusion criteria to their advantage, enrolling patients the authors of the trial would have excluded."

Sam and Harlan had long maintained that the main reason the FDA had rejected their drug was that the IRAC panel had not done its job right, and so ImClone had not been able to provide the agency with the "proper documentation." But writing in *The Cancer Letter,* Dr. Howard Ozer, director of the Oklahoma University Cancer Center, pointed out that the IRAC wasn't even part of the original trial protocol, and wasn't established until after Study 9923 was underway. The IRAC, he wrote, was an attempt at "some kind of overall quality control on the protocol, but this is a retrospective manipulation, and that's inappropriate methodology in clinical trials . . . A retrospective analysis introduces a bias."

The author of the Erbitux trial protocol is an unidentified person at ImClone. But Harlan Waksal was in charge of ImClone's science and clinical trials, and was ultimately responsible for the way it was written and implemented. Harlan had no comment to make about *The Cancer Letter*'s latest revelation.

The true believers held steadfast. "I still believe that there is a 99 percent chance that the FDA decides to approve Erbitux in a few months," Hemant Shah, a drug analyst with HKS & Co., told Adam Feuerstein. Shah added that oncologists with experience using Erbitux had told him they believed in it, and had convinced him it was an approvable cancer drug. Most important, Shah said, he believed in the drug's lead investigator, Len Saltz, of Memorial Sloan-Kettering.

"My father told me to have faith in great men," Shah said. "And Dr. Saltz is a great man."

CONGRESSIONAL INVESTIGATORS were beginning to tighten the screws. On February 21, Alan Slobodin sent a letter to seven drug firms that had reviewed ImClone's Erbitux data, prior to the Bristol deal, as a prelude to a possible strategic alliance. None of those other deals had come to pass, but several of those companies had done due diligence on ImClone and thus were privy to the kind of information about Erbitux that Bristol had based its $2 billion deal on.

The subcommittee's letter—sent to Pharmacia Corporation, Merck & Company, Eli Lilly & Co., Johnson & Johnson, Chiron Corp, Amgen Inc., and Abbott Laboratories—requested "all records including internal audits, investigations, and/or reports relating to ImClone Systems."

THE MEETING went surprisingly well. If the FDA had insisted on a whole new, larger clinical trial, it could have set Erbitux back by at least two years, and might have been the end of the historic Bristol-ImClone deal. But when representatives of ImClone, Bristol, and the agency met on February 26, the FDA agreed to consider "reanalyzed clinical data" from ImClone's Study 9923, as well as new data culled from a clinical trial conducted by the company's German partner, Merck KGaA.

ImClone and Bristol had pulled out all the stops to impress the agency. They had gathered CT scans and MRIs of 105 of 120 of the patients in the colorectal cancer Study 9923. The companies agreed to submit the data to a new IRAC panel.

As a gesture of goodwill and a way to dampen the ongoing criticism of Sam's unofficial compassionate-use program, the companies had invited an outsider to observe the meeting. He was Robert L. Erwin, a patient advocate for the Marti Nelson Cancer Research foundation, named after his late wife (he is also CEO of Large Scale Biologics, a biotech firm). A soft-spoken but determined man, Erwin said: "Both the FDA and ImClone seemed to be working together in a constructive, not hostile, way to move Erbitux along. The Waksals admitted that mistakes had been made, but they committed to correct them. When the FDA saw that attitude, they got specific about what needs to be done. The encouraging news is that it looks as if the drug will be available sooner than I thought."

A Merck KGaA spokesman chimed in: "We consider it a great day—the FDA opened the door for our data." The German company had enrolled 225 colorectal cancer patients in its clinical trial and said it hoped to launch the drug in Europe by 2003.

Peter Dolan didn't say anything more about ousting Sam and Harlan, for the moment. BMS and ImClone jointly issued a revised agreement that changed "certain economics of the agreement," and an expansion of Bristol's role in the development of Erbitux. Andrew Bodnar, a Bristol senior vice president already on the ImClone board, would oversee a "joint team" to shepherd Erbitux through the regulatory process. The new agreement capped royalty payments at 39 percent, delayed Bristol's milestone payments to ImClone, and cut them to $200 million—$100 million less than originally agreed on.

The market breathed a sigh of relief. Finally, it looked like the worst of the storm had passed. The deeply frozen partnership appeared to be thawing out, as Bristol and ImClone began to work at bringing Erbitux to market as expeditiously as possible. ImClone shares rose $5.01 on the NASDAQ, and Bristol was up almost $2 in NYSE trading.

The equanimity wouldn't last, though. It couldn't. Not with Sam in the picture. Equanimity wasn't really his thing.

\*     \*     \*

ON MARCH 14, *The New York Times* reported that a mysterious SEC document, called a Form 144, had come to light. It had been filed on January 25, 2001, by Merrill Lynch, for a stock trade made on December 27, 2001. It indicated that Aliza Waksal—Sam's youngest daughter, an aspiring actress who did not work at ImClone and had no real income to speak of—had sold 39,472 shares of ImClone Systems, Inc. Priced at about $62 a share, the transaction netted Aliza a total of some $2.46 million. The trade was executed the day before the FDA had faxed ImClone the RTF letter. If the trade had taken place a day later, Aliza's take would have been significantly less. Was her timing a lucky coincidence? Or was it a classic case of a family member trading on inside information?

The details were fuzzy. According to the SEC filing, it appeared that Aliza held 79,797 shares pledged by her father to Merrill Lynch as collateral for a loan. The form showed that Sam gave Aliza the shares as a "gift" on December 28, although they apparently remained as his collateral to Merrill Lynch. "Who knows what's going on?" said Paul Elliott of First Call/Thompson Financial, which tracks stock moves by corporate insiders. "This doesn't look good."

A WEEK AFTER the *Times*'s disclosure, the congressional Subcommittee on Oversight and Investigations sent another letter to Sam Waksal:

> Over the past several weeks, the Committee staff repeatedly requested in telephone conversations with the O'Melveny and Myers lawyers ("O'Melveny"), who are representing ImClone Systems in this investigation, that they obtain answers from you concerning questions about Waksal family relatives trading ImClone shares in the day(s) on or before the Food and Drug Administration (FDA) issued a refuse-to-file letter on December 28, 2001, to ImClone relating to the filing of the Erbitux application. In addition, the Committee staff verbally requested that O'Melveny obtain answers as to whether you controlled or had working control over third-party accounts trading in ImClone shares, and whether you controlled or participated in any off-shore accounts trading in ImClone shares. We trust that O'Melveny conveyed the Committee's questions directly or indirectly to you. To date, the Committee has received no response to these questions.

Signed by Tauzin, Dingell, Greenwood, and Deutsch, the letter asked Sam for details of his financial accounts, his telephone logs and appointment calendar, and information on his family's ImClone stock trades. The committee asked for this information by April 1.

ImClone protested that the company "has and will continue" to co-operate with the House subcommittee, but after two months of silence from Sam the protest rang hollow.

FOR BMS, it was a time of "negative surprises," as they say on Wall Street. Now Bristol's stock price had sunk from a 52-week high of $60 a share to a new low of $40. Dolan's triumphantly announced "Mega double" turnaround was rapidly unspooling into a sloppy, knotted embarrassment. Analysts were calling it, and him, "an utter debacle."

What happened? Many things, none of them good, one after the other.

There had been the disappointing results of clinical trials for Vanlev, a hypertension drug that Bristol had touted as a possible $3 billion-a-year product; it now looked to be a dud.

There had been the expiration of patent protection for three solid blockbusters—Taxol, anxiety drug BuSpar, and diabetes treatment Glucophage—which resulted in billions of dollars of annual revenue trickling down to mere millions as generic drugmakers produced cheaper versions.

There was the fact that Bristol's vaunted and expensive in-house laboratories had not managed to create a single blockbuster for more than a decade (most of Bristol's best-selling drugs are licensed from other companies or the government; but the licensing market was growing so competitive that Bristol has not had many successful deals lately).

There was increased competition all around and the failure of some promising drugs—Avandia, Tequin, Serzone—to live up to expectations.

Most glaringly, there was the controversy over Bristol's "channel stuffing," a 2001 program overseen by the aggressive Rick Lane, in which wholesalers had been incentivized by discounts to buy more drugs—some $930 million worth—than they needed, resulting in a serious blow to 2002 sales.

All of this, plus the Sturm und Drang at ImClone, had Bristol insiders talking of a "less-than-perfect execution" by CEO Peter Dolan. Analysts griped that Bristol's earnings could plummet by as much as 47 percent.

Bristol even retained Goldman Sachs as an adviser, as takeover rumors began to swirl around the world's fifth-largest pharmaceutical company. "The bottom is dropping out of this thing," said Barbara Ryan, of Deutsche Banc Alex.Brown. "It's unbelievable."

IN MID-MARCH, Peter Dolan was summoned for a face-to-face meeting with the Bristol board of directors and informed that his job was hanging by a thread. This was not made public, although there were certainly people outside of the company calling for Dolan's head. The board had not formally voted to put Dolan on notice, a knowledgeable person would later explain to *The Wall Street Journal,* but, "any CEO who has to go through this series of misfires is on probation."

Fred Schiff, Bristol's 54-year-old CFO and a company veteran, was also put on notice.

The Bristol board was "encouraged" that Dolan had accepted responsibility for the spate of problems and "understood the severity of what's going on." But the directors were also furious and determined to put an end to the serial bungling.

Stoic Dolan did not offer to resign. Nor did he offer to restate the company's 2001 earnings. And when word of the board meeting later leaked out, coupled with the news that Dolan had earned $2.3 million for the year—including a $1 million base salary and $1.3 million bonus "for meeting 2001 earnings estimates," despite the missteps—critics began to howl. Characteristically, Dolan remained mum.

In the meantime, a shareholder named Ira Gaines filed a lawsuit in Manhattan federal court, contending that Bristol-Myers knew "all along" that ImClone's drug application was flawed, even before the FDA had issued the RTF letter. By choosing not to reveal that the Erbitux BLA was insufficient for approval, Gaines claimed, the companies had misled investors like himself.

In coming weeks, more class-action suits would pile up. One claimed that "Bristol-Myers and certain of its officers and directors made false and misleading claims about progress on its Erbitux cancer drug." Another argued that Bristol had "engaged in a scheme to mislead the investing public" about its ability to maintain revenue and earning growth, its future prospects, and its sales and revenue levels for fiscal year 2001.

*     *     *

ON MARCH 20, Sam Waksal refused to give a sworn deposition to the SEC regarding his December trades of ImClone stock. The next day, ImClone's directors decided to expel him as president and CEO. The day after that, Sam reversed himself and agreed to testify before the SEC. The directors, in turn, reversed themselves and decided to leave Sam in place. Not everyone was happy with the decision.

On March 28, Richard Barth, the former chairman, CEO, and president of Ciba-Geigy, who had served on the ImClone board since 1996, sent a handwritten note, in which he resigned in apparent protest:

*Dear Mr. Goldhammer,*

*This is to confirm my telephone advice to you . . . that I will not stand for re-election to the Board.*

*Under the circumstances I do not consider it appropriate to continue as a director. Accordingly I will resign from the Board after I have had the opportunity to vote on the minutes of the March 25, 2002 meeting, which need to reflect my position of dissent from the Board's actions.*

Barth's resignation took place out of public view and was not widely reported at the time. What was widely discussed, however, was the view on Wall Street that "things" at ImClone—meaning management—had to change. It started as a whisper in January and by the spring had become a loud, insistent chant.

"I don't think the Waksals will be around by the middle of 2003. Their credibility is shot," predicted Morningstar analyst Todd Lebor. "When you are dealing with a drug company, trust in management is very important. ImClone is lacking that."

BY APRIL, Peter Dolan had fired his CFO, Fred Schiff, as well as his flashy lieutenant, Rick Lane, whose duties as president of the worldwide medicines group Dolan personally took over. Somehow, Brian Markison, Bristol's president of oncology and virology, and the point man on the ImClone deal, had managed to hang on. But Dolan was the only remaining member of the company's senior executive team.

Bristol's stock continued to sink. Now it loitered at about $31 a share. Earnings per share for the fiscal year ending in January 2003 were expected to fall more than a dollar below Wall Street's estimate of $2.28

a share. Top-line sales were predicted to drop $1 billion below the company's 2001 revenue, $19.4 billion.

"We had a plan in December that we believed in," Dolan intoned on a conference call in early April. But now, he admitted, Bristol-Myers's core business, prescription drug sales in the United States, was "dramatically off-track." The company's performance "is unacceptable," he added. "Both at the level of strategic planning and in daily execution, we need to do a better job, and I will personally lead this effort."

Analysts suggested that Bristol's best hope was to be bought out by another firm—Novartis and Pharmacia were the two companies most frequently mentioned—although others scoffed at the idea. "With all of those lawsuits and problems, not to mention an empty pipeline [for new drugs], why would anybody want to buy Bristol?" asked one exasperated fund manager. "It's a horror show!"

SAM MET WITH investigators from the House Subcommittee on Oversight and Investigations in mid-April. The meeting lasted four hours, and Sam used a lot of words and time to say not very much of substance. The investigators were able to ask only a few of their many questions about Erbitux, the collapse of ImClone, and Sam's possible insider-trading scheme. Sam agreed to return in early May for further questions and answers. But when the time came, he never materialized.

It was like flashing a red cape at an already agitated bull. "If you thumb your nose at our committee," barked Ken Johnson, Billy Tauzin's brash press secretary, "you risk being thrown in jail."

THEN ON May 22, 2002, Sam released a statement:

> Serving as Chief Executive Officer of ImClone Systems has been an honor and a privilege for the past eighteen years. In light of recent events and the distractions they have caused, I am withdrawing myself from the daily operation of the Company in the confidence that ImClone Systems will be able to maintain its focus on the advancement of our clinical development and research programs. I fully believe that our product candidates, the most advanced of which is Erbitux, will have a profound effect on the way that patients with cancer are treated.

It had all finally caught up with him. He had cofounded ImClone, led it through thick and thin, personified the company for nearly two decades, spotted Erbitux as a diamond in the rough and championed it when no one else would, and now . . . well, he was going away to deal with his troubles out of the limelight. He had been forced out. He had no further public comment. Sam Waksal was now the ex-president, chief executive officer, and a director of a well-known New York biotech company.

Goldhammer stated: "The Company owes a great deal to Sam's scientific and operational leadership, as well as to the inspiration, guidance and support he has provided our talented employees."

Harlan said: "The issues surrounding Sam have become a significant distraction to him and to the company . . . He felt it was hurting the company and its ability to get its message across."

The disappointments of the 2002 ASCO conference, held in Orlando, Florida, had been the last straw for Sam. ImClone had presented new Erbitux data from a pair of clinical trials in colorectal cancer: a small, 29-patient pilot study testing Erbitux in combination with a three-drug chemo mixture; and another small trial testing Erbitux alone. Results had been subpar. A third trial of the drug, conducted by an independent research organization, the Eastern Cooperative Oncology Group (ECOG), tested the effects of the chemotherapy cisplatin versus a combination of cisplatin and Erbitux on 123 patients. Because the ECOG study was late stage, blinded, randomized, and independent of ImClone, it carried great scientific clout. And although the drug showed some promising activity in this trial, it did not meet its clinical endpoints. The press made much of that.

A fourth small trial, involving 75 patients with advanced head-and-neck cancer—the disease that was supposed to express huge amounts of EGF—was sponsored by Merck KGaA and was led by Dr. Jose Beselga, John Mendelsohn's star researcher at Sloan-Kettering, and now a cancer specialist at Vall d'Hebron Hospital in Barcelona, Spain. In Beselga's clinical trial, only eight, or 10.67 percent of patients showed tumor shrinkage of at least 50 percent; for patients who responded to Erbitux, the median survival time was three months more than for the typical victim of head-and-neck cancer. This was a short—but to the patients, significant—extension of life. "It represents a clinical benefit when you consider the extremely poor prognosis for patients" with head-and-neck cancer, Beselga said.

These were all small clinical trials. Andrew Bodnar, the Bristol vice president who had been deputized to oversee the development of Erbitux, said they were designed to show the drug's early promise. Many of the oncologists at ASCO still believed in the EGFr class of drugs. But the FDA wanted evidence that showed Erbitux was effective in large, carefully designed, and scrupulously conducted trials. The data provided at ASCO 2002 did not give the agency what it required.

Part of the problem in Orlando was that Sam's myriad troubles had caused people to view ImClone with suspicion, and thus, Erbitux supporters complained, the results of the small clinical trials were viewed through an unjustifiedly negative light. Dr. Kris Jenner, money manager for T. Rowe Price, believed that ImClone's data had been unfairly judged. "The attention on him [Sam] was greater than the attention on the drug," Jenner said. "I felt like their data was clearly not as negative as it was portrayed."

At one point during the ASCO conference, Sam turned to Harlan and said: "This disconnect just doesn't want to go away."

Then he resigned. Now Harlan was CEO.

# TWELVE

# Who Knew What and When?

After her usual three or four hours of sleep, Martha Stewart awoke early on the morning of Friday June 7, 2002, to discover that her name was in the newspapers again. *All* of them. But not in a good way this time. She was deeply chagrined. She had not asked for this, but there was little she could do to control it. It seemed that someone was trying to embarrass her, or use her, or make an example out of her. She hated it.

As far as she was concerned, she'd done absolutely nothing wrong. She'd been running her homemaking empire, taping her TV and radio shows, editing her magazine, appearing in her regular plum spot on CBS's *Early Show*, tending to Turkey Hill, and planning new and exciting ways to extend the Martha brand. Her ImClone trade on December 27 was strictly routine, not to mention small potatoes: when the stock dipped below $60, Merrill Lynch had sold all of her holdings in Sam's company, as she and Peter Bacanovic had agreed they would do at that price. (He says their oral agreement was reached in mid-December, she says it was in late November.) But now all of this morning's newspapers were claiming that she was under suspicion of insider trading.

It was Sam's ImClone mess, which seemed to besmirch anyone and everyone who touched it. It was also Enron, Arthur Anderson, World-

Com, and all of that, too. The nation was obsessed with corporate scandal and skeptical of high-flying CEOs; now lawmakers were on a witch hunt. Guess who made the perfect target?

Somebody in Congress had seized on Martha's name as an easy way to generate headlines for their investigation. How had this happened? Why? According to all the leading papers—*The New York Times, The Wall Street Journal, The Washington Post,* not to mention the flesh-eating tabloids—Sam's lawyers had, within the last few days, told congressional investigators about her sale of ImClone stock. The articles implied that before her trade, Sam—or someone else, like Peter Bacanovic—had tipped her off to the impending RTF letter, and that she had therefore profited illegally.

It was painful. She had always tried to do well by doing good; she'd been smart, worked hard, taken risks, succeeded as few ever had, and had been well compensated for it. Maybe some were jealous, but most people appreciated her, as the success of her business clearly demonstrated. But in these articles, and the widening gossip about them, she felt a distinct change in tone, like a sudden chilling wind shift.

Martha was a creature of the mass media, and her internal barometer was finely tuned to subtle shifts in temperature and wind direction in that very particular ecosystem. She hoped the ImClone thing would fizzle, like just another tempest in a teapot. But she knew how fluky these things could be. ImClone could just as easily whip up into a black hurricane.

Certain people—especially politicians and the press—it seemed, were tapping into an incipient anti-Martha sentiment, and fueling it, to further their own agendas. She found it offensive. What was really going on here was that they were trying to take away her success. Or tarnish her personally. She wouldn't stand for it. No, she had too much pride for that. The men of Congress—and all but one (Diana DeGette, Democrat of Colorado) of the investigating subcommittee were men—saw smiley blonde Martha on TV and thought they could easily manipulate her, just as the men of Time Warner and Wall Street had once thought they could simply walk all over her. But they had underestimated her. They had not bothered to find out who they were really dealing with. Martha was no pixie; she was physically strong and extremely determined (something that other women liked about her). Through sheer force of will she had molded herself out of the lumpen clay of a lower middle class family from Nutley, New Jersey, into Martha Stewart, ubiquitous arbiter of style and billionaire global icon. She would not stand idly by while the mean-spirited bashed her for sport. She took the morning's headlines personally. It was an ad hominem attack and she would fight it tooth and nail.

Her attorneys had already fired the first salvo. John F. Savarese, of Wachtell, Lipton, Rosen & Katz, was quoted in the papers saying: "There is absolutely no evidence whatsoever that [Martha] spoke to Sam, or had any information from anybody from ImClone during that week. I am absolutely sure that there was no communication of any kind between her and Sam, no passing of any information from him to her."

That was her message: I did no wrong, now leave me alone.

Her plan was to bury herself in work, as usual. At the moment she was focused on taking MSO to the next phase, with the launch of a new digest magazine, *Everyday Food,* and a new line of furniture. Like other successful people—her friends Bill and Hillary Clinton, for instance—she was lucky because she had the ability to compartmentalize. She had thick skin. She was the kind of person who could be concerned *and* productive. So her plan was to ignore the ImClone problem as much as possible and hope that it would disappear as quickly as it had arrived.

In coming months, however, the ridicule and vilification and investigations of Martha would only grow worse. The tabloids were mean, especially the *New York Post,* which ran mocking headlines about her and one humiliating photograph after another—here's Martha with her hair blowing across her face, here she is looking old and sour, here she is looking fat and sour, here she is with wet hair at the salon. *Newsweek* and *People* and then seemingly every other publication under the sun got into the act, too.

The storm continued to build and build, and the general public seemed to be fascinated and amused by her comeuppance. Friends began to use the word *schadenfreude* to describe this gloating over her bad news. Martha knew how to spell the word, she pointed out, and she knew what it meant: "enjoyment obtained from others' troubles." She began to hear that word, like, every day.

Martha grew haunted by a question: What if the ImClone hurricane didn't blow itself out, as she had been telling everybody it would—what would it do to Martha Stewart Living Omnimedia, the company that was her life?

BY THE END OF MAY, ImClone stock had dropped to a new 52-week low of $8.90. This was the first time since January 1999 that the stock had been priced under $9. (In February 2000, ImClone shares had soared to an all-time high of $131.37 a share; now it was down 79 percent since the beginning of 2002.)

The problems at ImClone, compounded by a deepening recession, had cast a pall over the entire biotech industry. Bank of America downgraded AstraZeneca PLC to market performer from buy, based partly on questions about its targeted lung cancer treatment, Iressa. Like Erbitux, Iressa is a drug that could be used on tumors that express the epidermal growth factor (EGF) protein. "The EGF category is being questioned to a far greater degree than in the past," said David Gruber, a buy-side analyst with WPG Farber. "The mechanisms with Erbitux are a little different [than Iressa] but both are EGF inhibitors, so that raises some questions."

Gruber was also concerned about ImClone's management. Sam's resignation didn't mean that everything was suddenly okay, he said: "Having one of them leave doesn't solve the question of management's credibility. His brother is still there."

IN THE COURSE of an intensive, six-month investigation, the House Subcommittee's small team of investigators had reviewed thousands of pages of documents and interviewed two dozen officials from ImClone, Bristol, other pharmaceutical companies, Merrill Lynch, the FDA, the SEC, and the DOJ. They had a pretty good idea of what had happened at ImClone in late December, but were still trying to fill in gaps in the puzzle. Sam held the missing pieces. But he and his attorneys were apparently too busy to return their calls or answer their letters.

When the scandal first broke, a friend said, "All Sam cared about was what people thought. He asked, 'Are people saying I'm a terrible man?'" But now he was starting to go out on the town again.

"Sam's been out at dinner parties every night. He's always been about keeping up appearances . . . he's acting like nothing's wrong, like it's all under control and he knows something nobody else knows that will make it okay."

Said another friend: "Sam came over to the house. He said to me, "Why would I have told Aliza to sell, and not told Elana?' "

He couldn't stand to be alone. Aside from meeting with lawyers on a nearly daily basis, Sam spent his time lunching with groups of friends, attending openings and receptions in Manhattan, and going to parties in the Hamptons. Sam had much to say about a wide variety of subjects, although the details of the last 18 years at ImClone was not a subject at the top of his list.

By early June, Sam's half-answers and evasions had become so unsatisfactory that the congressional committee subpoenaed him to testify in Washington, D.C., under oath. The hearing was set for June 13. This was a serious development. If Sam failed to appear before Congress, as he had failed to appear for his second session with the investigators in May, then he could be sent to jail on charges of contempt.

"We have tried repeatedly to get Mr. Waksal to cooperate, but he has refused," said Tauzin's press secretary, Ken Johnson. "We are trying to determine if investors got short-shrifted. We haven't been able to get straight answers . . . and that has prompted this formal investigative hearing."

ImClone put out a press release saying that it "continues to work closely with, and cooperate fully with, the subcommittee." Ken Johnson grinned like a pit bull, and allowed that while the company had indeed cooperated, "we'd like to hear some of their answers under oath."

ImClone was trading listlessly now in the $7 doldrums.

IN CHECKING brokerage account records, government investigators had noticed that every member of the Waksal family, save Sam's mother, Sabina, had traded ImClone shares in December, just before the FDA issued the RTF letter. From the outside, it looked like a textbook case of insider trading: the Waksal family had apparently taken care of itself at the expense of nearly everyone else.

Phone and financial records indicated that: Harlan Waksal, Im-Clone's COO, had cashed out to the tune of $54,432,490 on October 29, and a further $50,358,000 on December 6 (two days after Lily Lee's visit to George Mills at the FDA). After a phone call from Sam on the night of December 26, Jack Waksal—referred to in SEC documents as "Family Member 1"—sold 110,000 shares of ImClone stock on December 27. He used three different brokers, and the orders were executed between 9:45 and 10:02 A.M., at prices ranging from $61.25 to $62.16 per share. Earlier that morning, he'd ordered Prudential Securities to sell 1,336 shares of ImClone owned by his daughter, Patti (whose investments he controlled)—"Family Member 3"—at about $62.20 a share. Then, at 9:29 A.M. on December 28, Jack placed a final order to sell 25,000 shares of ImClone stock, at $57.19 a share. In total, Sam's father sold 135,000 shares just before the FDA issued its RTF, and grossed over $8 million. Sam's sister, Patti, grossed $83,099.

Sam called his younger daughter, Aliza—"Family Member 2"—on the morning of December 27. At 9 A.M. she sold 39,472 shares of ImClone stock, in four blocks, at prices ranging from $62.28 to $63.20 a share. She reaped $2.5 million.

The previous evening, December 26, her father had attempted to transfer an additional 79,797 ImClone shares to Aliza. In his request to Merrill Lynch, Sam had written: "It's imperative this transfer take place tomorrow morning, December 27, first thing." He would explain to investigators: "I believe this was just the way it was written, just to make sure that they would do it very quickly. [Sam's accountant] was going away and he was making sure that it was done immediately. I don't believe that there was any imperative associated with it."

Sam's older daughter, Elana, and her husband, Jarrett Posner, had sold about 10 percent of their ImClone holdings as the stock dropped in panic selling on the 27th. Her broker was Peter Bacanovic. "My client did nothing wrong," her lawyer said.

In depositions before the SEC in April, Sam was asked: "Did you ever instruct [Jack or Aliza] to sell their shares of ImClone?"

Under oath, he answered: "No."

Indeed, every member of his immediate family denied he had been tipped off about the impending RTF letter. Each proffered a reason for selling his ImClone stock that had nothing to do with being tipped by Sam or Harlan. With the exception of Jack Waksal (who did not provide information to the committee), attorneys for each of the family members admitted that their client sold stock on or around December 27,

2001, but asserted that they received no nonpublic information about ImClone and each had a reason why he sold the stock on that particular day.

Although phone records and logs obtained from Sam and Harlan, covering the period December 26 to 28, suggest that both men had conversations with each other, and may have had conversations with members of their family and friends, the Waksal brothers denied that they had tipped off anyone about the RTF.

Ken Johnson was unimpressed. "There was a *lot* of stock dumped in the 48 hours before the FDA acted," he harrumphed.

Experts on insider trading were also skeptical, and noted that such a pattern of sales by so many people related to one or two individuals was not typical behavior. When the SEC judges an insider trading case, it usually asks whether a reasonable person would believe that the sellers would dump their shares for any reason other than having foreknowledge that the stock price would drop. In the Waksals' case, nobody could come up with an alternate answer that made sense to investigators. For most of 2001, Sam and Harlan had strenuously assured the world that Erbitux was going to be approved by the FDA and would soon become a blockbuster cancer drug. Many people believed them and had invested accordingly. The claim that all five Waksal relatives suddenly, of their own volition, decided to sell their ImClone holdings just before the RTF was issued strained credulity.

"These are circumstances that certainly would warrant an investigation for insider trading," said John H. Sturc, the former head of the SEC's enforcement division, now in private practice.

Congressman James Greenwood, the subcommittee's chairman, observed, dryly: "What we know is that if you make a trade because you know something that is not public, and that other stockholders don't know, that's insider trading . . . We've been tracking the precise chronology of the [ImClone] sales, and how that compares with who knew what and when."

VEE KUMAR, a normally soft-spoken, 47-year-old school psychologist from Kirkland, Washington, was so angry she could barely talk about it. Not just at Sam and Harlan, although mostly at them, but at the media and the FDA and Bristol-Myers, too. She felt that the news coverage about ImClone had focused almost exclusively on the trivia of money and celebrity—how much the Waksals had made, how much Martha Stewart might lose—with hardly a word about the cancer patients like her who were dying because they couldn't get their hands on a drug that everybody claimed worked like a miracle. If Erbitux did not work, then the Waksals shouldn't have told everyone it did.

"There is no excuse for ImClone raising patients' hopes and then not delivering," she seethed. Her academic reflex kicking in, she added: "They really ought to have done their homework better."

AT FIVE O'CLOCK in the morning on June 12, Sam Waksal was awakened in his SoHo loft by four armed FBI agents. Three more agents waited outside, two around back so that no one could slip away. Sam was groggy from sleep, or lack of it, and still dressed in his pajamas. They had a warrant for his arrest on charges of insider trading.

His youngest daughter, Aliza, and his father, Jack, were also in the apartment that morning. Perhaps they had convened to strategize.

Sam asked the agents not to handcuff him in front of Aliza. They agreed, and handcuffed him in the hallway, out of her sight. Then they led him downstairs and outside through a throng of pushing, shouting reporters, who had been thoughtfully alerted before the raid.

In photographs from that morning, Sam has a light stubble on his chin; he wears a blue-and-white striped Oxford shirt tucked into chinos with no belt, and an expression of rueful bewilderment.

Jack Waksal, the octogenarian Holocaust survivor, was not handcuffed. He was photographed punching a CNN cameraman as his son was led away to be arraigned. Later that day Harlan and others posted Sam's bail, a $10 million personal-recognizance bond, and he was released.

IT WASN'T QUITE nine in the morning on June 13, and the white marble hallways of Rayburn House—a large, squat structure on Independence Avenue, across from the mall and the Capitol, in Washington, D.C.— were jammed. Six months after the RTF and Sam's disastrous stock trades, the first congressional hearing into ImClone Systems was about to get underway. The hearing would take place in Room 2123, the very same chamber that showcased the subcommittee's Enron hearings in February. There was an electric, adrenalized feeling in the crowd, a surging anticipation that today's hearing would be equally dramatic, if not more so, than the Enron inquisition.

In a way, the scene at Rayburn House was the inverse of one of Sam's fabulous loft parties: here big science, serious money, national politicians, and celebrity representatives had gathered not to fete Sam and ImClone, but to prosecute them. There were lawyers and cancer patients and spin controllers and biotech consultants and Big Pharma operatives and government bureaucrats and journalists all milling about.

In the lobby, Congressman Billy Tauzin was happily feeding the beast. A Louisiana Republican from a largely Democratic and Cajun district, he was a populist with a florid face, a full head of light and dark gray hair, and a bright red tie. Tauzin cocked his big head back, smiled slyly, and squinted at a throng of TV cameras and radio microphones and madly scribbling print journalists. In a reverberating baritone, he said: "It appears, as our Committee investigation has revealed, that ImClone was so excited by preliminary response rates in *very sick colon cancer patients,* it tried to take a mediocre clinical trial and *gussy it up,*" he drawled. "But when it came to crunch time to get FDA approval, the *failure* of ImClone's key *executives* to ensure the quality of its clinical trials collided with the *hype*. And, aaalllll the whilllle, ImClone's insiders were lining their own pockets with *millions,* as ImClone's publicly-traded stock soared on *false, public promises!*"

Tauzin's press secretary, Ken Johnson, stood next to him beaming. Dressed like a gunslinger, in a black suit and black cowboy boots, Johnson stirred up questions, prompted his boss, and dropped a certain name as often as possible: "We find it curious that Sam Waksal was apparently in his office that Thursday [December 27], but didn't return phone calls to close friends like *Martha Stewart.*"

The reporters ate it up, jostled each other, and shouted more questions.

So much was happening at once that it was hard to keep track. Just yesterday, Sam had been arrested at dawn by the FBI and formally charged by the SEC with insider trading. Also, a report compiled by FBI Special Agent Catherine M. Farmer had come to light, which showed that at the time of his arrest Sam had been in a far worse predicament than even his critics had realized: by December 26, 2001, he was carrying a *personal* debt of more than $80 million—$65 million of which was on margin, secured by his ImClone shares. The debt service alone was costing him a staggering $800,000 a month. This revelation suggested that, at best, he had been living out a Walter Mittyesque fantasy of a multimillionaire biotech tycoon, with no concession to reality; at worst, it suggested that Sam had been totally out of control.

"How can you sleep at night knowing you are $80 million in debt?" wondered a fresh-faced congressional aide loitering in the hallway. "I sure couldn't. I mean that's, like, mind-boggling."

"That's why you're not Sam Waksal, dude," replied his friend. "No wonder he wanted to cash out."

In the meantime, Martha Stewart had released a statement through her lawyer—"My transaction was entirely lawful"—and had withdrawn from public view. But the congressional committee let it be known that phone and brokerage account records seemed to belie her statement.

It would later be revealed that on the morning of June 13, just hours before the ImClone hearing began, Martha's lawyers had tried to bend the arm of Billy Tauzin to enter Martha's letter into the committee record and issue a statement exonerating her. This strategy backfired badly. Ken Johnson would announce to the press: "We were stunned. We couldn't believe what they were asking us to do."

A spokesman for the New York Stock Exchange would neither confirm nor deny a report that Martha, who had been named a director of the Big Board just the week before, was being investigated by the exchange. This only drove the tabloids to further frenzied speculation.

And when a Merrill Lynch spokesman was questioned about Peter Bacanovic, he would only say: "We do not discuss possible client relationships, nor do we comment on investigations except to say that we cooperate fully."

SECURITY WAS TIGHT at Rayburn House and it took awhile for everyone to pile inside Room 2123 and find a seat, every one of which was filled. Congress was busy wrangling a homeland security bill in another chamber, and so the ImClone hearing was recessed until 10:30, which only added to the crowd's anticipation. The energy level began to ramp up from hyper to frenzied, as if there was about to be a shoot-out or an execution. Rumors and questions were flying up and down the hallways.

*Is Martha here? No, but her lawyer is. Which one is he? Is Sam actually going to appear today? Will he plead the Fifth? Do you think Peter Dolan will have a job after this? What's going to happen to that guy from Merrill?*

Paul Goldberg was there, dressed in black with a yellow cell phone hanging off his belt. So was Andy Pollack, of *The New York Times,* and Geeta Anand of *The Wall Street Journal,* and Justin Gillis of *The Washington Post,* and many, many others. At one point, Goldberg, Pollack, and I ran into a cluster of ImClone people and their crisis-management advisers from Abernathy MacGregor. The journalists almost didn't recognize Andrea Rabney, who had made $1,710,896 from the exercise of options and sales of ImClone stock: she sported a fabulous new haircut and was dressed in a spangly white suit. She took us in with a half-smile and said: "Well, now, *here's* a rogue's gallery."

Then she turned away. She seemed more thrilled than upset by the proceedings.

Finally, Representative James Greenwood, the low-key, 51-year-old Republican chairman of the Subcommittee on Oversight and Investigations, commenced the hearing. With silver curly hair, the courtly and professorial-looking chairman adjusted his glasses and read his opening statement in a soft but insistent voice:

In the past, when Americans of my generation have thought about the development of life-saving miracle drugs, the images most likely to come to mind have been those of self-effacing men of science like Alexander Fleming and Jonas Salk. In 1952, when Salk was convinced that he had developed a vaccine for the deadly scourge of polio, he didn't rush out to the marketplace with effusive praise either to the drug's efficacy or its moneymaking possibilities. Instead he vaccinated volunteers, including his wife and three sons. And only when it became clear that even though the volunteers had developed antibodies to the disease, none had become ill, did he finally publish his findings, the following year, in the *Journal of the American Medical Association.* Now flash-forward to 2001. Another doctor, this time with a Ph.D. in immunology, claims that his company is bringing another miracle drug to the market.

Like Salk in 1952, the disease he is researching strikes down roughly 60,000 thousand Americans each year. That disease is colorectal cancer. The name of this new drug is Erbitux. Here the similarity comes to a glaring halt.

It appears that instead of concentrating his focus on the need to carefully conduct clinical trials that the introduction of a breakthrough medicine demands, ImClone seemed more focused on the sales pitch. Dr. Samuel Waksal is quoted as having said that Erbitux was, "going to be the most important new oncology launch ever." Investors and hopeful patients alike were told that the results of ImClone's pivotal clinical trial were, "knock-your-socks-off exciting."

While others who had invested and hoped and perhaps prayed for a cure were busy having their hopes dashed, Dr. Waksal and others close to him appear to have been too busy cashing out to pay attention to those for whom the success or failure of Erbitux represented the difference between life and death.

Today the Subcommittee examines the unraveling of ImClone, whose highly publicized race to develop and market what some thoughtful researchers still consider to be a promising therapy failed so spectacularly. . . .

How did a highly-touted drug like Erbitux, which attracted the interest of Bristol-Myers Squibb to the tune of $2 billion, stumble so completely before even arriving at the regulatory starting gate? Cancer patients and their families want to know. And this Subcommittee Chairman wants to know. . . .

One of our chief concerns is assuring public confidence in our biotechnology/pharmaceutical industry and the FDA process. When there is a suspicion that we are not getting all the facts about a new drug, investment dries up and clinical trial enrollments stall. We must look seriously at whether the secrecy of the FDA approval process can be—or has been—abused and exploited for personal gain, and whether useful drugs are delayed because of flawed development strategies and internal FDA confusion.

The saga of failures like ImClone leads to a loss in confidence, not only in the possibilities of the science, but in the firms that seek to bring new cures to market and the public officials who must approve these cures and regulate these markets.

The hearing got off to a bang with revelations about ImClone executives' financial gains from the Bristol deal, and an explication of why the

Erbitux clinical trials were so badly flawed. Frank Papineau, the committee's detailee, explained that the structure of the ImClone-Bristol deal was unique: "A number of experts . . . told Committee staff that there is no precedent in pharmaceutical-biotech alliances for the BMS and ImClone deal, which resulted in the immediate personal enrichment of top executives through a tender offer to existing shareholders."

Dr. Raymond Weiss, an independent expert in oncology with 37 years of experience, was hired by the committee to review ImClone's clinical trial and to assess the efficacy of Erbitux. A trim man who answered questions precisely, Weiss found that Study 9923 was flawed and its results were "very suspect." There were three main reasons for this.

First, 37 patients (26.6 percent) of the 139 patients enrolled in the study were not eligible: that is, for various reasons they were not qualified to be in the study at all. Weiss found this "incredible," because typically only 5 or 6 percent of patients in such a study will be found ineligible: "It doesn't happen 27 percent of the time," he said. Such a large number of ineligible patients, "automatically makes the results . . . subject to question."

Second, Weiss found it highly unusual that 15 patients in Study 9923 were given "exemptions," meaning that once they were enrolled in the study something changed so they no longer fit the trial's entry criteria; they should have been excluded from the study, but weren't. The patient in Case no. 643, for example, had been treated with irinotecan in 1999, and then switched to oxaliplatin, a different chemotherapy, for three months. Because no chemo other than irinotecan was allowed in the study, this patient should have been excluded from Study 9923. Yet he was entered in the study in March 2000. Case no. 644 showed regression of the metastatic lesions in his lungs, thanks to the Erbitux/irinotecan cocktail, but at the same time tumors were sprouting in his pelvis— another violation of the study criteria. Case no. 615 did not receive the required two courses of irinotecan prior to his entry in the study, and thus should not have been eligible. And Case no. 683 showed that while Erbitux helped shrink the cancer lesions in his liver for a short time, "such a short . . . response would be expected from a drug with modest antitumor efficacy, but not one that had been espoused as another blockbuster anticancer agent."

"Once these criteria are set, exemptions are *not* given . . . If this is done, it could invalidate the results of the study," Weiss wrote in his report. "Eligibility exemptions are forbidden in all the clinical trials with which I have experience."

Third, he had major concerns about the dose and the administration of the irinotecan used with Erbitux in the drug cocktail. According to the trial's protocol, each patient was required to be administered with the same dose of irinotecan, and with the same frequency of treatment, as when he had previously "progressed" or failed the chemo treatment without Erbitux. Weiss discovered that 17 patients in Study 9923 were given different doses and/or different schedules of administration as they were given prior to the study.

"That's a major deviation," he said. "You couldn't separate the effect of increasing the dose of one drug from the effect of the combination of . . . Erbitux and/or irinotecan . . . Again, you make the results of the study subject to question."

Weiss went on to note that ImClone had misled the FDA about which trial protocol was being used. And he found that Sam had lied to Bristol when he'd claimed that the FDA was so "pleased" with ImClone that it had scheduled the company for an ODAC meeting on February 28. "We were very clear that no statement like that was ever made [by the FDA] to Sam Waksal," Weiss testified.

"I don't think FDA could agree that [9923] is a study that clearly makes a case for Erbitux as a drug that should be allowed on the market," Weiss said. "I would not describe [Erbitux] as a major breakthrough. I would describe it as an interesting drug with some activity apparent in colon cancer that makes it worthwhile to study further. We have many such drugs in the field of oncology."

Later, when questioned by Representative Ernie Fletcher, Republican of Kentucky—a doctor whose family has experienced colorectal cancer—Weiss said he didn't know why Bristol had gone ahead with its $2 billion deal. "I do not dismiss the study substantially," Weiss testified. "I say there are so many problems it is hard to know whether the drug really works. And I do not know why the BMS people went ahead with it, but I guess that I could use the analogy they thought they were getting a diamond and they turned out to have gotten zircon."

AT 12:45, the tall doors in back of the hearing room swung open and there was an audible gasp in the crowd, followed by the *click-click-click* of cameras on autoshoot. Sam had arrived.

He was surrounded by a phalanx of five lawyers in dark suits. They marched down the aisle in single file and sat in a row facing the bench filled with the men and women of Congress. Four television cameras lined up, and wall-mounted TV screens reflected the blank faces of Sam and his team. He wore a dark suit, white shirt, and light blue tie. His gold-rimmed glasses were tilted to the right.

At Greenwood's request, Sam stood and raised his right arm and was sworn in. His frail body was stooped, his face was gray and drawn, his mouth turned down at the edges; his left hand nervously fluttered around his pants pocket, in and out.

Greenwood said: "Thank you, Dr. Waksal. You are now under oath, and may give a five-minute statement for the record if you choose. Do you care to, sir?"

One of Sam's attorneys, Lewis Liman (a son of Arthur Liman, famed as the special counsel to the Senate's investigation of Iran-Contra), of Wilmer, Cutler & Pickering, answered for Sam, saying he would invoke his Fifth Amendment right not to testify. Instead, Liman submitted a letter to the subcommittee, which read:

> Dr. Waksal firmly believes that any allegations against him are un founded and that he did nothing improper. He also recognizes that this Subcommittee's hearing room is not the constitutionally appropriate venue to resolve those accusations. One of Dr. Waksal's major goals has been to make available a drug that would prolong the lives of people with cancer.

Greenwood nevertheless recognized himself for questioning of the witness. He had a point to make.

"[Study 9923] turned out to be riddled with severe problems with no apparent quality control by ImClone . . . Given . . . the financial gain of $111 million for you and your brother before the FDA application was even filed, and the failure to deliver on your promise to thousands of very sick cancer patients . . . would it be fair to say that your strategy at ImClone was to put personal profiteering ahead of patients, sir?"

Sam stared up at the chairman. Then, in a raspy voice, he replied: "Unfortunately, upon the advice of counsel, I . . . respectfully decline to answer."

The gallery clucked, and, at 12:52, Sam and his lawyers trooped out of the chamber. He held his chin up as he walked, but his eyes were cast down and he looked neither left nor right.

Later, Mark Pomerantz, Sam's lead defense attorney, would complain that no lawyer would have allowed a client mired in a federal investigation to testify under these circumstances. The subcommittee had been told beforehand that Sam would plead the Fifth, Pomerantz said, but had insisted that Sam appear at the hearing "so they could pursue the spectacle of having him invoke his constitutional right in front of Congress." That, declared Pomerantz, was "an aspect of grandstanding that is inappropriate."

HARLAN WAKSAL, the new CEO of ImClone Systems, Inc., did not plead the Fifth. He wore a blue suit, white shirt, and dark tie. He rested his hands on the table and clenched and unclenched his fingers tightly. He looked at the committee over the tops of his glasses, which had slid down to the flanges of his nostrils. He was determined to defend himself and ImClone as vigorously and precisely and politely as possible.

Harlan had worked very hard and taken huge risks without much compensation, relatively speaking, for years. Yet he had maintained faith in himself, in Sam, in their company, and in Erbitux. Many times—in 1989, 1999, 2000—he and Sam had pitched various joint ventures, or even an outright sale of ImClone to potential partners, but they had never closed a major deal. It had been immensely frustrating. Finally Bristol had come along with a tremendous $2 billion offer. It was a dream come true. But he didn't trust it. He had been down this road so many times with so many other companies that until the deal was actually inked he hadn't given it more than a 50 percent chance of happening. But it did happen. And once he had tasted success Harlan wasn't about to concede it or apologize for it.

Asked about the fortuitous timing of his $50 million stock trade on December 6, 2001—two days after George Mills had broadly hinted to Lily Lee that Erbitux would be rejected—Harlan replied that he had no foreknowledge of the RTF at the time. They asked repeatedly about the meeting on December 4, and he answered that the Mills had simply explained all of the options to Lily Lee, and had not hinted that an RTF was likely. "There was not material information, in my opinion, at the time . . . my transaction was quite independent of everything else taking place," Harlan testified.

He added that he had informed his board of his intention to trade 700,000 shares of ImClone in October, and insisted that he "did not have any inkling until after December 12" that ImClone would receive an RTF.

Representative Cliff Stearns, Republican of Florida, snorted at this and began hounding Harlan about his remuneration. Harlan defended himself by saying, "I have invested 18 years of my life in building this company from the ground up, and I believe the stock options are reflective of the effort and the time and the hard work." He walked the committee through the details of his ImClone holdings, drawing raised eyebrows when he mentioned that his 3.6 million shares, stock options, and warrants had been worth $210 million at the height of the market— nearly twice what many had thought they had been valued at.

Stearns questioned how Harlan could be so "intimately aware of the money" yet had not been "paying attention" to the Erbitux clinical trials. Harlan bristled. "I think your confluence of information is a little questionable," he shot back. "I don't really see the point that we were not paying attention. We were, indeed. It happens to be that I differ on some of the opinions that you have raised."

Stearns pressed Harlan about the "hype" that he and Sam had generated for Erbitux, and pointed specifically to the *60 Minutes* story. Harlan replied that ImClone had nothing to do with Lesley Stahl's piece. "I looked at the story as a very negative one for the company, sir," he answered curtly.

At this, the press corps on the left side of the chamber began whispering.

"Oh, puh-leeze! Harlan doth protesteth too much!" muttered a wire service reporter, rolling her eyes dramatically.

Harlan's claim was disingenuous. While it is true that ImClone had not suggested the story to Lesley Stahl, the fact is that ImClone received enormous publicity from *60 Minutes,* which is one of the most watched shows in the history of television. Not only does the program reach an audience of 14 million every Sunday night, but Stahl's emotionally fraught segment on two cancer-stricken mothers "begging for their lives" was widely discussed and written about after it aired. This raised ImClone's profile even further. Sam said that after *60 Minutes* aired, the company had been inundated by thousands of new requests for Erbitux, although the segment was hardly complimentary to his unofficial expanded access program. Indeed, later in the hearing Harlan tacitly acknowledged the value of *60 Minutes* when, in a little-noticed aside, he mentioned that Amy Cohen, the surviving cancer patient from Stahl's segment, was in the hearing room and was prepared to give a testimonial on the benefits of Erbitux. It was a play for sympathy and recognition reminiscent of the way Sam had urged Shannon Kellum to testify before the Burton committee one year earlier. Tauzin and Greenwood's committee, however, ignored the offer to hear from Ms. Cohen.

(At this hearing, Harlan didn't mention, nor was he asked about, his phone call to Fred Santino, the widower of Ruth-Ann Santino, whose cancer had killed her on the eve of the show's airing.)

Then came the questions about the company's loans to Sam. In 1992, *Barron's* had reported, ImClone loaned him $70,000, then gave a cash advance of $90,000, and then a further $275,000—which, on top of his salary and bonuses, had made Sam one of the best-paid CEOs in biotech, despite the fact that ImClone had never turned a profit. Sam had used this company money to fix up his apartment. In 1993, when *Barron's* had asked about these irregular loans, Robert Goldhammer said that Sam had repaid the money, with interest, and had agreed that no further personal loans would be made. Yet according to SEC filings, Goldhammer's hard line proved fungible and ImClone continued to make loans to Sam over the years.

"I don't know the context of the [*Barron's*] interview, but I do know that loans were given after [Goldhammer's] comment was made," Harlan said. He added that as CEO he'd instituted new corporate governance rules that precluded such loans.

But Stearns wouldn't let it go, and Harlan snapped: "I have the presidency of the company! I am telling you that there will not be further loans to officers of this company!"

The hearing wasn't going well for him. As the day wore on, committee members grew visibly irritated with Harlan and their questioning grew increasingly acerbic.

Harlan vehemently denied accusations that ImClone had misled the FDA, investors, or cancer patients. "There was no deception on our part," he testified. "It is a surprise to me that it's suggested we were somehow trying to fool [the FDA]."

Eventually he was forced to concede that ImClone's clinical trial had been mismanaged and that the RTF letter was "a tragedy." "We're a small company," he said. "We didn't have the resources to do some of the quality checks that needed to be done."

Like his brother, Harlan blamed most of the problems with the Erbitux application on the outside consultants, the IRAC. "We worked with outside groups. Clinical research organizations . . . Unfortunately, that's where the errors took place. In the quality."

HARLAN'S TESTIMONY was a revelation. This was the first time that many in the chamber had seen ImClone's new CEO in action, and they were suffering a cognitive dissonance. Harlan had been described in the press as a serious, self-effacing, conservative scientist—"a male soccer mom," as one observer memorably put it to Reuters. But this flesh-and-blood Harlan spoke loudly, in a clear, and at times strident voice, with absolute self-confidence. Perhaps he was nervous.

To ImClone's supporters, he appeared "strong" and determined, a person close to the company said. To Alan Slobodin he appeared to be "a well-coached witness." To others, Harlan appeared querulous, patronizing, and unrepentant. His answers to the committee carried a note of condescension, as if to say: *You congressmen simply don't understand what you're talking about. ImClone is involved in complex science and high finance. You must believe what I tell you because I am smarter than you.* It was as if the sheep's mask had suddenly slipped to reveal a harder, more lupine and predatory face beneath.

But then, near the end of his testimony, Harlan, in a moment of apparent humility, said: "We now know that we could, and should, have done a better job. We let patients down. And for that I am truly sorry."

HOVERING BEHIND TAUZIN and Greenwood, whispering in their ears, pointing to key documents, the wide-shouldered and intensely focused investigator Alan Slobodin did not testify that day, but his prodigious research informed the committee's line of questioning. Dressed in a black suit, white shirt, and dark tie, his thinning hair neatly combed back, Slobodin looked like a G-man out of a classic black-and-white TV show. In the course of their six-month inquiry, the investigators had laid bare a series of internal notes, e-mails, and documents that threw into question ImClone's and Bristol-Myers's assertions that they had been forthright in their portrayal of the FDA's concerns about Erbitux.

A handwritten note by Daniel Lynch, the biotech company's CFO, dated December 27, details a phone conversation he had with a Bristol executive. In the event of an RTF, he scribbled, the reaction should be: "No press release by BMS . . . Our press release should be as vague as possible."

In grandiloquent style, Billy Tauzin read aloud a confidential e-mail between two Bristol employees, Adriann Sax, an oncology drug executive, and Nancy Goldfarb, a public relations executive: "Nancy, I agree that some a lot [*sic*] of Sam's comments are misleading. At this point, we should continue to be silent."

Eyeing Bristol's Brian Markison, Tauzin asked, slyly: "What's the meaning of that kind of an e-mail, Mr. Markison?"

"Well, sir, these are the comments of two people . . . I'm not sure they represent the entire company," Markison answered, miserably. A stocky and confident man, he was now awkwardly hunched over his microphone and sweating. "We were struggling with new information."

"Mr. Chairman," Tauzin addressed Greenwood, "I suspect we've got some real problems with the way the [fast-track] system works."

Greenwood asked Markison when he first suspected that the FDA would send ImClone an RTF letter. It was a deceptively simple question. Markison shrunk further into his seat. With convoluted syntax, he replied that it was the meeting on December 4 between Lily Lee and the FDA—when George Mills explained ImClone's four options—that had raised a red flag for Bristol. Groping for a safe way to convey this, Markison said: "There was an inkling [on December 4], sir, quite frankly, that was in essence the beginning, in my mind, anyway, of—"

"It was an inkling in your mind?"

"It was an inkling in my mind, yes."

"And how did that inkling get into your mind?"

"That it [the RTF] was mentioned as a possibility."

Greenwood stared at him. Markison was saying that by December 4 Bristol suspected that Erbitux would be rejected by the FDA. This directly contradicted Harlan's testimony, which was that he had no suspicions of an RTF until December 12, and that his $50 million sale of ImClone stock on December 6 had not been predicated on any inside information.

Harlan was seated next to Markison. They did not look at each other.

* * *

LAURIE SMALDONE, BMS senior vice president of Worldwide Regulatory Science, is a slim woman with short brown hair and a serious demeanor. Seated between Harlan and Markison, she, too, was in an awkward position. Congressman Bart Stupak, Democrat of Michigan, zeroed in on the e-mail Smaldone, an experienced oncologist, had written in June 2001, in which she characterized the ImClone deal as "a very high risk opportunity."

She testified that Bristol still believed in Erbitux: "It has promise and has activity as an anti-tumor agent." Prior to signing the $2 billion partnership, Bristol did a worst-case scenario study of the results of the 138-patient study, which found insufficient data on 11 of 27 patients that ImClone had claimed responded well to Erbitux. Even so, Smaldone said, BMS decided that the resulting 13 percent response rate would be good enough to carry the drug through the FDA review. It was a gamble, but one based on precedent: Iressa had been approved by the FDA with a 13 percent response rate.

But Smaldone conceded that there were "substantive" problems with ImClone's FDA application that were "more than documentation." She said she had never seen an RTF before ImClone's, and she agreed that it had been justified. Bristol, she added, would never have dared to send an application of the quality of ImClone's Erbitux BLA to the FDA.

Smaldone did not look at Harlan and only criticized his work indirectly. "We did a very extensive due diligence review . . . there are, however, certain levels of expectations on the part of the proposed partner that . . . good clinical practice and quality assurance would be conducted as . . . with any pharmaceutical company . . . With total hindsight at this point, some of those expectations were not met."

IN THE MORNING Dr. Raymond Weiss had testified that Study 9923 had "all sorts of flaws," and in the afternoon Laurie Smaldone, along with several representatives of the FDA, agreed with him. Even Harlan Waksal had admitted that "there were problems" with the clinical trials. But what was barely hinted at in the hearing was that some of those who shared the blame for the faulty work on Erbitux were among the top oncologists in practice today.

There were, for example, the notable scientists on the ImClone scientific advisory board (SAB), which had not convened in years—such as John Mendelsohn (who would appear at a second congressional hearing in October), Vincent DeVita (the former head of the National Cancer Institute, and former executive director of the Yale Cancer Center), and Arnold Levine (the former head of the Rockefeller University). These three are highly-accomplished scientists. Their names lent great credence to the promise of Erbitux. And they had profited from ImClone's touting of Erbitux. (From options and the sale of ImClone stock, Mendelsohn—who always mentions his ownership of ImClone stock—made $6.31 million; Levine made $93,030; DeVita made $9,030. Yet they allowed ImClone's flawed application and Sam's rosey claims for the drug to roll on, apparently without challenge.

Although the SAB's inactivity was not raised in the hearing, the committee's report reprinted a letter of February 21, 2002, written by Dr. P. Frederick Sparling, of the University of North Carolina at Chapel Hill School of Medicine:

*Dear Harlan and Sam,*

*I have not heard from you regarding my previous suggestion that the SAB [scientific advisory board] should meet to review the situation regarding the clinical trials.*

*I think it is advisable for me to resign from the SAB effective immediately. I am sorry to do this because we have had such a wonderful long-term relationship and I consider you my personal friends. Indeed, I wish the very best for the company. I just do not believe I can be useful as a member of the SAB, and the long-term inactivity of the SAB suggests the SAB is not useful to the company.*

Another person with a degree of responsibility for the Erbitux data was Dr. Leonard Saltz, Memorial Sloan-Kettering's star oncologist, who was the lead investigator of Study 9923. In the spring of 2001, he announced that the Erbitux data was "knock-your-socks-off exciting," at ASCO. While Weiss was careful to point out that he knew and admired Saltz, and skillfully avoided answering questions about Saltz's role, he also made it clear that Study 9923 could have been conducted with greater care and rigor. (Memorial Sloan-Kettering, an institution that receives public money for cancer research from the NIH, refused interview requests for this book.)

\*     \*     \*

THE THIRD PANEL of the day was made up of representatives of the U.S. Food and Drug Administration, a group of scientists who are usually cloaked in bureaucratic anonymity but who now found themselves caught in the glare of television lights, politics, and a federal investigation.

Agency officials are not allowed to make public statements about a drug under review. Secrecy rules ensure the sanctity of the reviewers' work, and protect drug companies' proprietary intellectual property. That's the way it's always been done. One result of this policy was that the congressional subcommittee had been compelled to subpoena five FDA officials to get them to testify on June 13. As a result, the hearing provided the public with an unprecedented view of the inner workings of the FDA, warts and all.

Dr. Richard Pazdur, the director of the oncology branch of the FDA's Center for Drug Evaluation and Research (CDER), was a tall, thin man with a mustache, who cut a striking figure in a steel-blue suit. While some of his FDA colleagues tried to soften their criticism, or tiptoe around agency politics, Pazdur cut right to the chase. ImClone's clinical trials, he said, had been rife with "sloppy work" that put Erbitux in jeopardy of being rejected.

"This drug does show some activity," Pazdur observed. "But its life story is just beginning." He said that the FDA had urged ImClone to conduct more robust, controlled clinical trials to better understand the drug, but the company had ignored the suggestion.

Although he was not directly involved in reviewing the Erbitux BLA, Pazdur is a highly regarded oncologist whose specialty is colon cancer; he had worked under John Mendelsohn at M. D. Anderson before joining the agency in 2000, and had recently been proposed as head of the FDA. His words carried weight.

Chairman Greenwood was perplexed by his testimony. "If you tell the world that you have in your possession the Holy Grail of cancer treatments, and then . . . you have this haphazard conduct [of clinical trials]. I can't get these two things to compute. How does that happen?"

"It's called good drug, bad development plan," Pazdur answered. "And there's nothing you can do about it at the present time . . . For example, we may have a meeting with the company, talk to them about a [drug] development plan. They could walk out of this office and do another development plan if they wish. I cannot take a gun to somebody's head and say, 'You must do what I say here, okay?' Nor do I have any recourse to publicly address that issue."

He was referring to the contentious issue of FDA secrecy.

The FDA reviewers in charge of the Erbitux application testified that even though they had "cringed" at Sam Waksal's aggressive promotion of the drug, they were precluded by secrecy rules from responding in public or offering a more balanced analysis. Some in the agency are happy with this policy, saying in effect, "It's not our job to police press releases; our job is to study the data and ensure that a drug is safe and effective." Others in the FDA wish they had more resources to properly monitor companies' claims about unproven drugs.

The FDA does have an arm that monitors the promotion of drugs on the market. But when an experimental drug like Erbitux is still in clinical trials, the FDA usually doesn't have access to the data—or the resources—to monitor every statement made about it. Or, as Billy Tauzin put it: "The FDA is restricted, while the company can go out and hype [a drug] and take advantage of it financially."

One of the hearing's most significant revelations was that ImClone had used a different protocol (Version 2.0) to enroll Study 9923 than the one the FDA had okayed for fast-track status (Version 1.0). The difference between the two was that the eligibility criteria had been changed. This was critical. Without carefully defining which patients are eligible for inclusion in a clinical trial, the results of the study will be subject to biases and rendered meaningless.

In Version 1.0, the eligibility criteria for Study 9923 stated the patient must have demonstrated "progression of disease [metasteses] after completing a minimum of two courses of a regimen containing irinotecan." In Version 2.0, the criteria were changed to say that a patient had to have "documented stable disease [must have received a minimum of 12 weeks of irinotecan therapy] or progressive disease at any time after receiving an irinotecan-containing regimen."

In other words, ImClone's Study 9923 did not test whether Erbitux worked alone. That issue was at the core of the FDA's rejection of the BLA. It is important because chemotherapy is toxic and leaves patients with debilitating side effects. If Erbitux does work as a single agent, then patients could avoid using chemo altogether.

The FDA reviewers had apparently missed the fact that ImClone was using a different set of criteria. And ImClone did not correct the agency's misperception.

Dr. Patricia Keegan, a slight woman with short hair, was the deputy division director of the FDA's Center for Biologics Evaluation and Research (CBER), and was the senior reviewer of ImClone's drug application. Asked by Greenwood to explain "the enormous gap" between the "highfalutin' buzz" around Erbitux and the "fizzling dud" that the drug had become, Keegan explained that she had been impressed by ImClone's "compelling" claim of a 20 percent response rate. Erbitux, the data seemed to show, had tremendous promise as a new therapy for stage 4 colorectal cancer patients. "That is why we were willing to listen to the company in August 2000, and why we pursued this," she said, defensively.

To their disappointment and anger, the FDA reviewers later discovered that some of the claims made by ImClone at the crucial August 11, 2001, meeting were inaccurate. "They told the group at the meeting that the information in the application would satisfy us, that we would find [it] compelling and convincing," said Keegan. "I felt misled, personally."

To back their contention that Erbitux worked best in combination, Sam and Harlan had presented data from animal studies that showed Erbitux worked best when combined with irinotecan. That was "a very risky venture," Pazdur averred, because human studies can have quite different results than animal studies. Further, ImClone had asked patients to continue using irinotecan even though their tumors continued to grow and spread while using it. "This," thundered Pazdur, "violates every principle that I know in medical oncology."

Pazdur criticized his FDA colleagues' compromises with Im-Clone—such as allowing the company to conduct a small single-agent trial of its drug. "[Study 9923] was a flawed trial," he said. "It never really answered the question: Do you need irinotecan with Erbitux? And that is a critical question to be answered here . . . ImClone needs to show this drug works. They need to conduct a randomized trial. If they really believed [they] needed a combination, they needed to . . . look at irinotecan plus their drug, versus Erbitux alone. That would be the correct way of developing this drug."

Looking up from his notes, Greenwood blinked and said this is "pretty damning information . . . That's language even I can understand."

*　　*　　*

AT 5:03 THAT AFTERNOON the subcommittee was adjourned. The over-riding impression from the hearing was that in their rush to get the drug to market and cash in, Sam and Harlan had acted with great cupidity and short-sightedness. Their Erbitux data was fatally flawed but the FDA had not objected loudly enough. Now they might have to start their clinical trials all over again.

Generating and running a new clinical study would now be an especially steep climb for ImClone. Wall Street had been badly burned and would not forget it. Sam was in deepening legal trouble. Harlan was an unknown as CEO. Bristol was humiliated and angry. The FDA was also angry and had made it clear that for Erbitux to gain approval ImClone would have to conduct a large, well-constructed, carefully executed randomized trial. This would take months, if not years, to accomplish, not to mention millions of dollars. Furthermore, such a delay would allow competitors' drugs to close the gap on Erbitux. Now ImClone's survival was a perilously open question.

A few days later, a lifeline was thrown from an unexpected quarter. Merck KGaA, ImClone's German partner, had enrolled 330 patients for a randomized study of Erbitux—exactly the kind of trial that Pazdur and others at the FDA had called for. This study would compare the effectiveness of the drug as a single agent versus the combination of Erbitux and irinotecan. The Germans said the data could be ready by the end of the year. Although the criteria for European clinical trials differs from the American, ImClone might be able to use Merck's data to show that Erbitux worked.

The FDA indicated that if the Merck data were properly presented, the agency would consider it useful. Suddenly the European study became the make-or-break element for the resubmission of the Erbitux application.

# THIRTEEN

# *Coincidences Piling Up*

On Friday, June 14, Peter Bacanovic flew to London to visit a friend. It was supposed to be a quick, weekend-long trip. But just as his plane lifted over the Atlantic, the press was starting to connect the dots that linked him to Sam Waksal and Martha Stewart. Bacanovic was the mystery man in the middle, the missing link in Sam and Martha's ImClone stock trades of December 27.

"Who is Peter Bacanovic?!" bayed the tabloids and TV shows. "How much does he make?" "Where does he live?" "Is he covering up for Martha?" "Who are his other clients?" "And, by the way, who is this guy Douglas Faneuil?"

Bacanovic heard all these questions echoing across the pond, and by the end of the weekend had decided to extend his stay in London indefinitely. It was just a simple misunderstanding, he told SEC investigators in New York and his Merrill Lynch superiors in London. What happened, he said, was that he and Martha had previously agreed that when ImClone hit $60, he would sell her shares. And that was exactly what had happened. He had not been tipped by Sam. There was no conspiracy or illegal conduct. He was being portrayed unfairly simply because Martha had made money while others had lost it. End of story.

In New York, Martha's lawyers were saying exactly the same thing:

she and Peter Bacanovic had agreed to divest her ImClone holdings if the stock hit $60 a share. When it did, the stock was sold. Further, they pointed out, her ImClone trade should be viewed in the context of her many other transactions at the time. Martha is a billionaire CEO who was consolidating her many individual stock holdings and selling them off. In 2001, she had accounts at Morgan Stanley, Bear Stearns, and with Bacanovic at Merrill Lynch. Each of these stockbrokers had to get Stewart's personal approval for every trade, and Martha was growing tired of dealing with their calls. Towards the end of the year, she decided to consolidate her stock holdings with Bacanovic at Merrill Lynch, then sell off the bulk of them and hire a professional money manager (who would not need to call her about every transaction) to monitor her wealth. Stewart's holdings in the consolidated Bacanovic account totaled a reported .04 of 1 percent of her personal fortune, which mostly consisted of her MSO holdings and real estate.

"I approached her in November 2001 and said, 'You've never sold any of your own stock. You should take some money off the table as an insurance policy. You're still paying mortgages on your properties," recalled Jeff Ubben, who manages a San Francisco–based investment partnership and is a member of the MSO board. "She was a reluctant seller. She asked me if I knew any money managers and said she was in the process of getting out of the stock market. The implication was that she was selling all of her individual stock holdings." And Martha's business manager, Heidi DeLuca, confirmed to investigators that Martha sold "a lot" of stock in late 2001.

The mutually reinforcing alibi was interpreted to mean that Martha had placed a "stop-loss order" with Bacanovic, meaning that there would be a computer record of their client-broker agreement. But there was a snag. Merrill Lynch could find no record of a stop-loss order in its system. Instead, Bacanovic offered up a slip of paper with "$60" scribbled in the margin. He said that his agreement with Martha had been made verbally. Martha concurred. But there was another snag: she said they had made their agreement in November; he said it was made in December.

Was this more innocent misunderstanding?

"I've got to tell you that coincidences are just piling up, one after another," Billy Tauzin announced. He added that the congressional committee had yet to find definitive evidence linking Martha to an ImClone tip-off. But, "when you look at everybody dumping stocks . . . and their family and their friends . . . it's hard to believe that there was no insider trading."

The chronology of trading in ImClone shows that the stock price had dipped below $60 well before Martha's sell order was executed.

ImClone first rose above $60 on October 22, 2001. Three days later, it nearly hit $63, but then it dropped down to $56 on October 30. It surpassed $60 again the next day, then dipped under the bar again on November 1, 9, and 12. If Martha and Bacanovic agreed to a $60 stop-loss order before November 12, then the trade would have been executed by the 12th. Based on her statements, she must have entered her stop-loss order sometime after that, in the six-week period between November 13 and December 25.

In a letter to Attorney General John Ashcroft, members of the House subcommittee noted that Martha was "a former stockbroker . . . and sophisticated businesswoman," and said that their findings "cause us to be deeply skeptical of Ms. Stewart's accounts, and raise a serious question as to whether those accounts were false, misleading, and designed to conceal material facts."

Wall Street judged Martha "guilty" of insider trading very quickly: after news broke of her ImClone transaction, MSO shares dropped from $19 to about $14 a share, losing a quarter of their value. One of the market's chief concerns was whether a company so closely identified with its founder, leader, and "human brand" had a future if Martha were indicted, heavily fined, or even sent to prison.

She put a brave face on it and continued to loudly proclaim her innocence.

TO THE SKEPTICS it was obvious what had happened. On December 27, Sam, or perhaps Aliza Waksal, had tipped their broker Peter Bacanovic to the impending RTF letter. Or perhaps Bacanovic saw the Waksals bailing out of the family business and figured it out for himself. Either way, he told Martha Stewart, who was by far his most important client, that ImClone was going down fast. They quickly jettisoned all of her ImClone holdings and made a tidy profit a day before the bad news hit. When their hand got caught in the till, they concocted a phony story about a $60 stop-loss order.

This scenario sounded plausible, but where was the proof? Also, which part of this was prosecutable? There were no clear answers.

Bacanovic and Martha steadfastly stuck to their story; there was no "smoking gun" indicating a conspiracy. And even if she knew that Waksal was dumping stock, that is not the same thing as breaking insider-trading laws, which are very tightly written.

"Insider trading is misuse of information by someone who has an obligation to keep that information confidential," said William R. Baker III, the SEC's former associate director of the division of enforcement. "Insider trading is a form of fraud, and you have to have some fraudulent intent. If you don't know that the information is acquired in breach of some legal duty, you lack the intent necessary to show insider trading." Thus, to prove that Martha was tipped off, the government would have to show: that she received information from someone legally bound to keep it confidential, that she understood the disclosure was improper, and that she traded on the basis of that information. It is a high hurdle for prosecutors. And so legal experts pronounced that the authorities would have difficulty proving Martha had engaged in insider trading of ImClone—unless, that is, some new piece of evidence came to light.

WHILE PETER BACANOVIC was hunkered down in London, his assistant, Douglas Faneuil, was subjected to 20 hours of intensive questioning by Merrill Lynch lawyers and compliance officers in New York. After a week of grilling, Faneuil broke. He said that to his knowledge there was no stop-loss order between Martha and Bacanovic, and never had been. It was all a fiction, he said, to cover up Martha's insider trading. He told investigators that Bacanovic had pressured him to lie about the agreement, and in return had paid him off with a free airline ticket and extra vacation time.

Was Faneuil credible, or was he a scared young man who had told investigators what they wanted to hear in order to save himself?

On Friday, June 21, Merrill Lynch suspended both Bacanovic and Faneuil, citing "factual inconsistencies" in their conflicting accounts of what had happened. The bank handed over the results of its investigation to the congressional committee, the SEC, and the U.S. Attorney's office in Manhattan.

Bacanovic was said to be crushed by what he considered Faneuil's betrayal. "Peter has no enemies," a close friend told *New York* magazine, echoing Bacanovic's own confusion. "He lives in a world where he is nice to people and people are nice to him." It is a worldview that is reminiscent of Holly Golightly's in *Breakfast at Tiffany's*.

Having broken Faneuil, the investigators now began to squeeze Bacanovic. They wanted to use him to nail the big prize: Martha Stewart. It is possible that a plea bargain was dangled as bait. The pressure on Bacanovic to recant grew intense, but he refused to turn against his most important client and steadfastly maintained his innocence. No deal was worked out.

Douglas Faneuil's world was in disarray. He spent his days with lawyers and tried to work out a deal with the government; he was shadowed by a troop of paparazzi. He couldn't bear the pressure, and so he slipped out of New York and took refuge at his mother's house in a suburb near Boston.

Bacanovic eventually returned from London, and in New York he, too, became a marked man. For days, a brown station wagon filled with photographers was parked in front of his townhouse (where *Breakfast at Tiffany's* was filmed). He tried to maintain a low profile and sometimes hid out at a friend's house. He escaped to Los Angeles for a while, where he was not so easily recognized on the street. Brad Gooch said. "[Peter] seems sad now. He used to have this optimistic, peppy view of the world, an innocent relish of the social game. This experience has punctured that optimism."

Bacanovic's days, like Sam's and Faneuil's, were used up in attorneys' meetings—some of which lasted as long as five hours. He phoned friends and tried to live as normally as possible in a stressful and abnormal time. He was "irritated" at Martha for not selling her ImClone holdings earlier, as he had long told her she should.

To ward off the melancholy, he stealthily ventured out on the town. But it wasn't like walking Nan Kempner to a black tie affair, or attending an opening at the American Ballet Theatre.

A friend observed of Bacanovic's purgatory: "It is a supreme irony that someone so cautious, who plays by the rules so much, who is so skillful at not putting a wrong foot forward, gets wound up in something where he didn't do a thing wrong but suddenly is on CNN globally."

It was the Martha factor. It had changed, and charged, the ImClone case. The heady mix of scandal, celebrity, Wall Street, biotech, and a congressional investigation had transformed ImClone into a global media phenomenon that was featured prominently on the front pages of leading dailies across Europe, Japan, and even in India.

HARLAN WAKSAL had always stood in the shadow of his older brother. While Sam jetted around as the public face of ImClone, Harlan, long the COO and chief scientific officer, spent years tending to the Erbitux clinical trials and running the company on a day-to-day basis. But now he was CEO. Near the end of his testimony before Congress he had said: "We now know that we could, and should, have done a better job [with Erbitux]. We let patients down. And for that I am truly sorry." It was a striking mea culpa, not least because those were exactly the words that many people had longed to hear from ImClone, but that Sam had never deigned to utter. Other than to say, "We screwed up," at H&Q, Sam had never acknowledged his responsibility for the ImClone disaster or for the consequences of his words and actions on cancer patients and investors. There remained a deep and intractable anger about this. Harlan was beginning to put that to rest.

It may have been that he deliberately chose the very public forum of a congressional hearing to establish a new tone for ImClone. Intentional or not, it was a wise strategic move. The RTF was a large black mark that could not be quickly erased. To reestablish ImClone's credibility, ingratiate himself to Wall Street, and pave the way for the FDA's approval of Erbitux, Harlan *had* to acknowledge the company's errors and apologize before moving ahead.

He took further steps to distance himself from Sam. One of them was to clean up ImClone's muddled corporate governance policies. Board members would protest that this was a process the company had begun of its own volition, months earlier, but it appeared that the congressional hearing forced ImClone's hand. After the hearing in June, the House subcommittee was planning to interview five ImClone directors—Robert Goldhammer; John Mendelsohn; Vincent DeVita; David Kies, a partner at Sullivan & Cromwell; and Paul Kopperl, president of Delano & Kopperl Inc. about what they knew of the botched Erbitux BLA, and how and when they had sold their ImClone stock.

"How could the company have submitted data to the FDA that was so incomplete that it was refused without the board of directors being aware of that?" asked Congressman Greenwood.

ImClone announced that it had enacted a new governance rule—it banned directors who aren't officers of the firm from having other financial arrangements with ImClone—and terminated its $100,000-a-year contract with Vincent DeVita and its $12,000-a-year contract with John Mendelsohn. The company also withdrew from an agreement with Concord Investment Management, the money managers of which Robert Goldhammer was a partner. In 2000, ImClone had paid Concord a $412,000 fee to manage its debt-security portfolio.

The net effect of these changes was the impression that ImClone was finally growing up, that the "serious" Waksal brother was in charge, that there would be no more Sam-style shenanigans. Yet the big questions remained: Who, exactly, was Harlan Wolf Waksal? Would he prove any more trustworthy than his brother?

"I THINK HARLAN is doing an incredible job as CEO," said Norma Robert, Sam's old friend and a former ImClone employee. "Harlan's very, very bright. A family man. He has a different demeanor. He's more based in reality than Sam, who's more of an imaginative, dreamer-type of person."

"The two brothers are very different," affirmed Shirley Flacks, Sam's former mother-in-law. "Harlan is far more conservative."

"I've heard that Harlan's the real scientist," said one of Sam's New York society friends. "But who is he? What's he like? I have no idea. I've known Sam for 20 years and I've never met Harlan. He lives, you know, in the *suburbs.*"

"Harlan is clearly not seeking to be in the hip inner circle of New York society," says Richard Beleson of The Capital Group, an investment management firm that once invested in ImClone. "He's the guy who's done the day-to-day block and tackling to keep the company going. He's a family man. He was very embarrassed by the whole [RTF] thing."

"Harlan isn't stupid. But I never thought he should have been the scientific director of the company," said a former ImClone employee. "He doesn't have Sam's intuition or charisma. He's not quick on his feet. I mean, Harlan could never have done a $2 billion deal like Sam did. He could barely take a piss without Sam telling him how to do it. Harlan did the boring stuff. He'd sit on people, and make them do their assays and expense accounts over and over again."

"I like Harlan, but I do not have a high regard for him as a scientist. And as for what he knows about running a company? . . ." said another former employee. "He took his orders from Sam, but he's not a pathetic little brother. He's not 'Mikey' [from the old Life cereal ad]. Harlan eats 'the cereal' because he does everything for Sam and the family. Harlan is no innocent."

Another former ImClone employee said: "He and Sam have a symbiotic relationship. He knew everything that was going on."

A biotech investor who shorted ImClone stock and profited handsomely from the ImClone scandal recalled: "A lot of people on Wall Street weren't aware of Sam's problems in academia, but they knew about Harlan's cocaine bust. There were rumors for years. It was kind of an urban legend that always dogged him."

IN FEBRUARY 1981, Dr. Harlan W. Waksal, a 28-year-old physician in the third year of his internal medicine residency at New England Hospital, flew from Boston to Fort Lauderdale to spend two days at his parents' condominium and to pick up 2.2 pounds of cocaine.

According to one version of events, Harlan had met a person named Robert Johnston in a Boston cocktail lounge sometime over the previous year. Harlan would say he was "fascinated by [Johnston's] desperado type of a thing," and agreed to help Johnston smuggle some coke. Johnston arranged everything and told Harlan that given his looks and the fact that he was a doctor, he would not be suspected of being a drug mule. Harlan agreed, noting that he'd never been stopped in an airport.

In another version of events, which Harlan allegedly told the police just after his arrest, he had been lying by the pool at the family condominium on Hallandale Beach Boulevard, when an unknown person asked him to transport some cocaine to Boston. Harlan agreed. The arresting officers expressed doubt about the veracity of this story, but, they later testified, Harlan had insisted that this is how he came to possess the cocaine. At his trial, Harlan denied that this was what had happened and that he had ever told such a story. "Told them that I obtained [the cocaine] at a swimming pool? No, I did not," he testified.

In any event, at approximately 4:30 on the afternoon of February 14, 1981, Harlan met a yacht broker named Curtiss "Buster" Hayes at River Bend Marina, near Fort Lauderdale, to discuss chartering or possibly buying a sailboat. "My brother and I are both sailing advocates," Harlan explained. "We spend a great deal of time trying to sail. We have a small boat of our own, and I have spent some time sailing, and I go on quite a few charters down in the Caribbean area."

Harlan spoke to Hayes, who had been recommended by Sam, for several hours. They spoke about sailing and scuba diving in the Caribbean.

Earlier that day, at about noon, Harlan became aware that someone had placed cocaine in his carry-on bag. At about 3:00 or 3:30, Robert Johnston and another man named Joe placed two more bags of cocaine in two sets of underwear, which Harlan then put on. "It seemed like the most reasonable place to carry it." Later, Harlan testified, another person gave him a resealable plastic bag containing an additional three grams of cocaine, which Harlan put in his jacket pocket. All told, the 1,131 grams of cocaine he was carrying had a street value of some $45,000. It was to be delivered to one person in Boston, and Harlan was to be paid $2,000 for the job. Although he had a couple of drinks that day, Harlan says he did not buy or use any of the cocaine, nor was it meant for his use. "I was merely carrying the cocaine." This was the first time he had ever transported narcotics, he said.

At 6:00 that evening, Harlan and the yacht broker walked a couple of blocks from the marina to Hayes's house. They stayed there until 8:30, when Hayes gave Harlan a ride in his car to the airport. His flight to Boston was due to leave at about 10 P.M.

Deputy Sheriffs Ralph Capone and James Carl were standing against a glass wall in the Delta terminal at the Fort Lauderdale International Airport that night, working the undercover narcotics detail. At about 9:00 P.M., they noticed a youthful, nervous-looking man enter the Delta Airlines ticket area. This was Harlan. He was dressed in a white shirt, a tie, a blue blazer, and a pair of light-colored dress slacks. (Ever since becoming a doctor, Harlan had dressed this way when traveling by airplane, he said.) He carried a briefcase and a carry-on bag with a shoulder strap. He scanned the terminal constantly, used cash to purchase a one-way ticket to Boston, and did not check any luggage.

Officer Capone, who had made 110 cases using the drug courier profile, decided that Harlan's behavior fit the pattern of a drug courier.

(In a similar case, *United States v. Smith,* the court states: "The Miami–Fort Lauderdale area is known to DEA agents as the most significant source of cocaine in the United States.")

Harlan later said that he had bought his one-way ticket with cash because he didn't own any credit cards. And he didn't use checks, either, because due to his peripatetic studies, his ID cards were from various places in Ohio and Massachusetts. So he used cash.

After purchasing his ticket, Harlan and Hayes began to walk away from the counter. They were talking and going to have a last drink before Harlan's departure. Harlan recalls that he wasn't nervous; he was aware that he was taking a risk, but really didn't think it was possible that he'd be stopped and searched.

Officers Capone and Carl approached and identified themselves as police officers. Carl stood to his left and Capone stood directly in front of Harlan, opened his wallet to show a badge and ID card, and said something like: "We are narcotics officers. Are you aware of the drug trafficking problem in southern Florida?"

"No," Harlan replied. "What does that have to do with me?"

"We are surveying the situation. We would be interested in seeing your identification and ticket and looking in your luggage."

"I don't understand. I am a physician from Boston," said Harlan, who could see no due cause for them to stop him.

"You look too young to be a physician," one of the officers said.

Harlan showed them his Ohio driver's license and the Delta ticket. Then he showed them a second ID, his New England Medical Center card, and said, "Well, I *am* a physician. There's my identification." Harlan found the officers' tone sarcastic, condescending, and authoritative. "During their entire conversation with me they were pretty much laughing at the fact that I was a physician. They really didn't believe . . . that it was a possibility."

Capone said: "We would still like to search your luggage."

"What's going on?" asked the yacht broker, Hayes.

"We're just conducting an investigation," Capone said. Then he asked Harlan: "Is he with you?"

"He drove me here, but he's not with me," Harlan replied. Then he either said something like, "go ahead and look" at the carry-on bag, or he pointed a question right at the policeman: "And if I refuse to let you look in my bags?"

Capone, who was blocking Harlan's path, said: "We'll hold you and obtain a search warrant."

Harlan put his bags down. They had his ticket and identification and they were blocking his exit. He felt that he was essentially under arrest. "I guess that doesn't give me any choice."

"No, it doesn't. But we don't want to search your bag here. Why don't you come with us."

Hayes turned and left the terminal without a word.

The officers escorted Harlan to a small room just off the Delta ticket area, where air kennels are usually stored. At this point, Harlan said, he was clearly nervous, although he didn't show it. He'd later explain that his symptoms of nervousness are manifested by a "shakiness of the voice, probably a change in the blood pressure, increased pulse rate," and so on. But that "there was no point that I showed overt nervousness." This coolness under pressure, the ability to mask his true emotions, is something that he took evident pride in (although he denied this when asked directly by the prosecutor). He explained it to the judge this way: "I happen to be under quite stress [*sic*] situations oftentimes in the hospitals. And showing nervousness and feeling nervousness are very different. I usually control myself very well. Under these circumstances, I did the same. I really might have been nervous when I was confronted by them, but I had no indication that they had the right or would continue in their search."

In the back room, Harlan was instructed to put his hands on a table directly in front of him and to spread his legs. While Officer Capone frisked him, Officer Carl searched his briefcase and carry-on bag. In the bag, Carl discovered three clear plastic bags containing a white powdery substance.

"How did *that* get there?" Harlan exclaimed, according to the officers.

Harlan denied saying this. He claimed he said: "Oh, shit, this is going to destroy me."

Capone read Harlan his Miranda warning—"You have the right to remain silent; anything you say can be used against you . . ."—placed him under arrest, and handcuffed him. Then he patted Harlan down for weapons and felt a large bulge in Harlan's crotch. Pulling down the doctor's trousers he discovered that Harlan was wearing two pairs of underwear, each of which contained a resealable plastic bag containing a powdery white substance.

"Do you realize what you've done to me and to my career?" Harlan recalled saying.

"Well, we didn't place this cocaine on your body," Officer Capone replied.

Capone left the room to call for a police car to transport Harlan to an airport substation. At this point, Harlan grew distraught. "I can't believe this is going on," he said. "This is going to destroy my life." He was scared to death but he didn't show it. While waiting in the little room with Officer Carl, Harlan asked what the policemen would have done had he not consented to speak to them, or to the search.

"We have alternatives," Carl said.

At the sheriff's airport substation, Officer Capone again read Harlan his Miranda warnings and Harlan again asked what the officers would have done had he not submitted to the search or stopped to talk to them. Someone replied that they could have called for a drug-sniffing dog and gotten a warrant for a search, or they could have allowed him to board the airplane and alerted the authorities in Boston.

After further searching at the substation, the officers discovered three more grams of cocaine in Harlan's jacket pocket.

Harlan found an attorney that night, posted bail, and was released. The first attorney was replaced by a second, Donald L. Ferguson, who would defend Harlan over the next two and a half years.

What began as a routine drug arrest turned into an extended inquiry into the validity of "drug courier" profiling, the voluntary nature of airport searches, the honesty of Officers Capone and Carl, the tainting of witnesses by hypnosis (the policemen were hypnotized by a psychiatrist who had once hypnotized Sirhan Sirhan), the exclusion of evidence, and what constituted suitable punishment for a young man of great promise who had suffered an egregious lack of judgment.

The courtroom grew tense at times. Ferguson argued that the search was illegal, that Capone was "less than candid," and that Carl "had plenty of motive to be less than truthful."

Bruce Zimet, the assistant U.S. attorney prosecuting the case, defended the deputies and said: "If Dr. Waksal was trying to sell swampland in the Everglade and convince someone to build condominiums on it, he would sound the same way [as he did in court]. The whole case comes down to [questions of] credibility."

Harlan chose his words with care, qualified and requalified his statements, and limited the characterization of his actions. He painted a pitiable self-portrait: his career in ruins, abandoned by his friends, and suffering endless sleepless nights, he asked U.S. District Court Judge Norman C. Roettger for mercy. But a hint of smugness shone through his mostly sober testimony. When asked about how exactly the cocaine had come to be in his possession, he replied: "The two officers were questioning me about it, and I simply avoided answering any questions."

So adept was Harlan, that it struck the court that he may have had legal training or expert coaching. When asked about this, Harlan said he had discussed his predicament with two lawyers, his girlfriend, and his family.

Sam attended the hearings and took a very active interest in the proceedings. In the hearing of October 29, 1981, Judge Patricia Jean Kyle, of the U.S. Southern District, noted Sam's presence in the courtroom: "I find it amazing that [Harlan] Waksal's brother, every time one particular legal point is made, shakes his head. Is he a lawyer?"

"I don't think so," replied Ferguson.

Court documents show that Harlan, who had posted $125,000 bail and surrendered his passport, was permitted to travel only to Florida, Massachusetts, and Ohio. In June 1982, the court granted Harlan permission to travel to the U.S. Virgin Islands, as long as he remained in the presence of his attorney or his brother.

Harlan said he had taken directions from Johnston and Joe and had not questioned the wisdom of smuggling cocaine. "I was told to put it in my luggage or on my person, and that I would have no trouble getting it back to Boston."

"And were you told what to do in the event that you came in contact with any law-enforcement agents?" wondered the federal prosecutor, Bruce Zimet.

"No, I was not . . . It wasn't an issue."

"So you essentially were acting . . . just out of your own common sense and your own knowledge?"

"I think it would be more accurate to say 'out of my own stupidity' . . . There was never a discussion about how I was going to do it. It was more a point of my just doing it, and I agreed to do that." Smuggling cocaine was a mistake, Harlan conceded. "I was very upset about the whole situation to myself, as well as my career . . . I realized that I had done a stupid thing and that I was in a lot of trouble . . . I felt that I was completely down the drain."

In February 1982, responding to Harlan's attempt to suppress his statements and the evidence, 2.2 pounds of cocaine, Judge Roettger wrote:

> The court found defendant rather intelligent, as was expected. The court had some difficulty with some aspects of defendant's credibility. Defendant does not come across as "street smart." Yet, he insisted from the witness stand repeatedly that he was not at all nervous at the airport while also maintaining he was carrying cocaine for the first time. Not only human experience but a number of years of presiding at numerous trials involving narcotics cases, compel the court to conclude that Dr. Waksal's testimony in that regard is lacking in credulity.
>
> Defendant contends that Hayes, his airport companion, supports Waksal's position. Hayes testified that Waksal was not nervous but was "pissed off"; the court suspects the latter was undoubtedly true.
>
> The expectation that a physician would not actually be searched is suggested by the Government as the theory the doctor was following . . . the role is carried out by a physician outraged and indignant at this affront of being stopped, and being accused of being part of the drug problem. The court finds . . . the scenario painted by the Government is credible.

Judge Roettger agreed to let Harlan suppress statements made after his arrest and before his Miranda warnings were given, but he denied the motion to suppress the evidence.

In a wrenching hearing on April 27, 1982, in a Miami federal court, Judge Roettger wrestled with the nature of the crime and the appropriate punishment. Mercy pleas were entered by Sam, his wife Cindy, and Harlan's lawyer—who argued that his client had already paid a high price and that no state medical board would grant him a medical license. It was a nonjury trial. Judge Roettger decided to sentence Harlan to nine years in federal prison for possession of cocaine with intent to deliver.

"I am not unmindful of the abilities, talents, and skills of this defendant," Roettger said. "However, a doctor who violates the law and commits a serious felony is no more sacrosanct than a lawyer, an outstanding teacher, or a businessperson who is a pillar of his community." He recommended that Harlan serve time in the federal penitentiary in Springfield, Missouri, a prison hospital, where, he said, "[You] may be able to utilize your talents during your period of confinement." Judge Roettger wished Harlan luck: "I hope you put this behind you. You can get your medical license back and utilize your considerable talent in the field of medicine."

Harlan appealed. On July 11, 1983, his conviction was overturned by the U.S. Court of Appeals for the 11th Circuit, on the grounds that the search "resulted from an illegal seizure without a valid consent." The ruling invalidated the evidence; the case was never retried and Harlan served no time. As a result, he was not compelled by the SEC to disclose the incident when ImClone went public. Nevertheless, the episode has shadowed the brothers ever since.

A 1993 article in *Barron's* reports that at least three potential investors shied away from ImClone specifically because of Harlan's drug bust. And a surprising number of people mentioned it to me without prompting. (I was never able to speak to Harlan Waksal. He canceled three separate interviews and refused to return my phone calls.)

When *Barron's* asked Harlan about the drug bust, he maintained that he'd never used drugs and that this was the "only time" he'd ever transported drugs: "It was a dramatic mistake in judgment. I did it as a favor for someone, and it's a favor I have obviously regretted."

When I asked Sam about Harlan's drug bust in early 2002, he became visibly upset and said: "This is a very difficult subject, one that I prefer not talking about. It's a matter of public record. Harlan was never convicted of anything. He had an unfortunate incident when he was very, very young." Sam added: "All the bankers, the lawyers, the board always knew about it. But if we ran around talking about it, it would be very hurtful to somebody. It hurts me that he has to continue hearing about it."

In pleading for leniency for his brother, Sam had asked Judge Roettger: "Why would [Harlan] commit such a stupid and terrible act?"

"I've asked that myself so many times," the judge answered.

\*     \*     \*

As the investigation into ImClone gained momentum, some observers suggested that the government would attempt a "divide-and-conquer" strategy, pitting one Waksal brother against the other. But a former employee scoffed at the idea: "No way. It would never work. No matter what, Sam will never turn against Harlan, and Harlan will never turn against Sam. Blood is thicker than water."

# FOURTEEN

# In the Light of October

Martha Stewart's name was first publicly linked to the caterwauling ImClone scandal in an Associated Press story that ran on the evening of June 6, 2002. The wire story mentioned that she had traded ImClone stock, but at that point Alan Slobodin and his staff at the House Subcommittee on Oversight and Investigations weren't paying much attention to her. On June 5, a subcommittee staff member had contacted Martha's attorney to ask basic questions about her conversations with Sam and her ImClone trade on December 27. But the investigators considered Martha a sideshow, a celebrity distraction. They were focused on more weighty matters, such as understanding the botched Erbitux clinical trials, the timing and legality of the ImClone insiders' trades, and the apparent regulatory confusion at the FDA.

On June 12, the subcommittee received a letter from Arnold & Porter, an influential Washington, D.C., law firm. The law firm, it turned out, had been retained by Martha Stewart and was reaching out preemptively on her behalf. In a confidential letter, the attorney James F. Fitzpatrick wrote:

> There have been press reports in connection with the sale of Im-
> Clone stock by our client Martha Stewart. I wanted to provide you

with the following [information] which will make clear that her actions had absolutely nothing to do with any nonpublic information about . . . ImClone . . . At no time did Ms. Stewart ever receive from anyone any information concerning any action by the FDA with regard to ImClone . . . Shortly after placing the order to sell her remaining ImClone shares, Ms. Stewart placed a call to Dr. Sam Waksal's office . . . Dr. Waksal never returned the call.

I trust that this will clarify the sequence of events and the factors, [*sic*] which led to Ms. Stewart's decision to sell ImClone shares. As you can see, her transaction was entirely lawful.

In subsequent conversations, Arnold & Porter attorneys repeated the message: Martha's trade on December 27 had nothing to do with ImClone's RTF or with Sam Waksal; it was simply an unfortunate coincidence of timing; her trade was based on a preexisting agreement to sell ImClone at $60 a share. She was entirely innocent, they insisted, so please do not call her. The congressional investigators were happy to oblige, and remained focused on preparing for the ImClone hearing the following day.

AFTER THE SUBCOMMITTEE hearing of June 13, it was reported that Sam and Aliza Waksal shared a stockbroker at Merrill Lynch, a guy named Peter Bacanovic. Big deal, the investigators thought. They were already looking ahead to the second hearing on ImClone, which would take place in October, with a different set of witnesses. They had a lot of research to do. But the press, meanwhile, was busy connecting the dots. And toward the end of June it was revealed that not only was Peter Bacanovic the stockbroker for Sam and Aliza Waksal, he was also the stockbroker for Martha Stewart. *And* he was a college friend of Alexis Stewart's, Sam's former girlfriend. *And* Bacanovic had once worked at ImClone.

"Wait a minute—*what?!*" said Alan Slobodin. This was the first he'd heard of all these interconnections. Now he was very interested in this Merrill broker.

Martha Stewart had said that she traded phone calls with Bacanovic on December 27, the day of her ImClone stock trade. Now it looked as if he was the key guy in a textbook insider-trading case. Did Bacanovic know what had happened that day? Was he the one who'd made it happen? It looked awfully suspicious; it looked as if he had been the conduit of information from Sam to Martha. Slobodin wanted to talk to this guy. He contacted Merrill Lynch in New York and asked for a list of Peter Bacanovic's clients and assistants, his trading records, and his phone records; he also asked to see all trades in ImClone stock from December 3 though December 28, 2001.

In the meantime, members of Congress—one eye on the serious allegations being lobbed in the ImClone affair, one eye on the TV cameras and daily headlines—had all of a sudden decided that they very much wanted to speak to Martha Stewart, too.

SHE HELD A GLINTING, broad-bladed, sharp knife and brought it down with force and precision against the side of a head of white cabbage, *whock-whock-whock,* lopping off slices for a chicken and shredded-cabbage salad with noodles and peanut sauce. It was the morning of Tuesday, June 25, and Martha was on the kitchen set for her weekly cooking segment on CBS's *Early Show.* She was dressed in a loose, pale pink shirt with a tiny black microphone attached by the second button. Her blonde hair was parted just to the right of center, and hung straight down to her shoulders, partly obscuring her left eye. Her look of calm composure was belied only by a slightly tight jaw and a look of fatigue that the makeup could not fully obscure.

Jane Clayson, the CBS host, who was dressed in an orange shirt and a gray suit, introduced the segment with a summary of events thus far in the ImClone story. The network deems *The Early Show* a news program, and in order to appear in her regular segment Martha had agreed to discuss the farrago at ImClone. Clayson spoke about Sam and Erbitux and the FDA, and photos of Martha with Sam and Martha with Peter Bacanovic flashed on the screen. In the background, the sound of Martha's methodical cabbage shredding—*whock-whock-whock*—punctuated the litany.

Clayson finished and looked at her guest. Martha flashed a momentary smile, and with a hollow laugh, said, "Hi, well, if we're going to make salad, ah-ha-ha—"

"We *are,* but first let me ask you a few things about all of this," Clayson interrupted; this was a news program, and she was determined not to be charmed out of asking tough questions. "What do you say about all of the allegations here?"

"As you understand, I'm involved in an investigation that has very serious implications," Martha replied, calmly. She didn't seem angry; she didn't look at the camera. She looked at Clayson and spoke in a soft voice inflected with notes of put-upon innocence, between-us-friends complicity, impatience with the slowly churning wheels of justice, and steely resolve. "I'm not at liberty at this time to make any comments whatsoever."

Clayson pushed.

"Well, the investigation *really* centers on ImClone and its cancer drug, Erbitux, which many of us thought had—and it probably still has—great potential for curing cancer in seriously ill patients," Martha said, deftly turning the conversation away from herself. The knife in her hand continued to work methodically, slicing ribbons of yellowy-green cabbage. "I certainly *hope* the matter is resolved in the very near future, and I will be exonerated of any, ah, *ridiculousness.*"

This last word she practically spat out.

Clayson looked down at her papers and mentioned that the week before, Peter Bacanovic had been suspended by Merrill Lynch. "Are you worried that what he did might further complicate matters for you?"

With a sigh, and in a nearly apologetic voice, Martha answered, "Again, I have nothing to say on the matter."

Clayson noted that MSO's stock had dropped and asked how the bad press and governmental inquiries might affect Martha's image.

"Well, I'm *in* the media business," Martha replied with an uncomfortable smile. "I've been the center of very *fair* reporting and very *unfair* reporting. So, this is not new to me. I chose to go ahead with my work, concentrate on the good work my company is doing. My employees and I are hard at work making this the best omnimedia company in the world, Jane. We will continue to do that and—now I want to focus on my salad, because that's why we're here!"

"One more question, one more question about all of this," Clayson insisted. "In the media frenzy of the last week or so, how has it been to be in the middle of all that?"

Martha laughed and shook her blonde hair. "When I was a model—and I *was,* all during high school and college—you always wanted to be on the cover of a magazine. That's how your success was judged: the more covers the better. Well, I am the CEO of a New York Stock Exchange—listed company. And I don't want to be on any covers of *any* newspapers for a long, long time. That's the story. Thank you very much."

Somewhat awkwardly, the two then segued into the cooking segment of the show, where Martha demonstrated how to make a number of potluck salads. Trying to shift tonal gears—from probing news inquiry to innocent culinary delight—Clayson began to ask questions about salad ingredients and fat content. Martha laughed and used the soft voice to give the impression that all was back to normal. But the tension between the two women lingered and they rushed through the salad preparations as if they couldn't wait to get off the set and away from each other.

The segment was uncomfortable to watch and it soon became the butt of many jokes. Martha felt humiliated and frustrated. The following week, upon learning that CBS again intended to question her about ImClone, Martha temporarily bowed out of *The Early Show.* She has yet to return.

THROUGHOUT THE BLEAK early months of 2002, as the allegations against Sam Waksal seemed to grow more numerous, more spectacular, and more devastating every week, ImClone's board of directors decided that "for the good of the company" it would be best to retain Sam's services as president and CEO. To the board members, all of whom were distinguished older men, Sam *was* ImClone: he personified the company to outsiders; he kept the spirit of adventure burning inside; he and Harlan knew the staff and understood the company's multiple science projects and tangled inner workings better than anyone else. Sam, board member Paul Kopperl would later explain, was "largely indispensable."

Although the directors had "vigorous" discussions about Sam's leadership in those months, Robert Goldhammer, ImClone's chairman, never seriously entertained firing him. Sure, Sam had had a few problems with money and the truth over the years, Goldhammer would admit, and Sam was not temperamentally suited to run a big, mature enterprise but one way or another he had always found a way to repay the millions of dollars in loans extended by the company. More important, Sam's youthful zest for life kept ImClone going. "He was the spirit for our young research group," Goldhammer told Congress. "It was so important with a young company—you've just got to let them breathe. And he would do that. He would encourage them."

And so, to maintain continuity, to keep the development of Erbitux and ImClone's other drugs on track, and to save face, it made sense to them to keep Sam close by.

Yet the government's multipronged investigation could not be ignored. Nor could Bristol's obvious displeasure. Nor could the market's loss of faith, or the mounting shareholder lawsuits, or the glare of bad press, or the howls from cancer patients.

In January 2002, the board formed a special committee, which excluded the Waksal brothers, to look into the charges against Sam and the company. They were almost immediately confronted by a very serious new problem.

In early February, the special committee was informed that it was "possible" Sam had forged documents and a signature for two multimillion-dollar bank warrants. In April 1999, Sam pledged $44 million worth of warrants to buy ImClone shares as collateral for two separate lines of credit, one from the Bank of America, NA and the other from Refco Capital Markets. In the summer of 2000, Sam had secretly exercised the warrants, rendering them worthless. He did not tell his two creditors he had done this, which is illegal. Bank of America grew suspicious, and in January 2000 requested proof that its warrant remained valid. In November 2000, Sam concocted a fake legal document, called an "issuers letter," and for the second time forged the signature of his old friend John Landes, ImClone's senior vice president for legal affairs.

Landes learned of this forgery in February 2002 and confronted Sam. Sam did not deny what he had done. When Landes told the board about the forgery, the board's special committee instructed ImClone's outside counsel to "thoroughly investigate" the matter and report back. No one at ImClone reported this forgery, or Sam's 1986 forgery, to federal regulators.

DAYS AFTER ASSIGNING its attorneys to investigate the forgery, the already discombobulated ImClone office was spun into further turmoil when Peter Dolan suddenly demanded that Sam and Harlan stand down and that the biotech company renegotiate its agreement with Bristol-Myers Squibb. Faced with this external threat, ImClone closed ranks, stood behind the Waksals in public, and rebuffed its now thoroughly vexed partner.

Sam's forgery was quite obvious, but the attorneys' investigation dragged on for three months without reaching a conclusion.

By May 21, the ImClone board had decided that the bad news had become intolerable and requested that Sam resign. He did so the following day and was paid a $7 million severance. Sam's departure rendered the investigation into his forgery moot.

In mid-June Sam was arrested by the FBI on charges of insider trading. The next day he appeared before the congressional subcommittee and pled the Fifth. Six days after that, on June 19, ImClone received a "Wells Notice" from the Securities and Exchange Commission. This was a serious matter and it made headlines across the country. The Wells Notice warned that because of unanswered questions about suspicious trading of ImClone stock the previous December, the SEC was close to filing civil charges against the company. The Wells Notice gave Sam a chance to explain his, and his family members', trades and to persuade the commissioners not to file a lawsuit. In other words, it was Sam's last chance to clear his name.

The Wells Notice also put ImClone and its board in jeopardy. It would allow the SEC to seek an injunction against the company, levy fines against it, and seek penalties from its board of directors. Further, information unearthed by an SEC inquiry could be used in shareholder lawsuits against the company—of which there were already over a dozen, with more on the way. These lawsuits charged that ImClone executives had misled investors about the FDA's concerns over Erbitux and had caused them to lose a lot of money.

Members of the ImClone board understood very well what a Wells Notice meant for the company, and for them personally. It "was the last straw" for Sam at ImClone, Paul Kopperl would later tell Congress.

When Sam refused to answer the SEC's questions about his December trades, the board convened an emergency meeting. Asking Harlan to abstain, the directors—including longtime Waksal supporters like John Mendelsohn and Robert Goldhammer—voted unanimously to sue Sam to recoup the $7 million severance package he had been paid when he resigned.

Sam was being sued by ImClone—*his* company, the company that he had founded, and that his younger brother now ran—for breach of contract and for breach of fiduciary duty. This set Sam reeling. With a personal debt of some $80 million, not to mention all of his legal and public relations expenses, plus his usual high cost of living, he needed all the money he could get.

"He told the board he was cooperating with the government investigation," an ImClone spokesman announced. "With these new revelations, it appears he has not been telling the truth."

ON JUNE 27, 2002, Sam invoked the Fifth Amendment 223 times and was accused of impersonating a mime. This was in a private deposition for a civil suit. It had been filed against him and Scientia Health Group, Inc., a side venture he'd cooked up that was based in Bermuda but run out of ImClone's offices. From June through November 2001, James W. Neal Jr., an experienced banker and biotech executive, had served as president of Scientia; then his contract was voided on a technicality. Now Neal was suing, alleging that Sam had engaged "in illegal, unethical and fraudulent conduct."

Sam had established Scientia in late 2000 as a holding company to invest in and fund biotech and health-care companies. It was a good idea, and Sam managed to raise $40 million from 48 backers—many of whom were also backers of ImClone. The first person on the list of Scientia's "Founder" shares was Aliza Waksal; she was followed by the lawyer Allen Grubman, the ImClone PR woman Andrea Rabney, the banker and bon vivant Arthur Altschul, the Hamptons builder Ben Krupinksi, and a long list of other familiar names—Martha Stewart; Carl Icahn and his wife, Gail; financiers Leon Black and Nelson Peltz; Dr. Bart Pasternak; Jack Waksal; Elana Waksal and her husband, Jarrett Posner. John Mendelsohn was on Scientia's scientific advisory board. Zvi Fuks, of Memorial Sloan-Kettering (who had put Sam and Mendelsohn together), was a shareholder, and so was an Israeli woman named Sonia Ben-Yehuda.

Sam invested $7 million in Scientia. The Continental Casualty Company put in $5 million. The biggest investor of all was Softbank, a Japanese company that invested $10 million (after it had fared poorly in Internet stocks, Softbank had decided to branch into biotech).

Sam sprinkled Scientia shares like candy among his pals—to Harvey Weinstein of Miramax, to the film producer Keith Barish, and to the art dealer Larry Gagosian. Founding investors paid just one-tenth of a penny for each of their shares. Thus, Martha Stewart's 3,500 shares cost her $3.50 and Gagosian's 6,000 shares cost him $6. Gagosian wrote to the *New York Observer:* "I, along with dozens of Sam Waksal's social acquaintances, was solicited to invest in a start-up company called Scientia. Aside from the fact that Scientia is in the biotech field, I know very little about the company . . . My total investment is six dollars." When *The New York Times* called members of the company's prominent scientific advisory board, several of them were nonplussed. "I have no idea what that is," said Brigitte Huber, a professor at Tufts University Medical School. When reminded, she recognized the name Scientia but said that she had never attended a meeting.

James Neal's complaint charged that, "During his employment [Neal] became aware of certain illegal and unethical conduct engaged in by Waksal, both in connection to Scientia and his other business interests." (The complaint does not specify what the conduct was, and all parties refused to comment on the case.) "In addition, [he] witnessed Waksal make outright misrepresentations to potential investors on numerous occasions." Neal, the complaint said, "made clear to Waksal, and others, that he would not stand by silently while Waksal engaged in such misconduct . . . Waksal, in turn, concluded that he did not want to be hampered by an immediate subordinate who might expose his illegal, unethical and fraudulent behavior. Waksal thus wished to remove plaintiff from Scientia for his own personal benefit."

The suit further alleged that Neal's two subordinates at Scientia, Sonia Ben-Yehuda and Peter Getz, plotted with Waksal against Neal; then they persuaded Robert Takeuchi, Softbank's senior officer in America, to go along with their scheme.

Sam countercharged that several of his investors, notably Softbank, had objected to Neal's $350,000 salary and $250,000 bonus, and that Neal's refusal to take less pay was hurting the company. In November 2001, Neal was let go. That same day, Scientia completed its financing and closed its $40 million investment pool.

At Sam's deposition, Joseph Lee Matalon, Neal's attorney, asked whether Sam had commingled his own money with Scientia's. Sam invoked the Fifth Amendment. Matalon asked if Sam had transferred funds offshore—Waksal had accounts in Switzerland, Amsterdam, and the British Virgin Islands—"to put them out of reach of Mr. Neal in obtaining a judgment." Sam invoked the Fifth Amendment. Matalon asked about a $5 million loan from the Bank of America to Scientia. Sam invoked the Fifth Amendment. Indeed, Sam refused to admit that he had heard of Scientia (he was the founder and CEO) or that he received health benefits from the company. After taking the Fifth 223 times, Sam, Matalon noted, had done an admirable "impersonation of Marcel Marceau."

In July 2002, the court ordered Waksal not to transfer any more of his assets. The next day, he sold a piece of beachfront property in Sagaponack, New York, for some $3.12 million (the asking price had been $5 million). He claimed he had not known about the court's order. In the meantime, he'd also put up a house he owned in Wainscott for sale, at an asking price of $4.9 million. The house was taken off the market, for the moment.

Neal's suit stretched out for sometimes bizarre reasons. Matalon charged that the defendants were intentionally stalling the proceeding while trying to find a way to close down Scientia and avoid paying Neal. At one point, Sonia Ben-Yehuda, Scientia's executive vice president for business development, claimed that she had to fly to Israel to assist her sister, who had a "medical emergency"; she'd be unable to attend a deposition scheduled for September 19, she said. But at 11 o'clock on the morning of the 19th, Neal happened to run into Ben-Yehuda in Rockefeller Center; she was carrying two shopping bags from Saks Fifth Avenue. Her plans had changed, she said.

"This is the woman who was supposed to be in Israel and was shopping on Fifth Avenue!" blurted out Judge Ira Gammerman. "She lied to her lawyer!"

"It's unfortunate that you are left with a bad impression," said Ben-Yehuda's attorney.

In December 2002, Neal obtained a judgment of more than $2 million against Waksal and Scientia; the parties later settled the case for an undisclosed amount.

IN AUGUST 2002, Waksal was indicted on 13 counts over the ImClone scandal by a federal grand jury in New York. Aside from the charge of forgery, the indictment contained a remarkable set of new allegations—that Sam had erased computer records and shredded documents detailing his offshore accounts, defrauded the two banks, lied to investigators, duped his shareholders, and obstructed a federal investigation. He was now facing millions of dollars in fines and up to 30 years in prison for the bank fraud charge alone.

Sam's lead attorney, the bearded and barrel-chested Mark Pomerantz, called the indictment a "painful chapter" in his client's life. He cautioned the public not to jump to hasty conclusions: "Like all Americans, he is presumed to be innocent."

Sam pleaded not guilty. At an impromptu press conference outside the U.S. District Court building, in lower Manhattan, he exuded confidence. Although the case had been "extremely challenging and emotionally draining for me, my family, and my friends," he said, he continued to believe in the promise of Erbitux and in the leadership of his brother, Harlan. "ImClone," Sam predicted, "will grow, prosper, and continue its very important work."

Despite his upbeat words, Sam could not catch a break. A few days after he proclaimed his innocence, the press revealed that Sam had donated $26,000 to a soft-money account established on behalf of Hillary Rodham Clinton by Democrats during her 2000 run for the Senate seat vacated by Daniel Patrick Moynihan. Sam had donated $2,000 to her election campaign, and in 2001 he had donated $5,000 to her political action committee, HILLPAC. At first, Senator Clinton's camp said she "has no plans to return the money." Then she reversed course and said she would donate the $7,000 received by her senate campaign and HILLPAC to a charity, and would recommend that those in charge of her soft money account do the same with the remaining $26,000.

Although Sam has reportedly given over $160,000 to various Democratic politicians, he had not forgotten to hedge his bets with the GOP. In April it had been reported that ImClone had paid Libby Pataki, the wife of New York's Republican governor George Pataki, a $10,000 "consulting fee." It was not clear what sort of consulting she might be qualified to do for the biotech firm, but after questions were raised over the fee's propriety Ms. Pataki returned the money.

THERE IS NO BLUNTING the power of the market, and by the summer of 2002, Bristol-Myers Squibb was in the midst of one of the worst moments in its 115-year history. Three of the company's best-selling drugs had gone generic, resulting in enormous losses of annual revenue: the diabetes drug Glucophage IR had plummeted from $511 million in 2001 to $11 million in 2002; Taxol dropped from $160 million to $38 million; and the antianxiety medicine BuSpar fell from $82 million to $3 million. The company's licensing agreements had become a tangled mess, and its costly labs had once again failed to produce new drugs to fill its empty pipeline. When the company announced that it was being investigated by the SEC for "channel-stuffing" and improperly inflating 2001 revenue by $1 billion, investors balked and began to sell off the stock.

Bristol's share price dropped to just above $20, a six-year low. This represented a loss of over 70 percent of value in just 18 months. In an industry where profit can rise 10 to 15 percent a year, Bristol had warned analysts that its earnings would be off 46 percent from the year before.

Peter Dolan was now under intense pressure to turn the company around. He remained stoic in public. "We are dealing forthrightly with the tough issues facing the U.S. prescription business, most importantly the work-down of wholesaler inventory," he said in a midsummer conference call.

Then he let go Peter S. Ringrose, Bristol's chief scientific officer and president of its Pharmaceutical Research Institute. An Englishman, Ringrose had been with the company since 1997.

"What's sad about this is that once upon a time [Bristol] was a well-run, well-respected company," observed Matt Stephani, a portfolio manager at Idex Great Companies–America Fund. "That credibility is not something you reestablish two quarters down the road. It's going to take years—especially in this environment, where everybody is tired of getting burned."

Bristol wasn't the only Big Pharma company reeling that summer. The global pharmaceutical industry was in a funk and some investors had forsaken it entirely, believing that it was due for a major shakeout. But there were sporadic success stories, a couple of which were haunting to Peter Dolan.

In June 2001, the FDA unexpectedly rejected a drug called Zelnorm, for irritable-bowel syndrome, developed by Novartis AG, of Basel, Switzerland. The year before, Novartis had made news with Gleevec, a targeted treatment highly regarded as a breakthrough leukemia drug. Novartis's CEO, Dr. Daniel Vasella, had staked his reputation on Zelnorm and was taken aback by the FDA's rejection. Two days later he was further shocked when he received a fax from his marketing partner: in a terse letter, Peter Dolan announced that Bristol-

Myers Squibb was withdrawing from the deal to jointly market Zelnorm.

Vasella was insulted. He was angry that Dolan had terminated the agreement by fax, and had not even had the decency to call and talk it over. Vasella felt that a business relationship should be akin to a marriage: partners should be willing to stick together in both good times and in bad. Vasella strongly believed in Zelnorm's potential as a treatment and as a strong product.

But Peter Dolan was in desperate straits. There was hardly any good news coming out of Bristol, and his job was in question. He had been put on notice by the company's high-powered board of directors, which included the legendarily tough Louis V. Gerstner, the man who had saved IBM. Short on time, money, and patience, Dolan had decided to cut his losses with Zelnorm and move on.

"We are not looking back," a Bristol spokeswoman told the press in a final bridge-burning statement.

Fifteen months later Dr. Vasella had his revenge. Novartis appealed the FDA's ruling on Zelnorm, and had presented the agency with a more complete data package. And in late July 2002, FDA reviewers reversed course and approved the drug. Two years earlier than analysts had thought possible, Novartis began to sell Zelnorm and was gearing up for a major, American-style marketing campaign—complete with TV ads, patient surveys, and a flood of free drug samples for doctors. Good press followed and Novartis's stock surged. Soon, analysts began to predict that Zelnorm could become a $1 billion-a-year drug. Dolan, meanwhile, whose company had not had a single new drug approved in 2000–01, did not receive a penny from Zelnorm's success.

Even worse, seven months after ImClone's Erbitux had failed to pass muster, the FDA granted accelerated approval to a rival colon cancer drug called oxaliplatin (also known as Eloxatin), made by the Paris-based Sanofi-Synthelabo, Europe's seventh-largest drug company. Already used in more than 55 countries, "oxali's" FDA review took only seven weeks to complete. This was the shortest review ever for a cancer drug, beating the 10-week review in 2001 for Novartis's Gleevec.

In a clinical trial involving 463 patients, the combination of oxaliplatin and 5-FU shrank tumors by at least 30 percent in 9 percent of patients, while either 5-FU or oxaliplatin alone did not help any of the patients. The combination of oxaliplatin and 5-FU also kept tumors from starting to grow again for 4.6 months, or 2 months longer than for 5-FU alone. To the outside world, this may not sound like much of a benefit. But to cancer patients and their families, a few more weeks of life are meaningful. It was approved in mid-August 2002, when news about ImClone and its drug was all bad.

Two years earlier, oxaliplatin had failed to impress the FDA as an initial treatment for colorectal cancer because it did not seem to prolong cancer patients' lives. But new data presented at the 2002 ASCO showed that when oxaliplatin was combined with chemotherapy, it did indeed extend survival. "The whole history of oxaliplatin indicates how difficult it is" to win FDA approval, said Stephen K. Carter, a cancer drug consultant. He said the approval was "better late than never, but it's late."

Patients whose hopes had been raised and dashed by Erbitux lauded the FDA's quick approval of oxaliplatin. The press picked up on this and so did Wall Street and Washington. Indeed, the drug's record-breaking approval time had a political subtext: it was done, some said, to respond to criticism of the agency since it had rejected the Erbitux application, and to mute Big Pharma's complaints that FDA reviews of new drugs were too slow and cautious.

Dr. Richard Pazdur, who oversees oncology drugs at the FDA and was one of the stars of the first congressional hearing into ImClone, said that the agency had moved quickly because once the two existing chemo drugs for colorectal cancer patients—5-FU and irinotecan—stopped working, patients were left without recourse. "There really is no treatment option, and these people are desperately seeking treatment for this disease," he said. Furthermore, he said, Sanofi-Synthelabo's clinical trial, a three-arm randomized trial, was superior to ImClone's for Erbitux. The FDA was intentionally sending a message to drugmakers, he said: "The point that we want to get across was the value in doing randomized trials."

These events conspired to shove ImClone back into the spotlight. Oxaliplatin's approval had raised the bar for Erbitux: Harlan Waksal now had to show that his colorectal cancer drug was not just effective but superior to oxaliplatin, or that it would work in patients who did not respond to oxaliplatin or the two chemotherapies. Harlan played down the competition, saying that Erbitux and oxaliplatin were different drugs that worked in different ways. Two-thirds of the patients in a European trial of Erbitux had failed to respond to oxaliplatin, ImClone said; furthermore, the company had designed upcoming Erbitux trials with an approved oxaliplatin in mind. But the inescapable fact was that Sam and Harlan's mistakes had cost Erbitux, and Brstol-Myers Squibb, its "first-mover" advantage.

For YEARS, biotechnology companies have complained that the FDA's approval of their new drugs had moved much more slowly than that of traditional drugs. They have also complained that the agency's biologics division and its drug division used inconsistent standards and burdens of proof when reviewing drugs. Big Pharma generally considered the drug division to be better managed and quicker to respond to questions than the biologics division. But defenders of the biologics division say that because these drugs are derived from living organisms and the latest science, they are often more complex and less well understood than traditional drugs; reviewing them properly takes time.

At the June hearing into ImClone, members of the House subcommittee found that the biologics division "needed improvement." As a result, major changes in the FDA bureaucracy were put into motion for the first time in years. Congress asked the agency to create consistent standards for the biologics and drug divisions so that drugmakers will know in advance what the requirements are for drug approval. For a federal bureaucracy that is averse to change, this was a watershed moment.

It wasn't only drug companies and Congress that had gripes with the FDA. The influential editorial page of *The Wall Street Journal* had taken to bashing the agency—which it scoffed at as a "bureaucratic maze"—for moving too cautiously on new drug approval, and for "nit-picking bureaucrats" like Richard Pazdur who are "callous" toward terminally ill cancer patients. The agency's message, the *Journal* opined, was, "FDA to Patients: Drop Dead."

The newspaper was particularly irked by the delay in approval of a drug called Iressa, made by the Anglo-Swedish concern AstraZeneca PLC, for patients with advanced lung cancer.

Like Erbitux, Iressa is an epidermal growth factor (EGF) inhibitor, which works to disrupt the chemical signals that spur cancer tumor growth. In small clinical trials, AstraZeneca reported encouraging results: Iressa shrank tumors in about 10 percent of lung cancer patients who had not responded to chemotherapy and had improved the symptoms—such as the ability to breathe freely—of 36 percent of patients. While not a breakthrough, the drug at least showed some activity in patients without many treatment options. The American Cancer Society estimates that some 172,000 new cases of lung cancer are diagnosed every year, and that the disease kills about 157,000 people annually. The standard treatment for lung cancer is doses of toxic chemotherapy; once a patient has run through those drugs, though, there are no alternative therapies to turn to.

But Ralph Nader's consumer watchdog group Public Citizen asked the FDA to keep Iressa off the market because it had caused deaths in Japan, where the drug was already being sold. Japan's health minister announced that deaths and side effects from Iressa declined once his government enforced strict rules about how it was to be used.

In a lukewarm review in the summer of 2002, the FDA said that AstraZeneca had not conducted controlled studies of Iressa against a placebo, which made it impossible to measure the drug's effect against tumors, or to know whether it improved patients' quality of life. In declining to approve Iressa, the agency's reviewers said that it showed only "hints" of effectiveness. AstraZeneca's American depository receipts immediately dropped 15 percent.

Iressa's setback set off a ripple effect in the marketplace. Investors began to question the viability of the whole EGF class of drugs and began to sell off biotech stocks indiscriminately. OSI Pharmaceuticals, which (along with partners Genentech and Roche) is developing a promising targeted cancer therapy called Tarceva, saw its share price drop by 56 percent, even though there had been no news about its drug. Shares of Abgenix, which is also working on a promising cancer drug, ABX-EGF, dropped 13 percent. ImClone's stock dipped a further 9 percent, to $6.11.

When a third highly anticipated drug, Genentech's Avastin—an antiangiogenesis drug that blocks the flow of blood to cancer tumors—stumbled in September, alarm bells went off around the industry. In clinical trials, Avastin had failed to extend the life of late-stage breast cancer patients. This news again raised concerns that the highly touted new biotech oncology drugs might not work as well as advertised, if at all. What exactly was the problem? Was it the science behind targeted treatments? Was it the way these drugs were being tested? Was it unrealistic expectations from desperate cancer patients, Wall Street, and the media? Was the FDA judging these compounds too harshly?

In late September, an ODAC panel surprised nearly everyone by voting 11 to 3 to grant accelerated approval to Iressa, the AstraZeneca cancer drug. This decision was based on the notion that the drug's 10 percent response rate in patients with advanced lung cancer was a good predictor of future clinical benefit. The FDA agreed to green-light Iressa in the belief that while it helped only 10 percent of lung cancer patients that was better than helping none.

Perhaps the most persuasive argument in Iressa's favor came from an unexpected source: participants in AstraZeneca's compassionate-use program. In the course of developing the drug, the company had provided some 18,000 patients with Iressa outside of those in its clinical trials. At the ODAC hearing in September 2002, a parade of impassioned lung cancer patients came forward to praise the drug. Many of them claimed that if it were not for Iressa they would no longer be alive. It was a difficult testimonial to ignore.

Then Iressa became a media darling of Erbitux-like proportions: A 2002 *Forbes* cover story about the drug focused on the remarkable turnaround of Adriane Riddle, 18, "a fierce water polo player," whose lung cancer "had vanished" thanks to Iressa.

The sudden rise of Iressa set off a new ripple effect, as investors, thrilled to finally hear some positive news about EGF cancer drugs, began to bid up the same biotech companies they had recently knocked down: ImClone shot up 32 percent, OSI was up 28 percent, Abgenix was up 17 percent, and both AstraZeneca and Genetech were up 4 percent.

A few weeks later, AstraZeneca, which is Europe's second-largest pharmaceutical firm, released further data indicating that Iressa was more effective than previously believed. This had two results: it seemed to confirm that the FDA's decision to grant the drug accelerated approval was correct, and it further underscored ImClone's vulnerability to competition.

"The horse race between Iressa and C225 [Erbitux] is a lot closer than most people think," judged Catherine Arnold, a drug analyst at Sanford Bernstein.

\*       \*       \*

By July 2002, federal prosecutors had gathered enough evidence to charge Sam Waksal, his father, Jack, and his daughter Aliza with insider trading. They were aggressively pushing for an indictment. To the Waksals, for whom family was paramount, this was the worst possible scenario. Jack had always been Sam's "hero" and protector, and now the son had shamed the father and exposed him to the possibility of ending his life in jail. Jack was 81 years old: a prison sentence, even a short one in a "nice" facility, would be tantamount to a death sentence. This is not how his life was supposed to end.

Aliza, 27, an aspiring actress with a pale face, dyed blonde hair, and black designer-framed glasses, looked at her father, and in a plaintive voice, asked: "Why am I involved in this situation?"

Sam hung his head, incapable of returning his daughter's stare. Her question, and the obvious answer, was like a dagger to the heart. Feelings of shame, recrimination, and despair echoed inside of him all day every day and poisoned his fitful dreams at night. He felt himself slipping into a cold black hole, as if he'd suffered a momentary death. Staring at his gaunt face in the mirror, he asked himself, wretchedly: *Who am I? What have I done?*

Federal law stipulated that Sam had to be indicted by a grand jury within 30 days of being charged with insider trading, or else be granted a hearing at which evidence could be presented against him. This gave Sam something to fight against, a target to aim all of his excess energy at. He was determined to shield Jack and Aliza from prison. On this he was absolute. He'd rather lie down in front of a train than allow his father and daughter to go to jail. Nor would he turn on Martha Stewart.

Trying to buy as much time as possible, his defense lawyers engaged the prosecutors in a dialogue about the possibility of a "global settlement": Sam would agree to plead guilty to certain crimes, they said, as long as all charges against Jack and Aliza were dropped. The prosecutors were not inclined to accept the offer. To them, it was plain as day that Sam, Jack, and Aliza Waksal had phone conversations about the impending RTF, had engaged in insider trading in ImClone stock on December 27, and had lied about it when questioned by the SEC. Now they should face the consequences of their actions.

The public supported the government's position. In light of the parade of revelations about Enron, Arthur Anderson, Tyco, WorldCom, and Wall Street analysts, the American public was fed up with the rich and powerful getting away with brazen self-dealing. With the entrance of Martha Stewart into this case, ImClone had now become one of the most high-profile of the white-collar crime cases of 2001–02. The prosecutors were determined to make an example of Sam—and, if need be, his father and daughter.

The calculus seemed to be: squeeze Jack and Aliza to get Sam; squeeze Sam (and Douglas Faneuil) to get Bacanovic and Martha.

"I got the sense that . . . if [the prosecutors] could have Martha, they would be unbelievably happy campers," Sam would say later. The discussions between prosecutors and defense dragged on, antagonistically, for weeks. Finally, with the clock ticking, the judge reluctantly granted Sam a two-week extension to reach a plea agreement.

PETER BACANOVIC was 40 years old. In the decade he'd spent as one of the most trusted brokers, confidants, and escorts to some of Manhattan's wealthiest and most prominent names, he had never imagined himself being grilled by the Securities and Exchange Commission about his business practices. He was viewed by his clients, and he viewed himself, as the personification of discretion. Yet on January 7, 2002, he had received a call from attorneys at the SEC, who began peppering him with questions about Martha's ImClone stock trade.

In the course of this conversation, Bacanovic recalled that in his December 20 phone call with Martha, they had quibbled over ImClone (he wanted her to sell immediately; she didn't want to sell); she had eventually agreed to sell the stock when it hit $60 per share. He also recalled that he and Martha spoke on December 27: he told her that Imclone had dropped below $60 and she had instructed him to sell her holdings. Investigators from the SEC, FBI, and U.S. Attorney's Office would later allege that Bacanovic's recollections of this phone call were false and misleading.

On February 4, Martha Stewart was likewise questioned about her trade by the agents from the SEC, FBI, and U.S. Attorney's Office. They interviewed Martha by phone. Her lawyers were at her elbow and she was not under oath. She confirmed Bacanovic's statements about their conversations and her ImClone sale, and added that she did not know whether the phone message he'd left for her was recorded in the phone

log kept by her assistant, Ann Armstrong. She added that while convers-
ing, Bacanovic had told her that the SEC had questioned Merrill Lynch
about her trades, but she said, he hadn't mentioned that *he*'d been interviewed by the investigators. Martha said that since December 28th,
she'd only had one conversation with Bacanovic about ImClone—a discussion that had only covered matters in the "public arena."

In an indictment unsealed a year and a half later, the investigators
would charge that Martha's statements in this interview were false and
misleading. She and her broker, they alleged, had schemed "to provide
false information," "to fabricate evidence," and "to obstruct justice,"
among other serious charges.

CONGRESSMAN BILLY TAUZIN, the chairman of the House Energy and
Commerce Committee, is also the author of the Cajun cookbook *Cook
'N Tell*. Beaming, dressed in a tall white toque and a spotless white
apron, he had appeared on Martha Stewart's television show in 2000,
where he instructed Martha on the genuine bayou technique for cooking crawfish. By all accounts, Tauzin enjoyed himself immensely, and as
a memento has kept a photograph of himself and Martha on his office
wall ever since.

When asked about the photograph by reporters, Ken Johnson
quipped: "I wouldn't read too much into that. He's got 12 trophy deer
heads on his wall, too."

On August 6, Tauzin's committee wrote to Martha Stewart, asking
for additional information about her phone calls, copies of her e-mails,
and the records of her business manager:

> Since [the Arnold & Porter letter] of June 12, 2002, the Committee
> has learned of several developments raising questions about the accu-
> racy of statements made by your legal representatives concerning the
> circumstances of your . . . trade of ImClone stock . . . We acknowl-
> edge and appreciate that you have voluntarily produced some records
> and information to the Committee. However, these efforts and the
> pace of these efforts are not sufficient for our mutual interests in re-
> solving these issues expeditiously, fairly, and comprehensively . . . We
> have been informed that on advice of your counsel you will not agree
> to be interviewed by the Committee at this time under any condition.
> We sincerely hope, and urge, you to reconsider your position. Al-

though your trade began as a peripheral issue to the ImClone investigation, your trade and its circumstances and statements made on your behalf are now serious ones. We want to assure ourselves that you have not attempted to mislead this Committee with the intent to obstruct an investigation.

The following day, shareholders filed a lawsuit against Martha and her company, Martha Stewart Living Omnimedia, in federal court. Spurred by press reports that Douglas Faneuil, the Merrill Lynch trading assistant, had told Martha to sell her ImClone stock on Bacanovic's instruction, the suit alleged that Martha had misled investors and federal authorities about her stock sale. "Once Stewart chose to address these issues publicly, she had an obligation to . . . speak the whole truth. Instead, Stewart . . . made materially false and misleading statements about" the sale of her ImClone holdings, the suit said.

Representative Bart Stupak, Democrat of Michigan, and a member of the House subcommittee, said on the *Today* show that if Martha had not responded to Congress by August 20 she should be forced by subpoena to appear. "Bring her in and if she wants to take the Fifth [Amendment] that's her right," he said. "We've asked Martha Stewart and her broker to put forth the stop-loss order to verify her version of what happened . . . We always had promises . . . that she would come forward . . . As this thing has unraveled, they have drawn further away from the table. It's really in Martha Stewart's court right now."

"THERE'S GROWING evidence to suggest that Sam Waksal repeatedly lied to our investigators," Ken Johnson announced in August. It had been discovered that just as the government initiated its multipronged investigations, in early January, Sam had ordered two paper shredders. The investigators had uncovered the e-mail request for the shredders and had a copy of the receipt for the shredders. The investigators had also discovered that Sam had asked someone at ImClone to erase certain computer files detailing his telephone calls and his personal financial records. Jim Greenwood wrote to Harlan: "We are writing to express our grave concerns that Samuel Waksal or others at ImClone may have obstructed the committee's investigation by ordering or carrying out the destruction of certain records and documents."

Harlan replied that the shredders were an innocent purchase, bought in the course of "normal work activity." He had not destroyed any documents or erased any records, he said, nor was he aware of anyone in the company doing so "other than what has been attributed to Dr. Samuel Waksal."

Turning his attention to Martha, Greenwood said he had trouble understanding why, after months of polite but persistent requests by the subcommittee, Martha "would not be able to come forward and set the facts forward to clear her own name . . . I have no great heart to badger or persecute anyone." But, he added, "because you are rich and famous doesn't mean you get a pass on this." The subcommittee would be glad to exonerate Martha if she could provide exculpatory evidence, he added. "We would have preferred, and still prefer, that Ms. Stewart come in and talk with our investigators. We did not subpoena her to the hearing. We've tried to be as respectful as possible." If she refused to answer Congress's questions, he said, then he would subpoena her after Labor Day.

Martha refused to bend. Since early June her legal team—which by now included attorneys from Wachtel, Lipton, Rosen & Katz, in New York, and from Arnold & Porter in Washington, D.C., in addition to at least two PR/crisis-management firms—had provided government investigators some 1,500 pages of documents.

She steadfastly maintained that her ImClone stock sell-off was "prompted solely" by a preexisting stop-loss order.

But Billy Tauzin and Jim Greenwood had grown annoyed at the continual "tweaking" of Martha's story. They had discovered that Peter Bacanovic had made not one call to Martha on December 27—as he and she had claimed—but that he'd made several urgent efforts to reach her that morning, even while ImClone stock was trading well above $60 a share, the supposed stop-loss moment. This was significant because it seemed to indicate that the Merrill Lynch broker had advance knowledge that the FDA would issue its RTF letter the next day. Ken Johnson griped that with the preemptive Arnold & Porter letter of June 12, she "tried to sandbag us."

Martha declined to comment, which had the effect of inflaming suspicions. MSO stock had dropped 65 percent by this point, and there was rampant speculation that she was planning to step down as CEO of her eponymous company. *The New York Times* reported that MSO was shopping around for a replacement CEO, but the company's board of directors denied this was true.

The Labor Day break came and went, and still Martha refused to play ball with Congress. In early September, the Tauzin committee debated its options: subpoena Martha Stewart, hand its investigative files over to the Department of Justice, or simply drop the case against her.

It would be difficult to prove an insider-trading case against Martha, yet the committee had uncovered evidence of inconsistency in her various accounts of her ImClone stock trades. Billy Tauzin scheduled a news conference for 2:30 P.M. on September 10, at which he would make an announcement about the Martha Stewart investigation. At 2:00 that afternoon, committee members were still locked in an intense negotiation with her attorneys, as Congress attempted to arrange some sort of an interview with her. But Martha's legal team maintained that if subpoenaed she would take the Fifth Amendment.

Clearly frustrated, and worried about a public relations disaster, Tauzin decided not to order her to appear. Jim Greenwood said that the committee didn't want to create a Martha "media circus" when their real objective was to understand what had gone wrong at ImClone and to clarify the FDA's procedures for drug approval. "She's a sideshow; she's a collateral issue," he said.

Tauzin announced that Congress would hand over its Martha Stewart inquiry to the Justice Department. The evidence his investigators had gathered, he warned, "raises a serious question as to whether Ms. Stewart's accounts were false, misleading, and designed to conceal material fact." In a letter to Attorney General John Aschroft, the subcommittee wrote: "These unresolved issues implicate serious policy issues concerning the financial markets and whether the FDA drug review process lends itself to misbehavior by corporate insiders or other 'favored' persons."

The decision to hand off the Martha probe was criticized by some in the press as a pass-the-buck gesture, just as it had rankled certain members of the subcommittee itself. Bart Stupak, the Michigan Democrat, said: "I don't think we've done our job, and I think we've left a lot of unresolved questions. I really think if Martha Stewart wants her reputation back, she should come before the American people, before our committee, and finalize this matter once and for all."

Martha's lead criminal-defense lawyer, Robert G. Morvillo—a verbose, plainspoken former assistant U.S. attorney who has defended Merrill Lynch (in a separate case), politicians, oil magnates, and billionaires—was more sanguine. "I strongly disagree with the analysis of the committee and this staff, but am pleased that the matter will now be exclusively in the hands of professional law enforcement authorities [at the SEC and DOJ] . . . I'm glad that the political aspect of this matter will now terminate and am confident that the investigation will lead to Ms. Stewart's exoneration."

ON SEPTEMBER 25, Douglas Faneuil agreed to become the government's star witness against Peter Bacanovic and Martha Stewart. In the course of weeks of negotiations, his lawyers had attempted to trade Faneuil's testimony for immunity from any prosecution. But the scared, 26-year-old former Merrill Lynch assistant had changed his story so many times by now that the U.S. Attorney's Office had threatened him with felony charges for making false statements. Finally, a deal was brokered: in return for his cooperative testimony, Faneuil would be allowed to plead guilty to a single misdemeanor charge.

Merrill Lynch had informed the SEC that it had blocked Sam's various attempts to sell his ImClone shares in late December 2001. When the securities firm undertook a more in-depth investigation, it discovered a suspicious pattern of other investors dumping ImClone stock just before the RTF letter was released—including Martha Stewart's sale on December 27, a sale that had been handled by Faneuil. On January 2, Merrill provided the SEC with "new information" about the case. The next day, SEC investigators interviewed Faneuil.

He told them that Martha had sold her ImClone shares for "tax reasons," described his conversation with her as "curt," and said that she had asked for price quotes on several other stocks. In a later meeting with prosecutors, Faneuil altered his story slightly: now he said that Martha's ImClone sale had been triggered by the $60 stop-loss order. He stuck to this version of events until June, when Sam was arrested at dawn by the FBI, Martha was implicated, the House subcommittee held its first hearing, and the ImClone investigation had kicked into high gear. Faneuil told his Merrill Lynch superiors that Martha had not in fact had a stop-loss order, and that Peter Bacanovic had pressured him to lie about it.

Faneuil's deal with the government, observed John Coffee, a Columbia University law professor, is "a means to an end—and that end means catching a bigger fish."

EARLY ON THE MORNING of Thursday October 3, Martha Stewart had a conversation with her friend Richard Grasso, the chairman of the New York Stock Exchange (NYSE). She had joined the 27-member NYSE board with much fanfare in June, just before her connection to the ImClone scandal exploded into public. Lately, members of the august Big Board had grown restive: they were not pleased that one of their own was under investigation by the FBI, DOJ, and SEC, and was appearing in the tabloids on a daily basis. Martha got the message: she was becoming an embarrassment. Later that morning she resigned from the NYSE.

"It has been a great honor and privilege to sit on the board," she wrote. "But the rigors of my own very busy and demanding corporate life require my full attention at the present time."

After the resignation was made public, shares of MSO tumbled 8 percent, to close at $6.21, their lowest price ever.

DR. JOHN MENDELSOHN sat at the far left corner of the witness table with his hands folded, his eyes blazing, and his lips set in a sour scowl. Paul Kopperl was seated in the center. Robert Goldhammer, the chairman of ImClone's board, sat on the right. As congressman after congressman thumped the podium and enumerated Sam Waksal's misdeeds, recited the company's habit of extending favorable loans to select executives, and detailed insiders' lucrative stock trades just before the RTF letter was issued, the three ImClone board members did not look at each other. Mendelsohn stared stonily off to his left. Kopperl, a trim man with high cheekbones and sharp eyes, leaned back and stared up at the ceiling. Goldhammer, burlier than the other two, leaned forward to toy with his glasses and wristwatch while he stared down at the table.

It was October 10, 2002, and once again the House Energy and Commerce subcommittee had convened for a hearing on the "ImClone Cancer-Drug Story" at Rayburn House, in Washington, D.C. Although this hearing attracted fewer congressmen, lawyers, journalists, and other spectators than the one in June, there were just as many fireworks.

Jim Greenwood began the day by scolding both ImClone and the FDA for delaying Erbitux's entrance to the market: "Profits before patients and regulatory incoherence is a betrayal of cancer patients, and is at odds with the federal mission of promoting the public health."

Billy Tauzin focused on two highly politicized aspects of the Im-Clone case: the perceived shortcomings of the FDA and the issue of corporate governance:

> The public should not forget that potential flaws in FDA's drug-approval process have been at the center of this investigation all along. These flaws allowed a study of questionable quality to become the basis for fast-track application. They allowed irresponsible hyping of a promising drug as FDA silently stood by—thus raising and dashing hopes of thousands of cancer patients.
>
> I am encouraged that since the June ImClone hearing, the FDA has reorganized pharmaceutical product reviews to enhance consistency and performance. This is a good first step and we are very interested to learn how FDA envisions this reorganization will improve the drug-approval system, especially for cancer drugs. . . .
>
> There's clearly room for improvement. We know this from FDA's own work. Consider Eloxatin [Iressa] . . . Eloxatin shows a company can get accelerated approval just as fast as ImClone had hoped its drug would be approved, and with better data. Perhaps the Eloxatin case can be a useful model for the future. It clearly suggests that ImClone's experience might have been different, if there had been better communication between FDA and ImClone. . . .
>
> We have now learned that for years ImClone did not trust Sam Waksal with the company's corporate credit card. It actually installed special procedures to ensure he did not charge the company for his personal expenses.
>
> Why would ImClone management have trusted Dr. Waksal?
>
> The media have already reported his financial problems, and his past firings for allegedly misleading and even falsified scientific work. . . .
>
> Are we to believe that ImClone management was totally unaware of these issues? Did the Board and management act properly in light of these red flags?

As the hearing got underway, subcommittee members questioned a broad spectrum of issues—from the changes in the way the FDA reviews drugs to the rehabilitation of the Erbitux BLA. Most of all, the congressmen were astounded by ImClone's lax corporate governance and inability, or unwillingness, to curb Sam's exuberant spending.

"I've dealt with a lot of corporations, and I've got to be honest, I've never seen a document like this where the . . . board of directors has got to tell the CEO that, for example, they can only charge $50 to $100 of wine per bottle [*sic*], or that they can't buy sporting tickets except under exceptional circumstances, or that under 'Lodging' . . . five-star European hotels . . . are inappropriate," said Representative Diana DeGette, Democrat of Colorado, about Sam's abuse of the firm's American Express card. "Have you ever seen a corporate travel policy that goes into these specifics, Mr. Kopperl?"

"I have not," replied Kopperl, stonily.

DeGette went on to observe that despite policies about legitimate expenditures, the board's attempt to bridle Sam's spending was feeble. "It's like you guys kept doing stuff, but it never changed," she said. "Here you have a forgery . . . in 1991. Then you have a whole systematic taking out of money and loans, abuse of credit card charges . . . for almost a ten-year period. Then you have another forgery. Then you have insider trading around Christmas of last year . . . And it still takes the board almost six months to fire the guy, and he's only fired two weeks before criminal charges are brought. I'm—I'm just—I'm stunned."

In asking about Sam's forgery of the $44 million in bank warrants, Representative Peter Deutsch, Democrat of Florida, grew agitated over Kopperl's lawyerly obstinacy. "Did you ask Samuel Waksal if he forged this signature?" Deutsch asked.

"We turned it over to our special counsel, sir," Kopperl replied.

"Did they ask him that question?"

"I honestly don't know."

"And wouldn't that have been an appropriate question to ask?"

"Very possibly."

Deutsch's cheeks turned red and he began to sputter: "Very *possibly* it would be appropriate? You can't say yes or no? That's the most ridiculous answer I have heard in a very long time up here. And we've had everyone—we've had Enron, we've had WorldCom . . . I mean, 'very possibly'? Your CEO, the head of the company, forged—this is wacky. I mean, this is *wacky*. A guy's forging documents and you're keeping him in charge of the company?"

Greenwood followed up by asking: "Why wasn't Samuel Waksal fired immediately?"

Mendelsohn said nothing. Kopperl stared off into the distance. Goldhammer mumbled that they had turned the matter over to the company's outside counsel, and had asked for an investigation to be done "as quickly as possible."

"What did you learn from that investigation?" Greenwood asked.

"We never . . . the investigation was not complete by the time Sam was asked to resign."

Greenwood then quizzed John Landes about Sam's 1986 forgery of his signature. Landes said that he had chosen not to report that transgression to the board or to the government because "my understanding was that this was really a misunderstanding on Sam's part."

"My children know better than that, Mr. Landes," said Greenwood.

Then, in a riveting series of questions and answers, the subcommittee chairman demolished the hapless attorney. Greenwood noted that Sam had paid Landes a "consulting" fee for his work on Tribeca Company, a company investigating herpes drugs, the ownership of which Landes had a difficult time identifying. The implication was that Sam had used such fees to buy Landes's devotion, or silence. He noted Landes's conflict of interest in instructing his deputy, Cathy Vaczy, to clear Landes's carry-forward sale of $2.5 million worth of ImClone stock in December 2001. "Did you see any problem with your subordinate being able to clear your trade?"

"I did not," Landes replied weakly.

Shortly after the congressional hearing Landes resigned from ImClone. Of the original founders, he and Sam were gone; only Harlan and Goldhammer remained.

The subcommittee had released records showing that from October 29 through December 31, 2001, many ImClone directors, officers, and employees dumped millions of dollars of company shares—some $244 million worth, including $73.8 million in November and December alone. "If all of these people believed Erbitux was the next miracle drug, why were they all selling stock instead of buying more of it?" Ken Johnson had wondered. "The real miracle is that so many people got rich at a company that never turned a profit."

Harlan, who had been ImClone's CEO for 100 days, testified that it was simply a "coincidence" that so many senior and midlevel executives had suddenly begun to trade in large blocks of company stock—5,000 to 32,212 shares at a time—between December 12 and 21. This 10-day period was a crucial moment in ImClone's history: it begins the moment Lily Lee sensed a "change in tone" at the FDA on December 12, includes December 20 when the FDA's refusal to answer any more questions set off warning bells at ImClone, and ends with the institution of a "blackout" period just before the market closed on the afternoon of Friday December 21. The FDA issued its RTF on December 28.

Harlan brushed off questions about improper trading. "We looked into whether or not there was any sense of insider trading, and the conclusion that we reached . . . was that these trades were not based on . . . nonpublic, material information, and they were done for personal, individual reasons," he said.

Landes's deputy, Cathy Vaczy, concurred with her CEO: "It was by no means . . . an unusual number of employees engaging in option exercises and sales in December than in prior months. We didn't consider it unusual activity."

Admitting that ImClone was "a very small company" that had "clearly" provided the FDA with "faulty documentation," Harlan vehemently defended the science that he had overseen as COO: "I don't believe that the protocol [for the Erbitux clinical trial] was flawed . . . I strongly believe we were doing sound science and appropriate science the entire time." He added, "there are no problems with Erbitux . . . there were problems with the application" to the FDA.

Harlan denied that the company had overpromoted Erbitux. He denied that ImClone had misled journalists and investors and cancer patients. He replied with forceful conviction that "there was no tipping [by the FDA] of any type to us" before the issuance of the RTF. Asked about his brother's checkered academic career, as detailed in *Vanity Fair* and *The Wall Street Journal,* Harlan testified that he had not been aware that Sam was ousted from four prestigious labs for questionable work. Greenwood alluded obliquely to Harlan's cocaine bust when he asked about the story of Sam wearing his brother's lab coat and doing Harlan's medical rounds at the Tufts New England Medical Center while Harlan was detained in Ft. Lauderdale by the police. Harlan denied the story about Sam and rhetorically tiptoed around the question of his own predicament. "Well, I know that I was not there [at Tufts] at the time. I do know that Dr. Samuel Waksal, not masquerading as Harlan Waksal, did speak to a patient that had been under my care."

As in the June hearing, Harlan held forth with an unwavering cocksureness and seemed determined to prove that he was a different kind of CEO than his brother. "Yet even as we deal with these challenges, we have turned a new page," he insisted.

Near the end of the hearing, Representative Ernie Fletcher, a doctor with experience in clinical trials, observed: "You know, one of the things we learn in medicine is that the most dangerous people are the people that don't know what they don't know."

"That's very true," Harlan agreed. He went on to make a jocular aside—"I was here four months ago—and hopefully I won't be back in another four months to talk about this!"—that elicited laughter in the chamber. It seemed a self-deprecating and amusing thing to say at the time. But the joke would have a bitter punch line: six months later, Harlan would no longer be ImClone's CEO.

Representative Peter Deutsch kept hammering away on the Enron/ImClone connection, and John Mendelsohn looked peeved. He had always bent over backward to avoid even the appearance of a conflict of interest in his work, he said. He had repeatedly explained that his board membership at Enron and ImClone was just an unlucky "coincidence." But the Florida congressman wouldn't let it go. "Would you tell us whether you feel you did your job successfully?" Deutsch asked Mendelsohn, in a line of questioning about the Enron board's oversight of management. "What happened? Did the system fail?"

"We're here, I believe, to talk about ImClone," Mendelsohn said, in a steely voice. In the case of both Enron and ImClone, he said, "I believe that I have fulfilled my duties and that management has fulfilled its duties."

Mendelsohn's pain at being called before the U.S. House of Representatives to defend himself, his drug, and ImClone was as clear as it was poignant. And so was the dilemma that had badgered him since he had agreed to go into business with Sam Waksal over breakfast with Zvi Fuks, back in 1992.

"Sam Waksal's personal failures should not detract from what is really important—that Erbitux shows great promise," Mendelsohn said in his opening remarks. "Although questions rightfully abound about why the FDA did not accept the Erbitux BLA for filing, each study that has been conducted strongly suggests that Erbitux is an active anticancer agent in end-stage colon cancer. I am disappointed that Erbitux will not be available for patients who need it as soon as we had originally hoped. I joined, and continue to work with ImClone, because I believe that its scientists have the vision, the desire and the capability to get this new treatment to patients. My personal goal remains to do everything in my power to bring Erbitux through the approval process and to patients with cancer."

*Of course* he had been concerned about who licensed C225 in 1992, Mendelsohn told the subcommittee, but he had not had a lot of choice in the matter. "The license had been held by [Eli Lilly, which] did not move the antibody forward . . . I had talked with a number of other pharmaceutical companies who were not interested . . . And, frankly, I was delighted when I met Dr. Samuel Waksal . . . [he] was somebody who seemed to have the energy and the vision to try to bring this forward. [ImClone] was a small start up company instead of a big drug company, but I had no one else to do it."

FIVE DAYS AFTER THE HEARING, on Tuesday, October 15, 2002, Sam Waksal pled guilty to 6 of the 13 counts against him. Speaking outside the courthouse in a loud and tremulous voice, he said: "I've made some terrible mistakes."

It was the end of the road, but as usual Sam was doing things his own way. Most white-collar defendants negotiate a deal with the government: in exchange for pleading guilty, they are given more lenient fines or sentences. Federal guidelines suggest a sentence of seven to nine years in prison for the crimes Sam had pled guilty to. But Sam's plea was not a negotiated settlement. It was, instead, a characteristically risky gambit—one with echoes of the infamous case of Michael Milken, who was sentenced to prison for illegal junk-bond trades in the early 1990s.

The idea was that Sam's partial plea would shield Jack and Aliza from criminal charges, and perhaps win him a reduced prison sentence. His attorneys, led by Mark Pomerantz, were in effect gambling that the sentencing judge would be more lenient than the prosecutors.

But his opponent, Assistant U.S. Attorney Michael Schachter, asserted that the plea was not a "full acceptance of responsibility," and that he would seek a stiffer sentence of at least 10 years in jail for Sam.

If the prosecutors insisted on a presentencing hearing they could include testimony about Aliza or Jack, and they could also present evidence of other crimes to which Sam had not pled guilty, thus increasing his chances of a much longer prison sentence. Schachter said that he would present new evidence in such a hearing, "to ensure that Dr. Waksal is held accountable for *all* criminal conduct he engaged in." And he gave a tantalizing peek at some of the cards in his hand. On December 27 and 28, an as yet unidentified friend of Sam sold $30 million in ImClone stock, Schachter said, a sale that had begun "within minutes" of a phone call between Sam and the mystery investor before the RTF was issued. And there was a second unnamed "close friend of Dr. Waksal" who had made a suspiciously well-timed trade of $600,000 worth of ImClone stock. All of this would be detailed if a presentencing hearing were held.

"The Waksal plea is, to say the least, highly unusual," said Robert Katzberg, a white-collar defense attorney. "It is potentially very dangerous," for Sam.

But Pomerantz backed Sam's gamble, saying, "We're confident that when the sentencing judge hears all the relevant facts and circumstances, the sentence will be a fair one."

Sam faced a "Fatico hearing," named after a 1979 case in which the government wanted to introduce new evidence of crimes at the sentencing of Daniel Fatico, who had pled guilty to theft. This was ruled permissible, as long as the sentencing judge held a hearing where the defendant could rebut the allegations. (In Fatico's case, it was his alleged involvement in organized crime.) The idea is that by revealing a defendant's wider pattern of behavior, the judge is better able to set an appropriate sentence.

Until Sam Waksal's trial, the only time a Fatico hearing has been used in a high-profile white-collar criminal proceeding was in the case of Michael Milken, the junk-bond king. In October 1990, Judge Kimba Wood presided over such a hearing to determine if there was evidence of crimes beyond the six that Milken had agreed to plead guilty to. The hearing proved anticlimactic, as Ivan Boesky was not called as a witness, but it ultimately strengthened the government's case. Judge Wood ruled that while prosecutors had persuaded her that Milken had attempted to obstruct justice, they had not proven all of their claims. She gave Milken 10 years in prison, a sentence that was later reduced to two years.

After Sam had entered a guilty plea, his parents released a statement that read: "Jack Waksal and his wife are deeply saddened by today's events and the fact that their first-born son is now facing imprisonment. They will pray for his well-being."

Standing outside the courthouse in the opaque light of mid-October, Sam's face was ashen. In a hoarse voice, he said that he regretted that the bad publicity had "cast a shadow on ImClone, a wonderful company with talented and dedicated scientists." He said that he hoped Erbitux would be approved and would go on to help cancer patients. And then, his voice beginning to quaver with emotion, he added, "More than anything, I regret having involved my daughter Aliza, who has done nothing wrong and who has suffered so much as a result of my action . . . I deeply regret what has happened. I was wrong."

PART FOUR

# THE ONCE AND FUTURE MIRACLE DRUG

# FIFTEEN

# *Art, Death, and Taxes*

Jennifer McNeillie was a 44-year-old hydrologist from Florida. For Christmas in 2000, she and her husband went to visit his mother in Massachusetts. As a treat, Jennifer decided to have a lobster roll, a New England delicacy that she had a weakness for. When she got the sandwich, she brought it halfway to her mouth and felt an overwhelming nausea. *This is strange,* she thought, feeling "disconcerted." It was true that she had been feeling tired lately, and vaguely ill after meals; a routine physical had detected a lump in her rib cage, but she thought it was a gallbladder problem and hadn't dwelled on it. Jennifer was physically fit, an outdoors person. In her work as an environmental consultant she visited well sites and conducted environmental audits; on vacation she loved to ski. But now something was definitely wrong. She couldn't eat one of her favorite foods. Her husband, Steven Walker, drove Jennifer to a nearby hospital, where a battery of tests revealed that she had cancerous tumors in her liver and colon. She fell into a kind of shock.

Back in Florida three days later, Jennifer began to bleed internally. She was rushed into the hospital for an emergency operation in which a six-inch piece of her colon was removed. The doctors told her that her tumors had been growing for a long time, perhaps as long as 10 years, and were now too big to remove surgically. She began her cancer treatment with the Saltz regimen (a chemo cocktail of 5FU-leukovorin mixed with irinotecan, the standard treatment named for its inventor, Dr. Len Saltz). She did well on that for eight months, but then the tumors grew huge and Jennifer's ovaries had to be surgically removed. She switched to Xeloda, a once-a-day pill that made her feel sick, left her fingers tingling, and made her feet feel as if they were on fire. The cancer spread into her lungs and abdomen. Now, in addition to the Saltz regimen, she took oxaliplatin, an intravenous drug that required her to strap a pump around her waist. The pump made it difficult to sleep; she was very thin and felt constantly ill; she suffered from ascites, the painful accumulation of fluid between tissues and organs in the abdomen.

By September 2002, Jennifer McNeillie had stage 4 colon cancer, and the doctors didn't give her long to live. Then, at the end of the month, she was accepted into a small clinical trial for Erbitux.

Within two days the pressure in her abdomen began to lighten. Within two weeks, she was feeling much better and the tumors in her liver and lungs were reduced. By the third week of her treatment, Jennifer's cancer was almost completely eradicated. "Amazing," the doctors said. Other patients in the trial had encouraging results, but Jennifer was their best responder. By late October she was putting on weight, and she and Steven did some traveling. In December they skied in Colorado, twice.

"I kept feeling better and better," she said. "It felt just wonderful to be able to do things again." Her only side effect was a slight skin rash. "It was absolutely due to the Erbitux," she recalled. "Nothing else worked for me."

IN EARLY OCTOBER 2002, just as Jennifer McNeillie was starting on Erbitux and the second congressional hearing into ImClone was about to convene, ImClone and Bristol-Myers Squibb announced that they had initiated three new clinical trials designed to rehabilitate the Erbitux application at the FDA. These included two large, randomized phase 3 clinical studies to test the drug in combination with chemotherapies; and a 250-patient phase 2 trial designed to test Erbitux as a stand-alone treatment. The trials were due to finish in the third quarter of 2003. Wall Street viewed these as essential steps toward FDA approval, and jumped ImClone's share price by 7 percent in a single day.

Those gains were immediately erased three weeks later when Adam

Feuerstein reported in *theStreet.com* that Erbitux "may have failed" to reach its end points (or goal) in the critical European trial being conducted by Merck KGaA. Feuerstein cited an unnamed fund manager and an unnamed oncologist as his sources. With this revelation, ImClone's share price dropped 10 percent in a single day, to just over $7 a share.

"It is definitely not true," a Merck KGaA oncologist protested. And ImClone pooh-poohed Feuerstein's report as "unsubstantiated rumor."

But such was the cloud of suspicion around ImClone by now that Internet message boards flooded with brooding opinions and dark innuendo. "Here we go again!" posted a Raging Bull user. "And we thought the scandal was behind us!" Another poster captured the spirit of confusion, writing: "An unnamed IMCL [ImClone] cultist has reported that the unsubstantiated rumor of a retraction to the report that unnamed ill-informed informants reportedly heard from equally unnamed and ill-informed European informants somehow vaguely connected to the trials that we're in deep doo-doo is false (or is that true, I've gotten lost)."

Others harbored pet theories on what was *really* going on: "The hedge funds don't know when the trial results will be finalized—a piece of info crucial to their investment strategies—so they fabricate a story about how 'sources' are indicating now that the trial will fail. If the companies don't explicitly deny the rumors, then they've got a nice short-selling profit on their hands. And if the companies deny the rumors . . . then they've smoked out info from the companies that they otherwise might not have obtained. They also get a nice shorting profit."

What all the back-and-forth really underscored was investors' lingering hopes for Erbitux, their once-burnt skepticism of ImClone's bright promises, growing questions about the EGFR class of drugs, and the signal importance of Merck KGaA's clinical trial. This trial was already underway in Europe, and would produce data six months before the new ImClone/Bristol trial would. But clinical trials in Europe are conducted slightly differently than they are in the United States, which raised a host of questions.

One of the major reasons the FDA had rejected ImClone's application in December 2001 was that the company had failed to show whether or not Erbitux worked effectively on its own. This is always a critical question for a new cancer drug, one that clinicians and investors hoped the European trial would answer. Merck KGaA had enrolled 330 colorectal cancer patients in its Erbitux trial: two-thirds of them were given Erbitux plus irinotecan, and the remaining one-third took Erbitux alone. If the patients who received the combination therapy fared better than those using just Erbitux, then ImClone and Bristol could use the European data to reapply for approval in America. But if Erbitux proved to work well on its own, then the companies would be encouraged to seek approval for Erbitux as a single agent. This raised numerous issues: Would the FDA accept data generated in Europe to approve Erbitux in the United States? Even if it did accept the Merck KGaA results, would the FDA require ImClone and BMS to conduct additional single-agent trials? Did ImClone have patent protection for Erbitux as a single agent?

Although Merck had not yet released its trial results, the company had broadly hinted through its actions—especially in its decision to build a new manufacturing plant in Germany—that it strongly believed in Erbitux. But Merck cautioned that it was not prepared to reveal its latest Erbitux data until it had been reviewed by independent European investigators. If all went well, Merck KGaA would present its data at the 2003 ASCO conference, to be held on June 1, 2003, in Chicago. To the tea-leaf readers of Wall Street this meant one thing: the success of Erbitux in the Merck KGaA trial would signal whether it, and thus ImClone itself, would live or die.

ONE PERSON who was closely monitoring these developments was Harlan Waksal. When he took over as CEO in May 2002, he had stepped out from behind his charismatic older brother for perhaps the first time in his life. Harlan seemed to thrill in his new position, albeit in a quiet and workmanlike way. His main objective in the fall of 2002 was to smooth feathers on Wall Street, convince investors that the science behind Erbitux was sound enough to bring FDA approval, and to drum up new financing as quickly as possible.

The lack of money was becoming an all-consuming problem. In late September 2002, ImClone's stock bottomed out at $5.24, a 52-week low, and its cash reserves were dwindling.

ImClone was not an easy sell. Harlan began to take private meetings with institutional investors, a setting in which he reportedly excelled. In a series of one-on-one meetings with fund managers, he stayed consistently upbeat and on-message: ImClone and Bristol-Myers Squibb were working hand-in-hand to get the Erbitux application back on track, he said; it would take time, but they were making real progress.

Amid growing uncertainty about the Merck study and the direction of changes at the FDA, Harlan began to signal a shift in strategy. Originally the company hoped to get Erbitux approved in 2003 for use as a colon cancer therapy in combination with irinotecan. This made sense because the early test data had been compiled with this approach in mind, and because a combination therapy represents a significantly larger market. Now Harlan was floating a different approach, a Plan B, perhaps suggested by the FDA: to try to get Erbitux approved as a single agent. This would require waiting for data from the new clinical trials and would push regulatory approval back to 2004. But Harlan made the persuasive case that the slow steady advance of the tortoise was a safer bet than the sprinting rush of the hare. It was an argument that Sam would never have made, of course. But it seemed to strike a chord with investors. ImClone's stock gained 64 percent in two weeks, and by mid-November was selling for just under $12 a share.

There was one potentially serious problem with Plan B, however: ImClone only had enough cash on hand to last through the end of 2003. If the Erbitux application did not reach the FDA until sometime in 2004, it would not matter whether the drug was approved or not.

Harlan and his CFO, Dan Lynch, a former Bristol man, explained to fund managers that their intention was to raise a modest amount of bridge financing to get them from the end of 2003 to the point of Erbitux approval. Once the drug is approved, Bristol-Myers will pay ImClone $250 million; and if Erbitux is approved for a second cancer indication—to treat head-and-neck cancer, say—Bristol will pay ImClone another $250 million.

Harlan's goal was seemingly simple—get FDA approval—yet actually complex. At times it appeared so close that he could almost touch it, feel it, believe it; at other times it seemed to stay just out of reach, like a shimmering, taunting mirage. Harlan bore down: success would be his now, or possibly never.

THE FOOD AND DRUG Administration was also attempting to tame the whirling energies that its Erbitux RTF had unleashed. Not only were in-house critics like Richard Pazdur suggesting significant structural changes, but external critics continued to attack the agency's "nitpicking bureaucrats," blaming them for the slow approval of new drugs.

The central issue at the agency was that it had been leaderless for nearly two years now. The White House had faced withering criticism from both the pharmaceutical industry and consumer groups over this. The post had not been filled, in part, because of a standoff between President Bush and Senator Edward Kennedy, the Massachusetts Democrat, who had criticized the president's two previous nominees for being drawn from the ranks of industries the agency regulates.

Both sides agreed that the stalemate could not last, and late in the afternoon of Thursday October 18, the Senate unanimously confirmed Dr. Mark B. McClellan, a 39-year-old physician and economist with strong family ties to the Bush administration, as the new head of the FDA.

Boyish-looking, with a round face and a pointed chin, foxlike eyes, and short brown hair, McClellan is described as pragmatic, smart, and determined. He'd earned a medical degree from Harvard Medical School, a Ph.D. in economics from MIT, and a master's from Harvard's John F. Kennedy School of Government all at the same time. While teaching at Stanford, he had moonlighted at the treasury for President Clinton and as a health-care adviser for President Bush. The oldest of four boys, McClellan is from Austin, Texas, where he got to know the Bush family. His mother is Texas state comptroller; his brother Scott was the White House's deputy press secretary (and in 2003 took over from Ari Fleischer, as the White House press secretary). "Mark came into this world driven," said his mother, Carole Keeton Strayhorn. He "always has 20 plates spinning." When someone objected to the new commissioner's lack of regulatory experience, she said: "Man, you don't know Mark."

One of the first things McClellan did at the FDA was to wade right into the debate over the speed and rules for drug approval—which, largely because of the ImClone case, had become one of the most visible and pressing issues facing the agency and the industry. The new commissioner noted that it now costs an estimated $800 million, or more, to develop a drug, which is twice the cost of a decade earlier. That cost, which includes testing for safety and effectiveness, is passed down to the consumer.

The issue of cost had, along with the national debate over funding for Medicare and Medicaid, turned pharmaceuticals into a political football.

McClellan declared that his FDA would be doing things differently. He stated that he would cut weeks, if not months, off the drug-review process, make the agency more efficient and predictable, and encourage drug companies to innovate.

Under the current system, the FDA, in order to receive millions of dollars in user fees from pharmaceutical companies, must hew to certain time constraints when reviewing new drugs. Rather than give companies a clear yes or no answer about their drug within the proscribed period, FDA reviewers often ask for more information just before the deadline is up. While the companies dig up the required data, the FDA's clock stops ticking; it only resumes once the data is provided. In practice, therefore, new drug reviews take a lot longer than the FDA claims.

McClellan said that he intends to measure performance by the total time it takes to approve or reject a drug. Showing his business-school training, he plans to use a series of tools to streamline the system— using genetic markers, for example, to indicate whether a drug is converting a cancer cell into a normal cell, and doing a "root-cause analysis" every time a drug like Erbitux is given an RTF. Over time, McClellan said, he plans to do a lot more about drug review—like developing a series of guidelines that will spell out exactly what the FDA expects in terms of clinical trials and safety and efficacy information from drug companies.

Thus far, the new FDA commissioner's efforts have received mixed reviews. Some applauded McClellan's attempts to bring new tools and a sense of urgency to the agency, and note that his close ties to the White House will serve him well. But critics wonder if the FDA's budget is sufficient to keep pace with the commissioner's ambitions; they worry that any acceleration of the drug-approval process could stretch the agency too thin and threaten public health.

AFTER HER *Early Show* appearance in June, Martha Stewart had become the target of jokes, ridicule, and criticism. On the Internet, mock magazine covers with digitally altered photographs of Martha in handcuffs and titles like *Martha Stewart Living Behind Bars* were widely circulated. In print, cartoonists like "Doonesbury"'s Gary Trudeau mocked her, while the *New York Post* and *Newsweek* continued to run alarming paparazzi shots of the usually photogenic Martha. And on television Conan O'Brien quipped that according to Martha, "a subpoena should be served with a nice appetizer."

Her attempts to laugh it all off were not wholly convincing, and she withdrew from the public eye. Referring to the talk-show hosts David Letterman and Jay Leno, on whose shows she was once a regular guest, she said, wistfully: "My buddies Dave and Jay—I miss them."

In November Martha Stewart Living Omnimedia announced that third-quarter profits had dipped 42 percent. A company report said: "We have seen, and expect to continue to see, some negative impact on the company's business as a result of the inquiry involving Ms. Stewart, our founder and a central figure in our business." Aside from incurring the expense of Martha's attorneys and PR specialists, the report went on to say that MSO was experiencing "a more challenging environment" for its TV business, a "softening" in magazine circulation, "some impact" on ad revenue, and a "general uncertainty" about its future business.

December is usually a jam-packed month for Martha Stewart. But in 2002 she cancelled her annual Christmas TV special, blaming rising production costs, and continued to avoid CBS's *The Early Show.* Even so, Martha seemed determined to show her public, her detractors, and perhaps SEC and DOJ investigators, that she remained unfazed by the investigations. *Martha Stewart Living* was picked up for an 11th television season, and continued to reach 87 percent of the nation's markets, about the same as the year before. Only one station, the CBS affiliate in Atlanta, had been spooked enough by the bad publicity to drop her show from a morning slot to a postmidnight show time.

Martha's Plan B for the new year was to display a softer, warmer, more fun and imperfect persona. To make herself, in a word, more sympathetic. On-screen, her face looked far less pinched and painted than it did in June. She went out of her way to share the limelight, and began to disassemble the pretense that she single-handedly did all of the work on her many projects and never made a mistake. Whether it was admitting to a typo in a cookbook or dropping brussels sprouts down the drain (the kinds of mistakes that had been left unmentioned or were edited out in the past), Martha showed a new down-to-earthness—an implied vulnerability—that doubled as a shrewd recalibration of her public image.

Behind the scenes, meanwhile, Martha and her lawyers were playing hardball. Some would say that their inflexible approach was a strategic error. When the SEC requested documentation of her personal financial transactions, for instance, Martha dragged her feet and then finally provided them with crucial sections blacked out. This only succeeded in annoying the prosecutors.

In January 2003, feeling "frustrated by the bad publicity," she arranged a carefully stage-managed interview at Turkey Hill with Jeffrey Toobin, the legal affairs writer for *The New Yorker*. While touring him around the restored 1805 farmhouse, serving him Hunan chicken ("the best way to cook chicken in the whole world"), nuzzling with her chow chows and song canaries, Martha—monitored by unnamed advisers—described how baffling the last six months had been: "my public image has been one of trustworthiness, of being a fine, fine editor, a fine purveyor of historical and contemporary information for the homemaker. My business is about homemaking. And that I have been turned into or vilified openly as something other than what I really am has been really confusing . . . I mean, we've produced a lot of good stuff for a lot of good people. And to be maligned for that is kind of weird."

This story is said to have earned her another rebuke from prosecutors, who felt that she was trying to circumvent their investigation and romance the public (especially potential jurors, if her case ever went to trial).

Then, during a March earnings call with analysts, Martha let it slip that she was hopeful that her legal problems would be resolved in the near future. It may have been an innocent, off-the-cuff remark. The prosecutors interpreted it as a glad-handing attempt to influence the case. "The *New Yorker* story and her comments during that conference call, that really pissed them off," recalled a source. "After that, it was like they'd had enough of Martha."

In August 2002, the MSO shareholder Howard Rosen filed a class-action lawsuit against Stewart and her executives, claiming that MSO misled investors by failing to disclose that they sold $79 million worth of company stock while under federal investigation in early 2002. Martha shrugged off the charge, saying it was "without merit," and tried to have it dismissed. A judge allowed the suit to proceed.

There were calls for Martha to step down as CEO, in order to take the heat off of her company. Some observers said Martha could save herself a lot of trouble by admitting she'd made a mistake with her Im-

Clone trades and paying a fine; once that was done, they thought, she could move on. To Martha, these people obviously did not understand what was at stake: she believed the prosecution was an unfair attack, a personal affront, and she would fight it tooth and nail as a matter of principle.

"Quit a business that is my life?" she said. "Impossible."

In June 2002, L. Dennis Kozlowski, the large, bald, former chairman and CEO of Tyco International, was indicted for failing to pay $1 million worth of sales tax on the $13 million purchase of six paintings, including works by Renoir and Monet. The case made headlines across the country, in part because Kozlowski and Tyco's former CFO, Mark H. Swartz, were accused of fleecing their company and investors of some $600 million, and in part because ever since Alfred A. Taubman had been convicted of price-fixing at Sotheby's, the government had shone a harsh light on the wealthy, secretive art world.

The investigation of Kozlowski's tax dodge was pursued by Robert Morgenthau, the legendary Manhattan district attorney, who seemed to enjoy exposing a widespread pattern of tax evasion by art dealers and collectors. Morgenthau contended that dealers would pretend to ship artworks to other states—in Kozlowski's case, empty boxes were shipped to his home in New Hampshire, while the actual paintings were sent to his Manhattan apartment—in order to avoid paying New York's 8.25 percent state and city sales taxes. "There appears to be a culture out there in the art business—dealers and buyers think it's alright not to pay your taxes," the DA said. "We're trying to change that culture." When Morgenthau offered a one-time amnesty to tax cheats, more than 50 art patrons suddenly came forward with some $7 million in payments of New York sales tax. Many of them, a Morgenthau spokesman dryly noted, "were shocked to learn they had committed a crime."

Sam Waksal had dabbled in art collecting since the early 1990s, and through the painter David Salle had met the art dealer Larry Gagosian. Known as "Go-Go," the aggressive 52-year-old Gagosian had a distinctive head of short-cropped silver hair, was partial to designer suits, and had an uncanny ability to convince collectors to part with artworks they had no intention of selling. Considered "the most successful art dealer in the world" by some, Gagosian, the son of a Los Angeles city accountant and an actress, dated a supermodel and a dancer. He held court in a Madison Avenue carriage house or at Toad Hall, his Charles Gwathmey–designed spread in East Hampton. His empire of sleek art galleries extended from Chelsea and Madison Avenue in New York, to outposts in London and Beverly Hills. He showed A-list contemporary artists like Damien Hirst, Jeff Koons, and Julian Schnabel, to A-list clients, like S. I. Newhouse, Steve Martin, David Geffen, Peter Bart, and Charles Saatchi.

Sam Waksal desperately wanted to become part of this fabulous scene. "Sam was prepared, at whatever cost, to make that happen," said a friend.

Waksal flew on Gagosian's jet, vacationed with him on St. Bart's every Christmas, shared dinners with him in Manhattan, invited him to the parties at his Thompson Street loft, and even sold him $6 worth of shares in Scientia. Gagosian helped Sam build a collection of well-regarded paintings, at a steep price.

Between June of 2000 and October 2001, Waksal paid $15 million to buy nine paintings from the dealer, including works by Cy Twombly, Francis Bacon, and Francesco Clemente. Three of his purchases were considered major paintings: Mark Rothko's *Untitled (Plum and Brown),* for which he paid $3.5 million; a 1961 Franz Kline, *Mahoning II,* for $3 million; and a 1977 Willem de Kooning abstraction, *Untitled V,* for $2.4 million. Art world insiders gasped at some of these prices, noting that the $3.5 million Waksal paid for the Rothko was close to double its true value. As ImClone's stock plummeted in May 2002, Sam attempted to resell the painting but it failed to meet its $2 million to $3 million estimate at Sotheby's, and did not sell. At the spring art sales a year later, the de Kooning painting Sam had paid $2.4 million for sold for $1.9 million, and a Roy Lichtenstein he had paid $900,000 for sold for $792,000.

In the meantime, Waksal had been charged with avoiding New York sales taxes on his art purchases. He and Gagosian had reportedly had "a bitter falling out."

"Sam was so *not* a player in the art world," observed a member of the cognoscenti. "It was all about hanging out with Larry—trying to be a 'chick-magnet,' flying in the private plane, going to St. Bart's. All of the absolutely obvious, clichéd, macho rich-guy things. Sam's group, the flashy self-made guys, were all about running *here* and *there,* and going out to dinner, but never really talking about anything real. It was hideously superficial. Sam was so much cleverer than that, but he was so caught up in it he didn't care if he was overpaying for paintings. He refused to go to [a dealer other than Gagosian] and ask, 'What's this painting really worth?' I feel really sorry for Sam. He wanted to be one of the boys so badly. People would joke about it—'the nerd trying to be fast.' If he hadn't cared so much about all that stuff, he'd have had a really good thing going."

MARCH 3, 2003, was a late-winter day of glaring sun, deep shadows, blustery wind, and sharp cold in lower Manhattan. Up on the 11th floor of the sleek new, Daniel Patrick Moynihan United States Court House on Pearl Street, four courtroom artists sat in the jury box on the left side of a hearing room, nodding their heads up and down as they observed their subject and sketched quickly with pastels on large pads of paper. One of them, a woman with stringy blonde hair, observed Sam Waksal through glasses with bright red frames; another, a short woman in a multicolored sweater, strapped a binocular attachment around her head in order to scrutinize every pore and wrinkle and worry line on her subject's face.

The courtroom was close to full. Along with two dozen reporters, Sam had friends and family members there. One, a blonde woman dressed in a turquoise suit, stood up and took his photo with a point-and-shoot camera.

Sam looked around the courtroom with an untroubled expression. He was dressed in a gray pinstriped suit, a white shirt, and a steel-blue tie. He stood straight and answered questions in a clear voice.

Federal Judge William H. Pauley III asked how he wished to plead to two charges of fraud in avoiding $1.26 million in taxes in his art-buying spree. Sam bowed his head and said "Guilty, Your Honor."

Judge Pauley, a tall, lean man with the clinical diction of a surgeon, then asked him to explain what had happened. "We agreed that I would avoid paying sales tax by allowing the gallery owner to invoice me for the art as if it were delivered to me in New Jersey," Sam replied. The paintings had been addressed to him at ImClone's manufacturing facility at 22 Chubb Way, in Somerville, New Jersey. "In fact, the gallery owner had the art shipped to my apartment in Manhattan and had it hung there. On one occasion, the gallery owner was in my home and saw the art he had sold to me that day hanging on the walls."

Sam's attorney, Mark Pomerantz, said the scheme was not Waksal's idea, although he had willingly participated in it. (Larry Gagosian did not attend the hearing, and was identified only as "CC-1," or "coconspirator" in court documents; he had pled not guilty in the Waksal matter and said he was cooperating with the investigation.)

Because Sam had pled guilty the previous October to 6 of 13 counts of securities fraud, perjury, and obstruction of justice in the ImClone scandal, his art-tax case was investigated not by the Manhattan DA's office, as Kozlowski's had been, but by the FBI and federal prosecutors from the U.S. Attorney's Office. His chief antagonist in the courtroom was Assistant U.S. Attorney Michael Schachter, a slight, youthful-looking man with a tenacious courtroom style. Schachter would later describe Waksal's cover-up of improper stock trades as "numerous and distinct sets of lies," and had pressed for a stiff sentence. "It's important to send a message" to other would-be corporate crooks, he said.

Standing in front of a bank of TV cameras after the hearing, Schachter's boss, James B. Comey, the smooth, six-foot, eight-inch, dark-haired U.S. attorney for the Southern District, said: "Whether you are a purchaser or a dealer, come see us before we come see you. Because if the FBI comes knocking on your door, it won't be to admire your art."

The prosecutors were an ambitious bunch. It was Comey's team that had led the criminal case against Waksal the previous fall (the SEC was meanwhile pursuing civil charges against him), and who would later pursue Martha Stewart. Since his appointment in early 2002, the U.S. Attorney's Office had been quick to act on the public's disgust with white-collar malfeasance at a time when the economy was soft and many people were scraping to get by. While pursuing Waksal, Comey's office was also investigating the leaders of Adelphia Communications Corp. and WorldCom, Inc., and were building an obstruction-of-justice case against Frank P. Quattrone, a former star Silicon Valley investment banker at Credit Suisse First Boston. In New York, such cases were celebrated on the front pages of newspapers and took on a political dimension. Observers liked to point out that one of Comey's predecessors as U.S. attorney, Rudolph Giuliani, had used insider-trading charges against Ivan Boesky and Michael Milken in the late 1980s as a stepping-stone to the New York mayor's office. Many wondered if Comey intended to use his pursuit of corporate crooks from the late 1990s and early 2000s to achieve similar political ends.

"We have wrapped it up with Mr. Waksal," Comey announced at the conclusion of Sam's tax fraud hearing. Waksal's guilty plea marked the end of the criminal investigation of his misdeeds at ImClone, although Comey noted, investigations into other people's ImClone trades would continue.

In a few months' time, Judge Pauley would preside over Sam's sentencing. Federal guidelines suggested that for all of the crimes he had admitted to, Waksal should be sentenced to five to eight years in prison. Mentioning Sam's cooperation with government investigators, Waksal's lead defense attorney, Mark Pomerantz angled for the least amount of time for his client; Assistant U.S. Attorney Schachter, meanwhile, had argued that Waksal deserved more time than the guidelines recommended. Judge Pauley looked on impassively. Having grown tired of the attorneys' jockeying, and Sam's parade of surprise revelations, the judge made sure to ask: "Are there any other matters counsel wish to raise at this time?" Prosecution and defense agreed there was nothing more to say. Sam, it seemed, had finally revealed all. The hearing was adjourned.

A few minutes later, I was surprised to run into Waksal on the ground floor of the courthouse. Up close, he looked devastated. His face was pale, his forehead was wrinkled in concern, his lips were set in a grim line, and his right hand seemed to shake. This was the once irrepressible man who had taken me on a whirlwind tour around ImClone's Varick Street lab, made emphatic promises about Erbitux's multibillion-dollar future, and regaled me with tales of meeting Joe DiMaggio, Sean Connery, and Supreme Court Justice Antonin Scalia. When I said hello, Sam glanced quickly up and away with tired eyes, mumbled something, and fled down the echoing hallway like a wraith.

A WEEK LATER SAM reached a partial settlement with the SEC. Without admitting or denying any wrongdoing, he agreed to pay an $804,000 fine to settle two civil charges. In the first, the SEC charged that he had created an illegal profit by instructing his daughter Aliza to sell her ImClone shares on December 27 (she sold at $62.75 per share that day; on December 31, the first day of trading after ImClone had acknowledged the RTF letter, the stock traded at $46.46; the SEC calculated that the Waksals had thereby avoided a $630,000 loss). In the second charge, the SEC revealed that Sam had made a profit on 210 put options that he had purchased through Discount Bank and Trust AG, of Switzerland. He had bought the puts on December 28, 2001, and sold them on January 4,

2002, pocketing $130,130. In other words, once Waksal had learned of the FDA's RTF letter, he had bet against his own company.

"The case is not just about avoiding losses in advance of bad news, it's about trying to profit in advance of bad news," said Barry Rashkover, associate regional director of the SEC's New York office. It was a new low. Sam was ridiculed as one of the "Most Hated New Yorkers," and was pictured in the *New York Observer*'s "Hall of Shame 2003" alongside Osama bin Laden, and Saddam Hussein. The revelations dropped ImClone's share price further.

To settle the matter, the SEC forced the disgorgement, or repayment, of Sam and Aliza's profits and added another $44,000 in interest; Sam was barred from ever again serving as an officer or director of a public company. Two issues remain unresolved: Sam's alleged tipping of "another family member" [his father, Jack] and the payment of civil penalties for his illicit trades. Furthermore, the SEC's Wells Notice against ImClone still stands.

Just as the dust from this imbroglio began to clear. Harlan was suddenly confronted by a new set of problems. On March 31, it came to light that Sam had not paid some $60 million in state and federal taxes when he had exercised warrants and stock options at ImClone, nor had the company withheld those taxes, as it is legally required to do. This was highly unusual behavior for a chief executive, and now ImClone would have to pick up the tab. The company faced a charge of at least $23.3 million, and it would have to delay the filing of its 10-K annual reports (due on March 31), restate its 2001 financial results, and perhaps restate its results from previous years.

ImClone's independent directors were said to be apoplectic. An internal investigation discovered that Harlan, Robert Goldhammer, John Landes, and a few other ImClone insiders had also failed to pay the proper taxes. A person close to the company said that ImClone's failure to withhold taxes was rooted in confusion over whether taxes were actually owed on the options. There were two types of options, "qualified" and "nonqualified," as well as "founder's warrants," in dispute. At the time, ImClone's officers and legal advisers did not believe the options and warrants were taxable. Upon review, the company decided that they were indeed taxable.

Now the SEC opened an investigation into why ImClone had failed to pay the proper taxes. Then the NASDAQ Stock Market suspended trading in ImClone stock; the exchange threatened to delist ImClone al-together—meaning that it would now be more difficult than ever for the company to raise money and carry on its business—unless it quickly got its books in order. ImClone's share price slipped another 8.6 percent, to $16.77, and Wall Street expressed fresh disgust.

Jim McCamant, an analyst with Moors Cabot, who owned ImClone stock, reportedly said: "Waksal always seemed arrogant, but he was more arrogant than we thought. In retrospect, I should have been more suspicious than I was."

Harlan Waksal furiously scrambled to control the damage. ImClone officials held meetings with the IRS and New York tax authorities and rushed to revise their financial statements before the company was delisted by NASDAQ. "The integrity of management was at issue," said a person close to ImClone. "Harlan had to be removed as CEO."

TUESDAY, APRIL 29, 2003. On a conference call that morning, Martha Stewart addressed Wall Street with unaccustomed abashment: "During our last earnings teleconference this past March, I expressed that I was increasingly hopeful that my personal legal situation regarding the on-going governmental investigation of my sale of non-company stock would be resolved in the near future. Obviously that has not happened and I can make no predictions as to when it will."

The SEC had been displeased with Martha's optimistic predictions in March, and had evidently pressured her to clarify her status. Just as ominously, Martha announced that first-quarter revenue at Martha Stewart Living Omnimedia had dropped a surprising 15 percent, to $58 million, while its losses had spiked nine cents a share, three cents more than analysts had forecasted. *Martha Stewart Living* was the hardest hit of her businesses, with a 28 percent decline in ad pages. It wasn't difficult to guess why.

Although there was positive news to report—the success of *Everyday Food,* a new magazine launched in January, and a strong consumer response to the new Martha Stewart Signature furniture collection—the company had been stung by a lagging economy, an expensive Internet direct-commerce division, and the closing of hundreds of Kmart stores (the retailer's exclusive Martha Stewart Everyday brand was its best-selling label). But it was the SEC's investigation of Martha's ImClone stock trade that was "definitely the biggest factor dragging the company down," noted Laura Richardson, an analyst at Adams, Harkness & Hill. MSO's results were "certainly not the best," Richardson added. "The second quarter outlook is not as rosy as the investment community had assumed it was going to be. Problems are lingering . . . Maybe the public is becoming a little less enamored of the elaborate, formal Martha Stewart way of doing things for the home."

That afternoon, ImClone announced that Robert Goldhammer had resigned from its board and that Harlan Waksal had been demoted from CEO to chief scientific officer (CSO). Both men had been eased from their posts as a result of the federal tax probe and NASDAQ's threatened delisting of the company.

"A financial miscalculation of this scale made it untenable that Harlan Waksal and Robert Goldhammer continue in their posts," observed Steve Brozak, an analyst at Westfield Bakerink and Brozak. "This has been a terribly sordid affair, and one wonders why it took so long for Harlan to resign." Brozak spoke for a growing contingent who felt that Harlan bore considerable responsibility for ImClone's RTF and Sam's unchecked excesses over the years. Another issue that caused friction within the company was the highly unusual employment contract that Harlan had been granted as CEO: it automatically renewed itself on a daily basis. "There was no accountability," said a person close to Im-Clone, "I found it abhorrent."

Dan Lynch, a former Bristol man and ImClone's CFO, was elevated to "acting CEO" while a search for a permanent chief executive was undertaken. Goldhammer's role was taken over by David Kies, a partner at the law firm Sullivan & Cromwell who had joined the ImClone board in 1996; he eschewed the chairman's title in favor of being named "lead director." The company said it had cash reserves for another 10 months, but its liabilities remained murky.

The true believers held firm. "As far as Erbitux goes, this announcement doesn't matter," declared John McCamant, editor of the *Medical Technology Stockletter*. "The entire value of the company is tied up in Erbitux."

THE 2003 American Society of Clinical Oncology conference was held in Chicago over the first few days of June. This was ASCO's 39th annual meeting, and the theme was "Commitment, Care, Compassion, Honoring People with Cancer"—a phrase that alluded to oncology's focus on patients' quality of life. It had been one and a half years since the FDA's RTF letter derailed the Erbitux locomotive, and just over a year since Sam Waksal had been forced out of ImClone.

There were many innovative drugs and important papers to be presented in Chicago. In Washington, meanwhile, Mark McClellan, the new FDA commissioner, had begun to streamline and accelerate the agency's drug-approval process. A few weeks before ASCO the agency had surprised the market when it reversed an earlier ruling and suddenly green-lighted AstraZeneca's lung cancer drug Iressa, making it the first of the EGFr inhibitors to be approved for the U.S. market. The closely watched EGFr class were still considered "hot" drugs. The somnolent biotech business was suddenly growing animated again. The Amex Biotechnology Index had risen 36 percent in the last two months, and now stood at its highest level in over a year.

The usual carnivalesque atmosphere prevailed in Chicago. Large biotech firms like Genentech had plastered ads on bus shelters around town: "It's about time," the bright copy read. "Antiangiogenesis: ASCO 2003." Inside the cavernous exhibition hall, an enormous mock-up of the human colon rose above the crowd. Attendees were invited to crawl through the "Colossal Colon," inside of which was a tutorial on recognizing the warning signs of colorectal cancer; as they emerged from the colon, enthusiastic organizers snapped Polaroids and handed them to the surprised attendees as a souvenir.

Anticipation for Merck KGaA's trial data was high. Before ASCO opened, Merck had let it slip that its results were positive.

"The latest good news on cancer is that ImClone's Erbitux drug works after all," a *Wall Street Journal* editorial trumpeted. "Forgive us if we claim a little vindication, having defended the drug amid the howling about ImClone and corporate greed last year. The potential treatment for dying cancer patients always mattered more than Martha Stewart's ImClone stock trades. The continuing problem, however, is that every new cancer therapy has to endure a Food and Drug Administration obstacle course of needless delay."

On Sunday afternoon, June 1, Merck released the much-anticipated results of its Erbitux study. The trial's objective was to measure tumor shrinkage and the speed with which the disease progressed in colorectal cancer patients who had failed to respond to irinotecan. Of the 329 colon cancer patients who had been enrolled, two-thirds received the combination regimen, one-third received Erbitux alone. The result was a virtual photocopy of ImClone's discredited Study 9923.

In 2001, ImClone had declared that 22.5 percent of colon cancer patients who used the Erbitux-chemo combination saw their tumors shrivel. Later, the company's small single-agent study found that Erbitux alone had a tumor response rate of about 10 percent. In 2003, Merck showed that 22.9 percent of patients taking Erbitux in combination with chemotherapy saw a 50 percent reduction in tumor size, and 10.8 percent of patients taking Erbitux alone. As ImClone had said, the drug was shown to be more effective in combination than as a single agent.

ImClone's stock rallied sharply. Since the start of the year, investors had pushed ImClone's share price up 158 percent in anticipation of the good news from Merck. On June 2, the day after the European results were announced, the stock closed at $33.50 a share, a gain of 17.54 percent. As he waited to be sentenced to jail, Sam Waksal earned $2.62 million just from the uptick in ImClone's stock price.

Now the assembled oncologists wondered when the Erbitux application would be rehabilitated at the FDA. ImClone and Bristol-Myers Squibb refused to commit to a timetable, but the companies did say that with the agency's blessing they would use the Merck data along with revised data from their 2001 application to refile in late 2003. The buzz in Chicago was that Erbitux had a good chance of FDA approval, perhaps as soon as early 2004. "I think this is now likely to be one of the fastest approvals we have ever seen," predicted Hemant Shah, an independent analyst.

But not everyone found the Merck data convincing. Richard Evans, an analyst at Sanford Bernstein, wrote to investors: "Merck KGaA's Erbitux trial is strong enough to demonstrate that Erbitux works, but the poor trial design will likely render Merck KGaA's trial insufficient for Bristol-Myers to file with the FDA." He predicted that Erbitux would only be approved after further data was generated. Alan Venook, a professor of clinical medicine at U.C., San Francisco said: "Is this a potentially effective drug for cancer patients? Absolutely. But I'm not sure this data is enough to get a drug approved."

Indeed, the crowd's reaction to Erbitux in 2003 was noticeably less enthusiastic than it had been two years earlier. One problem was that Merck's trial lacked a control group or a comparison of Erbitux to conventional chemotherapies; as a result, the European study did not show "clear survival benefit." (New Erbitux trials were slated to begin, which ImClone and Bristol hoped would answer some of the lingering questions about the drug.)

By 2003, Erbitux had lost its crucial first-to-market advantage and rivals were closing. Now teams of biotech companies—notably Abgenix and Amgen, and their rivals Genentech and OSI Pharmaceuticals—were racing to bring their versions of targeted therapies to market. Abgenix's ABX-EGF was an injected monoclonal antibody like Erbitux, and had similar results (a 10 percent response rate as a single agent) to ImClone's drug; it may also be safer to administer than Erbitux. OSI's Tarceva, which is taken as a pill, showed encouraging results in lung cancer and brain tumor patients.

The unquestioned star of the 2003 ASCO was Genentech's antiangiogenesis drug, Avastin. It stole the show with data showing that it improved the survival rate of colon cancer patients, a feat that Erbitux had yet to match. In an 800-patient, phase 3 study, Avastin used with chemotherapy improved the survival of untreated colon cancer patients by 50 percent, or six months longer than those who used only chemotherapy. "To my knowledge, this is the largest increase in survival from the addition of a single agent," said a Genentech oncologist. Analysts predicted that Avastin could bring sales of $700 million to $1 billion in colorectal cancer alone. Investors bid up the company's shares 66 percent, to $62.61, adding some $13 billion to the biotech pioneer's value in a few weeks.

Adam Feuerstein, writing in *theStreet.com,* described Erbitux as the "warm-up act" to the "headliner" Avastin. And UCSF's Alan Venook characterized Erbitux as an "incremental" advance, while calling Avastin's "monumental."

JOHN MENDELSOHN viewed the many targeted treatments that were coming to market as both competitors and potential allies. "I really don't care, as long as we can help cure cancer," he said. "I want whatever works best for cancer patients." It is even possible, he mused, that some of these drugs could be used in tandem. Erbitux is being tested in combination with Avastin and with Iressa. "The combination therapies will probably be very important," said Mendelsohn. "But we still have a lot of work to do."

The larger issue is that despite the fact that these agents are remarkable scientific advances, they still only benefit some 10 to 20 percent of patients, and they only extend patients' lives by a matter of months. It is hoped that Mendelsohn's heirs will be able to use genetic tests to more precisely determine who benefits from which treatment, and to extend patients' lives beyond a few months.

For Jennifer McNeillie, the Florida hydrologist, Erbitux worked remarkably well for six months. But in early March 2003, the tumor in her liver began to swell and her abdomen grew tight again. She felt depleted. A terrible rash suddenly broke out all over her body. She began to take Thalidomide—the cell-starving drug originally used in the 1960s for morning sickness that led to severe birth defects in Europe. (It is now being reexamined as an anticancer agent when used in combination with other drugs.) In June, not long after the ASCO conference finished in Chicago, Jennifer died.

Her husband, Steven Walker, took the FDA to task for foot-dragging in a *Wall Street Journal* editorial:

> Those waiting for FDA decisions, mainly dying patients and those who care for them, view the agency as a barrier to new treatments that they desperately need to live. The agency's inability to recognize and adjust to the accelerating pace of medical research has tarnished its gilt. . . . Using a conservative estimate based on American Cancer Society numbers . . . about 14,500 Americans will be denied Avastin and about 28,500 will be denied Erbitux over the next six months while the FDA waits for and processes paperwork . . . the cost of human life adds up to about 14,300 years . . . My wife's battle with cancer and the setbacks she suffered at the hands of the system are typical of the challenges faced by all Americans fighting life-threatening diseases. Too many people are dying at the hands of a bureaucracy that does not have an approval mechanism that could ease the loss of life.

Working with a patient advocate group called the Abigail Alliance for Better Access to Developmental Drugs, Walker suggested that the FDA quicken the pace of approval for new drugs for those with "immediate needs," without weakening its standards. Exactly how this might be accomplished remains the focus of an intense and emotional debate.

*     *     *

AT THE SAME TIME that Erbitux was resurgent in Chicago, Sam Waksal was about to be sentenced in New York. His sentencing hearing had been set and reset numerous times—mid-May, late May—as the prosecutors and defense attorneys jockeyed for advantage. Judge Pauley rebuked both sides and warned them not to stall any further. At an April proceeding, Judge Pauley noted that Sam had provided only "vague" financial information about loans, taxes, and other liabilities to the probation department, which is in charge of sentencing recommendations. The judge asked Mark Pomerantz: "Do you really expect the court to believe that Dr. Waksal's monthly income and monthly expenses are in perfect equilibrium, down to the dollar?" Irritated, Pauley set a new hearing date: June 3, 2003.

At the end of May, Assistant U.S. Attorney Michael Schachter filed sealed papers detailing Sam's 1986 forgery of Sherwood "Woody" Weiser's ImClone stock certificate, by which Sam allegedly swindled his friend out of $90,000. Sam's lead attorney, Mark Pomerantz, replied to the charge: "Not so. Didn't happen." Schachter shot back: "We're told by ImClone's former general counsel [John Landes] that it happened." It was Landes's signature that Sam had forged on the document, after all, as Landes himself had explained to Congress in October. Neither side would elaborate on their jurisprudencial maneuvering, and they bickered about the length of Sam's sentence.

Judge Pauley sighed, and again set Sam Waksal's sentencing date: Tuesday, June 10, 2003. This time the date would stand.

# SIXTEEN

# *Icarian Actions*

Sam's 5,000-square-foot duplex penthouse in SoHo had 10 rooms, four bedrooms, four and a half baths, a library filled with books on every conceivable subject (friends claimed he'd "read them all"), a media room, a high-ceilinged living room with a fireplace, and a 5,000-square-foot terrace. While the lawyers haggled, and his friends worried about him, and the journalists sharpened their pencils in preparation for his sentencing, Sam flew his old friend Elizabeth Latham and her companion, the orchardist, from New Zealand to New York and put them up at his loft for a farewell celebration. There was no question that Sam would be going to jail: the mystery was for how long. He worried, but hoped for the best, perhaps a sentence of a year with community service. Lately he'd volunteered a bit at Housing Works, which helps homeless people with AIDS; maybe that would count with Judge Pauley.

When Elizabeth and the orchardist arrived at Sam's loft, they noticed that the phones sprinkled around the vast apartment were constantly ringing and Sam kept putting on his glasses to peer at the caller-ID box. Norma Robert had tried to get through; she knew he was there, and was annoyed that he wouldn't pick up her call. The orchardist was amused: "If he could have six or seven phones strapped to his body, he'd be quite happy," he quipped. The people calling were Sam's society friends, including Martha Stewart, to whom he remained close.

"I've heard that Sam has been 'abandoned' by his society friends, but these are all *incoming* calls, not outgoing," Elizabeth noticed. "The ones who matter still call. The others fall away."

She and her friend enjoyed extended, winey meals with Sam and his crowd, and described how, "even now, young, 35-year-old women are throwing themselves at him like sycophants."

She teased Sam: "Why don't you sign all your underwear and give them out to the women you've screwed?"

"Can't do it," he deadpanned. "Not enough underwear."

Beneath the wine and the apparent gaiety, Elizabeth worried about Sam. He was struggling to write a six-page letter to Judge Pauley, explaining who he was, the motivation for his actions, and why he believed he deserved a lenient sentence. His letter included references to the Talmud and Albert Camus's *The Stranger,* and it ended with a plea for community service "as part of my sentence so I can continue to make amends to society and let me keep giving back."

"Lots of people would love to see him go down," Elizabeth said. "He's the 'tall poppy.' He can be arrogant and say the most outrageous things. But the next minute, he'll tell a joke on himself. He's completely self-deprecating. He says to me, 'People think I've changed, but I'm no different now than I ever was. They just don't understand me.'"

When Elizabeth was told that cancer patients and ImClone investors felt betrayed by Sam, her cheeks flushed in anger and she snapped, "I totally resent that! To blame him for Erbitux not coming on the market is bizarre—the *FDA* stopped Erbitux, not *Sam.* People just like to blame other people. It's a fascinating indictment of humanity, really."

Elizabeth is one of the people who believed Sam had done nothing wrong: "He's definitely a scapegoat, and always has been. Sam ain't a bad guy. He's not morally corrupt. The only thing Sam did wrong was to call his daughter [after learning of the RTF letter], which is an entirely natural thing to do in those circumstances."

This is a view echoed by many of Sam's defenders, including his former mother-in-law, Shirley Flacks. "I really don't think he did anything wrong," said Shirl. "You know why they went after him? A, he's a Jewish boy. And B, he's a very public Democrat—he had dinner at the [Clinton] White House! I think it's a waste of human resources to put some-one like Sam in jail. He has so many talents. He should do community service."

Now, said Elizabeth, "family is the only thing that matters to Sam. I mean, he could've gone to court and fought this, but all he's interested in is protecting his father. He's being a martyr. And he could go away for a long while because of it."

If he received a one-year sentence, she said, "he'd be okay with that." But if it was any more time than that, "it will be difficult. He'll sell *everything.*"

She asked Sam if he'd researched what life is like in a white-collar prison. "No, I'm in denial," he replied.

MARTHA STEWART worked as a stockbroker for five years, from mid-1968 through mid-1973, at a small Manhattan firm originally called Perl-berg, Monness, Williams & Sidel. Although she worked for a time next to the actor Brian Dennehy and earned a good wage—$135,000 in her top year—it had not been a happy experience. Speaking to Charlie Rose in 1995, Martha recalled: "My father-in-law was a stockbroker, and he encouraged me to sort of gamble . . . I liked that little bit of life, too. And learned a lot about stocks. Went to work for a very interesting firm. No one was over 23 years old in my firm . . . I learned how to be really competitive there. It was a tough, tough environment . . . The movie *Wall Street* had nothing on this firm." By the summer of 1973, the market was in such decline that her commissions had dried up; furthermore, the brokerage was embroiled in the Levitz Furniture scandal (Martha was never implicated in any bad dealings; the brokerage went bust the following year). Martha would say that this experience turned her into such a "nervous wreck" that she quit and changed careers.

Having moved to suburban Westport, Connecticut, 1971, she rein-vented herself there as a caterer and author of books on entertaining—a move that would eventually lead her back to the public marketplace with MSO. But now, 30 years after she had fled Wall Street, Martha Stewart was again being tormented by the market and its regulators.

On June 3, 2003, the sky was a leaden gray over New York City and about 100 shareholders gathered at the Equitable Building for the annual meeting of Martha Stewart Omnimedia. The mood inside matched the weather. "Martha looked beleaguered and sad," a shareholder reported. The day before, Martha had received word from the U.S. Attorney's Office that it "intends to request the grand jury to return an indictment against her in the near future." What this meant was that in addition to the SEC's planned civil suit against her for insider trading, Martha would now face federal criminal charges.

She found this nearly incomprehensible. "I am not guilty but I feel sad, which is not a typical emotion for me," she'd say. "I keep saying 'Why, why, why?' This should never be a reflection on a business or a livelihood. It's terrible. For a creative person to be maligned like this is the worst thing that could happen. It takes away the joy."

She was without question the most high-profile target of the government's widespread probe of white-collar crime. Under mounting public pressure to take a "zero-tolerance" approach to corporate self-dealing, U.S. attorney Comey had for months pressured Martha to plead guilty to at least one of the crimes, generally thought to be the lesser charge of obstructing the investigation. Such a guilty plea would force Martha to step down as an officer of her company and would perhaps land her in jail.

She refused to buckle. As far as Martha was concerned, she was innocent and her prosecution was a politically motivated witch hunt. She had been taken for granted before, and in an odd way she relished the fight.

"I remember when I presented some of these concepts for the first issue of the magazine to the Time Warner people, and they said, 'There's too much in here; you'll run out of ideas.' Well, I haven't, and I won't," she recalled with a grin. "There is always another shape of cake to make. Living is a limitless subject." Turning somber, she added: "I have built this company from scratch, and I don't want to see anything destroyed. I am still very sure of my vision. I just want it all back on track, 100 percent."

Behind the scenes, her lawyers had spent months hashing out a settlement agreement with Comey's office. But at the 11th hour they delayed signing off on a deal in favor of going over the prosecutors' heads to appeal to the Department of Justice, in Washington, D.C. This was not an unheard-of tactic for a suspect in a high-profile case, but because it can backfire it is usually reserved for a last-ditch effort. In any event, the DOJ—headed by Attorney General John Ashcroft, who, like Comey, had been appointed by President Bush—rejected Martha's request for a meeting. This threw the case back to the now thoroughly antagonized federal prosecutors in New York.

MSO was tipping into crisis. Over the last two quarters, the company had lost money for the first time in its history. As the market predicted the effect this would have on products, its stock price continued to erode. "No matter what happens to Martha legally . . . they need to develop a plan for turning the business around," cautioned the analyst Laura Richardson.

Public interest in the case had grown frenzied, and rumors were swirling up and down the canyons of the city. After the annual meeting in June, Arthur Martinez, an MSO boardmember and the former chairman and CEO of Sears, Roebuck, was compelled to declare that it was "categorically untrue" that Martha had resigned: "Martha remains the chairman and chief executive," he said. Then MSO released a statement saying that its board members had been planning for "a number of possible contingencies, are evaluating the current situation and will take action as appropriate."

In fact, the night before, the MSO board learned that Martha would be arraigned. Under an emergency plan worked out in preceding months, Martinez had been designated to replace her as chairman if she were indicted. That night he had a change of heart. At an 8 A.M. board meeting (without Martha) the next day, Martinez said he would not accept the job, reportedly because Martha would retain control of the company and because Sharon Patrick refused to report to him. The crisis at MSO deepened.

Just before the annual meeting got underway, a shareholder named Joyce Francis put her finger on the nub of the problem: "The mistake was made long ago. They should never make a person a brand of anything."

JUNE 3 was also the day that Sam had originally been scheduled for sentencing. But Judge Pauley had pushed it back a week, and Sam held court that day over lunch at Nobu, the pricey sushi restaurant in TriBeCa. He looked good. Tanned and rested, dressed in a pale blue shirt and a navy blazer, he sat with a table-full of friends in a prime spot by the front window. He dominated the conversation, leaned in to make an emphatic point, gesticulated with his long fingers, and talked and talked and talked.

When the investigation had first started a year and a half earlier, Sam had been cowed. "Do people think I'm a bad man?" he'd nervously ask friends. But as time went on he adjusted to his notoriety and grew emboldened. "If I were in his shoes I'd be moving to Minnesota," said a longtime pal. "But he seems fine. He's out almost every night, cool as a cucumber. I don't blame him for having fun. If not now, when?" The gossip columns mentioned Sam dining at Elaine's, uptown, or loudly racking up a $700 bill with two friends at Da Silvano downtown; he was seen shopping at the Barefoot Contessa in the Hamptons (a gourmet food shop owned by Ina Garten, a former White House staffer and a contributor to *Martha Stewart Living);* he unabashedly turned up at the *Sopranos'* season premier, and at a book party for *The Cell,* a book about terrorism.

Before a defendant like Sam is sentenced, the probation department monitors him and writes a report, which the judge factors into his sentence. Sam hated his probation officer, a woman he found pedestrian and without humor, Elizabeth Latham said. Required to do a urine sample one day, Sam decided to have some fun with her. As he emerged from the bathroom, he handed the probation officer the filled plastic cup, then shook her hand in thanks. "Oops!" he said, and acted as if he'd had urine on his hand. Then he grinned and said, "Just kidding!"

She scowled at him, decidedly unamused. The probation department's presentencing report noted that despite his claims of penury, and many outstanding liabilities, Sam retained some $52 million in assets. It also noted that on a monthly basis he continued to spend: $7,300 on household help; $5,000 for a driver; $4,600 on restaurants; $4,925 on clothing; and $1,125 on golf.

IT HAD ALWAYS been important to Sam to be perceived as a Renaissance man—a smart scientist, a successful businessman, a cultured intellectual, a man about town, and a patron of Jewish culture. Indeed, he made much of his charitable contributions. He made substantial donations to Israel's Rabin Medical Center and New York's Metropolitan Jewish Geriatric Foundation; he gave to the Save the Children Foundation and served as chairman of the New York Council of the Humanities. But not all of his charitable giving went smoothly.

In May 1999, Waksal pledged $1 million to the Center for Jewish History in Manhattan; he later increased the gift to some $3 million. In return, the center dedicated a new building on West 13th Street to his parents. A plaque in their name was hung near the entrance to the building: "The Jack and Sabina Waksal Building." At the opening ceremony, in October 2000, people shed tears of gratitude, according the *The Forward*, a newspaper for the Jewish community. In speaking of Jack and Sabina Waksal, the chairman of the center's board, Bruce Slovin, said: "Here's a man and a woman who survived the Nazis, flourished in the United States, gave back to the community, and raised three wonderful children. That Jewish story is our story; that's what we all talk about. It's the American dream."

The Waksals' commemorative plaque remains on the building, but the center has yet to receive Sam's pledge. In August 2001, he transferred 3,480 shares of ImClone to the center, which sold the stock for about $158,000. But the center, which was counting on Sam's pledge to cover its construction costs, is not likely to ever receive its full payment. This has reportedly put the center in a tight spot, and caused great concern among its members. (My calls to the center were not returned.) According to the U.S. attorney's charge, the center's chairman repeatedly called Sam to ask that he make good on his pledge but Sam claimed he lacked the sufficient resources to pay his debt. Yet in 2001, Sam made over $72 million (which he failed to pay taxes on) and managed to buy $6.2 million worth of artwork for himself.

Sam is not the first to put such institutions in an unhappy position. In 1986, the Jewish Theological Seminary removed arbitrageur Ivan Boesky's name from its library after he was convicted of insider trading. But there is confusion about what to do about a wealthy-but-tainted philanthropist like Michael Milken, who, since pleading guilty to six felonies in 1990, has generously donated to Jewish and cancer research organizations as part of a concerted effort to rehabilitate his name.

"The Jewish organizations continued to line up and receive funding," Burton Visotzky, a professor at the Jewish Theological Seminary, told *The Forward*. "There's never a clear answer. Jewish institutions, quite frankly, depend on their donors, and the probity of their donors, not just the dollar. On the other hand, we yearn for an ideal: Purity. We like all of our teachers, our donors, to be like 'an angel of the Lord of hosts.' If they resemble an angel, good. If not, we try to avoid them. But that's an ideal—reality sometimes differs."

Sam Waksal took his duplicity a step further, the government claimed, when he deceived his own company about his charitable giving. In 2000, he exercised over $60 million in stock options. For most of that year, ImClone did not withhold taxes on those gains; but in October, the company changed its policy and started withholding income taxes on the gains recognized from the exercising of options. Once the new policy was in place, Waksal exercised another 200,000 stock options, with a taxable value of $10.4 million. Sam allegedly told ImClone that he was gifting the $10.4 million in ImClone shares to charity. In fact, he did not. Instead, he sent $7.5 million to his offshore account, $500,000 to the Gagosian art gallery, transferred $2 million to Refco Capital Management as part of a loan agreement, and pledged the remaining ImClone shares to secure a margin balance. After doing all of this, he signed an SEC Form 5, in which he claimed to have given the shares to charity. He then received several e-mails confirming his claim that he had gifted the shares to charity. Sam never revealed his lie.

"He's really proud of his Jewish heritage. But the stuff he did was so *not* Jewish," said Marcus Engelman, Sam's roommate at OSU. "He's smart, but he totally missed the morality and ethics of Judaism—the *heart*. He missed the part that could have saved him."

ON JUNE 4, the heavens opened up: New York's streets were gleaming wet and the sidewalks were filled with bobbing black umbrellas. At the federal district courthouse on Centre Street, downtown, an enormous crowd had gathered in the rain to watch Martha walk from her limousine into the imposing building to be arraigned. It was just possible to make out Martha's blonde head passing through the crowd. She was dressed in colors that popped out in the drizzle—a light beige pantsuit and a pale gray coat with a matching umbrella. As the paparazzi yelled and shoved cameras and microphones in her face, Martha attempted a smile, but she was visibly distraught. She was followed into the courthouse by Peter Bacanovic, who was dressed in a dark suit, white shirt, and gray tie; he held himself rigidly upright and stared straight ahead.

Inside Judge Miriam G. Cederbaum's chambers, Martha and her broker pleaded not guilty to conspiracy, obstruction of justice, and securities fraud. The judge released both without bail, asking Bacanovic to hand over his passport.

In a civil complaint, the SEC charged that Martha should have known that she received insider information when Douglas Faneuil, Bacanovic's assistant, told her the Waksals were selling ImClone shares: "From our perspective, this case involved insider trading," said an SEC spokesman.

But James Comey took a different approach. The 41-page grand jury indictment laid out an extensive set of charges developed by the FBI and the U.S. attorney's joint investigation. "I used my discretion," Comey said, in not charging Martha with insider trading. Although case law would support such charges, he added, it would be "unprecedented." Depending on how one interpreted the legal fine points, Comey had either a strong case or weak one. Because he had no smoking gun, the government had cobbled together a panoply of inferences, half-truths, and omissions to a case alleging that Martha had obstructed their investigation and committed securities fraud.

"Stewart and Bacanovic agreed that rather than tell the truth about the communications with Stewart on Dec. 27, 2001, and the reasons for Stewart's sale of ImClone stock on Dec. 27, 2001, they would instead fabricate and attempt to deceive investigators with a fictitious explanation for her sale," the indictment read.

Robert Morvillo, Martha's big, brash, cigar-chomping lawyer, suggested that prosecutors were simply trophy-hunting: "Is it for publicity purposes because Martha Stewart is a celebrity? Is it because she is a woman who has successfully competed in a man's business world? . . . Or is it because the Department of Justice is attempting to divert the public's attention from its failure to charge the politically connected managers of Enron and WorldCom?"

Comey countercharged: "This criminal case is about lying—lying to the FBI, lying to the SEC, lying to investigators. Martha Stewart is being prosecuted not for who she is, but because of what she did." He called the indictments "a tragedy" for Bacanovic, Martha, and her 580 employees. "It's a tragedy that could have been prevented if those two people had only done what parents have taught their children for eons—that if you are in a tight spot, lying is not the way out. Lying is an act with profound consequences."

In accusing Martha of securities fraud, the lengthy indictment referred to three statements she or her attorneys made about her stop-loss order and about her innocence, "in an effort to stop or at least slow the steady erosion of MSLO's stock price caused by investor concerns." On June 6, 2002, the Stewart camp told *The Wall Street Journal* that Martha's trade was "executed because Ms. Stewart had a predetermined price at which she planned to sell the stock . . . if the stock ever went less than $60." On June 12, Martha reiterated that an existing stop-loss agreement had led to her stock sale. MSO's share price gained 7 percent after the second statement. In a third statement released on June 18, after the market closed, Martha's attorneys repeated the message once again; when trading resumed the next day, MSO stock rebounded about 14 percent, the indictment said. "Stewart," the indictment alleged, "falsely stated she 'did not have any nonpublic information' regarding Im-Clone" when she sold her stock. As a result, she was accused of defrauding her own investors.

Among other charges, the government claimed that Martha had deliberately tried to cover her tracks once the SEC started to investigate the rash of ImClone trades. In January 2002, Martha sat down at Ann Armstrong's desk and deleted Peter Bacanovic's crucial phone message—in which he said that ImClone was "going to start trading downward"—on the computer log; but then she reversed herself, and reinstated the entry in its entirety.

In charging Peter Bacanovic, the government said it had even more compelling evidence of a cover-up. Comey charged that on December 21, 2001 (before Martha's trade), Bacanovic scratched the notation "@ 60" on a worksheet that listed Martha's stock holdings—meaning that she wanted to sell her ImClone shares at $60. Bacanovic had made this and various other markings on the worksheet in blue ballpoint pen. But, the prosecutors charged, the "@ 60" was made *after* January 2002, when Bacanovic learned of the SEC's investigation. "Peter Bacanovic altered the worksheet, using ink that was blue ballpoint, but was scientifically distinguishable from the ink used elsewhere on the worksheet," the indictment read.

Hours after Martha Stewart was arraigned, she announced that she was stepping down as chairwoman and chief executive of Martha Stewart Living Omnimedia. She would continue as a director of the company, and would remain a power behind the scenes with a new title, "chief creative officer." Sharon Patrick succeeded her as CEO. The chairman's role was taken by Jeffrey Ubben, a 41-year-old former Fidelity fund manager; his Value Act Capital Partners, which had invested in MSO shortly before the news of her ImClone trade broke, was the second-largest shareholder in MSO after Martha herself. Wall Street was skeptical of Ubben. Not only was he young, but he lived in San Francisco, far from MSO's headquarters in New York. Most of all, it was suspected that Martha remained in control of her company in fact, if not in name.

"If this is just a change in titles but not in roles, it won't be any different," said the analyst Laura Richardson. "If it is a true change in roles, it would be a step forward for them in coming out of this negative period."

Martha then launched a campaign to generate sympathy and to "clear my name," with the help of PR firm Sard Verbinnen. She established a personal Web site, *www.marthatalks.com*, in which she invited people to contact her. "I simply returned a call from my stockbroker," she explained in "A Letter from Martha" on the site. "The government's attempt to criminalize these actions makes no sense to me. I am confident I will be exonerated of these baseless charges."

If convicted on all counts, Martha potentially faced 30 years in prison and $2 million in fines, although the sentence would likely be much less. Her trial was scheduled for January 12, 2004.

Public interest in the case remained high. In a skillful bit of gamesmanship, Comey, the 42-year-old son of a Yonkers, New York, policeman, selected Karen Patton Seymour as the lead prosecutor in Martha's trial, to neutralize the gender issue. Martha's camp had exploited the notion that she was being railroaded because she was a successful woman. Seymour, 42, was a native of Big Springs, Texas; the chief of the criminal division of the Manhattan U.S. Attorney's Office, she oversaw 170 lawyers on such high-profile cases as WorldCom, Inc., and Adelphia Communications Corp., and was known to be cool under pressure. The gender issue was important. "They're clearly trying to make it appear as two strong women doing battle with one another," said Jo-Ellan Dimitrius, a jury consultant. "It's going to be a likeability call—how the female prosecutor may come across versus how Martha may come across" to the jury.

*　　*　　*

"*FAMILY BUSINESS* was a fun film, Sidney did a good job, but he didn't know how to end it," Sam Waksal said of Sidney Lumet's movie. "You loved it and you loved it, and then it just plunked. He crowded too much together at the end. I guess [filmmaking] is almost as hard as filing with the FDA."

*Family Business* ends with a rousing courtroom scene. As a packed courthouse looks on, the judge addresses Jessie (Sean Connery): "If there is a culprit in this case, you certainly fit the bill . . . Among other things, you've held up the development of an important new scientific discovery. But, as your lawyer points out, you are not a young man. It's not an easy matter to decide upon an appropriate sentence for someone of your years. I've had to think this out carefully."

With a *wham!* of the gavel, and the *clink* of handcuffs, the judge sentences Jessie to 15 years in prison—Members of the McMullen-Gruden family look on from the gallery, distraught. Jessie (who would ultimately die in the prison hospital) winks and grins at his grandson, and says: "Hey, if you can't do the time, don't do the crime."

EIGHTY-TWO-YEAR-OLD JACK WAKSAL was crying. And so was his grand-daughter Aliza, and his daughter, Patti. His wife, Sabina, was ill and was unable to attend. Harlan sat in the front row, grim-faced and silent. All eyes were on Sam, who stood up front, dressed in his usual dark gray suit, white shirt, and steel-blue tie; he betrayed no emotion.

It was June 10, 2003, a hot, clear Tuesday in New York, with a single puffy cloud loitering in a searing blue sky. By 10 o'clock that morning the tall court building that overlooked Chinatown was ringed by a huge crowd of TV and print reporters from all over the world, and curious onlookers. Upstairs, the air-conditioning in Judge Pauley's courtroom was not working well, and the standing-room-only hearing room was stuffy. The room was filled to capacity. Guards blocked the doors and a line of about 40 journalists snaked down the marble hallway, in various poses of frustration, boredom, and ennui, hoping against reason to be allowed in. Tensions flared. At one point, one of Sam's lawyers was barred by overzealous guards. At another point, the lead prosecutor, Michael Schachter, was not allowed inside. He just grinned and said, "Well, they can't start in there without me."

Finally, everyone who mattered was in place and Judge Pauley convened Sam's sentencing hearing.

In a lengthy appeal for an easy sentence, Mark Pomerantz told the court of Sam's "successful" career as a researcher, his parents' suffering in the Holocaust, his friendship with an ImClone janitor named Jimmy Carter, his "exceptional community service," his "empathy for the underdog," the burden of an intrusive media, and all the good he had done with Erbitux for cancer sufferers.

Sam was "a total believer in Erbitux," his lawyer said, who deserved a light sentence because he, "spent the better part of his life devoted to finding and developing a drug that would help people who had no other hope, people who without the drug would be dead."

> If you could turn back the clock and make it as though his crimes never happened, but you also had to erase his drug, it is not a bargain that he would make. And the reason is, Your Honor, it was not about money for this defendant. It was not money that made him devote his life to medical research. It was not money that led him to walk the halls of ImClone encouraging employees. It was not money that made him spend hours on the phone with cancer patients and relatives of people who were dying of cancer. He spent that time because it was his life's work. Because he loved it. Because he believed in it. And because he thought that he personally, as one human being, could do something to help. And that is in fact what he did. By advancing his vision of his effort, of his devotion, medical science has a drug that is going to be a powerful weapon . . . against cancer.

Pomerantz said that Sam had acknowledged that he had done wrong, and felt great remorse. "He should not have done what he did, to be sure," said the attorney. He should not have tipped off his daughter about the RTF; he should have not forged signatures; he should not have lied to the SEC; he should not have asked his secretaries to destroy documents; he did not mean to stiff charities, and he did not intend to burden ImClone with a huge tax bill. At heart, Pomerantz said, "this was a crime of weakness."

He characterized Sam's insider trading as "a matter of impulse . . .

not the cynical act of a corporate insider who knows that his company is really a house of cards and who wants to cash in on a Ponzi scheme so that he can make off with his personal fortune while everyone else is left holding the bag." Like many things Sam did, he added, "it was messy . . . It was done quickly in the faith that everything is going to turn out alright. And because he means well in the long term, he can cut a corner." Indeed, Pomerantz claimed, "The cover-up is worse than the crime."

He read excerpts from some of the 120 letters of support for Sam that had been sent to the court. The actress Lorraine Bracco, who played Dr. Melfi on *The Sopranos,* wrote a letter about how Sam had helped her through personal difficulties: "I don't pretend to know about Sam's business, but I do know that without Sam's guidance and support, I doubt I would be here to write this letter. To top it off, Sam has never made me feel in any way obliged to him, has never asked me for anything in return. He has allowed me my dignity." Speaking of her fund-raising for charities, she added, "Why do I do it? Why do I care? My answer has been and always will be that when I was hopeless, someone named Sam reached out to me."

Charles Dunn, of ImClone, wrote: "Reading the papers one might wonder how Sam could possibly have spent anytime [*sic*] at all in the office between jet-setting around the world with the hoi polloi [*sic*] and escorting Martha Stewart around New York. The boring truth is that Sam has always been a workaholic. He lived and breathed ImClone for almost 20 years, sacrificing personally to see that our drug succeeded."

And Paul Josefowitz, a cancer-stricken magazine publisher from London to whom Sam had given Erbitux, wrote: "It has now been 18 months since my diagnosis, and I think it's fair to say that without Sam Waksal's efforts and kindness, I would probably be dead. I hope some day I will be able to thank him in person."

Pomerantz added: "This defendant was the CEO of a public corporation. He did not have to involve himself with Paul Josefowitz or Shannon Kellum, or any of the other patients or relatives that have written this court. He never had to answer the phone. He never had to overrule his clinical staff and insist that ImClone would have a compassionate-use program." Sam had already paid heavily, his lawyer maintained. He was virtually penniless; he had inflicted terrible pain on his father and daughter. Yet Jack had to be dissuaded from addressing the court in his son's defense.

Pomerantz decried the government's "aggressive" prosecution, bemoaned the fact that Sam's crimes were lumped together with the likes of Enron and WorldCom, and regretted the government's disinterest in striking a deal; he noted that even a felon as notorious as Ivan Bocsky was only given a three-year sentence. Of Sam, Pomerantz assured the judge, "There is nothing the court can do to him that compares to the enormity of what he did to himself . . . I think most have rarely seen a situation in which a defendant has fallen so far, so fast."

Despite his youthful and easygoing appearance, Schachter vigorously struck back. "With all due respect, Mr. Pomerantz is simply wrong" he said. "Dr. Waksal's denial of the seriousness of his crimes, and of the harm that his crimes have caused nationally, may be a window to Dr. Waksal's true acceptance of responsibility here." He pointed out that as a CEO, Sam had "betrayed the sacred trust" of his investors and employees. Sam's lies caused "unsuspecting shareholders who were not armed with the same information" to lose some $10.6 million—and would have cost them an additional $5 million had his thwarted trades gone through. In buying put options through an anonymous Swiss account, Sam bet against his own company. Because he failed to pay his taxes, ImClone was stuck with a tax bill that exceeded its quarterly revenues.

Then Sam stood and made a brief statement:

Your Honor, I want to apologize for my wrongdoing. I want to apologize to my family. I want to say I'm sorry to my employees, to my colleagues at ImClone. I want to apologize to all the people that had confidence in me and whose confidence I may have betrayed . . . To cancer patients, I am so sorry for any delay that I might have effected in the approval of Erbitux because of my actions. I apologize to the shareholders of ImClone who believed in the drug, who believed in our company . . . Your Honor, I feel great remorse about what I did, but I do not feel bitter. I came to the United States and grew up in middle America and had been able to live and prosper in a country that allowed me to do all the things I ever dreamed of. I feel gratitude for everything this country has allowed me to do because of the accountability I felt [for] what happened to my parents . . . I know that life begins on the other side of moments of despair . . . I've learned from my mistakes, and I hope after all this is over to be able to move forward and to continue to do things that will have a positive impact on society.

At the end of the long, hot afternoon, Judge Pauley rendered a judgment against Sam that was expressed in subdued tones but tinged by a nearly Old Testament wrath. "The harm that you wrought is truly incalculable," he addressed Sam. "In the end, your spectacular success in building ImClone into a company worthy of inclusion in the NASDAQ 100 led you to disconnect from reality and, most importantly, from the rule of law. Your Icarian actions have consequences."

In a clinical tone, he picked apart Sam's defense point-by-point. Addressing Sam's "exceptional community service," he noted that Waksal had done some commendable things but nothing extraordinary for someone of his superb education and exalted position as a multimillionaire CEO. Indeed, Judge Pauley noted, that between 1999 and 2001, Sam earned over $132 million in income but gave only $157,451 in charitable donations—one-half of 1 percent of his adjusted gross income. He dismissed Sam's claim that he'd received "little financial benefit from his illegal conduct," and said Sam's "purported cooperation with the government . . . only resulted in additional charges against him."

Pauley made quick work of Sam's claim that "the constant media coverage" of his case warranted a lighter sentence: "This argument borders on the frivolous. For years, Dr. Waksal has sought out public attention. Any collateral effects [he] has suffered as a result of his illegal conduct is a circumstance he alone has brought down upon himself."

Summing up, the judge said: "Dr. Waksal, the serious crimes to which you've pleaded guilty are not simply a 24-hour window of catastrophically poor judgment, or a crime of impulse, as your attorney characterized it. Rather, those crimes are emblematic of a pattern of lawlessness and arrogance from your own self-described short-term cash flow needs. You abused your position of trust as [CEO] . . . and undermined the public's confidence in the integrity of the financial markets. Then you tried to lie your way out of it, showing a complete disregard for the fair administration of justice. On a more personal level, you even jeopardized the well-being of members of your family [for] your own ends."

With that, he sentenced Sam to the maximum prison term, 87 months—or seven years and three months—and the maximum fine under federal guidelines—$3 million, plus $1.26 million in restitution to the New York State tax commission. And now Samuel D. Waksal, who would turn 56 in September, became the first chief executive in the recent spate of corporate scandals to be sent to prison.

"It's going to be all right," Sam said, embracing his shaken father at the end of the day. Jack was a diminutive, square-headed man with tousled gray hair dressed in a dark suit. He wore tinted glasses, and he was nearly bowled over by the rambunctious media pack outside the courthouse. Moving slowly, he was supported on either side by Harlan, in a blue suit, and Aliza, who had dressed all in black for the occasion.

Half an hour later, Sam, an electronic monitoring bracelet strapped around his ankle, slipped out of the building, across the sidewalk into a waiting black car, which sped away into the shimmering traffic stream. He had come out so unexpectedly, and moved so quickly, that the pack of journalists were caught unawares; only one photographer had managed to snap his picture.

Until he went to prison, Sam would be confined to his loft 24 hours a day. The beautiful duplex had become Sam's gilded cage.

LOOKING BACK on the ImClone debacle, Irv Feit, the company's former patent attorney, said: "I was surprised when it all blew up. I still don't understand why it happened. Sam did what he'd set out to do: he took a risk and built a company with a lot of value, and he made a lot of money doing it. Why did he need more? He could have been remembered for having achieved something that very few people ever achieve—he brought a new cancer drug to market. I consider [the scandal] a tragedy."

In July, ImClone was relisted by NASDAQ and received a much-needed $6 million payment from Merck KGaA for Erbitux. On July 16, Robert Goldhammer resigned from the ImClone board.

A week later, Harlan Waksal resigned from the company. He faced a number of class-action lawsuits from shareholders who were convinced he was as culpable for the decline of ImClone as his brother. But Harlan left ImClone with some $97.5 million, and resolved to "pursue new challenges."

In his many court appearances, Sam had refused to admit that he tipped off his father, Jack, and repeatedly tried to shield Jack and Aliza from prosecution. Nevertheless, on October 10, 2003, the SEC indicted Jack Waksal for insider trading. The civil suit charged that in late December 2001, Sam told Jack that an RTF letter was imminent; Jack then sold $8.2 million worth of ImClone shares that belonged to himself and his daughter, Patti. (Jack controlled Patti's $83,000 worth of ImClone stock; she was named as a relief defendant who did not break the law but benefited from the illegal actions of others.) The SEC also charged that Jack had lied under oath to SEC investigators. It was a denouement right out of *Family Business.*

SHORTLY BEFORE HE LEFT for prison, Sam had invited Steve Kroft of *60 Minutes* to come by the Thompson Street loft for an interview. (It aired on October 5, Yom Kippur, the Jewish Day of Atonement.) Sam proudly showed off his apartment and his art collection, and appeared less remorseful than he had been in court. Speaking of his December 2001 stock trades, he admitted, "I was arrogant enough at the time to believe that I could cut corners, not care about the details or . . . consequences . . . Thinking I was the most honest CEO that ever lived . . . I could glibly do something [illegal] and rationalize it." He said he knew that the SEC was vigilant about monitoring stock trades by executives or members of their families, especially when a big price drop occurs. Nevertheless, he had induced Aliza to sell her 29,000 ImClone shares, and attempted to have her sell an additional 79,000 shares of his own. "Did I think about it at the time? Obviously not . . . I just acted irresponsibly." While he again expressed remorse for involving Aliza in his schemes, he never mentioned the cancer patients, doctors, or investors who had also relied on his word. In a flash of anger, he said "it was just wrong" for the government to "use my daughter" to induce him to plead guilty. But, he admitted, "I didn't think I would get caught at all."

Jim Comey refused to cut a deal with Sam that would protect Aliza and Jack Waksal from prosecution. In Sam's six-page letter to Judge Pauley, he wrote of his shame: "By allowing my daughter to lie in order to protect me, I tore my family apart. That punishment is with me every moment of the day. I dream about it. I can barely look at Aliza without questioning who I am. When she cried to me and asked me why she was involved in this situation, I died inside."

In fact, Sam had used Aliza without compunction for years. She had accounts at Merrill Lynch and Prudential Securities, but the U.S. attorney's investigation established that Sam directed every single transaction in them. In fact, Sam opened Aliza's account at Prudential on July 6,

2000, without her knowledge, by forging her signature. Later, his secretaries told investigators that Sam had them forge Aliza's signature on wire transfer requests and other financial documents. Sam used Aliza's account as a "nominee" account, to secretly trade in ImClone stock under the radar of Wall Street. He "repeatedly transferred millions of dollars worth of ImClone stock to his daughter's accounts, sold it, then caused the proceeds to be transferred back to him," the government charged. "He wanted to fool his shareholders into thinking that he wasn't selling his stock." On September 30, 2000, for example, Sam transferred 30,000 ImClone shares, worth some $3.36 million, to Aliza's account at Prudential; on October 10, he sold 20,000 of those shares for $2.1 million; he wired $1 million to his own account at Bank of New York, and $1 million to the Gagosian Gallery, to pay for artwork. Three days later, Sam sold the remaining 10,000 shares of ImClone in Aliza's account; on October 17, he transferred $1 million in proceeds to his own account.

The statements for Aliza's Merrill Lynch account, meanwhile, were mailed to Sam at ImClone, not to Aliza, and the same pattern of deception was revealed there. In just over two years, he transferred some $1.87 million from Aliza's Merrill account to himself or to companies like iBeauty.com and Scientia Health Group that he controlled.

On December 27, 2001, the most fateful day of his life, Sam told Aliza to sell all of the $2.4 million worth of ImClone stock in her Merrill account. He then transferred the proceeds to yet another account that he had opened in her name with a forged signature and without her knowledge, at First Republic Bank. And after Jack Waksal sold over $8.2 million worth of ImClone stock on December 27 and 28, 2001, Sam had his father transfer $2.85 million to Sam's account about two weeks later.

At Sam's sentencing hearing, Mark Pomerantz declared that Sam had not committed his financial crimes for himself but because he wanted to make sure Aliza's financial needs were met; he also said that Sam "never wanted to sell his own stock because he was a believer in the company."

But these claims, Jim Schachter charged, were "simply inaccurate." Schachter drove home the significance of such clandestine trading: "Dr. Waksal . . . may have been a believer [in ImClone and Erbitux], but he *did* sell stock, and he put it back in his own pocket. And he did it in such a way that investors were deprived of accurate information." Such crimes by a CEO of a publicly traded company, said Schachter, send "the message to investors that the game is rigged; that they are . . . competing against people that have inside information. And that is simply not fair." Waksal's crimes, Schachter added, "strike at the heart of our capital market system."

In a moment of self-pity, or perhaps of self-recognition, Sam told Steve Kroft: "It's very difficult for someone who thinks of himself as someone who does good things for society to be led away in handcuffs and thought about as a common criminal."

# Epilogue

July 22, 2003, the sky was overcast and the air was hot and densely humid in New York City. Large raindrops fell irregularly and spattered on the sidewalk. At 9:00 that morning, Sam Waksal climbed aboard an silver–gold S.U.V. driven by Harlan, and for the next three hours they drove in a south-westerly direction until they reached the town of Minersville, Pennsylvania. Situated in the mountains some 75 miles west of Philadelphia, Minersville is home to the Schuylkill federal prison, a minimum-security facility. Although it lacks the concentric rings of razor wire and towers with tinted glass and guards armed with scoped rifles of standard prisons, it is a bleak place. Before his sentencing, Sam had asked to be sent to the prison at Eglin Air Force Base, a white-collar penitentiary in Florida once rated by *Forbes* as "the best place to be incarcerated," and known as Club Fed for its supposedly easy living conditions. Sam said he had requested Eglin in order to be near his frail and aging parents, who live in Miami. The Bureau of Prisons sent him here, to Schuylkill, instead.

It's "not the worst place to be, but it's certainly not as nice as Eglin," said a lawyer who has had clients sent to Schuylkill. "It's going to get cold up there in the winter."

In the weeks leading up to this day, Sam had struck friends as newly reflective; he appeared to be wrestling with questions of responsibility and mortality. When Tina Brown dropped by the loft to see him, he said, "Do you know how much time one wastes in real life? Answering the phone? Going out to dinner? Trying to get laid?" He told a sardonic

*355*

story about a beautiful woman he had dated who was only interested in travel and presents. After ending the relationship, he walked away feeling guilty. She called out to him, and he turned, expecting tears and recrimination. Instead, the woman reminded him: "The water-ski instructor needs to be paid in cash."

One of his biggest concerns was that he'd grow bored in prison. He told friends that he planned to write an autobiography there, and that he was planning to teach himself Italian and ancient Greek. He also posted a Wish List on Amazon.com, so that friends and family could send him 50 books he had picked out (he wasn't allowed to bring anything with him into jail). The list included novels like *Atlas Shrugged* and *The DaVinci Code,* science-themed biographies like, *Darwin: The Life of a Tormented Evolutionist* and *Einstein: His Life and Times,* Judaica, like the *Kabbalah, Medieval Stereotypes and Modern Antisemitism,* and *Hannah Arendt and the Jewish Question,* and histories like *The Romans,* Herodotus's *Histories,* and Simon Winchester's *Krakatoa: the Day the World Exploded: August 27, 1883.*

One telling choice was Daniel J. Kevles's *The Baltimore Case: A Trial of Politics, Science, and Character*—about one of the most famous scientific scandals of recent years. In 1986, David Baltimore, a Nobel laureate in medicine, coauthored a paper with Thereza Imanishi-Kari on gene transfer in *Cell* magazine; when one of Imanishi-Kari's postdoctoral fellows, Margot O'Toole, could not duplicate their results, she accused Imanishi-Kari of fraud and implicated Baltimore. This touched off a decade-long controversy that split the scientific community and nearly cost the two senior researchers their careers. Ultimately, Imanishi-Kari and Baltimore were exonerated. Did Sam harbor the thought that one day he'd be exonerated, too?

On the eve of his departure for Schuylkill, Sam hosted a going-away party. A group of 40 friends, including the actress Lorraine Bracco and the hairstylist Frederic Fekkai, gathered at the Thompson Street loft to eat a cold buffet of cheeses, pâté, bruschetta, and other delicacies. As party favors, Sam handed out $600 bottles of Château Lafite-Rothschild from his collection, and he and his guests wore red baseball caps emblazoned with a white *S.* When Fekkai offered to send him a bottle of cologne, Sam replied: "Why would I want to smell good? I don't want some inmate coming up and saying, 'I like the way you smell.'" One of Sam's guests that night was an ex-con who was an adviser on prison etiquette. (He advised that to sit down on another inmate's bed is to signal that "you're interested sexually.") Bracco reportedly told Sam that she'd once toured a prison and learned that inmates kept their sanity by engaging in phone sex with their significant others. "There were some very pretty girls at the party," another guest recalled. Sam asked the girls: "If I call you, can we have phone sex?" With a laugh, they answered, "Sure!"

It would be the last party Sam ever threw at his storied apartment: he'd quietly put the loft up for sale at an asking price of $7.99 million.

At the gates of the Schuylkill federal prison, Sam was dressed in a blue blazer, a neatly pressed white shirt, faded blue jeans, white sneakers, and round, John Lennon–style dark glasses. He looked like a movie star on vacation, except for the worry lines in his cheeks and brow. Standing by the chain link and barbed-wire gate, he spoke in a weak voice to a small group of reporters, saying: "I deeply regret the mistakes that have brought me here today, and I'm ready to pay for those mistakes. I only hope that right now I can go on and continue contributing after this in a positive way for society."

Then he turned, hugged his brother, and surrendered to the waiting guards.

He was led inside. Strip-searched. His possessions were inventoried. He underwent psychological and medical screening. Then he reported to his unit and took up residence in an open, barrackslike building with rows of bunk beds and a small locker for each inmate. Soon he began working seven and a half hours a day scrubbing floors and mowing grass, five days a week, starting at 16 cents an hour. With good behavior, he could be released in about six years, when he is 62 years old.

I FIRST MET SAM WAKSAL at 10:00 on the morning of October 5, 2001. I arrived at ImClone's office at 180 Varick Street to interview him for a profile I was writing for *Talk* magazine. At the time, he was an unusual and charismatic biotech entrepreneur with a "breakthrough cancer drug." The story had been suggested by the magazine's editor, Tina Brown, who was a social acquaintance of Sam's and his occasional lunch partner at the Four Seasons. (I would later learn that Harvey Weinstein, one of *Talk*'s major investors, was not only a friend of Sam's but also an investor in ImClone.) Tina told me to "pick Sam's brains about his cancer drug and hot science stories." "He's got a really quick, febrile mind," she said. "He'll put you onto all sorts of stuff." She was right.

We sat in a long, narrow conference room. Sam was humorous and perceptive. He told me about his parents' Holocaust experience, dropped the names of friends like Kofi Annan, and suggested a number of stories I should look into. For instance, Sam said, every spring he and his friend Supreme Court Justice Antonin Scalia would meet in San Marino, Italy, to debate social and ethical issues in science. The talks were held under the auspices of Cardinal Antonini, "the Vatican's man on science." Sam's opinon was: "We're already at the point of Aldus Huxley's *Brave New World*. We can create a class of 'philosopher kings' and a class of betas, who work for the kings and we don't worry about if they aren't that smart."

Sam let it slip that he collected the works of painters like Twombly, deKoonig, and Rothko. He said he was involved in the National Endowment for the Humanities (NEH), with his friend Governor George Pataki. Actually, he *ran* the New York NEH, he said. And he was about to become president of the New York Biotech Association, too. Sam invited me to join him and a group of really interesting friends to drink wine and have a stimulating discussion at the next of the literary salons he held in his loft.

I left the building thinking that I had never met anyone quite like Sam Waksal. He was smart, funny, attentive, maybe a little odd but in a lively polymath kind of way. He was the kind of extraordinary person you meet in New York once in a while, the kind that make the hassle of the city worth it. I doubt I'd have been able to put this into words at that moment, but my general sense was that he had opened a door into an exclusive club, an inner sanctum, and, with an arm around my shoulder, had invited me inside. When I got back to my office and went over my notes I was dismayed to realize that Sam had spent the entire hour talking about everything *but* ImClone and Erbitux.

Since then, I've spoken to Sam Waksal at least a dozen times. I've interviewed him in his office, watched him charm a roomful of biotech analysts, run into him at one of the several parties he attended each week, and had numerous telephone conversations with him. I've also witnessed him take the Fifth Amendment before Congress, plead guilty to tax evasion, and duck out of his sentencing hearing with an electronic monitoring bracelet strapped around his ankle. After all that has happened, it is easy to demonize Sam Waksal from a distance, but the flesh-and-blood person was not so easy to write off. I witnessed flashes of his temper, and others have told me that he can be shockingly mean and vindictive, but he was nearly always gracious and entertaining with me.

In October 2001, when we first met, the news about ImClone and Erbitux was only positive. I had no reason to question his bona fides until the day he thrust a copy of his Ph.D. dissertation on me, along with his ImClone résumé. The dissertation, entitled *In Vitro Studies on Thymus Derived Lymphocytes: Differentiation of T-Lymphocytes and Their Function in Tumor Destruction,* ran 83 pages long, was neatly typed on onionskin paper, and came in a red leather binder with gold lettering. I hadn't asked for it, and tried to return it because it was dense with scientific jargon unsuitable for a general interest magazine. But Sam insisted I take it, and so I did. In retrospect, I have wondered if this apparently innocent gesture was in fact a challenge: "Catch me if you can."

Reading through the dissertation I noticed that it listed a different birthdate—September 8, 1947—than was listed on Sam's ImClone curriculum vitae, which said he'd been born on September 8, 1949. A company spokesman said the two-year difference was "probably a typo," and I laughed off the discrepancy. Many people lie about their age. But months later, after I had learned to question everything Sam Waksal said, I'd look back at his conflicting birth dates as the moment of peripeteia, the first hint that there was a different version of Sam Waksal than the one he had presented to the public. The next hint came with my discovery that he was actually raised in Dayton, not Toledo, Ohio. If he had lied about his birth date and his hometown, I wondered, then what about the more complicated subjects of science, finance, and the law in which he was involved? I began to call the people and institutions listed on Sam's résumé.

One of the first people I reached was Dr. Len Herzenberg, in whose Stanford University lab Sam had worked as a research associate in 1974. "Sam Waksal? A brilliant man, but he's not trustworthy," Len said. His wife, Lee Herzenberg, joined the conversation, and for the next 45 minutes they told me story after story about Sam Waksal. As I worked my way through Sam's résumé, I spoke to many people who had known him 10, 20, 30 years ago. Everyone had a story about him, some good and some not. Several people laughed outright when I called. "Sam Waksal! I haven't talked to him in thirty years, but I still think about him all the time," said one person. "He's not the kind you easily forget."

I am not a scientist, and I lack the expertise to critique the Waksals' pronouncements on ImClone's products, but I can report with some authority on the experiences of scientists and others who have worked with Sam and Harlan. I have interviewed more people involved with Im-Clone than any other journalist. And they made it clear that Sam's vigorous self-promotion frequently skirted, and sometimes crossed, the boundary separating fact from fiction.

In her controversial book *The Journalist and the Murderer,* Janet Malcolm writes:

> Every journalist who is not too stupid or too full of himself to notice what is going on knows that what he does is morally indefensible. He is a kind of confidence man, preying on people's vanity, ignorance, or loneliness, gaining their trust and betraying them without remorse. Like the credulous widow who wakes up one day to find the charming young man and all her savings gone, so the consenting subject of a piece of nonfiction writing learns—when the article or book appears—*his* hard lesson.

While this may sometimes be true, Sam Waksal demonstrated that the opposite can also be true: sometimes it is the subject of an article or book who is revealed to be, "a kind of confidence man, preying on people's vanity, ignorance, or loneliness, gaining their trust and betraying them."

Like all charmers, Waksal was adept at sensing the strengths and weaknesses of others; he tapped into deep human longings—the desire for life, the desire to help another person, the desire for attention or power or riches—and manipulated them for his own ends. In doing so, he managed to lay bare many of humanity's deepest impulses, and to tell us more about ourselves than we generally care to admit.

Ultimately, he wanted more than scientific acclaim, his photo in all the magazines, an invite to every party, and his name on the lips of every financier in the country. He wanted the world to admire and respect him—to love him.

In a letter to Judge Pauley, Cindy Nash wrote of her ex-husband: "Sam's place in the family and its tragic history have been both a blessing that inspired his strengths and a burden that placed huge obstacles in his path and contributed to his human flaws, one of which is a deep insecurity."

Sam has said of himself: "One of my great faults is I refused to deal with the everyday details that people have to deal with to make sure mistakes aren't made. And I think there may have been an arrogance where I didn't have to deal with details—that these details were meant for other people, not for me."

His fibs metastasized. Then they consumed him.

When I asked him about some of the less complimentary things I'd heard, Sam swatted away questions about the RTF, the many lawsuits against him, and his unhappy career in academia as if they were just minor annoyances. But when I asked about Harlan's cocaine bust, Sam turned bright red and angry; and when I asked if Sam had impersonated Harlan and done his rounds at the Tufts Medical Center, he grew cold and withdrawn. When I asked about the future of Erbitux, he suddenly brightened again.

I was in the midst of "closing" my story for *Talk* magazine in January 2002 when two things happened: Paul Goldberg printed excerpts of the FDA's RTF letter in *The Cancer Letter,* which set the ImClone crisis in motion, and *Talk* magazine suddenly folded. Luckily for me, Graydon Carter, the editor of *Vanity Fair,* picked up my orphaned story and encouraged me to keep reporting. (The resulting article, "Investigating ImClone," ran in the June 2002 issue of that magazine.) *Vanity Fair* arrived on newsstands in late May, just before Martha Stewart's name was linked to insider-trading charges, and just before the first congressional hearing into ImClone opened. By midsummer new revelations about Sam were appearing on a regular basis, and the ImClone story surged ahead with an increasingly destructive momentum.

By the time I returned to the subject for this book, in February 2003, much had changed. Sam had pled guilty to 8 of the government's 15 counts; Harlan was ImClone's CEO; Bristol was tightening its grip on the Erbitux development program; the prognosis for the drug's rehabilitation at the FDA was good, although investor expectations had been scaled back from the wild hopes of 2001; and Martha Stewart's alleged insider trading of ImClone stock had begun to dominate the news coverage.

IN THE FALL OF 2003, Bristol-Myers announced that its third-quarter profits had more than doubled from the year before. Peter Dolan was optimistic about Bristol's new slate of drugs, and said he hoped Erbitux would be green-lighted by the FDA in mid-February 2004. But the short-term good news masked a clutch of significant problems. In March 2003, Bristol-Myers admitted that it had engaged in "inappropriate accounting" for years: sales from 1999 to 2002 had been inflated by as much as $3.35 billion, while earnings had been inflated by $900 million; the company recanted its handling of many restructuring charges and asset sales since 1997. In 2001, Bristol engaged in "channel stuffing"—the practice of enticing wholesalers to buy more drugs than they needed; the tactic backfired the following year when wholesalers' purchase of BMS drugs dropped sharply.

In early 2003, agents from the Department of Justice, the SEC, the FBI, and the U.S. Postal Service quietly began interviewing more than 100 Bristol employees and former employees about Bristol's accounting practices. It was one of the first investigations—along with an inquiry into hospital chain HealthSouth—to be undertaken using the tough new antifraud statues of the Sarbanes-Oxley Act, which requires company leaders to swear to the accuracy of their financial reports under pain of severe penalties.

According to *The New York Times,* investigators seized Bristol documents, culled e-mail messages, and asked retirees pointed questions about four key players: Richard J. Lane (a former president of the BMS medicine business), Frederick Schiff (a former BMS CFO), Charles Heimbold, and Peter Dolan.

Rick Lane was dismissed from Bristol in 2002 for undisclosed reasons; later named CEO of a generic drugmaker in Florida, he refused to talk to the press. Fred Schiff, Bristol's former CFO, was also forced out; after being named CFO of a medical equipment maker in New Jersey, Schiff was sued by his predecessor there, who alleged accounting irregularities.

A spokeswoman for Charles Heimbold, the U.S. ambassador to Sweden, said: "Mr. Heimbold flatly denies any suggestion or innuendo that he participated in any inappropriate conduct," at Bristol. "During his tenure as chairman and CEO, no one at the company ever gave Mr. Heimbold any reason to believe that the company's accounting was erroneous or inappropriate in any way."

In 2002, Heimbold's protégé Peter Dolan revised Bristol's earnings estimates five times: in August, he swore that Bristol's financial statements were accurate; in October he disavowed those statements. Bristol insiders have said that Dolan was acutely aware of the company's channel-stuffing efforts. Moreover, Dolan was forced to write down nearly all of Bristol's investment in ImClone thus far. Meanwhile, twenty-nine state attorneys general had sued Bristol-Myers over Taxol, alleging that BMS's ferocious legal defense of its market exclusivity for the drug had violated federal antitrust statutes. In April 2003, the company announced it would pay $55 million, some to each state, to settle the charges. This was part of a much larger, $670 million settlement the company worked out to settle allegations that it unfairly delayed generic competition for Taxol and the antianxiety drug BuSpar.

Many have wondered how Peter Dolan managed to keep his job. Close observers noted that the real power on the Bristol-Myers board was Louis V. Gerstner Jr., whose aggressive accounting techniques at IBM resulted in his own well-publicized skirmishes with regulators. Although the Bristol board publicly expressed support for its CEO, Dolan was pilloried in the press and on Wall Street. James J. Cramer, the stockbroker and effusive media personality, labeled BMS "a suspect enterprise," accused Dolan of "accounting gimmickry," and called on the board to "ax him."

Dolan retreated from view for nine months. Finally, on April 29, 2003, he held a conference call with securities analysts. Sounding relatively chipper, Dolan maintained that BMS was moving "toward what I see as a business-as-usual period." Many of his listeners, however, weren't swayed. "You're listening to him on the one hand and thinking on the other that he's the subject of a major criminal investigation," Barbara Ryan, an analyst at Deutsche Bank Securities, confided to *The New York Times*. "That certainly doesn't help rebuild credibility."

As of this writing, the SEC's Wells Notice against ImClone remains unresolved. The company's financial reserves are not deep, and it has been through a major internal shake-up; it does not have a permanent CEO or a chairman of the board.

On Monday, September 15, ImClone held its 2003 annual meeting at its manufacturing facility in Somerville, New Jersey. It had been two years, almost to the day, since the biotech company had signed its landmark deal with BMS to develop and market John Mendelsohn's cancer drug. At the meeting, ImClone issued its latest proxy statement, and Dan Lynch, the company's acting CEO, and David Kies, the company's lead director, announced a few changes. First and foremost was that Dr.

John Mendelsohn, who had served on the ImClone board since 1998, had decided to leave the company. Mendelsohn had not been held responsible for the scandal, and insiders said that they had encouraged him to stay because he lent ImClone credibility. But he had decided not to stand for reelection. Mendelsohn's departure seemed curious, but the father of Erbitux said, "It was my idea. I have a big agenda here at M. D. Anderson and I want to focus my attention on that." He was confident that ImClone was righting itself, and remained cautiously optimistic that the FDA would approve Erbitux soon. "Whatever the FDA decides, there's still a *lot* of work to be done on this drug. There's going to be more bumps in the road, but in my small way I helped bring stability to ImClone and now I want to concentrate on new opportunities. The big challenge now is to identify the right patients for the right [targeted treatments]."

Reflecting on his long and arduous quest to "get Erbitux into patients," Mendelsohn said: "I'm the kind of guy who chooses to take on things I can get really committed to. I make mistakes. I don't do everything perfectly. I'm sure there are people who are not happy with all of my decisions. But I do approach things with the idea that I want to make it a better world."

Over the next several days, Mendelsohn's decision was widely reported on, but what was not picked up was that other members of ImClone's old guard had also left the company. Paul Kopperl, who had been one of the witnesses at ImClone's congressional hearing, did not stand for reelection to the board. Nor did Dr. Arnold Levine, a respected oncologist. In 2002 Levine had stepped down as the head of Rockefeller University due to "health reasons," although the tabloids revealed that he'd had a drunken fling with an attractive grad student. (She confirmed the rumors and posed provocatively for the newspapers' cameras.) ImClone's corporate attorney, John Landes, had been replaced. And his lieutenant, the vice president for legal affairs Catherine Vaczy, had also left the company.

By the fall of 2003, all of ImClone's founders and most of its long-serving senior executives were gone. The new regime had strengthened its corporate governance and internal auditing measures. The board, which once counted nine directors, now had six, including two new directors, including a former PriceWaterhouseCoopers CPA.

ImClone's lead director, David Kies, promised that from now on the company would "provide the highest standards of corporate management and governance."

ON AUGUST 14, 2003, New York City was dimmed and thrown into confusion by a blackout that rippled across much of the eastern seaboard. That day, Bristol-Myers and ImClone refiled the Erbitux application with the FDA; the package included data from the Merck KGaA trial in Europe. (Because of the power outage, they were unable to e-mail the reams of documentation to the FDA, and had to truck stacks of CDs to the agency in Washington, D.C.) This started a six-month regulatory clock ticking: the FDA was required to rule on the drug by no later than February 13, 2004.

On October 10, the same day that Jack Waksal was sued by the SEC for insider trading, BMS and ImClone issued a press release stating that the FDA had accepted the companies' biologic license application for Erbitux (meaning that the data was complete), and that the application would be reviewed for accelerated approval.

Many people believe that Sam Waksal will be proven right about one thing, at least: Erbitux will be accepted by the FDA, will prove itself capable of helping thousands of very sick cancer patients, and will soon earn millions, if not billions, of dollars a year.

I hope this dream comes true. Nevertheless, significant questions remain. Will the latest data package prove convincing to the FDA? Does ImClone have patent protection for Erbitux as a single agent, or only as a combination therapy? Having lost a two-year lead on competing therapies, like Avastin and Tarceva, how will Erbitux fare once they all come to market? (ImClone's drug works differently than the others, and it is possible that Erbitux could be used in combination with one or more of them.)

IN THE SPRING OF 2002, Shannon Kellum had described ImClone as "a fairy tale that turned into a nightmare." The scandal had saddened and concerned her. "I'm in shock," she said. "Erbitux is a miracle drug for some people. But now I feel like after all the hard work we're going *backwards.* We really don't want that." Her oncologist, Dr. Mark Rubin, had recently discovered a tumor on her spine, she said. Shannon continued to use Erbitux and tried to remain upbeat, but said she was feeling "very, very nervous." Then she added, "I'll do everything I can to get this drug approved."

I spoke to her again in mid-June. Shannon said she was feeling good and that she planned to do some traveling over the summer. In September, I sent Shannon an e-mail (she had wanted to help write this book). The e-mail bounced back. I called her office and a pleasant woman said: "I'm sorry, she no longer works here," and transferred me to Human Resources. When I asked the woman in HR how to reach Shannon Kellum there was a long pause; then she sighed, and said, "I'm sorry to tell you that Shannon is . . . she's, uh . . . she passed away."

I mumbled something, and glanced down in sadness.

Shannon Kellum died on August 12, 2002. She was 32 years old. This time, Shannon did not make national headlines. Her local newspaper ran a brief obituary. Two months later the *Miami Herald* ran an article about her. When the *Herald* called ImClone, the company released a statement under Harlan's name: "We were sad to hear that Shannon passed away. . . . She showed great strength with her fight against cancer, and the company is proud of the role that Erbitux played in that fight."

The news of Shannon's death came as a shock but not a complete surprise. She suffered from a particularly deadly form of cancer. She had been extremely brave and determined, had been an inspiration for many other cancer patients—especially young ones, and had made the most of her situation. Although Shannon had arguably saved Erbitux, it did not save her in the end. She accepted this and harbored no bitterness. She credited the drug with extending her life far beyond what others had believed was possible. "It's the only thing that worked for me," she said many times.

Thelma Hinkle, Shannon's mother, said: "She was working right up to a month or two before she died. [Erbitux] didn't have many side effects. . . . She was at the end of her rope. I think the drug gave her some extra time."

I called Shannon's oncologist, Dr. Mark Rubin, to express my condolences, and to discover how and why Shannon's health had taken a sudden turn for the worse. But Dr. Rubin had retreated behind a mysterious wall of silence. Perhaps Shannon had asked him to keep the details of her waning days private, or perhaps he had simply had enough of talking about ImClone and Erbitux.

*Epilogue*

One of the last things Shannon said to me was: "Maybe the Waksals do have a shady past, but let's look at the *drug*. We know it works. It's just not available. Meanwhile people are dying—young and old—all because they couldn't get it quick enough. That seems like such a miniscule excuse to us patients. It's *sad*. When you have cancer, the last thing you have is time."

# *Notes*

Most of this book is based on the hours of interviews I conducted with the people named in these pages. The vast majority of these interviews were conducted on the record; some interviews were conducted on a not-for-attribution basis, but with the understanding that the text could reflect facts, observations, or events that the interviewee was privy to. Most of these interviews were tape-recorded and I have written notes of all of them. I also reviewed countless court documents, including transcripts of court proceedings, phone records, grand jury indictments, and internal company e-mails or memos collected during the government's investigations of ImClone. In addition, I read many news reports, from the *New York Post* to *Chemical Engineering & News,* relating to Erbitux, the Waksals, Bristol-Myers, and Martha Stewart.

My descriptions of a person's state of mind came from the person to whom it is attributed, either from an interview or sworn testimony. Quotations came from the speaker, someone who heard the remark, or from notes, recordings, and transcripts. In disputed cases I have sometimes included more than one version of events. I have attempted to use anonymous quotations only when absolutely necessary.

The investigations of ImClone by the Department of Justice, Securities and Exchange Commission, and Federal Bureau of Investigation were very thorough and provide an excellent resource. An especially good overview of the case, and many surprising details, can be gleaned in the hearing transcripts and full investigative report of "An Inquiry Into the ImClone Cancer-Drug Story" conducted by the House Committee on Energy and Commerce's Subcommittee on Oversight and Investigations of the 170th Congress (hereafter, the House subcommittee report). The full report is available at: http://www.access.gpo.gov/congress/house.

## Prologue

In the fall of 2001 I spent considerable time observing and talking to Sam Waksal, and heard him give several versions of his standard pitch: "Erbitux is going to be *huge*. It will alter the way cancer therapy is done from now on . . . it will be a $1 billion-a-year drug."

Details of the phone calls and stock trades made by members of the Waksal family and Martha Stewart were made public in various court filings, including: *Securities and Exchange Commission v. Samuel D. Waksal,* United States District Court, Southern District of New York (March 11, 2003) (hereafter, *SEC v. Sam Waksal*); and in the grand jury indictment, *United States of America v. Samuel Waksal,* United States District Court, Southern District of New York (hereafter, *USA v. Sam Waksal*); and in the grand jury indictment *United States of America v. Martha Stewart and Peter Bacanovic,* United States District Court, Southern District of New York (hereafter, *USA v. Stewart and Bacanovic*).

Details of how Sam Waksal established nominee accounts in Aliza Waksal's name, and how he repeatedly had her signature forged, are in "Government's Memorandum in Opposition to Defendant's Memorandum in Aid of Sentencing," from *USA v. Sam Waksal,* filed June 10, 2003, by James B. Comey, United States Attorney, Southern District of New York, attorney for the United States of America (hereafter, the opposition memo).

Several articles described how on December 26, 2001, Sam learned that an RTF letter was likely while he was on St. Bart's and flew back to New York City. See, for example, "What Martha Knew," *New York,* July 8, 2002, pp. 23–27.

In an interview with CBS's *60 Minutes* that aired October 5, 2003, Sam Waksal indicated his state of mind on December 27, 2001: "I was arrogant enough at the time to believe that I could cut corners . . . I didn't think I was going to get caught at all."

# PART ONE: THE $2 BILLION ANTIBODY

## Chapter One. Cancer Cells Are Smart

Although I have never met Dr. John Mendelsohn in person, I have interviewed him by phone several times. He provided biographical and physical details, fact-checked my writing on the antibody C225 (Erbitux), explained his feelings at various moments in time, corrected a number of things that had been written about him in the past, and gave me a brief tutorial on cancer research.

For descriptions of the party at the Zweig apartment, I relied on Mendelsohn, as well as "The Birth of a Cancer Drug," *Business Week*, July 9, 2001.

There has been much written on the history of the biotech industry, and in compiling an overview I consulted a wide range of material. Especially useful were two books: Robert Teitelman, *Gene Dreams: Wall Street, Academia, and the Rise of Biotechnology* (New York: Basic Books, 1989), and Stephen S. Hall, *A Commotion in the Blood: Life, Death, and the Immune System* (New York: Henry Holt and Company, 1997). I am indebted to Karin Duncker at the New York Biotechnology Association, and Mitch Gipson, Executive Director of the Audubon Business and Technology Center at Columbia University, for steering me to valuable reference material.

## Chapter Two. The Idea of the New

For the story of Genentech and my continuing overview of biotech, I relied on the sources mentioned above, especially Teitelman, from which much of the discussion of interferon is drawn (Teitelman, *Gene Dreams,* pp. 27–35).

*Life* magazine on interferon is from Hall, *A Commotion in the Blood,* p. 178, as are the observations of Charles Weissmann, Ibid, pp. 184–5, and the story of A. J. Goertz, Ibid, pp. 203–5.

Characterization of Sam and Harlan in the early 1980s comes from my interviews of Sam, his friends and colleagues, and news accounts.

Jack and Sabina Waksal's experience in the Holocaust is taken from *USA v. Sam Waksal:* Memorandum on Behalf of Samuel Waksal in Aid of Sentencing, filed by Waksal's Attorney, Mark Pomerantz, of Paul,

Weiss, Rifkind, Wharton & Garrison, LLP, June 10, 2003 (hereafter, Waksal memo).

Sam told me the story of Jack fighting with "the Polish resistance" and hiding under a corpse in a stone sarcophagus during World War II; but none of his friends recalled this story, and it is not mentioned in the Waksal memo. Jack Waksal and his attorney did not return calls seeking clarification.

Norma Robert, one of Sam's old friends, recalled seeing a blue concentration camp tattoo on Sabina's arm. All information about Norma is from my interview with her, March 17, 2003.

Sabina Waksal's "strange sense of humor," from my interview with Sam.

The stories that Sam and Harlan told at ImClone about their upbringing were recounted by a former ImClone colleague.

Shirley Flacks, from my interview.

Dr. Marcus Engelman, from my interview.

All of the information about Elizabeth Latham (hereafter, Latham) and her relationship with Sam and Harlan comes from my interview with her.

Dr. Irv Weissman, from my interview with him.

Lee and Len Herzenberg from my numerous conversations with them, both on the phone and in person, 2001–03.

Dr. Boyse, from Geeta Anand, "Four Prestigious Labs Ousted Waksal for Questionable Work," *The Wall Street Journal,* September 27, 2002 (hereafter, *WSJ* ).

Dr. William Terry of the NCI. Ibid.

Dr. Robert Schwartz of the Tufts University School of Medicine, Ibid.

Sam at the Tufts lab and "Disco Techs," from my interviews of people who worked with him at Tufts.

Dr. Schwartz, "Watch out for Waksal . . . creating an illusion" in Anand, "Four Prestigious Labs Ousted Waksal for Questionable Work," *WSJ,* September 27, 2002.

Sheldon Wolff at Tufts, Ibid.

Alexandra and Constantine Bona; Sam's file at Mount Sinai is sealed under a confidentiality agreement and Dr. Sherman Kupfer in Ibid.

Sam "big fights at Mount Sinai . . . arrogant and abrasive," in Edward Wyatt, "Outside the Lab: Biotech CEO's Lifestyle Raises Investor Eyebrows," *Barron's,* June 28, 1993, p. 14 (hereafter, *Barron's*).

Dr. Stave Kohtz, from my interview.

Sam on therapy, from my interview.

"Institutionally we're under the gun," from Anand, "Four Prestigious Labs Ousted Waksal for Questionable Work," *WSJ,* September 27, 2002.

Naming the company "ImClone," from my interview.

Harlan on "make some products, get rich, and retire early," from Catherine Arnst, "The Birth of a Cancer Drug," *BusinessWeek,* July 9, 2001.


## Chapter Three. Family Business

I interviewed Martha Stewart on November 7, 2001. Once she was implicated in the ImClone scandal, however, her lawyers refused to allow me to talk to her. She has been the subject of many articles and, more recently, legal filings. For background on her, I consulted Jerry Oppenheimer, *Martha Stewart—Just Desserts: The Unauthorized Biography* (New York: William Morrow and Company, Inc., 1997) and Christopher Byron, *Martha Inc.: The Incredible Story of Martha Stewart Living Omnimedia* (New York: John Wiley & Sons, Inc., 2002).

Martha met Sam at a charity event, from Oppenheimer, *Martha Stewart—Just Desserts,* p. 333.

John Landes refused to return my calls. Background on him, from informed sources and his congressional testimony; the House subcommittee report.

Norma Robert, from my interview. Years later, Sam would arrange a rapprochement with Norma, by hosting her 60th birthday in his loft and footing the bill for the party. "He was very nice; he didn't say anything about the fight," she said.

That Sam initially ran ImClone out of his apartment and an office at 9 West 57th Street is the recollection of a person who worked at ImClone in its early days.

Robert Goldhammer refused to return my calls. Observations about Goldhammer, from my interviews with people close to ImClone.

Information on Hugh and Charles Dunn comes from former ImClone employees. Charles Dunn's $3.88 million from the exercise of

ImClone stock options in 2001 is drawn from the House subcommittee report, p. 306.

The ethos of Genentech, Swanson, and Boyer is taken from various sources, including Teitelman, *Gene Dreams.* Genentech "Clone or Die" T-shirts, from Hall, *A Commotion in the Blood,* p. 191.

ImClone's first three products, from interviews with former Im-Clone employees.

Lee Compton, from my interviews.

Merck KGaA's $14 million deal for IL6 is mentioned in filings and press releases on the company's Web site, www.imclone.com. It is also mentioned in a letter from John Landes to Sherwood Weiser dated April 23, 1991, reprinted in the House subcommittee report, p. 318. A former employee told me about Sam's ill-fated trip to Germany.

Ian Alterman, from my interview.

Characterization of Harlan Waksal, from informed sources.

I spoke to Alexis Stewart about Sam Waksal on December 12, 2001. Like her mother, Alexis has been the subject of many articles, and her relationship with Sam is mentioned in both Oppenheimer, *Martha Stewart—Just Desserts,* and Byron, *Martha Inc.* Former ImClone employees were the source for some of my stories about Sam and Alexis.

Andy Stewart left Martha for her personal assistant (Robin Fairclough), from Byron, *Martha Inc,* p. 117.

Sam put Alexis up in an apartment, from Lauren Barack and Katy Byron, "Martha & Sam: The Inside Story," *New York Post,* June 15, 2003 (hereafter, *NY Post*).

"Dr. Waksal's" medical note for Alexis in filings for *USA v. Sam Waksal.*

Peter Bacanovic's lawyers would not allow me to interview him. However, Bacanovic did answer some of the questions I posed in an e-mail sent through an intermediary. Like Martha and Alexis Stewart, Bacanovic has been the subject of numerous articles.

Brad Gooch, from Landon Thomas Jr. and Beth Landman Keil, "Who Knew?" *New York,* July 8, 2002, pp. 22–27.

"Seminal discoveries in science," from my interview.

Information on ImClone's alliances with American Home Products and Abbott Laboratories from the ImClone Web site, www.imclone.com.

*Family Business* directed by Sidney Lumet is based on the novel by Vincent Patrick, released in 1989. Waksal, from my interview.

In June 1986, Sam Waksal forged Harlan Waksal and John Landes' signatures on the "Woody" Weiser stock certificate. Correspondence and Sam's affidavit is reprinted in the House subcommittee report, pp. 309–21.

Testimony of Harlan Waksal, Goldhammer, and Landes, from the House subcommittee hearing on October 10, 2002; transcripts printed in Ibid.

"Crazy thing to do," from *USA v. Waksal.*

Elana Castaneda, from my interview.

Charles Antell, from the case file, *Charles Antell v. Samuel Waksal,* Supreme Court of the State of New York. Includes court filings, Sam's handwritten note, and a copy of the bounced check for $85,000.

"Evidence of falsified scientific results," from my interviews of a former ImClone manager. Harlan Waksal refused to return my phone calls to corroborate this story.

Solomon Brothers anecdote, from my interview with a former Im-Clone employee.

The company was facing bankruptcy in 1992, from my conversations with Sam Waksal and several former ImClone employees.

## Chapter Four. The "Miracle"

Description of the breakfast meeting of April 1992 and subsequent recollections, from my interviews of Sam Waksal and John Mendelsohn.

Chugai deal, from ImClone documents and my interview of a former ImClone scientist.

Pyramidal crystal paperweight engraved with the SAS motto: from my observation of the items in a cabinet at the ImClone offices; Sam was proud to tell me about his jumbled collection of Roman oil lamps, ancient Jewish coins, signed baseballs, and the crystal paperweight.

Sam was caught with his hand in the till, from my interview with an informed source. Goldhammer did not return my call.

Antiangiogenesis and the work of Dr. Judah Folkman, from Gina Kolata, "Hope in the Lab: A Cautious Awe Greets Drugs That Eradicate Tumors in Mice," *The New York Times,* May 4, 1998, p. A-1 (hereafter, *NYT*). Reaction to the Kolata story from David Shaw, "Overdose of Optimism: A Case Study in How a Story Can Set Off a Frenzy," *The Los Angeles Times,* February 13, 2000, p. A-29 (hereafter, *LA Times*).

Sam rewrote a press release in the mid-1990s, from my interview of a former ImClone employee.

Dr. Mendelsohn at M. D. Anderson, from my interviews with Mendelsohn, supplemented by Jim Atkinson, "Miracle Workers," *Texas Monthly,* September 2002, and Geeta Anand, "Ties to Two Tainted Firms Haunt Top Doctor in Houston," *WSJ* December 12, 2002.

Sam declared the 1994 ASCO meeting was "pivotal," from my interview.

Dr. John Mendelsohn reacted to this comment, from my interview.

Harlan's "Make or break" and "We could have licensed (C225) . . . following our lead," from an informed source.

The Waksals felt insulted by low bids from Big Pharma, from Arnst, "The Birth of a Cancer Drug," *BusinessWeek,* July 9, 2001.

The Waksals' optimistic claims about ImClone's science, from an informed source. Harlan refused to return my phone calls.

Cadus Pharmaceuticals has been mentioned in many articles about Sam Waksal, Carl Icahn, Martha Stewart, and ImClone; Bart Pasternak has also been mentioned in such articles. See, for example, Christopher Byron, "Martha Spins a Web," *NY Post,* July 3, 2002.

Carl Icahn and Princeton, from a Princeton news release, "Icahn Family Foundation Gives $20 Million for New Genomics Laboratory," Princeton University Office of Communications, October 21, 1999.

Harlan, "I was sure that . . . have the money," from Arnst, "The Birth of a Cancer Drug," *BusinessWeek,* July 9, 2001.

Sam, "end of ImClone," from my interviews with him.

I spoke to Shannon Kellum perhaps seven or eight times over the course of 2001–02, and the information here came from those interviews. The outlines of Kellum's story have been told in numerous articles, such as Arnst, "The Birth of a Cancer Drug," *BusinessWeek,* July 9, 2001. (NB: while generally excellent, this article got one important fact wrong: Shannon Kellum was never made "free of" cancer, as the article claimed.)

Colorectal cancer facts, from news clippings and the American Cancer Society. A good resource on the subject is the Colon Cancer Alliance at: www.ccalliance.org.

I spoke to Dr. Mark Rubin three times in November 2001, and the information here is taken from those conversations. In preparing this book I called him numerous times in 2003, in an attempt to fact-check and clarify; for reasons that remain unclear, he never returned my calls. I wish he had. Previously, Rubin's work with Shannon Kellum had received much media attention: the doctor and his patient were the focus of Tim Friend's "New Drug Targets Cancer Cells," *USA Today,* May 22, 2000; the next day they appeared together on ABC News's *Good Morning America,* where they were interviewed by Diane Sawyer, May 23, 2000.

## Chapter Five. Small and One-Armed

ImClone's declining reputation and financial state, from informed sources; also in Wyatt, "Outside the Lab: Biotech CEO's Lifestyle Raises Investor Eyebrows," *Barron's,* June 28, 1993.

The unprecedented nature of ImClone's Study 9923 is detailed in the House subcommittee hearings and report. See the report and testimony of Ray Weiss and the testimony of Richard Pazdur, June 13, 2002.

Much has been written on the history of the Food and Drug Administration (FDA). For this account I relied on the voluminous material on the agency's Web site, www.fda.gov, various news articles, and in the useful Philip J. Hilts, *Protecting America's Health: The FDA, Business, and One Hundred Years of Regulation* (New York: Alfred A. Knopf, 2003).

Morris Fishbein and cancer quacks, from www.quackwatch.org, a site devoted to exposing medical quackery—including cancer cure charlatans like Harry M. Hoxsey.

Congressman John Dingell's 1989 hearings into the FDA, the rise of David A. Kessler as FDA commissioner, and the Kessler-Gingrich battle over the agency are detailed in Hilts, *Protecting America's Health,* pp. 255–337.

Greenwood, Ibid.

Description of ImClone's visit to the FDA in August 2000 was culled from congressional testimony by FDA and ImClone personnel, as detailed in the House subcommittee report. Pazdur, from his testimony, June 13, 2002. Also see Stacey Schultz, "The Drug That Could Have Been," *U.S. News & World Report,* August 19, 2002.

Ruth-Ann Santino and Amy Cohen, from Lesley Stahl, "Controversial 'Compassionate Use,' " CBS's *60 Minutes;* air date May 6, 2001. Transcript available online.

Details about Ruth-Ann Santino, from my interviews of Fred Santino.

Sam's "Compassionate use is a very difficult topic for ImClone," from my interviews.

Harlan described the *60 Minutes* segment as "very negative" in his congressional testimony on June 13, 2002: see the House subcommittee report, p. 90.

Jane Reese-Coulbourne, from my interview.

Mark Pomerantz, from testimony in *USA v. Sam Waksal* and Sam's sentencing hearing on June 6, 2003.

Pharmaceutical industry statistics, from several news clippings, such as David Leonhardt, "Health Care As Main Engine: Is That So Bad?" *NYT,* November 11, 2001; or Gardiner Harris, "Why Drug Makers Are Failing in Quest for New Blockbusters," *WSJ,* April 18, 2002.

That BMS considered licensing C225 for $100,000, from an informed source.

I interviewed Bristol-Myers Squibb's Brian Markison by phone on December 11, 2001; after that conversation he, and indeed everyone at BMS, refused to return my calls.


## Chapter Six. A Very High-Risk Opportunity

The history of Bristol-Myers Squibb was taken from the company's Web site, www.bms.com, and various news clippings. Facts about the company in 1984, from Teitelman, *Gene Dreams,* pp. 143–5.

Discussion of cytotoxic chemotherapies, and Dr. Stephen Carter's work, in Ibid, p. 146.

Description of Taxol, and the work of Mansukh Wani and Munroe Wall, from Linda Raber, "Anticancer Research Honored at RTI," *Chemical Engineering & News,* May 19, 2003 at: http://pubs.acs.org/cen/acsnews/8120/8120acsnews.html.

Tom Jordan at BMS, work on Taxol, from my interview of Tom Jordan and an informed source. Taxol facts at: www.bms.com.

Stephen Carter memo from an informed source.

Because Taxol has proven the best-selling cancer drug in history, and because of controversy over how the NIH allowed BMS to develop it, and BMS's ferocious legal defense of its exclusivity to the drug, many articles have been written about Taxol. See, for instance, Maggie Fox, "U.S. Government 'Gave Away' Cancer Drug—Senator," Reuters, June 6, 2003.

Bristol's Physician Advisory Board, from an informed source.

Squibb Corporation, from www.bms.com.

Peter Dolan background, from Gardiner Harris, "Bristol-Myers Names Peter Dolan as CEO," *WSJ*, February 8, 2001; Greg Winter and Reed Abelson, "The Optimist Leading Bristol-Myers," *NYT*, May 12, 2002. Dolan did not return my calls seeking clarification.

BMS insiders warning about Taxol since 1994, from an informed source.

OSI Pharmaceuticals, from my interview with Dr. Colin Goddard, osip.com, and numerous articles. See Geeta Anand, "Best 3-Year Performer, OSI Pharmaceuticals," *WSJ*.

The process by which Bristol and ImClone negotiated their history-making deal came to light in various legal filings, including an SEC Schedule 14D-9, filed September 28, 2001, that explains in great detail the history of the transaction (www.sec.gov/edgar.shtml).

Len Saltz's presentation at ASCO on May 3, 2001, made headlines, such as Adam Feuerstein, "ImClone's Spot at the Podium May Be a Tip-Off It Has a Cancer Drug Hit," *theStreet.com*, April 4, 2001.

Congressman Dan Burton chaired the hearing, "Compassionate Use of Investigational New Drugs: Is the Current Process Effective?" before the Committee on Government Reform, of the 107th Congress, on June 20, 2001. (transcript at: www.house.gov/reform).

Sam Waksal was the only drug company executive to testify that day (he claimed that ImClone had terminated its compassionate-use program in January 2001, although as *60 Minutes* and others revealed he continued to make Erbitux available to certain people after then). And while other cancer treatments, like Iressa and Gleevec, were mentioned in the hearing, Erbitux was highlighted in the testimony. Indeed, Shannon Kellum, who was ImClone's star colon cancer patient, said: "if it was not for C225, I would not be here right now . . . we need to get this drug approved." Other cancer patients and the families of cancer victims also testified that day, including Fred Santino and Frank Burroughs, and were clearly distraught over their inability to gain access to the seemingly miraculous Erbitux. The Burton hearing occurred at a critical time for ImClone: it was in the midst of filing a "rolling" biologic drug application with the FDA—an agency that was politically vulnerable—and Waksal had embarked on the secret negotiations that would result in an unprecedented, $2 billion deal with Bristol-Myers Squibb.

Congressman Dan Burton's trip to Germany in August 2001 in Juliet Eilperin, "Burton's German Trip Protested: Official Visit to Frankfurt Coincides with Wife's Treatment There," *The Washington Post,* August 11, 2001, p. A4. Dan Burton and his staff did not return my phone calls about this matter.

Phyllis Carter and Merck KGaA, from my interview.

Details of negotiations between Bristol and ImClone, from various news articles and the SEC Schedule 14D of September 28, 2001.

Characterization of Richard J. Lane, from informed sources.

The BMS due diligence report and Laurie Smaldone's "very high risk opportunity" e-mail of June 2001 were unearthed by the congressional investigation of ImClone; the House subcommittee report, pp. 44–45.

ImClone's multimillion-dollar loans to company insiders were revealed in Ibid, pp. 43–44, and later in numerous media accounts of the scandal.

Bristol's " 'go' decision," in Ibid, p. 45.

Complaints about the ImClone deal from inside Bristol came from knowledgeable sources. BMS did not respond to my calls.

## Chapter Seven. The $2 Billion Antibody

Background on the Kilimanjaro hike and friendship between Martha Stewart and Sharon Patrick, from many news accounts. See: James T. Madore, "The Woman Behind Martha," *Newsday,* October 7, 2002; or I. Jeanne Dugan, "Someone's in the Kitchen with Martha," *BusinessWeek,* July 24, 1997.

Martha's vision statement, from Byron, *Martha Inc,* p. 223.

Genesis of *Martha Stewart Living,* from Ibid, p. 191.

Chris Meigher, Ibid.

Syndication, Group W., and Richard Sheingold, Ibid, p. 202–14.

Byron does a good job of explaining the negotiations between Martha Stewart and Time Warner Inc. See pp. 220–69. The same goes for Oppenheimer, *Martha Stewart—Just Desserts*, pp. 335–58. Byron and Oppenheimer both cover Allen Grubman's successful negotiations with Time Warner on Martha's behalf, as do several articles.

History of Kmart, from various sources.

Charlotte Beers, from various sources.

The IPO for Martha Stewart Living Omnimedia was widely reported on, as in "Martha Stewart IPO at $18," on CNNmoney, October 18, 1999 and in Jeff Peline, "Martha's IPO: It's a Good Thing," CNET news.com, October 19, 1999. Three thousand brioche and croissants in "Martha Stewart's Troubled World," *NYT* op-ed page, June 5, 2003. *National Enquirer* suit in Byron, *Martha Inc.*

Martha to Tina Brown "I'm rich," from James Barron et al., "Public Lives," *NYT*, October 20, 1999.

Elizabeth Latham, from my interview.

Nancy Davis foundation, from *The Nancy Davis Foundation for Multiple Sclerosis (The Race to Erase MS) v. Samuel Waksal and ImClone Systems,* District Court, County of Pitkin, Colorado, filed September 29, 1995.

Sam's Restaurant, from *Stephanie Wallace v. Samuel Waksal,* Supreme Court of the State of New York, February 18, 1994.

Tina Sharkey in files from *Tina Sharkey v. iBeauty.com, Elana Waksal Posner, and Dr. Samuel D. Waksal,* Supreme Court of the State of New York, May 25, 2000.

Gabriella Forte, from *Gabriella Forte v. Dr. Samuel D. Waksal,* Supreme Court of the State of New York, filed August 13, 2001.

Sam on Gabriella Forte, from my interviews.

Sam buying paintings from Gagosian at a premium, from an informed source.

Sam Waksal on September 11 from my interview; letter of Cynthia Nash to Hon. William H. Pauley III, in Appendix to Waksal memo.

ImClone "just as much Heimbold's deal," from an informed source.

Adam Feuerstein, "Bristol-Myers Deal Gives ImClone Execs a Big Payday," in *theStreet.com,* September 19, 2001.

Harlan yelling at Feuerstein, from my interview with Feuerstein.

Harlan and Andrea Rabney anger at an analyst, from an informed source. Harlan would not return my calls for comment.

The October 2001 meeting of BMS's Physician Advisory Board and Tom Jordan's retirement, from informed sources.

## PART TWO: REFUSAL TO FILE

### Chapter Eight. The Letter

Lily Wailee Lee's unscheduled visit to George Mills and Lee Pai-Scherf at the FDA was recounted by all three participants in riveting testimony before Congress on June 13, 2002. See transcript of hearing in the House subcommittee report.

Descriptive details of Woodmont I and assessment of Mills's skill, from an informed source.

*BusinessWeek* inaccuracy about Shannon Kellum's health from my interviews with Dr. Mark Rubin (November 2001).

Lee described her conversation with the FDA to Harlan, from Lee's congressional testimony June 13, 2002, the House subcommittee report.

Beth Seidenberg e-mail in Ibid.

Sam Waksal's state of mind in December 2001 as described by him to me and other journalists.

Party at Tina Brown and Harry Evans's apartment, from my personal observation. Martha toppling into the azalea bushes: I recall Martha inadvertently stepping backward off the stone patio and into the bushes. See also Tina Brown, "Lunching in New York," *The Times of London,* October 3, 2002.

State of Martha's business and her planned sale of ImClone shares is detailed in press accounts, such as Jeffrey Toobin, "Lunch at Martha's," *The New Yorker,* February 2, 2003.

"Even though people complain Sam's a wacko . . . ," from my interview with Martha Stewart.

Description of Sam's Christmas party on December 6, 2001, from informed sources.

Sam's stock trades and $80 million debt are detailed in SEC reports and other government filings. See the House subcommittee report.

Elana Castaneda, from my interview.

Feuerstein, "Talk Is Cheap, but It's Making ImClone Pay," *theStreet. com,* December 19, 2001.

The location and actions of ImClone and Bristol-Myers personnel in late December 2001 come from their congressional testimony and news accounts. See transcript of hearings in the House subcommittee report.

*Los Angeles Times* story of December 26, 2001, in Ibid.

Sam's friends comment on his sudden departure from St. Bart's, from Thomas and Keil, "Who Knew?" *New York,* July 8, 2002.

Internal ImClone note, from December 27, 2001, from the House subcommittee report.

Ann E. Armstrong phone log, from the subcommittee Web site.

Martha's airborne breakfast, from Toobin, "Lunch at Martha's," *The New Yorker,* February 2, 2003.

Description of Sam Waksal pacing his office on December 28, 2001, from my interviews.

The FDA's Refusal-to-File letter excerpted in *The Cancer Letter,* January 4, 2002.

"I was in shock," from my interview with Sam on January 3, 2002.

John Mendelsohn and RTF, from news reports and my interviews.

Addison Woods, from my interviews.


## Chapter Nine. "We Screwed Up"

Reuters report of December 29, 2001, noted in the House subcommittee report, p. 46.

BMS internal e-mails, Ibid.

Sam Waksal on January 3, 2002, from my interview with him.

Paul Goldberg description, from my numerous interviews with him, 2002–03. Details of Goldberg's conversation with Sam Waksal on January 3, 2002, from Goldberg.

Parlor game, from informed sources.

Hambrecht & Quist conference and impact of *The Cancer Letter*'s leak of the RTF letter, from my interview of Adam Feuerstein.

Feuerstein, "Today's Main Course: Grilled ImClone Execs," *the Street.com,* January 9, 2002.

Discussion of the patent question, from Ibid.

Irv Feit, from my interview.

Description of H&Q and Sam Waksal, from Feuerstein.

Howard Ozer in Goldberg, "Imclone 'Screwed Up,' CEO Waksal Tells Conference; Stock Plunges," *The Cancer Letter,* January 11, 2002.

Nadine Wong, "Don't Write Off ImClone Just Yet," *theStreet.com,* January 10, 2002.

# PART THREE: CLINICAL TRIAL

## Chapter Ten. Inquiries

Alan Slobodin background, from my interview with Slobodin, my interview with Congressman James Greenwood, informed sources, and *The Almanac of the Unelected,* 2001.

Details of the congressional investigation of ImClone drawn from the House subcommittee report, material on the subcommittee's Web site at: energycommerce.house.gov/107/subcommittees/subcommittees.htm, interviews with informed sources, and my interview with Congressman James Greenwood.

Christopher Byron, "The Story of ImClone," *NY Post,* January 14, 2002.

Eight P.M. call from Sam Waksal on January 15, 2002, from my notes and a tape recording of the conversation.

Charles Miller et al. on effect of ImClone and Enron scandals on John Mendelsohn, from Geeta Anand, "Ties to Two Tainted Firms Haunt Top Doctor in Houston," *WSJ,* December 12, 2002. Supplemented by Atkinson, "Miracle Workers," *Texas Monthly,* September 2002, and my conversations with Mendelsohn.

Richard Lane, "No doubt it works," from Amy Barrett, "BMS Is Feeling Woozy," *BusinessWeek,* January 21, 2002.

Jon Alsenas, from Feuerstein, "ImClone Is Bringing Down the Biotech Neighborhood," *theStreet.com,* January 23, 2002.

Brian Markison, from my interview.

Peter Dolan's comments were made on a conference call that was widely reported on, January 24, 2002.

## Chapter Eleven. The Disconnect That Wouldn't Go Away

Peter Dolan's private dressing down of Sam Waksal in Michael Waldholz and Geeta Anand, "Recent Experience with ImClone Prompted Bristol-Myers's Stance," *WSJ,* February 19, 2002.

Description of BMS offices in Ron Winslow and Geeta Anand,

"Bristol-Myers Clashes with ImClone After Cancer Drug Hits Road-block," *WSJ*, February 7, 2002.

Dolan's public demand that the Waksal brothers step down was widely reported on. See Ibid.

The letters between BMS and ImClone were issued to the public by the two companies and were widely reported on.

Eric Hecht, from Geeta Anand and Vanessa Fuhrmans, "ImClone Directors Meet to Consider Bristol's Desire to Restructure Deal," *WSJ*, February 12, 2002.

Carl Icahn's large and curiously-timed investment in ImClone was widely reported on.

Icahn-Waksal "Towel snapping," from Frank DiGiacomo and Ian Blecher, "The Wacky Dr. Waksal," *New York Observer*, April 22, 2002.

The Carl C. Icahn Laboratory at Princeton, from news release from Princeton University Office of Communications, October 21, 1999.

Peter Crowley "optics or economics," from Dane Hamilton, "Merger Talk: Icahn Not Wedded to Buying More ImClone," Reuters, March 4, 2002. Lawrence Blumberg, Ibid.

Russell Glass's departure from Icahn Associates, from "Top Associate of Carl Icahn Resigns—Sources," Reuters, February 27, 2002.

Waksal's failure to report some 50 stock trades, from many articles, including in Toni Clarke, "ImClone's CEO Violates SEC Rules with Stock Filing," Reuters, March 26, 2002.

Peter Romero from Ibid.

Discussion of ImClone's clinical trial protocol, from Goldberg, *The Cancer Letter*, February 15, 2002.

Hemant Shah, in Feuerstein, "Cancer Experts Say ImClone's Tests Were Flawed," *theStreet.com*, February 15, 2002.

Robert Erwin from my interviews.

SEC Form 144, from *NYT*, March 14, 2002, as noted in the House subcommittee report, p. 539.

Congress's letter to Waksal, from the subcommittee Web site.

Peter Dolan summoned before the BMS board, from Geeta Anand and Joann S. Lublin, "Bristol-Myers Puts Its CEO on Notice Following Missteps," *WSJ*, April 15, 2002.

Richard Barth's resignation letter, reprinted in the House subcommittee report.

Sam Waksal's resignation from ImClone was widely reported on.

"This disconnect . . ." from Geeta Anand, "At the Center of Controversy, ImClone CEO Calls it Quits," *WSJ,* May 23, 2002.

### Chapter Twelve. Who Knew What and When?

Martha Stewart's state of mind on June 7, 2002, inferred from numerous interviews she has given journalists, such as Toobin, "Lunch at Martha's," *The New Yorker,* February 2, 2003. It is supplemented by my personal experience with Martha Stewart.

The congressional investigation of ImClone is explained in the House subcommittee report and on the subcommittee Web site.

Sam's "Are people saying I'm a terrible man?" from Thomas and Keil, "Who Knew?" *New York,* July 8, 2002.

The Waksal family's trades in ImClone stock are laid out in SEC filings and in the House subcommittee report.

John H. Sturc on insider trading, from Chris Adams and Geeta Anand, "Martha Stewart Sold ImClone Shares, but No Sign She Knew of FDA Action," *WSJ,* June 7, 2002.

Vee Kumar, from my interview.

Sam's arrest by the FBI on June 12, 2002, was widely covered. A photograph of Jack Waksal punching a CNN cameraman ran in the *New York Post* on June 13, 2002.

Congressional hearing of June 13, 2002, from my experience, numerous press accounts, and transcripts in the House subcommittee report.

*Barron's* prescient report on ImClone's loans to Sam appeared in Wyatt, "Outside the Lab," *Barron's,* June 28, 1993.

Merck KGaA clinical trials, from press accounts such as Adam Feuerstein, "FDA: We Gave ImClone Early Warning, *theStreet.com,* June 13, 2002.

### Chapter Thirteen. Coincidences Piling Up

Bacanovic questioned in London, from Thomas and Keil, "Who Knew?" *New York,* July 8, 2002.

"A reported .04 of 1 percent" of Martha's fortune and Jeff Ubben, from Toobin, "Lunch at Martha's," *The New Yorker,* February 2, 2003.

Representative W. J. "Billy" Tauzin said "coincidences are just piling up," from "U.S. Rep Tauzin: Lots of 'Coincidences' in ImClone Probe," Dow Jones Newswires, July 17, 2002.

William R. Baker III, from Toobin, "Lunch at Martha's," *The New Yorker,* February 2, 2003.

Douglas Faneuil broke under questioning, from media accounts, especially *NYT* and *WSJ.*

Bacanovic was devastated by what he considered Faneuil's betrayal, from Thomas and Keil, "Who Knew?" *New York,* July 8, 2002.

"Peter has no enemies," Bacanovic's purgatory, and Brad Gooch, from Ibid.

Harlan testimony, from the House subcommittee report.

Greenwood question in Ibid.

ImClone's new corporate governance rules, from press accounts. See Geeta Anand and Chris Adams, "ImClone Changes Board Rules As Probe Focuses on Oversight," *WSJ,* June 26, 2002.

Characterizations of Harlan Waksal, from informed sources.

The story of Harlan's cocaine bust is told in compelling detail in the court proceedings: *United States of America v. Harlan Waksal,* United States District Court, Southern District of Florida, October 29, 1981; and Ibid, February 19, 1982; and *United States of America v. Harlan Waksal,* United States Court of Appeals for the Eleventh Circuit, July 11, 1983. See also press clippings about the case, such as, Robert Barkin, "Judge to Rule on Airport Drug Search," *Fort Lauderdale News,* December 31, 1981; Barkin, "Judge Upholds Airport Drug Search," Ibid, February 23, 1982; Barkin, "Doctor Gets 9 Years for Possessing Cocaine," Ibid, April 28, 1982; Jack Brennan, "U.S. Asks for 2d Drug Trial, Defendant Calls it Harassment," *Sun-Sentinel,* October 13, 1983.

## Chapter Fourteen. In the Light of October

The back and forth between Martha Stewart's representative and congressional investigators is laid out in the letters they sent each other. See the House subcommittee Web site.

Martha's appearance with Jayne Clayson on CBS's *The Early Show,* has been widely written about; a webcast can be seen on CBSnews.com, June 25, 2002. On November 6, 2003, Martha told Barbara Walters on ABC News's *20/20* that "I think the last year and a half has been the most difficult part of my life . . . To tell you the truth, I have not been able to chop a cabbage since [*The Early Show* appearance]. No more coleslaw for me."

Kopperl and Goldhammer's high regard for Sam, from their congressional testimony.

Sam's forgery of Landes' signature on an issuers letter was widely reported on. In his congressional testimony on October 10, 2002, Landes discussed the incident and his subsequent interactions with Sam.

The grand jury indictment, from *United States of America v. Samuel Waksal,* United States District Court, Southern District of New York, August, 2002.

Sam's donation to Hillary Clinton, from news accounts, such as "U.S. Sen Clinton: Ex-Imclone CEO's Donation to Go to Charity," Associated Press, and in Deborah Orin, "Hill's Dirty Money," *NY Post,* August 9, 2002.

Bristol-Myers' troubles were covered widely in the press. Peter Ringrose's departure from BMS was announced by the company.

Novartis's Zelnorm, from Robert Langreth, "Crisis in the Cabinet," *Forbes,* December 10, 2001; and in Gardiner Harris and Vanessa Fuhrmans, "Its Rivals in a Funk, Novartis Finds a Technique to Thrive," *WSJ,* August 23, 2002.

Oxaliplatin's success from news sources, including Andrew Pollack, "Colorectal Cancer Drug Wins Quick Approval," in *NYT,* August 13, 2002.

*Wall Street Journal* editorials, from "Bullying ImClone," *WSJ,* February 13, 2002; "FDA to Patients: Drop Dead," from *WSJ,* September 24, 2002.

Iressa, from news accounts. *Forbes* cover story, from Robert Langreth, "Iressa: Conquering Cancer," *Forbes,* November 11, 2002.

Sam indicated his state of mind, and his guilt over Aliza, in numerous statements. See, for instance, Jerry Markon and Geeta Anand, "ImClone's Former CEO Pleads Guilty to Charges," *WSJ,* October 16, 2002.

Sam "I got the sense that . . . happy campers," from Steve Kroft interview with Waksal, *60 Minutes;* airdate October 5, 2003. Partial transcript available at: www.cbsnews.com.

Bacanovic's conversation with the SEC, from numerous press accounts.

Congress's communications with Martha Stewart on the House

subcommittee Web site and from press accounts. "U.S. Congressman Says Martha Stewart Could Face Subpoena," Associated Press, August 8, 2002.

Robert Morvillo, from numerous press accounts, including Jan Hoffman, "In Martha Stewart's Corner, a Tough Cookie," *NYT,* June 19, 2003.

Douglas Faneuil's flip-flops were widely reported.

The October 10, 2002, congressional hearing into ImClone, from my own reporting, supplemented by press coverage and the House subcommittee report.

Sam's guilty plea was widely reported on, as in Markon and Anand, "ImClone's Former CEO Pleads Guilty to Charges," *WSJ,* October 16, 2002.

# PART FOUR: THE ONCE AND FUTURE MIRACLE DRUG

## Chapter Fifteen. Art, Death, and Taxes

Jennifer McNeillie and Steven Walker, from my interview.

Feuerstein, "Is Another Setback in Store for ImClone?" *theStreet.com,* October 29, 2002.

"Here we go again," from Shawn Langlois, "ImClone Longs Rail Against Report," CBS.MarketWatch.com, October 29, 2002.

Harlan's shift in strategy from Feuerstein, "CEO Takes ImClone for a Walk Up the Street," *theStreet.com,* November 18, 2002.

Critics of FDA: "FDA to Patients: Drop Dead," from *WSJ,* September 24, 2002.

Dr. Mark B. McClellan from various news stories, including, "Bush to Nominate Physician to Head FDA, Sources Say," Dow Jones Newswire, September 24, 2002.

Martha's interview with Jeffrey Toobin, "Lunch at Martha's," *The New Yorker,* February 2, 2003.

Kozlowski, from press accounts.

Morgenthau, from "Manhattan DA Probing Art Collectors for Tax Evasion," Dow Jones Newswire, March 5, 2003.

Details of Sam Waksal's tax dodge on paintings, from court proceedings and press releases, such as "Waksal Pleads Guilty in U.S. Court to New Charges of Evading $1.2 Million in Sales Tax on Artwork Purchases," from the U.S. Attorney, Southern District of New York, March 3, 2003. See numerous media accounts, especially in *NYT* and *WSJ*. For details on Gagosian see Phoebe Hoban, "The Artful Dealer, *New York,* May 26, 2003, p. 27.

Characterization of courtroom, Judge Pauley, Schachter, Comey, Pomerantz, and Sam Waksal, from my personal observation.

Background of U.S. Attorney James Comey, from various articles, including Alexandra Wolfe, "Meet Martha's Prosecutor," *The New York Observer,* June 16, 2003.

Barry Rashkover of the SEC, from "Waksal to Pay $800,000 in Partial Deal with SEC," from *WSJ,* March 11, 2003.

Sam's failure to pay up to $60 million in income taxes, from news accounts such as Toni Clarke, "ImClone: Waksal Did Not Pay Income Taxes," Reuters, March 31, 2003.

Steve Brozak on Harlan and Goldhammer, from Victoria Griffith, "Resignations Add to Cloud Over ImClone," *Financial Times,* April 30, 2003.

Jim McCamant, from Toni Clarke, "ImClone CEO Chairman Resigns Over Probe," Reuters, April 29, 2003.

"Colossal Colon," Genentech's drug Avastin, and Alan Venook at 2003 ASCO in Chicago, from Feuerstein, *theStreet.com,* various reports, June 1–3, 2003.

*WSJ* editorial, from "Topic of Cancer," *WSJ,* April 2, 2003.

John Mendelsohn, from my interviews with him.

Steven Walker, "S.O.S. to the FDA," *WSJ,* August 26, 2003.


## Chapter Sixteen. Icarian Actions

Description of Sam Waksal's penthouse apartment on Thompson Street, from Braden Keil, "Gimme Shelter: Waksal Selling in SoHo," *NY Post,* September 6, 2003.

Elizabeth Latham and the orchardist, from my interview.

Shirley Flacks, from my interview.

Martha Stewart as a stockbroker, from Byron, *Martha Inc.,* p. 231. MSO shareholder meeting, from press accounts.

Martha "I keep saying, why, why, why?" in Shawn Sell, "Martha Stewart Looks Up," *USA Today,* September 2, 2003.

Martha's lawyers working on a settlement agreement with U.S. Attorney's Office, from news accounts. See *Financial Times,* Dow Jones Newswire; Constance L. Hays, "Martha Stewart Indicted by U.S. on Obstruction," *NYT,* June 5, 2003.

Arthur Martinez, from press clips, including Patricia Sellers, "Designing Her Defense," *Fortune,* June 23, 2003.

Sam Waksal at Nobu on June 3, 2003, from my observation.

Sam and his probation officer story was recounted by Elizabeth Latham.

Probation Department report stating Sam's $52 million in assets, from the opposition memo, *USA v. Sam Waksal.*

Sam's philanthropy, the Center for Jewish History, from Ibid; and from Lisa Keys, "Fallen 'Angel'?" *The Forward,* July 19, 2002.

Martha Stewart and Peter Bacanovic in Judge Cedarbaum's chambers, from numerous press accounts.

Robert Morvillo statement excerpted from MarthaTalks.com, Stewart's personal Web site.

Charges are laid out in the grand jury indictment, *USA v. Stewart and Bacanovic.*

Laura Richardson from Hays, "Martha Stewart Indicted by U.S. on Obstruction," *NYT,* June 5, 2003.

Ubben, from Sellers, "Designing Her Defense," *Fortune,* June 23, 2003.

Prosecutor Karen Patton Seymour in Stewart trial and comment from Jo-Ellan Dimitrius, from Laurie P. Cohen, "U.S. Wants 'Gender Card' Out of Martha Stewart Case," *WSJ,* July 7, 2003.

Comey's nomination as deputy attorney general from Benjamin Weiser and Eric Lichtblau, "Manhattan U.S. Attorney in Line to Be Ashcroft Aide," *NYT,* October 4, 2003.

Sam on *Family Business,* from my interviews.

Sam's sentencing hearing June 10, 2003, from my personal observation, media accounts, court filings, and hearing transcript.

Harlan Waksal's departure from ImClone was widely reported.

Jack Waksal's indictment by the SEC, from news clippings like Gail Appleson, "SEC Sues Waksal's Father in Insider Plot," Reuters, October 10, 2003.

Sam's "I was arrogant" interview with Steve Kroft aired on CBS's *60 Minutes* October 5, 2003.

Aliza's nominee accounts, from the opposition memo, *USA v. Sam Waksal.*

## Epilogue

Sam Waksal's arrival at Schuylkill federal prison was well documented in the press. His Amazon.com wish list can be viewed at Amazon.com and has been written about extensively.

Details of Sam's farewell party at his Thompson Street loft, from numerous articles, especially in New York's tabloids. See, for instance, Joe McGurk, Richard Johnson, and John Lehmann, "Sam's Farewell," *NY Post,* July 24, 2003.

Janet Malcolm, *The Journalist and the Murderer* (New York: Vintage Books, 1990.)

BMS investigation and Taxol settlement in news clippings. See Gerdiner Harris, "Will the Pain Ever Let Up at Bristol-Myers?" *NYT,* May 18, 2003.

Dolan and Gerstner, from James Cramer, "Keeping Its CEO Keeps Bristol-Myers in Limbo," *theStreet.com* May 23, 2003.

ImClone's 2003 annual meeting, from news clippings; details about personnel changes, from ImClone's 2003 proxy statement (SEC Form 14A), filed September 15, 2003.

John Mendelsohn, from my interview.

Shannon's death and quote from her mother, Thelma Hinkle, from John Dorschner, " 'Miracle Drug' User's Death Revives Doubts," *Miami Herald,* October 2, 2002.

Shannon Kellum, from my conversation with her, spring 2002.

# Index